People, environment, and place: An introduction to human geography

ROBERT P. LARKIN
University of Colorado,
Colorado Springs

GARY L. PETERS
California State University,
Long Beach

CHRISTOPHER H. EXLINE
University of Nevada-Reno

Charles E. Merrill Publishing Company
A Bell & Howell Company
Columbus   Toronto   London   Sydney

Published by
Charles E. Merrill Publishing Company
A Bell & Howell Company
Columbus, Ohio 43216

This book was set in Optima and **Benguiat.**
Production Editor: **Cherlyn B. Paul**
Cover Design Coordination: **Will Chenoweth**
Cover Photograph of Hong Kong harbor: **Gene Gilliom**

Library of Congress Catalog Card Number: 80–80724

International Standard Book Number: 0–675–08085–1

Printed in the United States of America

2 3 4 5 6 7 8 9 10—86 85 84 83 82

Preface

People, Environment, and Place was designed as an introductory college textbook for a one-quarter or one-semester course in cultural or human geography. Its purpose is to introduce students to the basic concepts of human geography and provide a geographical framework for the analysis of current world problems.

The first chapter introduces the discipline of human geography and discusses its traditions and place in today's world. The remaining fourteen chapters are divided into four sections.

The first section, chapters 2 through 4, deals with the nature of human populations. This includes an analysis of historical population patterns, the human population today and tomorrow, and the population of Anglo-America. The second section, chapters 5 through 8, deals with the mosaic of culture. It covers human reliance upon culture, race and religion as elements of the cultural system, language patterns, and politics and nation-states. The third section, chapters 9 through 11, analyzes the nature of resources, environment, and development by discussing natural resources as the basis for economic development, the road toward modernization, and the relationship between people, technology, and the environment. The final section, chapters 12 through 15, discusses economic activities and urbanization, including agriculture, industrialization, cities and an urbanizing world, and the urban environment.

Key terms are introduced in bold type throughout the text, listed at the end of each chapter, and defined in the glossary at the end of the book. Each chapter ends with a pertinent bibliography for further reference. Case studies are integrated throughout, examining in more detail such topics as population control, modernization in the developing countries, and the 1976 Tangshan earthquake.

It is impossible to acknowledge individually each of the many authors from whom we have learned; yet without their continued research efforts, textbooks could not be written. Of course, we alone are responsible for any shortcomings or errors the book may have.

Our thanks also to the editoral staff at Charles E. Merrill. Their guidance and suggestions have been most helpful. Administrative Editor Greg Spatz has made useful comments and suggestions from the book's inception. A special note of thanks to the Production Editor, Cher Paul, for her excellent work in the design of the book and her patience with its authors.

Robert P. Larkin
Gary L. Peters
Christopher H. Exline

September 1980

Contents

List of maps   ix

1 The geographic perspective   2

Fundamental views of human geography, 2; The four traditions of geography, 3;
Geography in today's world, 4; Key terms, 4; References, 5.

1 WORLD POPULATION   6

2 Population: Historical patterns   8

Measuring population growth and change, 8; World population growth, 11; Case
study: Population control by catastrophe: The Black Death, 19; Population theory,
23; Key terms, 27; References, 27

3 The human population today and tomorrow   28

World population today, 28; Population theories from today's perspective, 31;
Case study: Marxist theory: The case of the People's Republic of China, 36;
Migration, 39; Population projections, 41; Paths to population equilibrium, 44;
Culture, population growth, and family planning, 44; Key terms, 48; References, 49.

4 The population of Anglo-America   50

The population of North America before the Europeans, 50; Historical development
of the U.S. population, 50; Population growth in the 20th century, 52; Population

growth and environment in the U.S., 66; Historical growth of Canada's population, 70; Canada's population in the 20th century, 70; Key terms, 75; References, 75.

2   THE MOSAIC OF CULTURE   78

5   Human reliance upon culture   80

The concept and dynamics of culture, 80; The spatial expression of culture, 82; The material basis of culture, 87; Cultural diffusion and change, 94; The landscape as a cultural map, 100; Looking toward the future, 104; Key terms, 104; References, 105.

6   Elements of the cultural system: Race and religion   106

The concept of race, 106; Case study: South Africa: A study in conflict, 109; Religion and the landscape, 115; Key terms, 124; References, 124.

7   Language patterns   125

Language and evolution, 125; General functions of language, 128; Language as a social institution, 130; Distribution of languages, 134; Key terms, 138; References, 139.

8   Politics and nation-states   141

The nation-state, 141; Frontiers and boundaries, 147; Colonialism, neo-colonialism, and supranationalism, 160; Key terms, 166; References, 167.

3   RESOURCES, ENVIRONMENT, AND DEVELOPMENT   168

9   Natural resources: The basis for economic development   170

Recognizing natural resources, 170; The material basis of development, 177; Resources: A geographic survey of major categories, 179; Case study: The California drought of 1976–77, 187; Resource conflicts, 187; Key terms, 192; References, 192.

10   The road toward modernization   **194**

Modernization and development, 194; Development and modernization in a
cultural context, 195; Spatial organization and development, 199; Case study:
Modernizing the Masaii, 205; People, environment, and development, 210;
Children and the future, 213; Key terms, 213; References, 213.

11   People, technology, and the environment   **215**

The nature of ecosystems, 215; Pollution and ecosystems, 219; Environmental
hazards, 224; Case study: The Tangshan earthquake of 1976, 235; Key terms, 236;
References, 236.

**4   ECONOMIC ACTIVITIES
     AND URBANIZATION**   **238**

12   Land and livelihood: Sustenance from the earth   **240**

Food production systems in developing countries, 241; Agriculture in the
developed countries, 247; Food production and the growth syndrome, 254;
Imprints on the agricultural landscape, 262; Case study: The influence of values
and value systems on the cultural landscape, 266; Key terms, 269; References, 270.

13   An industrializing world: Patterns and prospects   **271**

The industrial revolution: A major event, 271; Locational factors for manufacturing
activities, 274; The world pattern of manufacturing, 280; World industrial regions,
283; Manufacturing regions in North America, 284; Case study: Taking stock—
geography and the market, 288; Manufacturing and the growth syndrome, 289;
Industrial impressions on the landscape, 290; Key terms, 292; References, 292.

14   Cities in an urbanizing world   **293**

The origin of cities, 294; Recent urbanization: regional comparisons and contrasts,
301; Urbanization in developing countries, 304; Key terms, 312; References, 312.

15   The urban environment   **314**

Elements of the urban ecosystem, 315; Case study: Urban evolution, 316; The
outer city, 331; Systems of cities, 334; Key terms, 339; References, 340.

Appendix: 1980 World Population Data Sheet—Summary 341

Glossary 345

Index 351

List of maps

2−3   The Fertile Crescent   **14**
2−4   Diffusion of agriculture and domestication   **16**
2−5   Meso-American preconquest economic and cultural centers   **18**

3−9   Population distribution of China   **39**
3−12   Cartogram of family planning   **46−47**

4−1   Native American population density   **51**
4−2   Population distribution, 1900   **54**
4−4   U.S. population density, 1970   **55**
4−5   Abortion rate per 1000 women of reproductive age, 1973   **57**
4−7   Alien address reports, 1976   **59**
4−9   Region-to-region migration, 1975 to 1977   **65**
4−10   Water deficit regions   **68**
4−14   Canadian population distribution, 1976   **74**

5−1   Cultural hearths   **83**
5−2   The Mormon cultural region   **86**

6−1   The Apartheid Plan   **113**
6−2   World distribution of religious groups   **118**

7−3   World distribution of languages   **135**
7−4   Major Asian languages   **136−37**

8−2   Shapes of states   **144**
8−3   Territorial expansion of royal authority from the core area of France   **145**
8−5   Feudal boundaries in the Low Countries, 1300   **152**
8−6   Types of boundaries   **153**
8−7   Chilean−Argentinian boundary dispute   **154**
8−9   International boundaries in the Great Lakes   **156**
8−10   Types of boundaries in the United States   **157**
8−11   Land-locked states   **158**
8−13   The world after the Colonial Revolution, 1972,   **161**
8−14   The world before the Colonial Revolution, 1945   **163**

9−3   California water projects   **180**
9−4   U.S. oil shale, uranium, and thorium deposites   **185**
9−5   The international flow of oil, 1976   **186**
9−6   Nuclear generating capacity, 1976   **187**
9−8   Strippable coal reserves in the conterminous United States   **189**
9−9   Cropland overlaying coal   **190**
9−10   Cropland and strippable coal reserves in Illinois   **191**

10−1   GNP per capita, 1980   **196**
10−4   Railway network of Ecuador, Peru, Bolivia, and Chile, 1974   **202**

11–7   Tropical Storm Agnes, 1972   **227**
11–8   Tropical cyclone regions   **230**
11–9   Major seismic belts   **233**
11–10   Seismic risk in the United States   **234**

12–2   Intensive subsistence farming   **244**
12–4   Comparison of actual land-use classes with patterns based on the Von Thünen model   **249**
12–6   General types of agriculture in California   **253**
12–7   Potentially arable and cultivated land, mid-1960s   **256**
12–8   Manure map of the world   **258**
12–9   Diffusion of shotgun houses   **263**

13–3   U.S. copper industry   **278**
13–5   World distribution of raw steel production   **282**

13–6   Major industrial regions   **284**
13–7   Distribution of manufacturing in the United States and Canada   **285**
13–8   North American manufacturing core region   **286**
13–9   Employment change, 1965–70   **287**

14–1   Early centers of urbanism   **296**
14–2   Ancient cities of the Tigris–Euphrates Valley   **297**

15–1   Rail transportation in the San Francisco Bay area   **317**
15–2   Small rail systems in the eastern Bay area   **318**
15–3   Urban realms of the San Francisco area, as indicated by major shopping facilities   **319**
15–5   Functional types of U.S. cities   **322**

People, environment, and place:
An introduction
to human geography

1

The geographic perspective

Familiarity with the world in which we live lies at the core of understanding human geography. At a time when the United States and other nations of the western world command great influence, we are essentially geographic illiterates. Our citizens know relatively little of other places and other peoples. Understanding the relationship between people, places, and the environment is essential to solving many crucial world problems.

FUNDAMENTAL VIEWS OF HUMAN GEOGRAPHY

When introducing geography or any other discipline at the college level, it is important to let students know what they are getting into. However, introducing geography presents difficulties not encountered by economists, say, or anthropologists, in introducing their subject. Geographers seem to suffer from image problems and lack of exposure, as well as from internal disagreements about what geography is.

One common saying is "geography is whatever geographers do," but we can't hope to get you, the reader, to accept such a broad nondefinition. Yet we would like you to understand that approaches to geography do vary, partly because geography, like history, is a discipline based on approach rather than on content. To some extent at least, *space* is to geography what *time* is to history. The word *space* as used by geographers does not refer to outer space, to the moon and planets, or to space ships, but rather to the surface of the earth (Robinson, 1976, p. 523). Whereas historians seek to know when and why some phenomenon occurred, geographers seek to know where and why. However, historians often care about where and geographers about when, and geography usually borrows time to understand why things are the way they are at any particular place.

Our own feelings about what human geography is most concerned with are apparent in our title for this book. We are concerned mainly with people and environments within the context of place. **Location,** both absolute and relative, is a principal element of geography. *Place* implies location, but connotes something richer to us. Places are created by people as they adapt to and, in turn, mold their environments through culture.

Places may at once be ***unique*** and ***general,*** depending on our perspective. New York and Paris, for example, are both major metropolitan cities offering many goods and services. Both are homes for universities, operas, commercial centers and cosmopolitan populations. Generally, they are called *cities,* but from another perspective they are individuals. There is only one Paris and only one New York, despite their functional similarities.

Geographers have approached their studies from both perspectives, uniqueness and generality, though currently the latter is more favored. The way geographic space is organized—the spatial arrangements of people and their activities and institutions, and the linkages between places—are central concerns in geography today. Yet the search for uniqueness, for features that identify regional differences between places, and for the sense of place is still pursued by many geographers.

Arguments about whether human geography is a social science or part of the humanities have gone on for decades and are likely to continue; many will be apparent as we proceed. Generally, we tend to agree with the following comment by Preston James, an eminent geographer:

> Whether geography is pursued inductively or deductively, or even whether it is pursued as an art or as a science, is perhaps less important than that it be pursued by honest scholarship, and that the results of this pursuit be communicated. (James, 1967, p. 24)

Geography as a social science

If a vote were taken today among the members of the Association of American Geographers, a majority would say that human geography is a social science, concerned primarily with geographic patterns on the earth's surface and explanations for these patterns. We rely heavily on the *scientific method* to solve geographic problems. Statistics and mathematics have gained a seat beside maps as tools for geographic research.

Geography borrows heavily from the other social sciences, especially from economics, sociology and anthropology. For example, suppose we wish to explain the location of steel production in the United States. At the very least, we would need to know what was needed for the production of steel, the costs of getting raw materials together at various locations, labor and management costs, and where the steel will be consumed. In other words, we would need to know about the demand for steel and the costs of supplying that demand. In this example the geographer would rely heavily on the ideas and concepts of economics.

Geography and the humanities

At the heart of the humanities we find such academic fare as philosophy, literature, history and the arts—all of which focus primarily on human thoughts and acts. Among geographers today, growing concern with a hu-manistic perspective is apparent, though the number of geographers professing such concern is still small. According to one humanistic geographer, Yi-Fu Tuan,

> Scientific approaches to the study of man tend to minimize the role of human awareness and knowledge. Humanistic geography, by contrast, specifically tries to understand how geographical activities and phenomena reveal the quality of human awareness. (Tuan, 1976, p. 267)

Humanistic geography considers the feelings and ideas people have about places—not just as locations, but as experienced landscapes. This is the *sense of place.* Places have meanings to people, which vary with scale or size, as well as with the degree to which the places have been experienced. Home, neighborhood, city, region and nation are all places; however, our familiarity with them tends to decrease as we move from home to increasingly larger geographic units.

Studies of place and the sense of place are uncommon, considering that an understanding of place is at the core of geography. Literature and art have also been concerned with a sense of place, so humanistic geographers are not alone in their search for an understanding of the unique character of places.

THE FOUR TRADITIONS OF GEOGRAPHY

Although geographers view their discipline in many ways, some common concepts emerge. William Pattison of the University of Chicago pointed out four common traditions of geography. These four distinct but affiliated traditions are seen as blinders that operate in the minds of geographers, preventing disarray in their collective efforts (1964, p. 211).

1. Earth-science tradition. This tradition is concerned with the study of the biosphere, the interface of land, water, and air. It is primarily an outgrowth of geology, and many early geographers associated with this tradition were considered geologists as well. *Physical geography* is a result of this tradition. A variety of college or university courses deal with this material, and curricula usually include such courses as landform analysis (geomorphology), weather and climate, and biogeography.

2. "Man–land" tradition. This tradition emphasizes the ecological nature of geography, that is, the interaction between people and the physical environment. During the 1970s, concern about human impact on the environment emerged from scientists in several disciplines.

Geography has long been concerned with this interaction, and during the latter part of the 19th century, many geographers, influenced by Darwinian ideas, thought that the physical environment actually determined human behavior. The concept of *environmentalism* or *environmental determinism* was firmly entrenched in the United States until about 1920. Since that time, however, most geographers have disavowed it as a viable geographic concept.

Although environmentalism is an outmoded idea, the study of the relationship between people and the environment is an important aspect of geography. The solutions to such world problems as pollution, natural hazards, and hunger are dependent upon knowing more about the human-environment interface.

3. **Area-studies tradition.** This tradition is concerned with the character of places and how they evolved to their present organization. Many interdisciplinary area-studies programs have sprung up in the past few decades at colleges and universities around the country. The study of places and their distinctive character, however, have been topics of concern to geographers for many decades.

4. **Spatial tradition.** This tradition deals with positioning and layout on the earth's surface and with the spatial arrangements or patterns of both physical and human phenomena. The map has been the geographer's principal tool in portraying spatial distribution patterns. It assists geographers in two ways: a map of a spatial distribution helps to *describe* and *explain* the particular distribution. Since the 1950s, statistics, mathematics, and symbolic models have played an increasingly larger role in geography, especially when used in describing and explaining spatial distributions.

GEOGRAPHY IN TODAY'S WORLD

Geography's four traditions both outline the historical evolution of geography and indicate some future problems and processes. Human geography in particular is constantly changing, and geographers throughout the world are attempting to cope with the problems associated with a rapidly changing world. Foremost among them is how to understand and cope with what American geographer Wilbur Zelinsky called the **growth syndrome.** According to Zelinsky, the analysis of the growth syndrome is "the most timely and momentous item on the agenda of the human geographer" (1970, p. 498).

What is the growth syndrome, why is it so important, and what role can human geography play in its analysis? The growth syndrome has been discussed and defined by many social and physical scientists. Essentially, it involves three basic parameters: continuing growth of the human population in both developed and developing countries, rapid increase in the production and consumption of commodities, and misapplication of old and new technologies, leading to an increasing abuse and pillage of the human habitat. Concerning the importance of the growth syndrome, Zelinsky says,

> Genuine progress in human welfare, ultimate success in the prolonged struggle to become fully human, and most immediately, evading disaster of a truly major magnitude for man and most of his fellow-passengers on Spaceship Earth may well hinge upon the promptest sort of corrective action.

Coping with the growth syndrome will involve a monumental effort by physical and social scientists. Although not the only components, the viewpoints and methods of analysis used by geographers will be important in understanding and mollifying the growth syndrome.

KEY TERMS

Space
Location
Uniqueness
Generality
Scientific method
Sense of place
Earth-science tradition

"Man-land" tradition
Environmentalism
Environmental determinism
Area-studies tradition
Spatial tradition
Growth syndrome

REFERENCES

James, P. E. (1967), "On the Origin and Persistence of Error in Geography," *Annals of the Association of American Geographers* 57, 1–24.

Pattison, W. (1964), "The Four Traditions of Geography," *Journal of Geography* 63, 211–216.

Robinson, J. L. (1976), "A New Look at the Four Traditions of Geography," *Journal of Geography* 68, 520–529.

Tuan, Y. (1976), "Humanistic Geography," *Annals of the Association of American Geographers* 66, 266–276.

Zelinsky, W. (1970), "Beyond the Exponentials: The Role of Geography in the Great Transition," *Economic Geography* 46, 498–535.

People are the basic units of concern to cultural or human geographers. Their importance in the world is not simply a matter of numbers, but rather a function of their cultural adaptations to and impacts upon the physical environment. People modify places to suit their perceived needs.

Before we begin to look at the human imprint on the landscape and impact on the physical environment, we must first understand population dynamics and the nature of population change and resultant spatial patterns and distributions.

Because our current world situation is closely tied to the past, we must outline the methods of analyzing population growth and change, then look at the historical evolution of world population. The principal cultural and spatial changes associated with population growth are also discussed.

An analysis of the world's population today, including discussions of distribution and structure, are also needed. Migration and the problems associated with population projections are investigated.

The final chapter in this section focuses closer attention on the growth and distribution of people within the context of a specific cultural region, Anglo-America.

World population 1

(World Bank)

2

Population: Historical patterns

The world population was around 4.4 billion in 1980. Rounding this figure to 4 billion and allowing one square yard of space for each person—enough space so each one could stand comfortably without touching a neighbor—we could pack the entire world's population into the state of Delaware and still have more than 25 percent of that state left over. Or, if we were to move that same population into the state of Texas, we would find that the **crude population density**—the number of people per square mile—would be somewhat less than that of San Francisco County, California.

However, imagine Delaware populated by 4 billion people; the image is the human equivalent of a modern cattle feedlot. Unlike cattle feedlots, of course, no outsiders could provide the necessary inputs, food and water, and remove the unavoidable outputs. Our imaginary Delaware-sized world would disintegrate into a chaotic morass of humans locked in a struggle for survival. In Darwinian fashion a few might survive, allowing the race to continue with a much smaller population.

Though life in Texas with 4 billion people would undoubtedly be an improvement, it would still be short-lived. To explain, suppose that we completely isolated San Francisco from the rest of the world, and it suddenly had to become self-sufficient. Again, a struggle for survival would ensure, followed by a population collapse to a level that could be supported by the available land area. Thus, in a Texas-sized world of 4 billion people, a population crash still seems unavoidable.

In both of these hypothetical worlds, the population exceeds the **carrying capacity** of the land, or the number of people who can be sustained by a particular land area at a given technological level. Obviously, if we allowed the 4 billion people to fan out across the globe, there would seem to be plenty of land for everyone. The total land area of the earth, including inland water and Antarctica, is approximately 57 million square miles. If our 4 billion people were equally distributed, each square mile would contain about 70 people. But the world's population has never been evenly distributed.

The study of **spatial variations** in the distribution of people is an essential part of population geography. Geographers are hardly alone in their interests in population, though the concentration of their interests differs from that of other disciplines. **Demography** is the scientific study of the human population, including size, composition, and distribution in space. Although both demography and population geography are concerned with the same topic, the study of human populations, the demographer usually emphasizes the measurement and analysis of population data over time, whereas the population geographer is usually more concerned with the location, arrangements, and spatial distribution patterns of people. However, both the population geographer and demographer share some concerns, such as the analysis of population movements.

MEASURING POPULATION GROWTH AND CHANGE

Demographers have developed many different rates for measuring population growth and change; fortunately, the simple rates will suffice for our purposes.

Early morning rush hour in Cairo. (World Bank Photo by Ray Witlin, 1975)

One of the fundamental characteristics of any population is its absolute size. Only two demographic variables can alter world population size, births and deaths; the size of smaller populations, such as those of nations, states, or cities, may also be altered by migration. National, regional, or local population growth over a given time period equals the number of births minus the number of deaths plus the number of people who moved in minus the number of people who moved out. This is the **basic demographic equation,** and all changes in population size may be understood through the contribution of the three basic demographic processes—births, deaths, and migration. The equation can be written as follows:

$$\begin{matrix} \text{Population} \\ \text{at some future time} \end{matrix} = \begin{matrix} \text{existing population + births} \\ -\text{deaths + in-migration} \\ -\text{out-migration} \end{matrix}$$

$$P_2 = P_1 + B - D + I_m - O_m$$

Rate of natural increase

The rate of natural increase equals the **crude birth rate** minus the **crude death rate** —the annual number of births and deaths, respectively, per 1000 people in a population—and is a measure of population change exclusive of migration. Thus, the rate of natural increase is the annual net change per 1000 people in a population. This equation can be written as follows:

$$\text{Rate of natural increase} = \begin{matrix}\text{crude birth rate} - \\ \text{crude death rate}\end{matrix}$$

$$RNI = CBR - CDR$$

Seeing that the crude birth rate for the world in 1980 was 28 and the crude death rate was 11, we find that the world's rate of natural increase in 1980 was 28 minus 11, or 17 per 1000. Similarly, United States rates were 16 and 9, respectively resulted in a rate of natural increase for 1980 of 7 per 1000. Note that the rate of natural increase is not necessarily equal to the rate of population growth, because the effect of migration is not included in the former. The world rate of natural increase equals, at least for now, the rate of population growth, because migration to and from the earth is nonexistent—the sojourns of astronauts and creatures of close encounters notwithstanding. The U.S. rate of natural increase is well below the actual rate of population growth because of a sizable net immigration.

Population growth rate

The population growth rate is a measure of the average annual rate of increase, usually expressed as a percent. Barring migration, it is possible to make the rate of natural increase the same as the population growth rate by simply converting the rate per 1000 to an annual percentage rate. The 1980 world rate of natural increase was 17 per 1000; this can be converted to an annual population growth rate of 1.7 percent by dividing the rate of natural increase by 10. Keep in mind, however, that the rate of population growth will usually differ from the rate of natural increase because of the migration factor.

The rate of natural increase in the United States amounted to an annual growth rate of 0.7 percent. Actually, the 1979 population growth rate for the United States was closer to 0.9 percent, with the difference between the two rates due to net immigration. Therefore, 75 percent of the growth of the United States population in 1980 was due to natural increase and 25 percent to immigration. These figures are still not quite adequate because they exclude the unknown effect of illegal immigration.

Doubling time

The doubling time of a population is the number of years required for a population to double in size, given that the population grows at a specified annual rate. Population growth is dynamically similar to the growth of money in a savings account; both involve compounded interest. We can closely approximate the doubling time for a population by dividing the annual rate of population growth into the number 70. Thus, with world population growing at 1.7 percent annually, the present population would double in about 41.2 years, assuming that the 1.7 percent growth rate continues over the entire period. The doubling time for

the United States, which is growing at 0.8 percent annually, would be 87.5 years. Mexico's 1976 growth rate was 3.5 percent; if that rate continued, Mexico's 1976 population of 62.3 million would reach 124.6 million in 1996, 249.2 million in 2016, and an astounding 1.99 billion by 2076, less than a century away. Lest such figures lead us to general panic, however, we should remember Mark Twain's warning about using present rates of change to calculate past or future changes:

> In the space of one hundred and seventy-six years the Lower Mississippi has shortened itself two hundred and forty-two miles. That is an average of a trifle over one mile and a third per year. Therefore, any calm person, who is not blind or idiotic, can see that in the old Oolitic Silurian Period, just a million years ago next November, the Lower Mississippi River was upward of one million three hundred thousand miles long, and stuck out over the Gulf of Mexico like a fishing rod. And by the same token any person can see that seven hundred and forty two years from now the Lower Mississippi will be only a mile and three-quarters long and Cairo and New Orleans will have joined their streets together and be plodding comfortably along under a single mayor and a mutual board of alderman. There is something fascinating about science. One gets such wholesale returns of conjecture out of such trifling investment of fact. (1960, p. 93)

Warnings to remember

The study of population is primarily concerned with the collection and analysis of demographic data. Such data necesitates that we proceed somewhat cautiously; demographer Leon Bouvier suggests four warnings.

> *Warning 1:* Do not use growth rates to indicate changes in birth rates because growth is a function of mortality and migration in addition to fertility.
> *Warning 2:* Do not use natural increase to indicate population growth, except in those areas where migration is nonexistent.
> *Warning 3:* Do not confuse numerical growth or decline with rates of population growth or decline. It is possible that in a situation where the growth rate (percentage) is actually declining the total numerical growth of that population could still be increasing. For example, although the growth rate of the U.S.

Soweto, South Africa. Most of these small, two-family houses are overcrowded; as many as 12 people live in some of them. (United Nations, 1975)

population has been declining in recent years the total population has still been increasing.
Warning 4:   Do not take population figures as gospel truth, especially if they come from areas with less than adequate data gathering facilities. (1976)

WORLD POPULATION GROWTH

In order to understand the current world population situation, as well as future prospects, we must first understand how the population reached its current level —a world of more than 4 billion people growing at an average annual rate of 1.7 percent. In 1980, 75 million people were added to what many already perceived as an overcrowded planet. To see this in perspective, the annual population increment is comparable to the population of Nigeria—77 million in 1980: each year the world absorbs another Nigeria, which currently is the ninth largest nation. It is unlikely that this rate of growth will continue indefinitely, or even for the remainder of this century. The current high rate of population growth is an anomaly, and lower growth rates must prevail again as they have throughout most of the past. The recent period of rapid population growth is unique in demographic history, both in terms of the absolute size and rate of growth. We are becoming increasingly aware of the conflicts between growing populations and finite resources, which will be mollified by reducing the rate of population growth.

For most of human history, population growth has been exceedingly slow; the annual rate of increase probably did not reach 0.1 percent until the seventeenth century. It then accelerated gradually until 1750. Most of our ideas concerning historical populations are conjectural; demographic detectives, using whatever clues they could find, have pieced together the story of the human population's slow but persistent

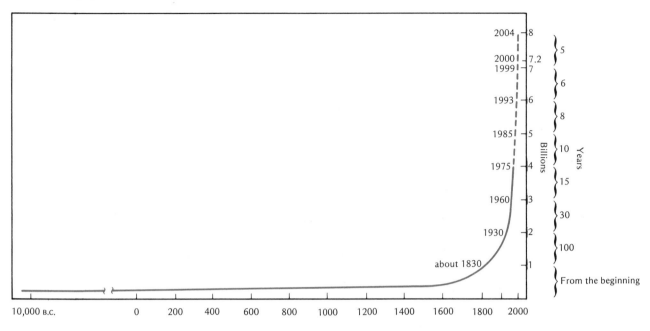

FIGURE 2–1 Arithmetic growth of world population from 10,000 B.C. to A.D. 2004; projected figures assume constant fertility level. (*Population Bulletin*, courtesy of the Population Reference Bureau, Inc., Washington, D.C. After Development Coordination Committee, *Development Issues*, 1975, p. 71. Washington, D.C., U.S. Dept. of State.)

expansion in both numbers and territory inhabited. What is known of historical population sizes and growth rates must remain speculative, because censuses and other collections of population data were nearly nonexistent before the middle of the eighteenth century. Earlier censuses had been taken in a few places, such as China, but the data are questionable at best. Even today we do not have reliable statistics for perhaps one half of the world's population.

Considerable variation can be found in the estimates of prehistoric populations, which are generally made on the basis of assumptions about the land's carrying capacity and the distribution of the human population. One study of prehistoric human population put 125,000 people on earth one million years ago, 3.34 million people 25,000 years ago, and 5.32 million people 10,000 years ago (Deevey, 1960). People lived by hunting and gathering, and their distribution was limited by the places which could provide them with an existence.

By 1 A.D., the world population had increased to between 250 and 300 million. People were more widely spread around the globe, and a number of relatively dense clusters of population existed. The average annual rate of population growth was probably about 0.05 percent. At this rate, doubling time would have been 1400 years, compared to 41.2 years for the current world population.

The world's population did not reach 1 billion until around 1820, with an annual rate of population growth of roughly 0.50 percent. Though all human history had been required to reach the first billion, only 110 years were required to add the next billion; in 1930, 2 billion people resided on this planet. The population more than doubled in only 47 years to 1980's 4.4 billion. Population projections suggest that, barring major catastrophes, we will add another 2 to 2.5 billion people by the year 2000. The reasons behind changes in population growth involve both changes in birth rates and, especially in previous centuries, changes in death rates.

An arithmetic graph of population growth, familiar to many people, clearly depicts the very rapid growth over the past three hundred years (figure 2–1). However, such a graph can be misleading. If the graph were to start with the year zero—the year that humans became recognizably human—instead of 1 A.D., what would it look like? Assuming that the year zero was

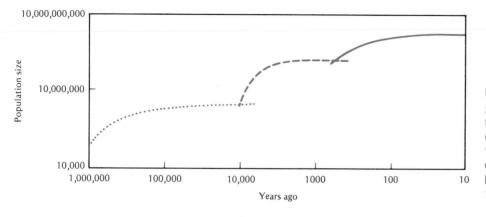

about 2 million years ago and that the graph depicted population growth for all of human history, such a graph would be impossible to make for student use. For example, if the graph had a scale of one inch per one hundred years (commonly used in such graphs), it would then be over 1666 feet long, or about one-third of a mile. Further, the line depicting population numbers would be flat for over 1665 feet and only rise in the last foot of the graph; only the last three inches of the graph would show the rapid rise in population during the past three hundred years. More will be said about these changes, but first consider a different graphic interpretation of population growth.

Figure 2–2, developed by Edward Deevey, views past population growth on a *logarithmic* rather than an *arithmetic* graph. The contrast between this and figure 2–1 is both striking and suggestive. Rather than a single period of population increase, we see three periods of rapid demographic increase, each followed by a slowing of growth rates. Deevey argued that each of these periods of accelerated population growth was a response to a revolution during which the earth's capacity to support populations was increased, sometimes rather dramatically. Human evolution has been mainly cultural rather than physical, and major changes in people's ability to utilize their environment allowed numbers to increase. It is also possible, of course, that increases in numbers forced the finding of new ways of utilizing the environment (Boserup, 1965). Either way, Deevey identified three major revolutions: the tool-making or cultural revolution, the agricultural revolution, and the scientific-industrial revolution. The term *revolution* continues to be used to describe these major events in our past, but we should

keep in mind that these revolutions, especially the first two, were slow to occur and slow to spread from their places of origin. Keep in mind also that early statistics are imprecise.

The cultural revolution

The cultural or tool-making revolution occurred in prehistoric time. The archaeological record is the only source of information about events in that era. The origin and evolution of humans continues to occupy the time and energy of many researchers; the skeletal remains of early hominids are periodically found, and new finds continue to push back the frontiers of our knowledge to even earlier times. The geographical search for early humans has established an African origin; skeletal remains recently uncovered suggest an age of 2.5 to 3 million years. Peking man and Java man roamed portions of the earth around 500,000 years ago and were undoubtedly early humans. However, as fascinating as such studies of early humans and their ancestors may be, little is known of their numbers except that there were undoubtedly few of them. As Deevey commented, "For most of the million-year period the number of hominids, including man, was about what would be expected of any large Pleistocene mammal—scarcer than horses, say, but commoner than elephants" (1960, pp. 197–198). Not only were their numbers small, but the rate of growth in those numbers must also have been exceedingly small.

Homo sapiens sapiens probably emerged 35,000 years ago. Skeletal remains found in France's Dordogne Valley were first considered those of cave-dwellers who were referred to as *Cro-Magnon Man*.

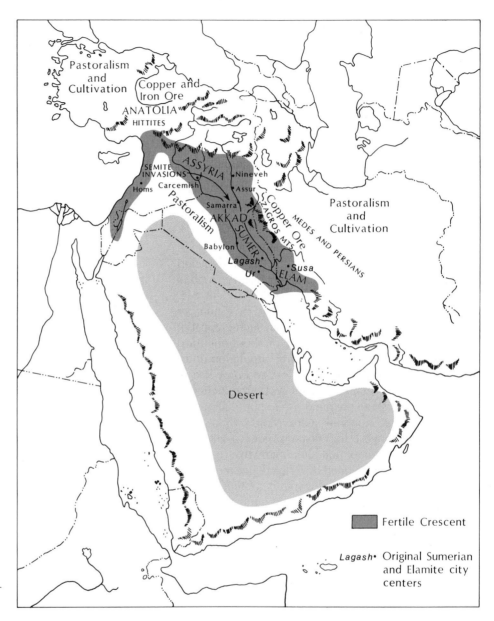

FIGURE 2–3 The Fertile Crescent.

The art left behind at Lascaux and several other caves in the Valley suggests a high degree of intelligence and awareness. The brain size and bone structure of *Cro-Magnon Man* was not significantly different from ours, and some researchers believe that *Cro-Magnon Man* was indistinguishable from our own species (Boughey, 1975).

The growth in numbers of *Homo sapiens sapiens* prior to the agricultural revolution was extremely slow.

Their existence, most likely a precarious one, was supported by fishing, hunting, and foraging. Population densities at the start of the agricultural revolution were small, and people were vulnerable to environmental changes. Actual estimates of population size are subject to wide margins of error. However, the order of magnitude seems reasonable. According to Deevey, the world's population 10,000 years ago was 5.32 million. Others have suggested that it might be twice that

Carl Sauer. (Dept. of Geography, Univ. of California/Berkeley)

amount. Thus, we can reasonably assume a world population of 5 to 10 million on the eve of the agricultural revolution, including all continents except Antarctica.

The agricultural revolution

It is likely that *incipient cultivation* and *domestication* developed somewhere around 10,000 B.C. in the Near East, the result of an extremely slow evolutionary process. One of the earliest areas to experience the new agricultural changes that would gradually burgeon into a major revolution was the rimland around the *Fertile Crescent* (figure 2–3).

There is, however, little doubt that people at other locations were developing at approximately the same time. One of America's most noted cultural geographers, Carl O. Sauer, postulated that Southeastern Asia was a more likely place for the earliest develop-

ment and subsequent diffusion of agriculture (figure 2–4) (1952).

An examination of the factors which influenced Sauer's choice of Southeast Asia provides an interesting insight into the manner in which a cultural geographer must consider the critical interplay between the physical environment and human activities. The fundamental aspects of Sauer's argument were:

1. Agriculture did not originate as the result of a chronic shortage of food. People close to starvation simply do not have the leisure for the reflection and experimentation necessary for the development of agriculture.

2. The area in which domestication originated must have been extremely diverse in terrain and possibly climate in order to provide the number and types of plants needed for the raw materials of experimentation.

3. The most primitive agriculturalist could not have coped with the periodic floods of the Near East river

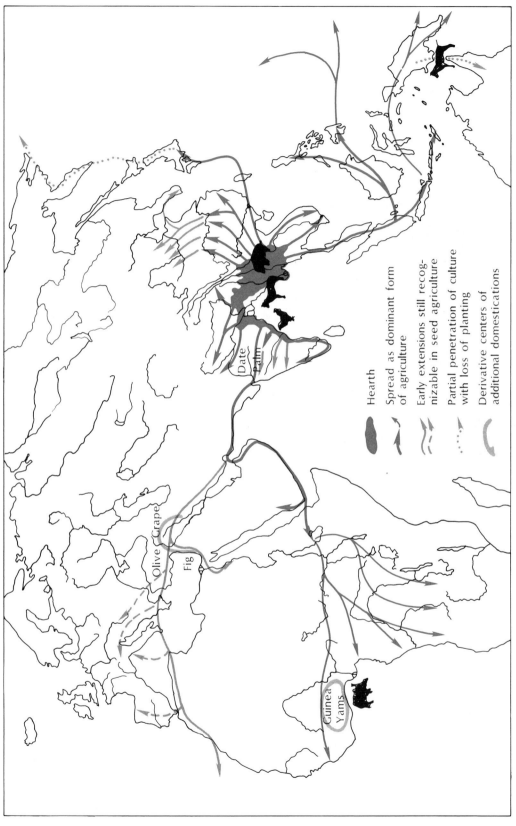

FIGURE 2–4 Diffusion of agriculture and domestication. (Reprinted from *Agricultural Origins and Dispersals* by Carl O. Sauer by permission of the M.I.T. Press, Cambridge, MA. © 1969 by The Massachusetts Institute of Technology), p. 27.)

valleys, so early Near East agriculture must have originated in hill or mountain lands.

4.   Woodlands would provide the most likely type of physical setting for early agriculture. The woodland soil, for example, could be more easily worked than the harder soils of the grasslands.

5.   The people who domesticated plants must have had a long history of the acquisition and development of the skills necessary for agriculture. These groups, in all probability, evolved from gatherers.

6.   The founders of agriculture were most probably sedentary. People who of necessity had to be mobile to acquire food, water, fuel or shelter would not likely have settled and remained at one location long enough for agricultural development to take place.

Sauer hypothesized that Southeast Asia met these requirements of physical and organic diversity. The region has a mild climate, abundant rainfall and a great many rivers, providing not only transportation and water but also a plentiful food supply. Fishing provided enough of a food surplus that some people were freed from the immediate daily chore of obtaining food, thus allowing time for experimentation and reflection. The type of plant multiplication and selection found commonly in Southeast Asia also favored that region as an early center of domestication. Unlike the grain crops associated with the Near East, the type of vegetation domesticated in Southeast Asia was largely associated with asexual plant reproduction; that is, a piece of a plant was set into the ground to form a new plant. This could have led to the discovery, by simple observation, that plant growth could be generated and regulated by human activity.

Although the question of the earliest site of agricultural development has not been totally answered, there can be little doubt that very soon the agricultural revolution was underway at several places in the Old World, and shortly in the New World as well.

With the evolution and **diffusion** of agricultural practices, humans were to experience tremendous changes, from the wandering and tenuous life of the hunter-gatherer to the more secure and sedentary life of the agriculturalist. However, these changes were gradual. Some possible domestication of plants took place in Mesoamerica between 7000 and 5000 B.C., followed by slow but consistent increase (figure 2–5).

The introduction of farming encouraged greater population density and probably produced the first grain surpluses. In turn, a few people were freed from the fundamental tasks of providing food. Many inventions and innovations followed, including irrigation, long-distance trade, metallurgy, and the development of village settlements, which increased the carrying capacity of the land.

The rate of growth of the world's population also increased because of these changes. As the agricultural revolution diffused to various parts of the earth's inhabited surface, its impact on population growth became increasingly significant. However, as Deevey's interpretation suggests, once the impact of this revolutionary increase in the earth's carrying capacity had completed its diffusion, the rate of population growth must have slowed.

We mentioned earlier that the earth's population was 250 to 300 million by the beginning of the Christian Era. Although the population continued to grow, its progress was slow and regional distribution varied. The overall pattern was one of growth; however, **cyclical changes** were common. The population growth rate was checked by food supplies and often interrupted by epidemics, famines, and wars.

The effects of famines were primarily local and their influence on the death rate depended on both the severity of the famine and the links between the famine-stricken area and other areas. Famines have occasionally been devastating, as in Eastern China between 1877 and 1879 when 9 million people died. However, as transportation linkages improved, the effects of local crop failures diminished.

The impact of wars on population growth rates is difficult to assess. Simply counting battlefield deaths would underestimate the demographic impact of most wars, because wars act as diffusion agents for numerous diseases and disrupt food supplies (Zinsser, 1967, p. 113).

Epidemics have often had a devastating effect on regional populations. Dramatic examples include the Justinian Plague of A.D. 541–544 and the Black Death of A.D. 1346–1350. The Black Death may have decreased the European population by 25 percent, with death tolls in some places reaching over 50 percent; the recovery of the European population was further impeded by the One Hundred Years War.

A gradual acceleration in the rate of population growth occurred around the 16th century in Europe, though localized periods of famine, war, and disease were still common. By then the world was approaching another major revolution, one which continues to im-

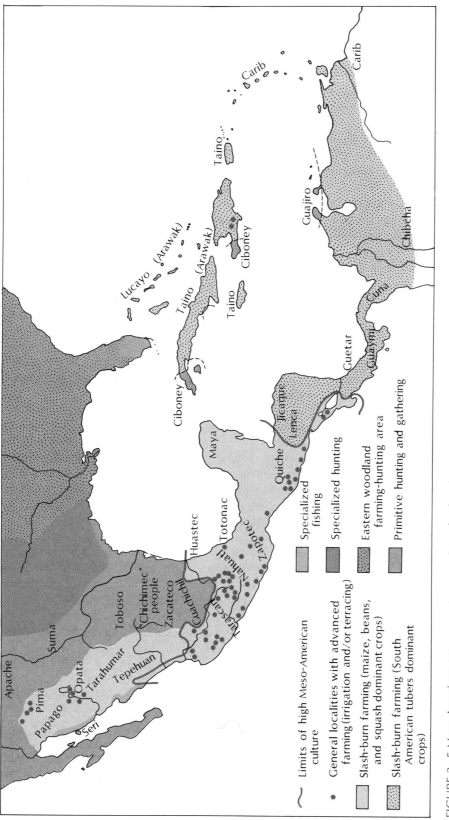

FIGURE 2–5 Meso-American preconquest economic and cultural centers, A.D. 1500. (Robert
C. West, John P. Augelli, *Middle America: Its Lands and Peoples*, 2nd ed., © 1976, p. 220.
Reprinted by permission of Prentice-Hall, Inc., Englewood Cliffs, NJ.)

Limits of high Meso-American
culture

General localities with advanced
farming (irrigation and/or terracing)

Slash-burn farming (maize, beans,
and squash dominant crops)

Slash-burn farming (South
American tubers dominant
crops)

Specialized fishing

Specialized hunting

Eastern woodland
farming-hunting area

Primitive hunting and gathering

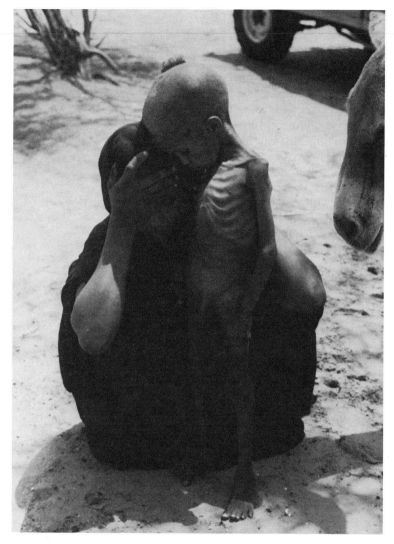

Sahelian drought victims in Mauritania. (United Nations, 1973)

pact world population growth and distribution. On the eve of the Industrial Revolution, life for most people was difficult. Crude death rates were high, average life expectancy was probably under 35 years, and in order to survive, most populations had high crude birth rates.

CASE STUDY:
Population control by catastrophe: the Black Death

A more frightful teacher than the plague, which swept over humanity with special fury in the middle of the fourteenth century, it is difficult to imagine.

Diepgen

The pandemic of plague, more commonly called the Black Death, was perhaps the greatest single calamity ever visited upon the human race.

The Great Dying, as the Germans called it, was responsible for the death of at least one-fourth of Europe's population between 1346 and 1350.

The plague was first introduced to the trading city of Caffa in the Crimea by the army of an invading Mongol prince in 1346. It spread to Constantinople by the spring of 1347, then quickly spread through Greece and the Mediterranean islands. By October it reached Sicily, and passed on to Naples, Genoa, and Marseilles by the end of 1347. It established itself in southern Italy, Spain, and France by early 1348. By June it was in Paris, and by fall, in England and Ireland. A little later Germany and the Netherlands succumbed, and by 1350 all of Europe, including the dependencies of Iceland and Greenland, were in the grip of the Black Death.

The exact cause of the disease *(Bacillus pestis)* is now well recognized. There are three highly fatal forms of the disease: the pneumonic form, which primarily attacks the lungs; the septicemic form, which brings about death by poisoning the blood; and the bubonic form, which produces *buboes,* a swelling of the lymph glands. Fleas, primarily from black rats and other rodents, carry the disease and transmit it to humans. It is usually fatal within five or six days. It produces agonizing pain, high fever, prostration, and the dark blotches resulting from skin hemorrhages from whence it got its name. Estimates are that 80 percent of those who contracted the disease died in agony within a few days. According to a study by William Langer, "The medical profession was all but helpless. . . . It is difficult to imagine the growing terror with which the people must have watched the inexorable advance of the disease on their community" (1964, p. 115).

The demographic impact of such high mortality varied from place to place. Some small communities experienced total decimation, whereas others, such as Milan, seemed to have escaped entirely. There was initial skepticism by modern scholars of the huge mortality figures recorded by chroniclers of the time, but recent detailed analyses have found that most of the reports were substantially correct. For example, two thirds of the residents of Hamburg died; the population of Florence was reduced from 90,000 to 45,000; and Siena's population declined from 42,000 to 15,000. The decline in western and central Europe was so great that nearly two centuries passed before that region regained its population of 1348 (figure 2 – 6).

The social and economic changes brought about by the plague were enormous. Epidemics of the 14th to 16th centuries produced mass migrations from the towns. Most of the migrants were the well-to-do, including princes, kings, emperors, merchants, the clergy, and even physicians. They left the common people behind to shift for themselves. Mass segregation occurred within the towns; when the plague hit, soldiers often would keep anyone from entering or leaving. Entire streets or blocks were cordoned off, and the sick were forced to stay in their neighborhoods or even their homes. Gallows were installed in many public squares to warn those who considered violating these regulations.

It was not uncommon for victims to die in the streets. Gravediggers, usually tramps or criminals, were paid fantastic wages. Often they did not discriminate between the dead and near-dead; the bodies of both were thrown into carts and dumped in large pits outside the town walls.

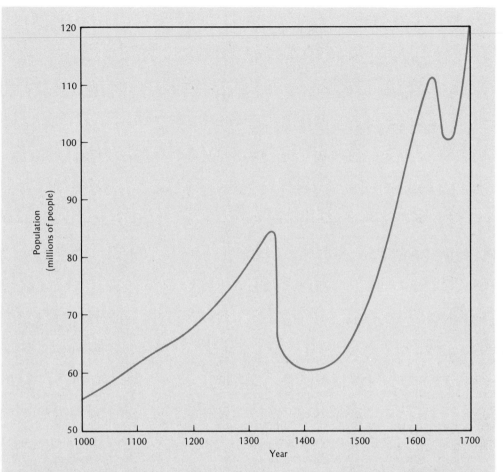

FIGURE 2–6 Population growth and plagues in Europe. (From William Langer, "The Black Death."

An outbreak of the plague would bring about two somewhat similar yet contradictory forms of behavior. A wave of violence and crime would accompany an outbreak of the plague. Robbery and looting flourished, and burial gangs stripped corpses of valuable possessions and looted the houses of the dead.

Just as some were driven to the complete abandonment of morality, others, perhaps the majority, were driven to pathetic religious and superstitious extravagances. This dichotomy was noted in the London Epidemic of 1625 by the poet George Wither:

> Some streets had Churches full
>   of people, weeping;
> Some others, Tavernes had,
>   rude-revell keeping;
> Within some houses Psalmes
>   and Hymnes were sung;
> With raylings and loud scouldings
>   others rung.

In their religious ferver, many people gave expensive gifts to the church or made extravagent vows. A spread in the belief in witchcraft occurred. In some places it was believed that the Jews had poisoned the world, and so people killed them; in other places cripples were scapegoated. Even physicians were stoned in France because they were said to be encouraging the spread of the disease.

The economic life of Europe also suffered from the Black Death. Prior to the plague, Europe was in a period of relative prosperity, rapid population growth, and territorial expansion. With the advent of the Black Death, Europe sank into a depression that lasted for more than a century. The economic decline was particularly evident in the rural agricultural regions. In the words of Petrarch, the fourteenth century poet, "a vast and dreadful solitude" encompassed the land. Although the economic revival of the 17th and 18th centuries cannot solely be attributed to the eradication of the plague, it certainly was an important factor.

The Industrial Revolution

The genesis of the Industrial Revolution occurred in England in the latter half of the 18th century and rapidly spread throughout western Europe and the United States. By the early 20th century, it had reached Russia and northern Italy. The first Asian country to experience the Industrial Revolution was Japan, where industry replaced agriculture as the major sector of the economy. The Industrial Revolution continues today and has only partially diffused to the developing countries.

Population growth had begun to accelerate by 1750 in England and Wales, and soon after in other countries as they began to industrialize. Crude birth and death rates tended to be high prior to this time; in average years there had been more births than deaths, and in bad years the reverse was likely. There was a greater fluctuation in death rates than in birth rates. In order to overcome the prevailing high death rates, high birth rates were probably considered necessary, though birth rates were generally not as high as they might have been.

Human ability to wrest a living from the earth increased during both the cultural and agricultural revolutions, but it was not until the Industrial Revolution that people began to gain control over death for the first time. Many changes resulted in this control over death rates, primarily by curbing the high peaks in their cyclical fluctuations.

Improved agricultural practices and better distribution systems decreased the localized effects of famines; agricultural practices often associated with the Enclosures Acts in England during the 1700s were of critical importance. The Enclosures Acts essentially fenced off the land, which meant that animals could not roam freely in the fields and destroy crops. Selective breeding became a widespread practice, and in a little over 100 years, the weights of animals in English slaughterhouses tripled. The availability of manure for fertilizer increased; New World root crops were introduced into Old World agriculture; and soil restorative crops like legumes (clover and alfalfa) were planted on fields in the fallow (nonuse) year.

The innovations associated with each of the three revolutions, particularly the agricultural and Industrial Revolutions, diffused outward. The speed and direction of diffusion was governed by such things as distance, intervening obstacles, nature of the environmental base, and receptivity of various social structures. One important point to remember is that the spread of these innovations was uneven; whenever innovations caught up with a society, there was a traumatic effect. They often necessitated new patterns of leadership, new forms of organization, and the acquisition of new skills, and usually resulted in rapid population increases.

The innovations of the Industrial Revolution have diffused at unequal speeds and at unequal intensities across the earth. The acceptance of new innovations is not always easy, and some cultures, like some individuals, are quicker to accept change than others. These innovations often greatly increased the carrying capacities of occupied lands; new tools, for example, increased agricultural productivity. No small part of this often traumatic change has been the growth of population and related changes in the population structure. Such changes have also left their imprint on the landscape, providing materials for such fields of study as industrial archaeology.

One further point to be emphasized from Deevey's interpretation of historical population growth is the nature of the curve for each revolution. After each relatively rapid spurt in population growth, the rates have slackened off—the numbers reached a plateau, and further additions were slow to be achieved. Each revolution, at least partially, removed some preexisting constraint upon population growth, but must also have set in motion the forces which eventually brought growth under control. Obviously, these forces are of urgent concern in our present circumstance.

Now for the first time, world population has entered a period of rapid and sustained growth. During the 19th century, this rapid growth was concentrated in the developed countries; by the middle of the 20th century, population growth in the developed countries had subsided, and it was accelerating in the developing countries. Before leaving the topic of population growth, we should have a closer look at some of the early theories of population change.

POPULATION THEORY

Population theories may be divided into two categories, primary and secondary. Theories formulated to explain demographic behavior are called *primary theories,* whereas *secondary theories* are formulated to analyze a much broader class of phenomena that have demographic implications. For example, a writer mainly interested in the concept of race, income, or some other nondemographic phenomenon may construct a theory with demographic significance; it would be considered a secondary theory. If the researcher's intent is understanding the specific factors related to fertility, mortality, or migration, the construct is a primary theory. The study of population as a professional specialty is relatively recent and, prior to the late 18th

century, did not receive a large amount of specialized attention. Most of the theories related to population were secondary.

Both primary and secondary theories may be further characterized as environmental or naturalistic. *Naturalistic* explanations are mechanistic, tending to stress the inexorable operation of biological processes and sometimes failing to allow for human adaptive ability. *Environmental* theories offer to explain demographic behavior through cultural processes.

Most population analysts place more emphasis on environmental theories. The term *environmental* refers to both the physical and cultural environment; although the part played by heredity (naturalistic theories) is recognized, the predominant view today is that human events are increasingly controlled by culture (Thomlinson, 1976).

Pre-Malthusian theories

Most major philosophers paid little attention to the topic of human population, and early views on population and the factors affecting fertility originated primarily in folklore (Eversley, 1959). Some of these basic notions were held by much of humankind throughout history.

Perhaps the most common notion prior to Malthus was that population decline is bad and growth is good. These equations recur throughout world literature. Wealth and material progress were largely dependent on manual labor, and an expansion in the size of the labor force was viewed as leading to prosperity. Since high mortality rates were common throughout most of human history, many children were necessary to overcome the "grim reaper."

Another legacy of great importance has been the persistence of the utopian dream. It was partially in response to this utopian dream that Malthus wrote his famous essay.

The Malthusian model

Perhaps more than any other population theorist, Thomas Robert Malthus has had a profound impact on ideas and attitudes about population growth. Thomas Robert Malthus was born in England in 1766 into a rather wealthy family. He lived during a time of major economic and social revolution. Preceding his lifetime, Europeans were conditioned to expect and accept a bitter lot and a short life, based on the assumption of limited material resources. Poverty was associated with God's will and individual merit, and the earth was viewed as a place of testing and punishment.

This, however, was a time of ferment, and the acceptance of deprivation was increasingly challenged. Liberty, equality, and fraternity were the new watchwords, and production and trade were rapidly increasing.

Out of this background came a rash of utopian schemes, visions of the future, and wild dreams. The future was seen as a time when many of the ills of humankind could be eradicated. It would be possible for the perfect society to evolve with a few changes and some luck. Malthus's father was enamored by these new ideas and had many discussions with utopians in his home. The young Malthus held the opposite opinion.

Malthus's first edition of his famous population essay was entitled *An Essay on the Principles of Population as it Affects the Future Improvement of Society, with comments on the Speculations of Mr. Godwin, Mr. Condorcet, and other writers.* It was not written as a text in demography or as an exposition of some new law of population growth; its purpose was to refute some utopian ideas and to reject the contention that society could be made perfect. The chief targets of Malthus's criticism were Mr. Godwin and Mr. Condorcet.

Concerning Condorcet, Malthus wrote, "I have read some of the speculations on the perfectability of man and of society with great pleasure. I have been warmed and delighted with the enchanting pictures which they hold forth. I ardently wish for such happy improvements . . ." (1959, p. 3). Unfortunately, Malthus then argued, the road to Utopia was always blocked by the "principle of population," which dictated that humanity must always press to the limit of subsistence.

The first edition of Malthus's *Essay* was rather straightforward, consisting only of two postulates and one assumption. The first postulate was that "food is necessary for the existence of man;" the second was that "the passion between the sexes is necessary and will remain in its present state." According to Malthus these two laws were fixed laws of human nature; having so far seen no change in them, he argued, we may conclude that they will persist. Subsequent editions of

Malthus's *Essay* elaborated on the two postulates but contained no substantive changes in his original thoughts.

Malthus assumed that population would increase at a geometric rate, whereas food production would only increase at an arithmetic rate. In Malthus's words, "population, when unchecked, increases in a geometrical ratio. Subsistence increases only in an arithmetical ratio. A slight acquaintance with numbers will show the immensity of the first power in comparison of the second" (1959, p. 9). Thus, "the human species would increase as the numbers 1, 2, 4, 8, 16, 32, 64, 128, 256, and subsistence as 1, 2, 3, 4, 5, 6, 7, 8, 9. In two centuries the population would be to the means of subsistence as 256 to 9; in three centuries as 4,096 to 13, and in two thousand years the difference would be almost incalculable." The grimness of the first *Essay* stems from these postulates and assumptions. According to Malthus, population growth would always press against the means of subsistence, unless it was prevented by some very powerful and obvious checks. These checks were moral restraint, vice, and misery. Malthus disagreed with Godwin's assumption that things would be perfect if we could only rid ourselves of private property and government. The principle of population was inflexible, inexorable, and inescapable, and its effect could not be removed by any exercise of reason.

Looking back on Malthus's theory, several weaknesses appear; according to demographer Ralph Thomlinson (1976), four are especially important. First, Malthus overemphasized the limitation of the supply of land; the nineteenth century revolution in agricultural methods, later development of chemical fertilizers, as well as changes in plant and animal breeding altered the carrying capacity of the land. Second, Malthus failed to fully recognize the possibilities industry offered for improving living standards. Third, he failed to consider the impact of innovations in transportation, which helped colonial empires provide additional raw materials, an exploitable labor supply, and new markets for manufactured products. Finally, his religious beliefs prevented him from grasping the possibility of widespread contraception; Malthus believed birth control was immoral and closed his eyes to its possibilities.

Though much discussion and controversy occurred after Malthus's book was published in 1797, his theory dropped from favor by the middle of the 19th century as the Industrial Revolution found ways to lessen the pressure of population. However, the rapid population increase during the mid-20th century, in conjunction with considerable malnourishment in many areas, has revived an interest in Malthus's ideas. These **Neo-Malthusians** feel that population growth will outrun the supply of food, and the world will not be able to continue to support a growing population.

Malthus's contribution was considerable. Its main success was in clearly and succinctly showing the dependence of population on subsistence. Furthermore, it pointed toward the many checks on population growth (Strangeland, 1904).

Communist-socialist theory

Although several historical population theorists disagreed with Malthus, his foremost critic was probably Karl Marx, who believed that overpopulation did not exist and that Malthus was a bourgeois clergyman who defended the established order of social inequality. Malthus was also accused of copying the ideas and writings of the classical school of economic theorists who proposed private property, self-interest, individualism, and unrestricted competition as solutions to Europe's population growth. Malthus was thus an archenemy of the worldwide socialist movement because he was considered an apologist for the exploiting class and a literary oppressor of the impoverished.

In the *Communist Manifesto* and other works, Marx expounded the familiar theory of class struggle—that an uprising by the proletariat would eventually lead to a classless, egalitarian society without private property. Marx believed that food and resource production was outstripped by population growth not because of any natural law that population growth would always be greater than subsistence, but rather because the poor, under the capitalist system, did not have control of food and resources. Furthermore, if the means of subsistence—equipment, knowledge, land, and an adequate share of the wealth—were controlled by poor people, their production of goods and services would be much greater than population growth. Private ownership of the means of production and exploitation by the rich blocked this solution. In essence, Marx felt that the problem lay in the distribution of resources and not in overpopulation.

This argument has been accepted by many socialists and communists. However, there is a basic difference between the socialists and the communists: "whereas Communists prefer to deny the existence of population problems, socialists acknowledge the problems but turn to revision of the social order for a solution" (Thomlinson, 1976, p. 44).

There has been a recent swing by both socialists and communists toward the acceptance of population *per se* as a source of serious problems. In 1965, a research worker at the Institute of Economics of the USSR Academy of Science, Boris Urlanis, called for another look and reevaluation of the classic Marxist view concerning the causes of population problems in developing countries. Also, the People's Republic of China has recently implemented a series of steps to lower its birth rate. These steps included legalizing abortion, raising the legal minimum age for first marriage, making contraception readily available, emphasizing the public responsibilities incurred by reproductive behavior, and rewarding families for not having children.

The Demographic Transition

According to Malthus, humankind is either unwilling or unable to exercise moral restraint, resulting in an increase in vice and/or misery and an associated rise in the death rate. Thus, the gap between the birth rate and death rate would be closed by a rise in the death rate. However, the Malthusian forecast has not worked as a valid historical generalization, for several reasons. First, food supplies have been, and may continue to be, increased faster than the arithmetic rate suggested by Malthus. Second, population growth has certainly been checked, at least in certain areas of the world, by declining fertility within marriage. The gap between the birth rate and death rate in Europe was closed by a declining birth rate, not by a rising death rate as forecasted by Malthus; a new kind of demographic stability was reached, first in northwest Europe and then elsewhere. This transition from high birth rates and death rates to low birth rates and death rates is known as the **Demographic Transition.**

The Demographic Transition Model postulates a necessary causal link between modernization—the complex of social, economic, political, and intellectual changes associated with industrialization—on the one hand, and fertility and mortality reduction on the other.

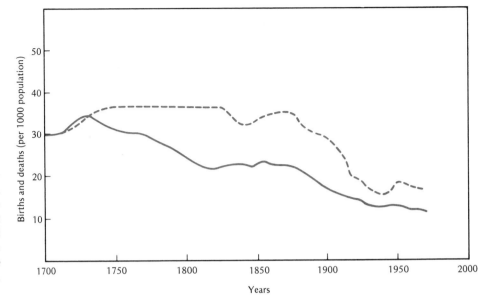

FIGURE 2–7 The Demographic Transition in England. (Adapted from Abdel R. Omran, 1977, "Epidemiologic Transition in the United States," in *Population Bulletin* 32, no. 2, p. 15. Courtesy of the Population Reference Bureau, Washington, D.C.)

Conceptually, it may be viewed as an idealized sequence of stages through which a given population passes, the end result being low birth and death rates. The transition model is based on data from the demographic experience of northwestern Europe, especially England and Wales (figure 2–7), and illustrates the changes in vital rates that have taken place in England and Wales over the past three hundred years. Prior to industrialization in the 18th century, this area experienced high death and birth rates, resulting in a relatively stable population. Around the middle of the 18th century, a decisive break occurred: the death rate began to decline. The reasons for this initial fall in the death rate are not completely understood, though most analysts agree that it was probably due to an increase in the food supply because of unusually good harvests at that time. The death rate also rose slightly in the beginning of the 19th century, probably due to the growth of factory towns and their squalid, unhealthy living conditions. After a few decades, however, the death rate resumed its decline, which has continued until the present day.

The birth rate, shown in figure 2–7, illustrates an initial increase directly related to the Industrial Revolution. Industrialization brought about the disappearance of the apprentice system: unskilled young people no longer faced long apprenticeship through the Guild system before they received compensation and therefore, could marry and start a family at a younger age.

For the next one hundred years, the birth rate stayed relatively constant, then started its major decline around 1870. The primary reason for the decline was not a change in marriage patterns, but a redefinition of the ideal family size. Several reasons for this decline in family size have been suggested. Children began to contribute less to family welfare, for example. Prior to industrialization, children contributed a great deal; since most people were agriculturalists, children could perform tasks such as weeding crops and fetching water or wood. Also, children worked in the mines and early textile factories because it was much cheaper to employ children than adults. Children were also a form of social security, and they were often the only means of support for their parents in their old age. However, children became a burden as more restrictions were put on child labor practices in the middle and late 19th century. The state also began to provide for older citizens with the development of welfare systems. The number of farmers dropped significantly with increasing industrialization, and the role of children was diminished.

Rising expectations was a second reason for the redefinition of ideal family size. A tremendous volume of goods and services came about as a result of the Industrial Revolution. Increasingly, people could shift from satisfying needs to satisfying wants. Social mobility and the attainment of riches were easier with fewer children, and some luxuries came to be viewed as necessities. More favorable attitudes toward family planning came about with the growth of knowledge. All of these factors led to a significant decline in the birth rate, and an equilibrium between birth and death rates was finally achieved.

Although figure 2–7 refers to the demographic experience of England and Wales, the same general trends can be found in most of the western world. Though the timing of the transition varied in other countries, the results were essentially the same. However, remember that the birth rate did not begin to decline until the industrialization process was fairly complete. Population patterns today reflect varying degrees of the demographic transition.

KEY TERMS

Crude population density
Carrying capacity
Spatial variations
Demography
Basic demographic equation
Crude birth rate
Crude death rate
Incipient cultivation

Domestication
Fertile Crescent
Diffusion
Cyclical changes
Primary vs. *secondary population theories*
Naturalistic vs. *environmental population theories*
Neo-Malthusians
Demographic Transition

REFERENCES

Bogue, D. J. (1969), *Principles of Demography*. New York: John Wiley & Sons, Inc.

Boserup, E. (1965), *The Conditions of Agricultural Growth: The Economics of Agrarian Change under Population Pressure*.Chicago: Aldine Publishing Co.

Boughey, A. S. (1975), *Man and the Environment: An Introduction to Human Ecology,* 2nd ed. New York: Macmillan Publishing Co.

Bouvier L. F. (1976), "On Population Growth," *Intercom* 4, 8–9.

Brackett, J. W. (1968), "The Evolution of Marxist Theories of Population: Marxism Recognizes the Population Problem," *Demography* 5, 158–173.

Brown, L. R. (1976), *World Population Trends: Signs of Hope, Signs of Stress,* Worldwatch Paper No. 8. Washington, D.C.: Worldwatch Institute.

Deevey, E. S., Jr. (1960), "The Human Population," *Scientific American* 203, 194–204.

Eversley, D. R. (1959), *Social Theories of Fertility and the Malthusian Debate*. London: Oxford University Press.

Fagan, B. W. (1974), *Men of the Earth: An Introduction to World Prehistory*. Boston: Little, Brown & Co.

Freedman, R. and Berelson, B. (1974), "The Human Population," *Scientific American* 231, 30–39.

Hernandez, J. (1974), *People, Power, and Policy*. Palo Alto, CA: National Press Books.

Langer, W. L. (1964), "The Black Death," *Scientific American* 210, 114–121.

Malthus, T. R. (1959), *Population: The First Essay*. Ann Arbor: University of Michigan Press.

McNeill, W. H. (1976), *Plaques and People*. Garden City, NJ: Anchor Press/Doubleday.

Sauer, C. O. (1952), *Agricultural Origins and Dispersals*. New York: American Geographical Society.

Strangeland, C. E. (1904), *PreMalthusian Doctrines of Population*. New York: Columbia University Press.

Thomlinson, R. (1976), *Population Dynamics: Causes and Consequences of World Demographic Change,* 2nd ed. New York: Random House, Inc.

Twain, M. (1960), *Life on the Mississippi*. New York: Bantam Books, Inc.

Zinsser, H. (1967), *Rats, Lice and History*. New York: Bantam Books, Inc.

3

The human population today and tomorrow

The historical evolution of the human population presents an overall picture of a slowly growing population for much of human history with a rapid increase at the advent of the Industrial Revolution. There were, of course, periods of rapid population growth associated with the cultural and agricultural revolutions, but since the base population was relatively small, its imprint on global economic and environmental systems was not great.

At the present time, the human population of over 4 billion people is spread throughout the globe. Large numbers of people with modern technology at their disposal have created our modern interconnected world. Changes in the number of people, the age structure of their populations, or their movement or migration patterns can have worldwide repercussions on both the economic and environmental systems. Without some understanding of the nature and distribution of today's population it would be impossible to solve the world's socioeconomic and environmental problems.

WORLD POPULATION TODAY

The historical record shows that the acceleration of world population growth started with the European countries and the lands Europeans settled overseas. However, in the contemporary world the so called *developing countries* in Asia, Africa, and Latin America are the locations for the most dramatic population growth; birth rates in these countries are nearly twice as high as those found in the **developed nations** of the world. A high birth rate coupled with a falling death rate creates a situation in which population increases rapidly, so it is not surprising that three-fourths of humankind live in the developing world.

Developed and developing regions. Various terms have been used to differentiate between rich and poor nations or regions. Currently, *developed* and *developing,* or *more developed* and *less developed,* are in common use. *Developed* and *underdeveloped* have been popular in the past and show some sign of becoming popular again. Generally, we have used the terms *developed* and *developing,* recognizing that no pair of dichotomous terms adequately describe the world's nations.

Our classification follows the United Nations division of the world into regions. The developed regions include all of Europe, Northern America (including Greenland and Bermuda), Australia and New Zealand, Japan, the U.S.S.R., and Temperate South America (Argentina, Chile and Uruguay). The remainder of the world comprises the developing regions.

The last 25 years have seen the world's population grow from around 2.5 billion to over 4 billion—an increase of over 1.5 billion people—as well as a change in the population shares held by selected regions and countries (figure 3–1). During this period, the growth rates of the major regions of the earth have varied significantly (figure 3–2). The demographic dis-

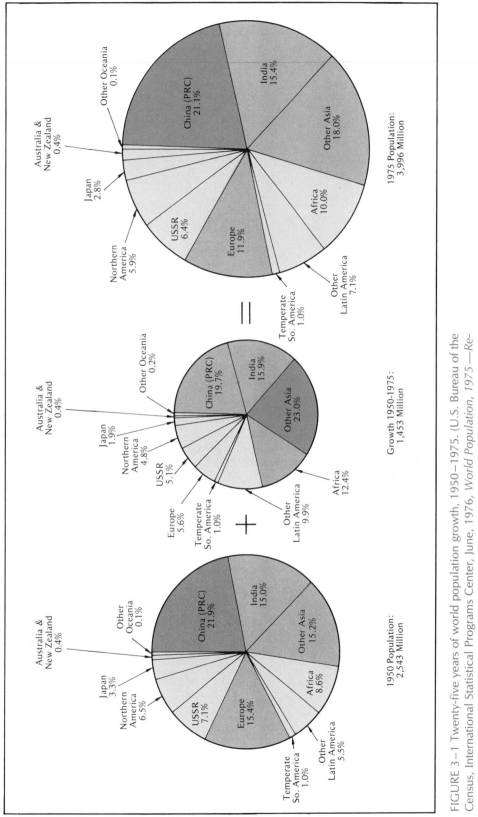

FIGURE 3–1 Twenty-five years of world population growth, 1950–1975. (U.S. Bureau of the Census, International Statistical Programs Center, June, 1976, *World Population, 1975 —Recent Demographic Estimates for the Countries and Regions of the World*. Washington, D.C., U.S. Government Printing Office, p. 11.)

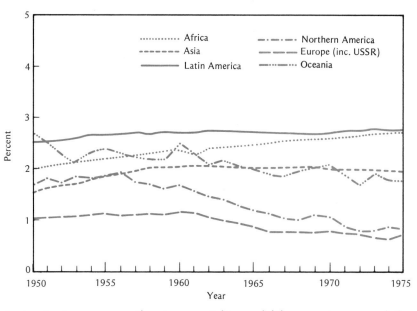

FIGURE 3–2 Average annual population growth rates by continent, 1950–1975. (U.S. Bureau of the Census, International Statistical Programs Center, June, 1976, *World Population, 1975 —Recent Demographic Estimates for the Countries and Regions of the World.* Washington, D.C., U.S. Government Printing Office, p. 10.)

crepancy between the developed and developing areas, illustrated in figures 3–1 and 3–2, means that world population will increase by six to eight billion in the next 25 years and that the vast majority of this projected growth will be centered in the developing countries of Africa, Asia, and Latin America.

Between 1750 and 1850, the developed countries grew at a rate of 0.5 percent, whereas the developing countries increased at an annual rate of 0.4 percent; from 1850 to 1950, the rates were 0.9 percent for the developed countries and 0.6 percent for the developing countries; from 1950 to 1975, the rates were 1.1 and 2.3 percent, respectively. Today about 75 percent of humankind lives in the developing countries (Demeny, 1974).

A *cartogram* of the world's population distribution (figure 3–3) illustrates some interesting facets of population distribution. Perhaps the most striking aspect of the cartogram is the numerical predominance of Asia's population—55 percent of the world total. Of the approximately 3 billion people in the developing countries, about 75 percent live in Asia, including 33 percent in south and west Asia, 28 percent in China, 14 percent in southeast Asia.

Age structure

Many interesting comparisons can be made between the population structures found in the developed and developing countries. The *age structure* of the population, for example, offers many clues to population growth rates, mortality and life expectancy, and the standard of living. A country with a rapidly growing population will have a large proportion of its residents in the younger age groups. An examination of the world population under the age of 15 provides further evidence, for instance, that Asia, Africa, and Latin America are growing rapidly, while North America, Europe, and Oceania, with a far lower proportion of young people, are growing less rapidly.

A population with a large proportion of older people will have different needs and requirements than a population with a great many young people. A *population pyramid* is a useful way to examine the age–sex structure and social attributes of the population concerned.

A population pyramid is essentially two bar graphs placed back-to-back with the vertical center line representing zero (figure 3–4). The horizontal bars represent the number of people in each age group by sex, and the vertical axis gives the different age groups in five year intervals. The shape of the population pyramid varies according to the country or community and the time period. A population pyramid is an important device for summarizing the demographic history of a country over the past two or three generations.

The pyramid's shape is determined by fertility, mortality, and migration. A population with a large number of children, the result of high birth rates, would have a pyramid with a wide base (figure 3–4), whereas a population with a falling or low birth rate has a small base (figure 3–5). The pyramid is also affected by death rates; low death rates usually are reflected in a pyramid with a large, elderly population. Population pyramids can also show evidence of great human tragedies; the population pyramid of Berlin shows a distinct lack of men in the 20–29 year age brackets (figure 3–6). This unusual configuration was most likely due to the great loss of life among soldiers during the Second World War. Migration can also be a factor in changing the shape of the population pyramid. A large in-migration of people of a certain age group can significantly alter the shape of a pyramid.

When the shapes of pyramids for several countries are compared, certain broad categories of population structure can be recognized, each coinciding with a particular sort of cultural development. There are basically four types of population structures (figure 3–7). The first type is the pyramid with a regular triangular shape, typical of a developing country with high birth and death rates. Few countries can be found today with this type of pyramid, though it was common during the 17th and 18th centuries. The second type has a narrow top, wide base, and concave sides; it represents a falling death rate, particularly in the youngest age category (0 to 5 years), and a high birth rate. This pyramid is typical for most of the developing countries in Africa, Asia, and Latin America. A beehive shape indicates a relatively stable population with low birth rates (a narrow base), low death rates (steep sides), and a high median age. Most European countries would exhibit this type of shape; England, Wales, and Sweden are good examples. The fourth type of population pyramid represents a country that has had a rapid decrease in fertility, giving a tapered shape to the bottom of the pyramid. This type is well illustrated by Japan.

POPULATION THEORIES FROM TODAY'S PERSPECTIVE

In the preceding chapter, the principal population theories were discussed in their historical development. In this chapter, we will examine those theories to see what changes have occurred since their original formulation.

Neo-Malthusian

As noted previously, the works of Thomas Robert Malthus have had a tremendous influence on ideas concerning the nature and impact of population growth.

Neo-Malthusians currently believe that, despite the promises of science, the rapidly rising population of the world will face dire consequences unless its growth is checked.

Although Neo-Malthusians generally agree with the ideas of Malthus, they do take exception to Malthus's opposition to birth control. They strongly support the concept of family planning and support programs which apply a broad range of modern innovations to reduce population growth rates. The large-scale implementation of family planning programs is typical of their approach.

The Neo-Malthusian point of view was forcefully expressed by Robert S. McNamara, then President of the World Bank, in an address delivered at the University of Notre Dame in 1969. McNamara, who was in favor of giving technical and financial assistance only to those nations with an official family planning program, stated that the population problem would destroy much of humankind's future unless family planning was instituted on a large scale. McNamara believed that many signs of an impending crisis were evident already; for example, half of the world is hungry, including millions of malnourished children who already have irreversible brain damage, and despondent masses huddle in the degrading conditions of third world slums—in short, we see the widespread misery predicted by Malthus.

The Demographic Transition

The Demographic Transition Model is based on the historical patterns of vital rates in western Europe. How relevant is the experience of western Europe for the rest of the world? Figure 3–8 represents the Demographic Transition Model as applied to various parts of the world today. *Stage A* indicates an area that has high birth and death rates, equivalent to preindustrial Europe. Only parts of Africa, with their high birth rates and relatively high death rates, fit this pattern, and even most of the African nations have recently begun to move into *Stage B*, which represents a population that has a high birth rate but a declining death rate. Much of Asia, excluding Japan and Taiwan, fits into this category. *Stage C* includes those nations with a high birth rate and a low death rate; they include tropical Latin America, where populations are growing at the fastest rate in the world. The fourth category, *Stage D*, shows a declining birth rate and a low death rate and includes countries in temperate South America, such as Argentina and Uruguay. The final category, *Stage E*, depicts

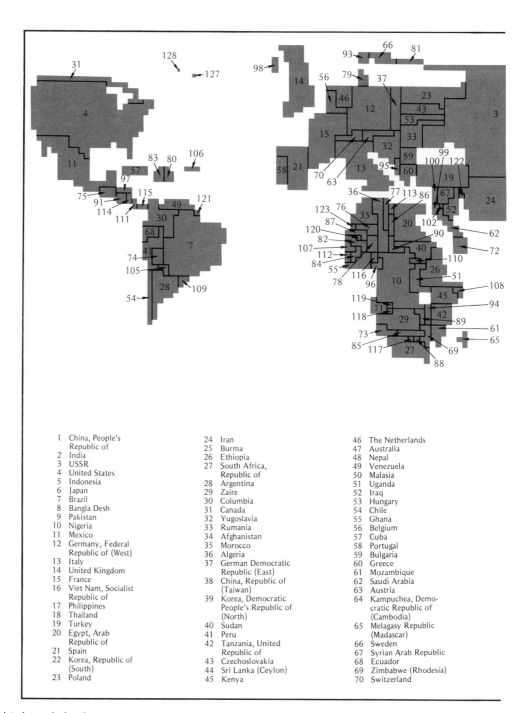

1	China, People's Republic of	24	Iran	46	The Netherlands
2	India	25	Burma	47	Australia
3	USSR	26	Ethiopia	48	Nepal
4	United States	27	South Africa, Republic of	49	Venezuela
5	Indonesia	28	Argentina	50	Malasia
6	Japan	29	Zaire	51	Uganda
7	Brazil	30	Columbia	52	Iraq
8	Bangla Desh	31	Canada	53	Hungary
9	Pakistan	32	Yugoslavia	54	Chile
10	Nigeria	33	Rumania	55	Ghana
11	Mexico	34	Afghanistan	56	Belgium
12	Germany, Federal Republic of (West)	35	Morocco	57	Cuba
13	Italy	36	Algeria	58	Portugal
14	United Kingdom	37	German Democratic Republic (East)	59	Bulgaria
15	France	38	China, Republic of (Taiwan)	60	Greece
16	Viet Nam, Socialist Republic of	39	Korea, Democratic People's Republic of (North)	61	Mozambique
17	Philippines			62	Saudi Arabia
18	Thailand	40	Sudan	63	Austria
19	Turkey	41	Peru	64	Kampuchea, Democratic Republic of (Cambodia)
20	Egypt, Arab Republic of	42	Tanzania, United Republic of	65	Melagasy Republic (Madascar)
21	Spain	43	Czechoslovakia	66	Sweden
22	Korea, Republic of (South)	44	Sri Lanka (Ceylon)	67	Syrian Arab Republic
23	Poland	45	Kenya	68	Ecuador
				69	Zimbabwe (Rhodesia)
				70	Switzerland

a population with low birth and death rates. This, of course, would include the western world and Japan.

If one accepts the Demographic Transition Model and believes that there is a necessary, causal link between modernization and a declining birth and death rates, then the best solution to rapid population growth is to modernize the world as rapidly as possible. However, if there is a progression from *Stage A* to *B* to *C*, and so forth, then the rapidity at which nations move through these stages is essential. Those nations in *Stage D* are proceeding in the right direction and will soon reach an equilibrium of births and deaths. Although the

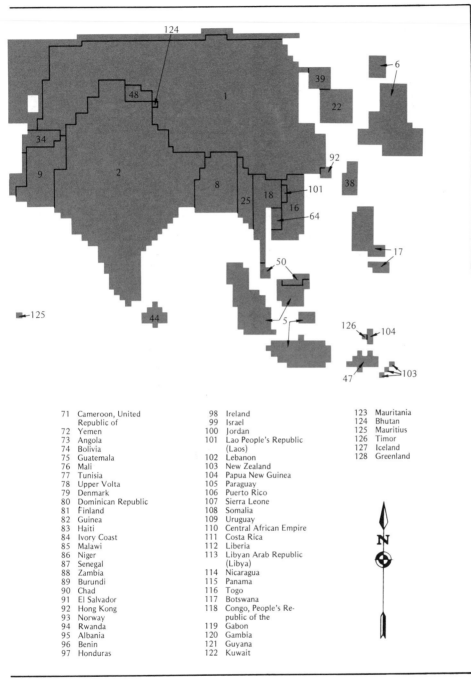

71	Cameroon, United	98	Ireland	123	Mauritania
	Republic of	99	Israel	124	Bhutan
72	Yemen	100	Jordan	125	Mauritius
73	Angola	101	Lao People's Republic	126	Timor
74	Bolivia		(Laos)	127	Iceland
75	Guatemala	102	Lebanon	128	Greenland
76	Mali	103	New Zealand		
77	Tunisia	104	Papua New Guinea		
78	Upper Volta	105	Paraguay		
79	Denmark	106	Puerto Rico		
80	Dominican Republic	107	Sierra Leone		
81	Finland	108	Somalia		
82	Guinea	109	Uruguay		
83	Haiti	110	Central African Empire		
84	Ivory Coast	111	Costa Rica		
85	Malawi	112	Liberia		
86	Niger	113	Libyan Arab Republic		
87	Senegal		(Libya)		
88	Zambia	114	Nicaragua		
89	Burundi	115	Panama		
90	Chad	116	Togo		
91	El Salvador	117	Botswana		
92	Hong Kong	118	Congo, People's Re-		
93	Norway		public of the		
94	Rwanda	119	Gabon		
95	Albania	120	Gambia		
96	Benin	121	Guyana		
97	Honduras	122	Kuwait		

FIGURE 3–3 Cartogram of population size. Each country's size is proportional to its population; thus, China dominates with 900 million people. The list identifies each country by number. (From *Population, An Introduction to Concepts and Issues* by John R. Weeks. © 1978 by Wadsworth Publishing Co., Inc., Belmont, CA 94002, pp. 40–41. Reprinted by permission of the publisher.)

nations in *Stage C* are experiencing a rapid increase in population, they are going in the right direction and will shortly experience a decline in birth rates and a concomitant decrease in population growth. The critical areas of the world are those found in *Stages A* and *B;* they have yet to reach their greatest increase in pop-

ulation, *Stage C.* Also, Africa and Asia already contain the largest populations, and if they duplicate the European experience, their populations will increase tremendously.

In order to ascertain the relevance of the Demographic Transition Model for the developing countries

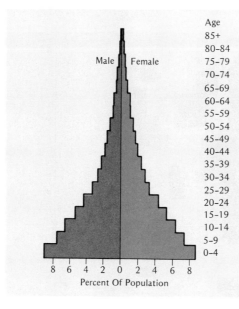

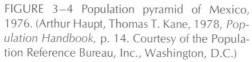

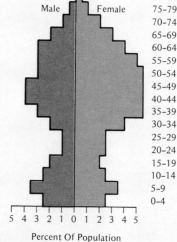

FIGURE 3–4 Population pyramid of Mexico, 1976. (Arthur Haupt, Thomas T. Kane, 1978, *Population Handbook,* p. 14. Courtesy of the Population Reference Bureau, Inc., Washington, D.C.)

FIGURE 3–5 Population pyramid of the United States, 1976. (Arthur Haupt, Thomas T. Kane, 1978, *Population Handbook,* p. 14. Courtesy of the Population Reference Bureau, Inc., Washington, D.C.)

FIGURE 3–6 Population pyramid of Berlin, 1946. (Reprinted from *Population Geography: Problems, Concepts & Prospects,* by Gary L. Peters and Robert P. Larkin, © 1979, with permission of Kendall/Hunt Publishing Co., p. 37.)

today, several questions must be answered. Is there a necessary, causal link between modernization and fertility decline? Is it possible for a nation to move through the stages of the Demographic Transition in a short time? The answers to these questions will certainly determine the demographic future of the world.

Demographic Transition theory in today's world. In recent years demographers have carefully analyzed the details of the Demographic Transition Model and have begun to question the explanatory and predictive

power of the model (Teitelbaum, 1975). The circumstances of developing countries today are significantly different from those of the western nations during their period of development and modernization.

The concepts of the transition theory have greatly influenced policy formulation for the developing nations, and to the degree that these concepts are validated, they will be useful in guiding policy development. There are, however, serious reservations about the applicability of the transition model stemming from the degree to which the developing countries will du-

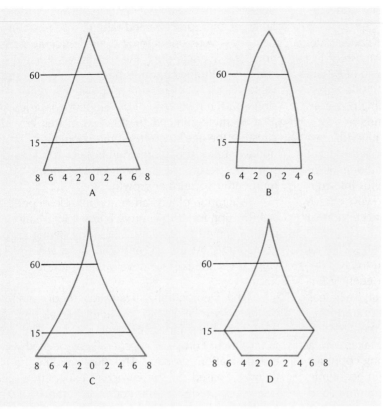

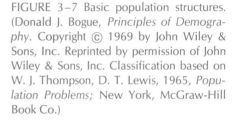

FIGURE 3–7 Basic population structures. (Donald J. Bogue, *Principles of Demography*. Copyright © 1969 by John Wiley & Sons, Inc. Reprinted by permission of John Wiley & Sons, Inc. Classification based on W. J. Thompson, D. T. Lewis, 1965, *Population Problems*; New York, McGraw-Hill Book Co.)

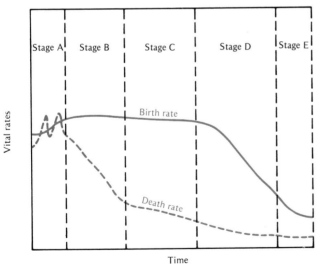

FIGURE 3–8 Stages of the Demographic Transition. (Reprinted from *Population Geography: Problems, Concepts & Prospects*, by Gary L. Peters and Robert P. Larkin, © 1979, with permission of Kendall/Hunt Publishing Co., p. 53.)

plicate the experience of the developed countries upon which the demographic transition theory is based. These differences between the European experience and that of today's developing countries may operate against moving through the demographic transition. Some of these differences and their implications for demographic change in the developing countries are outlined below.

1. *The pace of mortality decline.* The European nations experienced a gradual decline in mortality over an extended period of time; this decline was associated with the economic and social forces related to industrialization. Today's developing countries, however, have undergone a rapid decline in mortality, primarily related to the ease with which imported death-control technologies were applied in the developing countries,

and only peripherally related to the social and economic forces of modernization.

2. Fertility levels. The fertility levels of today's developing countries are much higher than those of Europe during its modernization. The birth rate of Britain during the early 19th century was generally less than 35 per thousand, whereas many developing countries today have birth rates over 45 per thousand.

3. Use of contraceptives. The decline in fertility associated with the European experience was the result of increased and more effective use of traditional fertility control measures like abortion and coitus interruptus. The developing countries of today, however, have more effective and safer means of contraception at their disposal.

4. The structure of society. The European society of the 19th century was much different from today's developing countries; for example, in 19th century Europe it was common to have a large family, whereas the "demonstration effect" of the European transition and its small family norm has diffused to many developing countries. Also, government has taken on a larger role, and many leaders of developing countries are now aware of the relationship between economic development and population growth. Economic and social development for many developing countries has proceeded more rapidly than in 19th century Europe, suggesting a more rapid completion of the demographic transition.

5. Population growth and migration. Today's developing countries are experiencing an increase in population at an unprecedented rate. When most European countries were undergoing their demographic transitions, the average doubling time was 90 years; today, many developing countries have a doubling time of 30 years. Rapidly increasing populations place severe stress on the resources of developing countries. It will also be more difficult to slow down this growth because of the age structure of the populations of developing countries: the large number of young people, itself the result of higher fertility, adds a great momentum for further growth.

Migration played an important role in population stabilization for 19th century Europe. International migration served as a safety valve for growing European populations. At the present time, however, this safety valve does not exist for developing countries.

The Demographic Transition theory—and particularly its relationship to today's developing countries—has been increasingly questioned. The decline of fertility in Europe was generally associated with the modernization process. The demographic transition theory is based on the European experience, and its success in predicting the course of fertility decline in today's developing countries may be limited. In some respects, today's developing countries have a greater ability to cope with rapid population growth, whereas in other areas they have more difficult problems to solve.

CASE STUDY:
Marxist theory: The case of the People's Republic of China

Since the establishment of the People's Republic of China in 1949, its population policy has undergone several changes. From 1949 until mid-1953, both state and party officials openly accepted the promises of Marxism at face value: a large population was a definite asset to the economic development of China—a belief espoused often by Chairman Mao. This optimistic viewpoint was based on the notion that the elimination of foreign capitalist exploitation and Chinese feudalism would bring about an increase in the productive zeal of the peasants.

Because of a decline in the production of foodstuffs in the mid-1950s, the early optimism of Chinese leaders regarding food and population gradually eroded away. The declining growth rate of foodstuffs, coupled with a rising population growth rate from a large base population, most assuredly posed economic problems for the Chinese leaders. The topic of population growth was first publicly mentioned at the 1954 National People's Congress. The Chinese Communist Party's Seventh National Congress issued a statement in

1955 giving limited support to birth control. But it was not until the late 1950s that a concerted effort was made—an effort which met considerable resistance. Apparently, the population was not yet ready for such a radical change in its traditional ethic, and the result was a minimal impact on fertility.

The birth control campaign probably reached its lowest point from 1958 to 1961 when the Great Leap Forward, with its emphasis on people's communes, de-emphasized the importance of population control. However, three successive years of natural disasters, from 1959 through 1961, not only brought an end to the Great Leap Forward but also created a continuing, acute food crisis. Thus, the second birth control campaign was the result of an environment in which the nation had concurrently experienced a severe food crisis and a population problem.

The second birth control campaign lasted from 1962 to 1966, when it was interrupted by the Cultural Revolution and the Red Guard Movement, which generally frowned on family planning. The turmoil associated with the Red Guard Movement subsided by 1969, and the birth control campaign was reactivated.

Today, the concept of the two-child family as the desirable norm is becoming more widespread. China's continuing effort to build a modern state and improve the living conditions of its people has given fertility control high status. The population program of the People's Republic of China has a number of interesting aspects (Tien, 1973).

Late marriage

A law setting the minimum age of marriage at 18 years for women and 20 for men was adopted as early as 1950. This law tends to delay childbearing and reduces births overall. More recently, Chinese women have been asked to postpone marriage until at least age 23 and men until 26; although not part of the law, this request is widely known and respected. Also, since premarital intercourse is strongly frowned upon in the Chinese culture, pregnancies among unmarried women are reportedly few. In such instances, there is often strong encouragement for the women to have abortions.

National family planning services

Fertility control is made relatively easy for married couples to practice. It is an integral part of a national health system. China has made great progress in setting up a nationwide family planning structure and in changing the public attitude in favor of small families.

At marriage couples are given detailed advice about contraception. All the conventional means of contraception are readily available, including oral pills, IUD's, diaphragms, condoms, and foams. Oral contraceptives are the most frequently used.

Contraception is backed up by readily available abortion. If a woman suspects contraceptive failure, she is expected to visit her health clinic for a diagnosis of pregnancy. If the tests are positive and she does not want to have a baby, an abortion is performed.

Sterilization is also widely used. There appears to be some reluctance among men to have vasectomies, but tubal ligation is well accepted by women, particularly by those between 35 and 40 who already have had two or more children.

Motivation

China's family planning program has been in operation long enough for a new generation to reach reproductive age. This group has widely accepted the teaching of Mao that limiting family size is a patriotic duty; this is evidenced especially by low birth rates in the cities. The older generation is reported as gradually accepting the change in norms governing family size. People know that they are not supposed to have big families, and most of them are influenced by this knowledge.

Population distribution and growth

The two well-known features of China's population distribution are that over 75 percent of the population resides in rural villages and that about 90 percent of the population is concentrated (although unevenly) on the approximately 40 percent of Chinese soil lying east of an imaginary line drawn from border to border and passing through Harbin (Harbin) in Heilongjiang (Heilungkiang) Province and Chengdu (Chengtu) in Sichuan (Szechuan) Province (figure 3 — 9). Because of this uneven distribution, measures were developed to transfer population from areas of high density (population surplus) to areas of lower density. The desire to increase productivity brought about policies that moved both industries and people away from the densely populated coastal provinces to the relatively sparse population of the western provinces.

In summary, the People's Republic of China has taken steps to reduce population growth and stabilize its population. Fertility control has obviously contributed to a slowing of population growth in China. However, with so little information on total population, it is difficult to estimate birth and death rates. Even if the recording of births were complete and available, uncertainty as to the population total precludes determination of vital rates.

It is relatively certain, however, that birth and death rates have declined considerably since 1953. United Nations demographers and U.S. Census Bureau experts all are in agreement that, in 1965, the birth rate was in the vicinity of 33 to 35 per thousand, whereas the death rate was approximately 15 to 17 per thousand. According to United Nations estimates, the birth rate for the 1970 — 75 period averaged 26.9 per thousand population, while the death rate was 10.3 per thousand. For 1980 the Population Reference Bureau estimated a crude birth rate of 20 and a crude death rate of 6. The drop in fertility in the past few years has been impressive, and the rate of growth in China at the beginning of the 1980s is near 1.4 percent annually, meaning a doubling time of about 50 years. The age structure of the Chinese population is such that continuing population increases can be expected. Despite advances in fertility control, China is still growing relatively rapidly, and it will be necessary for the birth rate to drop more for population equilibrium to be achieved within the next century.

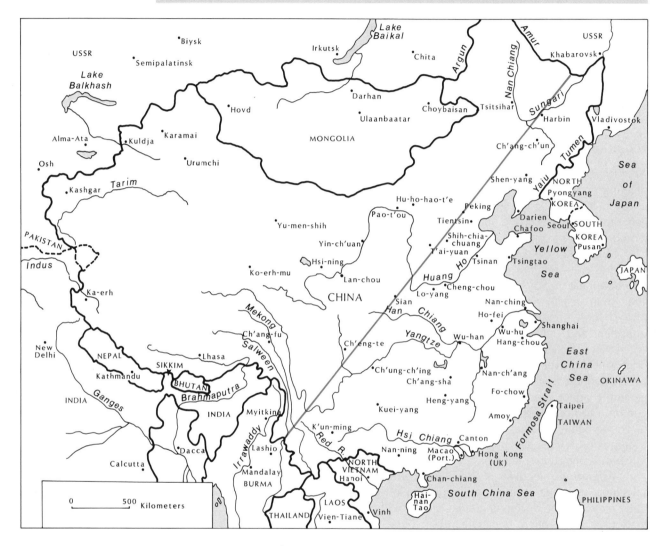

FIGURE 3–9 Population distribution of China; three-quarters of the population currently live east of the line. (U.S. Dept. of State.)

MIGRATION

The tendency of people to migrate, and the frequency and distance of these movements, are distinctive concerns of geographers. Human mobility is evidenced by the social, linguistic, and nationalistic mixing of much of the world's population. Although migration has al-

ways been a characteristic of humans, modernization and industrialization, with the associated technical and economic progress, has caused an increase in human migration. The ability of humans to adjust to major ecological changes through cultural adaptability and migration serves as a major social adjustment mechanism.

The 19th and early 20th centuries witnessed major international migration activity from the densely settled regions of Europe to areas where opportunities and land were abundant. Today, however, the major international migration movements are from the developing countries of Asia, Africa, and Latin America to the large industrial nations of western Europe and the United States. Furthermore, most migration today is internal, not international; rural–urban migration within countries has been an important mechanism for redistributing people in response to changing socioeconomic conditions.

Migration theory

Migration plays a dual role in population dynamics by deleting population from one region and adding it to another. It is an extremely important element in any geographic analysis of the population of a specific region or country.

Migration is selective. Migrants do not represent a general cross section of either the origin or destination populations. Some people are more likely to migrate than are others, and as a result, *migration differentials* are important. Age is perhaps the most important and universally accepted migration differential. Late adolescents and young adults usually predominate in movements within countries as well as between countries; young people can change jobs and generally adapt more easily to new situations. It is common to find a population with a large proportion of young adults in areas experiencing a great deal of in-migration, whereas areas that have experienced much out-migration usually have more older adults.

Migration selectivity is also influenced by marital status; marriage itself is usually a migration-generating event. In the developing areas of the world, migration is most often undertaken by young single adults. Historically, this was also probably true of the developed world; however, in today's developed countries, there is little difference between the mobility of the single person and that of the married person.

Sex selectivity is another factor related to migration, but a variety of factors determine whether the migration stream is dominated by males or females. In 19th century Europe, for example, the movement from rural to urban areas was primarily accomplished by young farm women who went to work as domestic servants in the cities. On the other hand, the frontier towns in America were largely male-dominated.

Education and occupation are also important variables associated with migration selectivity. Unskilled workers are less likely to be migratory than the skilled and semiskilled, and professional people are probably the most mobile occupational group.

Ravenstein's laws. People migrate for a variety of reasons, and a number of theories have been developed to help explain these migration patterns. E. G. Ravenstein pioneered the development of migration theory with his "Laws of Migration" (1885, 1889) in which he related migration to population density, size, and distance as a result of his studies in Great Britain. Although Ravenstein was a British civil servant most of his career, he was born in Germany and held an academic post briefly in England as a professor of geography. Ravenstein had few records of migrants in England, but in a fairly short time he extracted the essentials from these records and published this series of generalizations, most of which still hold true today.

1. Most migratory moves cover only a short distance. We have discovered this a thousand times since Ravenstein, but the idea that distance is an obstacle to migrants is one of the most firmly fixed generalizations in the migration literature.

2. Females predominate among short-distance movers; or, the greater the distance, the more likely males are more numerous in the migration stream.

3. For every stream there is a counterstream. Not a great deal is known about the counterstream except that sometimes its migrants contain more skills than those in the main stream. Counterstream migrants also are believed to have a higher median age.

4. Movement from the hinterland to the city is most often made in stages.

5. An economic motive is dominant; or, as Ravenstein put it: "Bad or oppressive laws, heavy taxation, an unnatural climate, uncongenial social surroundings, and even compulsion . . . all have produced and are still producing currents of migration, but none of these currents can compare in volume with that which arises from the desire inherent in most men to better themselves in material respects . . ." (1889, p. 286).

This does not exhaust the list of Ravenstein's laws, but it is surprising that from 1880 to the present, relatively few attempts have been made to extend these generalizations, or to devise additional ones, or to attempt to gather these into some theoretical framework. At least until recently, most migration models and stud-

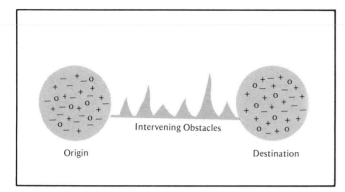

Origin   Intervening Obstacles   Destination

FIGURE 3–10 Lee's migration model, showing origin and destination factors and intervening obstacles. (Everett S. Lee, 1966, "A Theory of Migration," in *Demography* 3, No. 1. Washington, D.C., Population Association of America, p. 50.)

ies have emphasized the economic determinants of migration.

Lee's migration model. A recent set of hypotheses about the streams, volume, and characteristics of migrants was proposed by Everett S. Lee in a paper called, "A Theory of Migration" (1966). Lee categorizes the elements which influence migration as follows:

1. factors associated with a migrant's origin,
2. factors associated with a migrant's destination,
3. obstacles between the two which the migrant must overcome, called *intervening obstacles,* and
4. personal factors.

According to Lee, there are huge numbers of circumstances or forces in one's home area which condition one's propensity to move. In a book on population, demographer Donald Bogue (1969) devotes a whole page to a closely spaced list of things that stimulate migration, including jobs, marriage, and trouble with the law or in-laws. Similarly, there is an equally large number of influencing characteristics for possible destinations. The important thing is that people respond differently to these stimuli. Lee indicates that "good" climate is almost universally attractive, and "bad" climate repels almost everyone; but what is a good climate for someone passionately fond of skiing may leave an avid skinnydipper cold. A good school system is important to parents of school-aged children, and they might not even consider moving to an area with inferior schools; but to property owners without children, say retired people, a good school system may mean only high property taxes. Thus, the evaluations people make of various places, their perceptions of places, change as they progress through different phases of their *life cycle.*

It is important to keep in mind that people make migration decisions on the basis of what they perceive to be happening in different places. What they perceive may or may not agree with actual conditions. So *perception* is important when trying to explain why people move. People's perceptions of places are in turn affected by everything from age and sex to personal idiosyncracies.

Lee tried to summarize his ideas with a schematic diagram (figure 3–10). The circle representing the place of origin has pluses, minuses, and zeroes. A plus indicates favorable elements in the area which tend to hold migrants there; the minuses are elements which potential migrants dislike; and the zeroes are characteristics to which the potential migrant is indifferent. The same schema is used for the area of destination. Thus, when one adds up the pluses, minuses, and zeroes for both the origin and destination, the region with the greatest assets has the greatest influence on the decision to move. Before the migrant decides to relocate, however, another set of circumstances must be considered. Lee calls these *intervening obstacles;* they include such things as the cost of making the move and the psychic costs associated with breaking ties with family and community, both of which are related to distance. Thus, migration has a very complex relationship to population growth.

POPULATION PROJECTIONS

We have been viewing the present population mainly in the perspective of the past. A logical question, and an important one as well, is, what does the future hold for the world's population? It is difficult to answer such a question, but an immediate attempt, based on a set of assumptions about population dynamics over a given time period, is the *population projection.* Projections of future populations are hazardous and must be undertaken with caution; the longer the time period, the more skeptical we should be.

TABLE 3–1   Population of the world and 8 major areas (in millions)

Major area	1925	1950	1975	2000	2025	2050	2075
World total	1960	2505	3988	6406	9065	11,163	12,210
Northern group	1203	1411	1971	2530	2930	3084	3107
Northern America	125	166	237	296	332	339	340
Europe	339	392	474	540	580	592	592
U.S.S.R.	168	180	225	321	368	393	400
East Asia	571	673	1005	1373	1650	1760	1775
Southern group	757	1094	2017	3876	6135	8079	9103
Latin America	98	164	326	625	961	1202	1297
Africa	153	219	402	834	1479	2112	2522
South Asia	497	698	1268	2384	3651	4715	5232
Oceania	9	13	21	33	44	50	52

Source: U.N. Dept of Economic and Social Affairs, *Concise Report on the World Population Situation in 1970–1975 and Its Long-Range Implications,* Population Studies No. 56 (New York: United Nations, 1974, p. 59).

Demographers and population geographers are generally careful to differentiate between predictions and projections. A prediction suggests that we know, or believe we know, what some future population will be, whereas a population projection is based on a set of assumptions about the demographic processes that will affect population growth over a specific time period. A projection, then, will be only as good as our assumptions.

The simplest assumption to make is that population growth in the future will proceed at the present rate. However, this is unrealistic in most situations. A population projection usually begins with separate estimates for the death, birth, and migration rates, then combines them into a single projection for the future population. The projection is accurate only if the assumptions hold. Several times, a projection has altered people's reproductive behavior and set in motion events which will assure that the projection will be in error. Often a series of projections is made, using different assumptions about future death, and birth, and migration rates. Seldom, however, are these assumptions related to the size of areas, food supplies, and other realities in a concrete way.

World and major regions

Long-range population projections are based on assumptions which may or may not be accurate. As a recent United Nations' study stated,

> The affairs of men are often subject to swings of the pendulum, erratic fluctuations, sometimes even dramatic upsets. That unsystematic variations will also

occur in the future, particularly the long-range future, can be fairly taken for granted. But since these are intrinsically unforeseeable, only fairly smooth and systematic changes can be projected. In actual fact, these may, at the most, constitute a long-term average trend around which there will occur unpredictable ups and downs. The calculated smooth changes should reflect those factors in the situation which are likely to prevail in the long run. (1974)

The United Nations made several assumptions in conjunction with population projections, including: at least a minimal degree of social order and control will be maintained; efforts at maintaining or improving the quality of life will continue and will not be totally frustrated; and regional vital rates will change differently, but eventually everywhere mortality and fertility will fall slightly below the lowest levels now observed.

These United Nations population projections are shown in table 3–1 and figure 3–11. The four southern world areas have a greater potential for growth than areas of the north. Figure 3–11 is drawn on a logarithmic scale, so that equal steepness means equal growth rates. It is interesting to see that the population of south Asia will have surpassed the current world population by about 2030. The current world population will have tripled to just over 12 billion in one century.

The United States

Recent population projections for the United States have been published by the Department of Commerce. Three main projection series have been made, each beginning with the estimated population as of July 1,

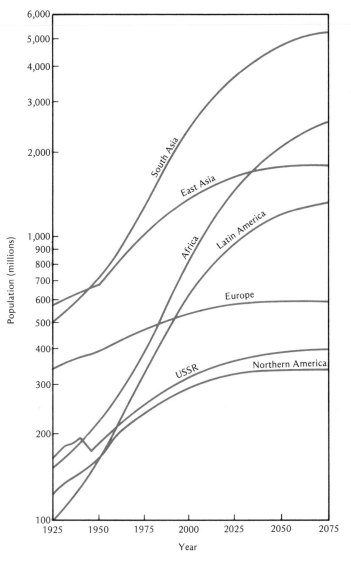

FIGURE 3–11 World population in major areas, 1925–1975, according to "medium" variant of long-range projections (charted on a logarithmic scale). (U.N. Dept. of Economic and Social Affairs, 1974, Population Studies, No. 56, *Concise Report on the World Population Situation in 1970–1975 and Its Long-Range Implications*, New York, p. 58.)

1974. Each series assumes an annual immigration of 400,000 and a slight reduction in the death rate. As with the United Nations projections, the differences between the projections result from variations in the assumed course of fertility. The final level of completed cohort fertility for Series I is 2.7, for Series II is 2.1, and for Series III is 1.7.

There is an immediate divergence in the three different projections as is apparent in table 3–2, though the total differences are quite small in 1975. The difference between the Series I and Series III projections is 12,919,000 by 1985, and it increases to 41,909,000 by 2000—a number approximately equal to the combined 1970 populations of California, New York, and Connecticut. These differences are extremely important when considered in the light of their

TABLE 3–2 U.S. population projections.

| | Variant (population in 1000s) | | |
Year	Series I	Series II	Series III
1975	213,641	213,450	213,323
1980	225,705	222,769	220,356
1985	241,274	234,068	228,355
1990	257,663	245,075	235,581
1995	272,685	254,495	241,198
2000	287,007	262,494	245,098

Source: U.S. Bureau of the Census, "Projections of the Population of the United States, 1975 to 2050," *Current Population Reports,* Series P–25, No. 601 (Washington, D.C.: U.S. Government Printing Office, 1975).

impact on employment, housing, education, and other needs, yet remember that this increase is slow in com-

TABLE 3–3   Population projections for Mexico with both constant and declining fertility

Year	Population in 1000s		Birth rate per 1000		Growth rate per 1000	
	High fertility	Declining fertility	High fertility	Declining fertility	High fertility	Declining fertility
1970	51,249	51,249	43.9	43.9	36.7	36.7
1975	61,758	61,758	43.3	43.3	37.8	37.8
1980	74,784	73,474	43.2	40.0	38.4	34.7
1985	90,651	86,166	43.5	37.4	38.7	31.9
1990	110,082	99,791	43.7	35.1	39.0	29.4
1995	133,863	113,896	43.9	32.1	39.2	26.4
2000	162,928	127,723	43.9	28.5	39.4	22.8
2005	198,404	140,410	44.0	24.7	39.5	18.9
2010	241,716	154,553	44.0	24.7	39.5	18.9
2015	294,535	169,745	44.0	24.7	39.5	18.8

Source: John Isbister, "Birth Control, Income Redistribution, and the Rate of Saving: The Case of Mexico," *Demography* 10, 1973, p. 91.

parison to population growth in the developing countries. One of the realities not included here is the potential rise in illegal immigration, which may be linked in turn to Mexico's continuing rapid population growth.

Mexico

Mexico's annual population growth rate is approximately 3.5 percent—a rate which will double her population every 20 years. A series of population projections for Mexico from 1970 to 2015 appears in table 3–3, with the assumed birth rates and resultant growth rates.

Two characteristics are readily apparent. First, Mexico's growth over the next four decades will be extremely large, as will be the task of providing for the population's day-to-day needs. Second, the high and declining fertility projections vary greatly—to 35,205,000 by the year 2000. Because of the power of exponential growth, the difference is a staggering 124,790,000 only fifteen years later, a number nearly as large as the population of Indonesia, the world's fifth most populous nation. However, considering the current high unemployment rates and low incomes for most Mexicans, such projections seem to be only abstractions. In recent years the Mexican government has supported family planning programs and encouraged lower fertility.

PATHS TO POPULATION EQUILIBRIUM

Most population analysts agree that rapid population growth cannot continue indefinitely; population growth must eventually stop. The most important questions are, *what* will stop rapid population growth, and *when* will it stop? Simply stated, there are three possibilities: birth rates can fall to balance low death rates; death rates can rise to balance high birth rates; or both can move toward an intermediate level of equilibrium.

Trying to predict what will stop rapid population growth, and when, is a difficult task. Several models have been proposed. One projects a rapid rise in population that levels off before the carrying capacity is reached. Another shows a rapid rise in population that overshoots the carrying capacity. This overshoot would lead to an increase in the death rate due to lack of food, which in turn would lead to a decline in population numbers to below the carrying capacity. Perhaps the most catastrophic model projects a rapid rise in population leading to a degradation of the carrying capacity, which then brings about a drastic reduction in population size. Yet another proposed model shows a continual increase in the carrying capacity, which keeps ahead of population growth most of the time; when population growth would occasionally overtake the carrying capacity, new innovations would soon lead to an increase in the carrying capacity. Which of these models will be most appropriate for the future is certainly a matter of speculation.

CULTURE, POPULATION GROWTH, AND FAMILY PLANNING

The United Nations designated 1974 as World Population Year and convened the World Population Conference, held in Bucharest, Romania in August of that

Family planning advertising in Jamaica. (James Pickerell for World Bank)

Victoria Jubilee Hospital in Kingston, Jamaica. New mothers hear a family planning lecture before going home. (James Pickerell for World Bank)

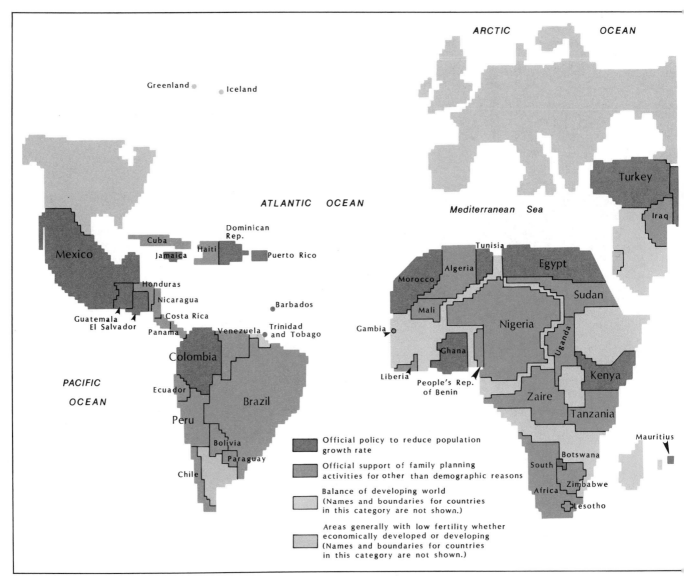

FIGURE 3–12 Cartograph of family planning, illustrating government positions on population growth and family planning, 1976. Country and regional size is proportional to the annual birth rate. (Dorothy Nortman, Ellen Hofstatter, October, 1976, "Population and Family Planning: A Factbook," in *Reports on Population/Family Planning*, No. 2, 8th ed., New York, The Population Council, pp. 52–53.)

year. The purpose of the conference was to discuss problems associated with population growth and to focus world attention on population issues. This was the largest international population conference ever held and included representatives from 136 governments around the world.

Although the existence of population problems was recognized by most governments, there was much disagreement and debate about the causes and solutions. Several countries attributed high birth rates to the lack of economic and social development, believing that development, and not population and family planning programs, should be emphasized. A slogan frequently heard at Bucharest was, "Take care of the people, and population will take care of itself." This view implicitly assumes the validity of the demographic transition model. Many countries, however—including the western European nations, the United States, and Canada—felt that reducing population growth

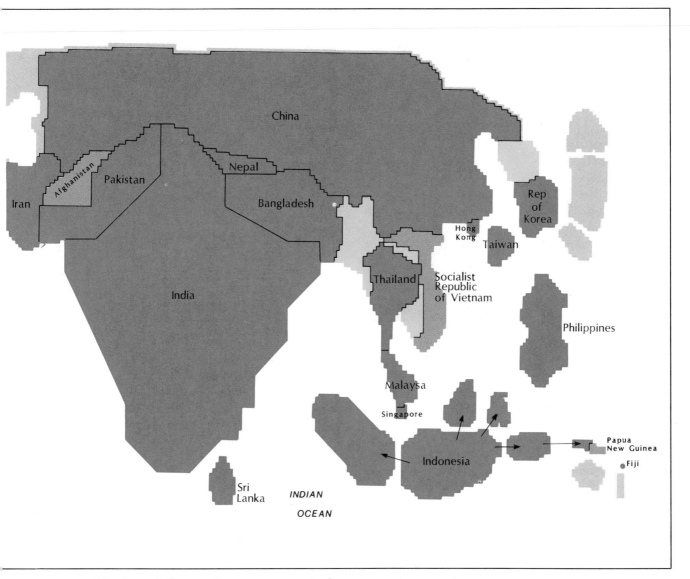

rates would substantially contribute to economic development.

The relationship between population–family planning and development was expressed by Dorothy Nortman and Ellen Hofstatter of the Population Council in that agency's October 1975 "Report on Population/Family Planning."

> Whatever the stance on the political stage, the most ardent family planning advocates recognize that contraception *alone* will not produce housing, schools, or steel mills; and among the staunchest supporters of the 'new economic order' many appreciate the demographic value of legitimate and government-subsidized family planning services.

Family planning

One response to controlling population growth is the establishment of a national family planning program. Almost unheard of twenty years ago, such programs have become increasingly common during the late 1960s and 1970s.

The primary objective of **family planning** programs is to lower fertility. However, such programs are often concerned also with maternal and child health and the reduction of illegal and nonmedical abortions. Though the precise components of family planning programs vary from place to place, all programs share certain common features. Usually such programs are

A maternity ward in Kingston, Jamaica. The shortage of hospital beds forces women to share with other mothers, as well as their babies. They must leave the hospital within 24 hours of giving birth. (James Pickerell for World Bank)

funded and administered by the government, though many receive outside help from such organizations as the United Nations or the Agency for International Development. The primary function of most family planning programs is the provision of birth control information and services to a target population.

Figure 3–12 depicts the status of family planning programs as of 1976. During the 1960s and 1970s, rapid population growth came to be seen as an obstacle to economic betterment, and countries often responded by initiating family planning programs of some type. The oldest of the national programs shown here is that of India, which was begun in 1952.

The establishment of a family planning program is not without difficulties, since opposition often comes from various groups within the population ranging from midwives to religious groups. Among the difficulties noted in Bernard Berelson's analysis of family planning programs were political, bureaucratic, organizational, economic, and cultural problems (1972, p.

209). Particularly noteworthy is the organizational capacity of family planning programs, or their ability to reach their target populations.

There is increasing evidence that family planning programs are at least partly responsible for declining fertility in a number of developing countries, including Hong Kong, South Korea, Taiwan, and more recently, China.

Quite likely, population projections will be adjusted downward as countries increase attempts to control their growth rates through family planning programs. For many of the poorest countries, demographic choices are limited as they find themselves perilously close to the old Malthusian dilemma. Limited food supplies and slow economic growth may ultimately result in population equilibrium via rising death rates if birth rates are not brought down. In the 1970s some areas experienced increased death rates, including parts of India and Bangladesh, as well as the Sahel region of North Africa.

KEY TERMS

Developing countries (nations)
Developed countries (nations)
Cartogram
Age structure
Population pyramid

Neo-Malthusian
Demographic Transition
Demonstration effect
Marxist theory
Migration

Migration differentials
Migration selectivity
Ravenstein's laws
Lee's migration model
Life cycle

Perception
Intervening obstacles
Population projection
Population equilibrium
Family planning

REFERENCES

Berelson, B. (1972), "The Present State of Family-Planning Programs," in Brown, H. and Hutchings, E., Jr. (eds.), *Are Our Descendants Doomed? Technological Change and Population Growth.* New York: Viking Press, 201–236.

Bogue, D. J. (1969), *Principles of Demography.* New York: John Wiley & Sons, Inc.

Clarke, J. I. (1972), *Population Geography,* 2nd ed. Elmsford, NY: Pergamon Press, Inc.

Demeny, P. (1974), "The Populations of the Underdeveloped Countries," *Scientific American* 231, 148–159.

Lee, E. S. (1966), "A Theory of Migration," *Demography* 3, 47–57.

Nortman, D. and Hofstatter, E. (1975), "Population and Family Planning Programs," *Reports on Population/Family Planning,* 7th ed.

Peters, G. L. and Larkin, R. P. (1979), *Population Geography: Problems, Concepts, and Prospects.* Dubuque, IA: Kendall/Hunt Publishing Co.

Population Reference Bureau (1976), *World Population Growth, 1965–1975.* Washington, D.C.: Population Reference Bureau.

Ravenstein, E. G. (1885), "The Laws of Migration," *Journal of the Royal Statistical Society* 48, 167–227.

Ravenstein, E. G. (1889), "The Laws of Migration," *Journal of the Royal Statistical Society* 52, 241–301.

Teitelbaum, M. S. (1975), "Relevance of Demographic Transition Theory for Developing Countries," *Science* 188, 420–425.

Tien, H. Y. (1973), *China's Population Struggle.* Columbus, OH: Ohio State University Press.

Trewartha, G. T. (1969), *A Geography of Population.* New York: John Wiley & Sons, Inc.

United Nations (1974), *Concise Report on the World Population Situation in 1970–1975 and Its Long-Range Implications.* New York: United Nations.

Young, L. B. (ed.) (1968), *Population in Perspective.* New York: Oxford University Press.

4

The population of Anglo-America

Our purpose in this chapter is to focus closer attention on the growth and distribution of population within a specific cultural region. The historical growth and distribution of people in Anglo-America, the international and internal movements of people, and the relationship between population growth and the environment are all considered, along with possible population policies in both the United States and Canada.

THE NORTH AMERICAN POPULATION BEFORE THE EUROPEANS

The first European arrivals to the New World found that the land was already inhabited by people who were to be known, from then on, as Indians. Though their numbers on the eve of European discovery were unknown, a likely estimate is that there were perhaps one million on the entire North American continent (figure 4–1).

Culture and languages varied considerably among these native inhabitants. Contact and interaction between separate groups was probably minimal. Groups ranged from the Eskimos in the north to the Indians on Mexico's central plateau. Their economic systems were closely adapted to their environments and varied from hunting and fishing to primitive agriculture. Some groups moved often in response to environmental changes or attacks from hostile neighbors.

HISTORICAL DEVELOPMENT OF THE U.S. POPULATION

As late as the 17th century, the land that is today the United States was sparsely populated. Numbers were limited by the nature of fishing, hunting and gathering economics, as well as by disease and conflicts. However, events were underway which would drastically alter the population geography of the United States— an alteration which continues today.

The European demographic situation

In the 16th and 17th centuries, sweeping socioeconomic changes were occurring. Europe was becoming linked by trade to Asia, Africa, and the Americas. The Industrial Revolution was beginning and would ultimately alter the socioeconomic fabric of societies in many ways. Accompanying gradual improvements in living conditions, improved sanitation, and new public health measures were gradual reductions in death rates. Without similar reductions in birth rates, populations began to increase.

World exploration, coupled with social and intellectual changes throughout Western Europe, created an atmosphere which encouraged economic, political, and territorial expansion. It was fortuitous that European population growth, with the resulting increased pressure on land and other resources, occurred at a time when the virtually empty lands of North America were being explored. A consequence of these events was the great migration from Europe across the Atlantic to the waiting shores of North America.

It was in the "peasant heart" of Europe, where an age-old structure was crumbling under the changes which accompanied the opening of the modern era, that the immigrant movement began (Handlin, 1951, p. 7). The social stability of European peasant societies

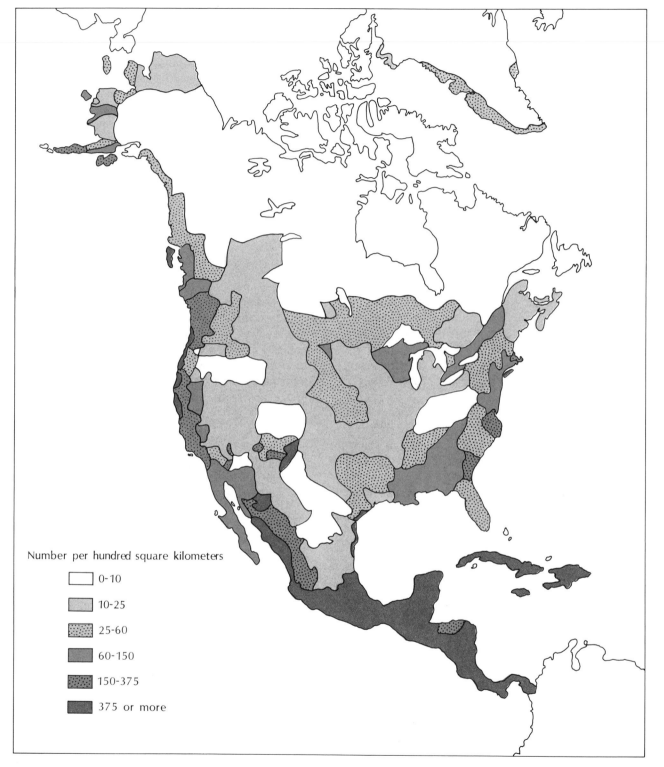

FIGURE 4–1 Native American population density. (Harold E. Driver, 1969, *Indians of North America*. Chicago, Univ. of Chicago Press, p. 566. © 1961, 1969 by The University of Chicago. All rights reserved.)

derived from their deep emotional, spiritual, and economic involvement with the land. They had a profound sense of place and derived meaning and identity from their local communities; the Industrial Revolution was an intruder. So began one of the greatest migrations in human history. It has been estimated that between the beginning of the 16th century and the early 20th century, over 60 million Europeans went overseas, mainly to the United States, Argentina, Canada, Brazil, Australia, New Zealand, South Africa, and the British West Indies.

Africa and Africans

Early European expansion led to contacts with Africa which were to have far-reaching effects on the population geography of the United States. Colonial America always needed labor, a need which was partly filled by slaves, procured in Africa, transported across the Atlantic, and sold in the colonies and elsewhere. Slaves were first sold in Virginia in 1619 and in Massachusetts in 1636; in 1705, a law was passed which classified slaves as a type of real estate. Unlike the European migration, the slave trade was a *forced migration.*

Slavery thrived in the plantation states where hand labor was needed for the cultivation of cotton, tobacco, and rice. In the hot and humid climate Blacks became a necessary part of the agricultural system, especially as cotton continued to expand. As Paterson observed, "Perhaps the greatest tragedy of all for the blacks was that the South committed itself so completely to cotton cultivation that in the end, in spite of many a voice raised in protest against the system, it *could not* discard slavery and survive" (1975, p. 33).

Population in 1790

The first official census in the United States was conducted in 1790; the total population count was 3,929, 214. Most people lived within 250 miles of the Atlantic Coast in 1790, and only a small percentage had ventured west of the Appalachians. This young American population still was closely tied to Europe, and even now the most densely populated portion of the United States is the Atlantic Seaboard.

Population in 1850

By 1800 a westward movement was already underway. Settlements had reached into New York's Mo-

hawk Valley, parts of Kentucky, and western Pennsylvania near Pittsburgh.

People continued pushing westward. Between 1790 and 1850 the population of the United States grew by over 19 million to a total of just over 23 million, most of whom lived east of the Mississippi River. Settlements had reached westward as far as Iowa, Missouri, Arkansas, and western Texas. Both natural increase and immigration contributed to population growth, though we know little about actual birth and death rates during this time.

Population in 1900

By 1900 the population of the United States had grown to nearly 76 million and was distributed as shown in figure 4–2. Westward movement had continued, and settlements stretched to the Pacific Coast. The area of continuous settlement had reached nearly to the 100th meridian; most areas west of it were still sparsely settled, though there were enclaves of considerable settlement. The frontier era in America had come to an end, though homesteading was to continue. As Billington commented, in discussing the addition of Oklahoma, Arizona, and New Mexico into the Union,

> Although the director of the census had spoken prematurely in 1890 when he declared that "the unsettled area has been so broken into by isolated bodies of settlement that there can hardly be said to be a frontier line," these events in the Southwest signaled the closing of an era of American history. Good lands scattered throughout the trans-Mississippi country still waited the settler's plow; actually four times as many acres were homesteaded after 1890 as before. But the day was drawing to an end when relatively cheap farms beckoned the dispossessed and the ambitious with the promise of a chance to begin life anew amidst nature's bounties. With the closing of the frontier the United States was on the threshold of a new era, where its people must face the problems of an expansionless existence for the first time in their history. (1959, p. 86)

Thus, by 1900 settlement had spread from coast to coast, though there was still a considerable amount of filling in to be accomplished.

POPULATION GROWTH IN THE 20TH CENTURY

From 1790 to 1890 population and territorial expansion were characteristic features of the changing pop-

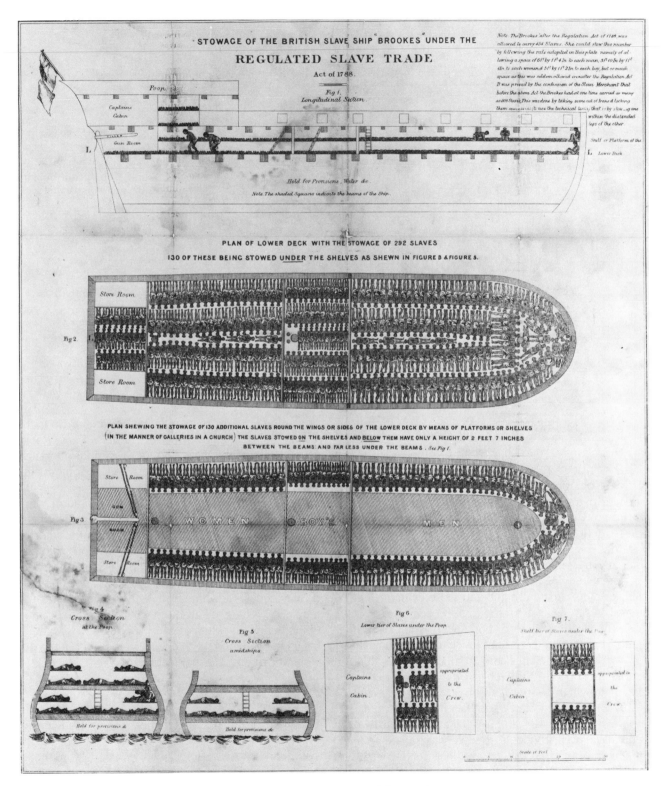

British ship in accordance with the Regulated Slave Trade. (Library of Congress)

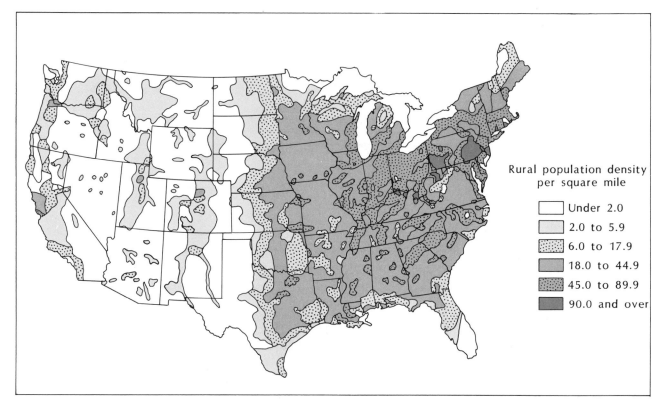

Rural population density per square mile

- Under 2.0
- 2.0 to 5.9
- 6.0 to 17.9
- 18.0 to 44.9
- 45.0 to 89.9
- 90.0 and over

FIGURE 4–2 Population distribution, 1900. (Conrad Taeuber, Irene B. Taeuber, 1958, *The Changing Population of the United States.* New York, John Wiley & Sons, Inc., p. 11.)

ulation geography of the United States. The 1890s was a decade of transition in population dynamics and economic growth. Rural–urban migration and **urbanization** rearranged the people; birth rates and death rates were declining. The years since 1900 have been characterized by rapid and often quickening change. In 1920 people living in urban areas (with populations of 2500 or more) first out numbered those living in rural areas.

The steady growth of population is apparent in figure 4–3. Despite periods of low fertility, such as the 1930's, the United States grew from almost 76 million people in 1900 to 222 million in 1980. The rate of population growth in 1980 was approximately 0.9 percent. In 1970 the United States population was distributed as shown in figure 4–4. In 1970 the average density of population was around 57 people per square mile, ranging from 0.5 in Alaska to over 950 in New Jersey. Overall, the highest **population densities** still appear in the manufacturing belt of the northeast. Westward

across the Mississippi, population densities drop in the Great Plains, then drop even further in the Rocky Mountains and the Basin and Range regions. Densities rise again near the Pacific Coast and in some of the adjacent inland valleys.

Between 1960 and 1970 the most rapid percentage increases in population occurred mainly in the western states. Nevada grew by 71 percent, California by 27 percent, Arizona by 36 percent, and Colorado by 26 percent; Florida was the only exception, where the population increased by 37 percent. Percentage increases are somewhat deceptive, however, because they don't reflect the absolute size of the base population. During the 20th century population dynamics have changed, and these changes are important in our view of United States population.

Mortality trends and patterns

During the 19th century death rates decreased considerably in the United States. Between the end of the 18th century and 1960, the decrease in mortality added over 40 years to the average life expectancy at birth; from 1900 to 1960 alone life expectancy in-

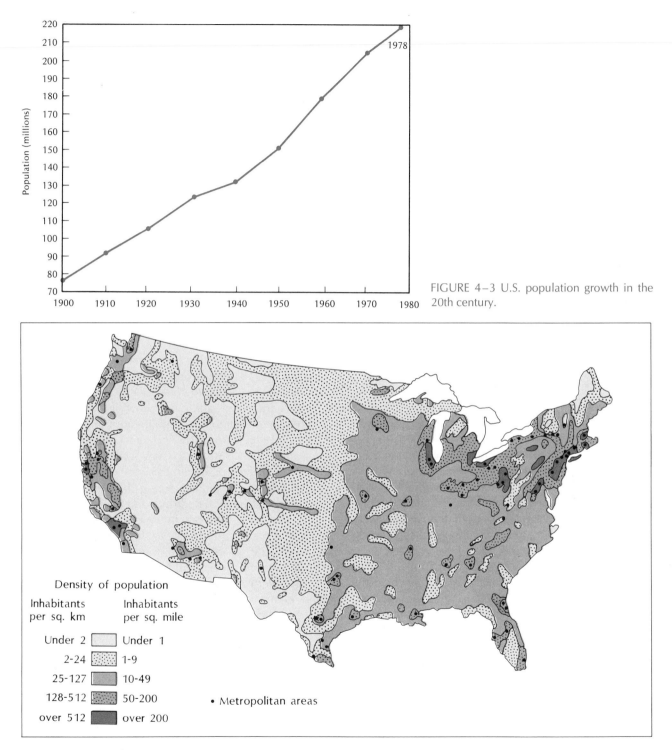

FIGURE 4–3 U.S. population growth in the 20th century.

FIGURE 4–4 U.S. population density, 1970. (David A. Lanegran, "Where Is Everybody?" in David A. Lanegran, Risa Palm, eds., 1973, *An invitation to Geography*. New York, McGraw-Hill Book Co., p. 154.)

creased 20 years for males and nearly 24 years for females (Kitigawa, 1972), mainly through higher infant survival rates. Declines in mortality since 1900 have been greater among infants and children than among the elderly. The long-term decline in mortality slowed in the 1950s, and in 1979 the crude death rate was around 9, compared with 9.6 in 1950.

Changes in mortality in the United States can best be understood by looking at what Abdel Omran termed the **epidemiologic transition** (1977). Omran suggested a three-stage model of epidemiologic transition:

1. The age of pestilence and famine. Though data for this stage are not readily available for the entire country, Omran suggested scattered records of epidemics confirm its existence in the 18th and parts of the 19th centuries. In the United States significant smallpox epidemics occurred in 1824, 1851, 1854, 1866, 1875, 1881, 1891, 1895, 1901, and 1902. Epidemics of other diseases included cholera, yellow fever, influenza, and scarlet fever. Endemic diseases like tuberculosis were often major causes of death. Famines were less important causes of mortality in the United States than in Europe, but dietary deficiencies contributed to mortality.

2. The age of receding pandemics. According to Omran this age lasted from the middle of the 19th century until about 1920. As the frequency epidemics decreased, mortality declined. Cholera and yellow fever disappeared, and scarlet fever was considerably diminished in severity. Pneumonia, influenza, and bronchitis remained important causes of death, though they were declining somewhat. Nutritional diseases such as ricketts showed little sign of decline.

3. The age of degenerative and "man-made" diseases. According to Omran this stage began in the United States sometime after 1920. Heart disease, cancer, diabetes, and stroke emerged as important causes of death, and remain so today.

In recent years the spatial pattern of mortality in the United States has shown significant variations from place to place, even after adjusting for age differences. Among whites mortality is relatively high in certain areas of the Northeast, the Appalachians, the south Atlantic coastal plain, the Gulf Coast, in and around the Chicago area, the cutover area of northern Michigan, and isolated mountain and desert regions of the West. For nonwhites the highest mortality occurs in the in-

dustrial Northeast, the Old South, and the border states.

Fertility trends and patterns

Although we have no accurate national fertility statistics for the United States prior to the 20th century, both historical and more recent estimates agree that birth rates were high in colonial America, with a crude birth rate of 50 or more. The average colonial woman probably gave birth to about eight children; these women married earlier than their European counterparts and produced larger families as well. A young population in an open land where opportunities were abundant could provide a reasonable basis for high fertility. As late as 1820 the crude birth rate in the United States still exceeded 50, but it subsequently began a long, though sometimes interrupted, journey downward, as the demographic transition was underway. It was a necessary adjustment to the emergence of an urban-industrial society.

By 1900 the crude birth rate had dropped to 32. During the 1930s it dropped slightly below 20, with the depression acting to curtail the desire to reproduce. Fertility increased abruptly following World War II, with the crude birth rate jumping from 20.4 in 1945 to 24.1 in 1946. Throughout the remainder of the 1940s and into the 1950s the crude birth rate remained around 25. From 25.3 in 1957 it began another decline, which accelerated during the 1970s. By 1979 the crude birth rate had dropped to about 15.

The crude birth rate in the United States does not vary considerably from state to state. Lower rates occur in the Pacific states, parts of the Midwest, most of the Northeast, and Florida. Higher rates occur in many of the southern states, other than Florida and Georgia, and in the Great Plains, Rocky Mountains, and the Great Basin.

Generally the movement toward lower fertility has been led by people in the upper socioeconomic group, and the lowest crude birth rates are still found there, though there are exceptions. For example, at very high income levels fertility rises somewhat.

There is an inverse correlation between the level of education of women and their fertility. Prolonged education is associated with delayed marriage and childbearing. The changing role of women in the labor force has also had a downward impact on fertility, because a working woman usually must forego her in-

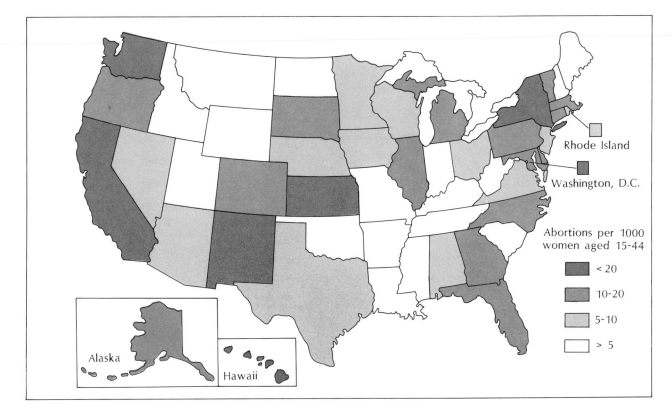

FIGURE 4–5 Abortion rate per 1000 women of reproductive age (considered to be 15–44), by state, 1973. (Edward Weinstock, Christopher Tietze, Frederick S. Jaffe, Joy G. Dryfoos, "Legal Abortions in the United States Since the 1973 Supreme Court Decisions." Reprinted with permission from *Family Planning Perspectives*, Vol. 7, No. 1, 1975, p. 26.)

come for some period of time during and following pregnancy. The traditional role of wife and mother is less appealing to many than increasingly available career opportunities.

Despite the availability of contraceptives and the education available to young people today, teenage pregnancies are alarmingly common. In 1977 about 1.1 million teenagers either gave birth, had miscarriages or stillbirths, or had abortions; another 200,000 got pregnant as teenagers, but did not give birth until they had reached 20. Most teenage pregnancies occur out of wedlock and are unintentional. Teenage fertility is higher for nonwhites than for whites, and the difference is most pronounced for girls aged under 14, where the nonwhite rate is five times greater than that for whites. For 19 year olds the nonwhite rate is less than twice that for whites.

Abortions.   Prior to 1970 it was relatively difficult for a woman in the United States to obtain an abortion. Subsequently, with the liberalization of abortion laws in New York and a few other states, 2,229,070 legal abortions were performed between 1972 and 1974. Figure 4–5 shows the spatial pattern of abortion rates in 1973. The highest rate, excluding Washington, D.C., was in New York, which had 53.7 abortions per 1000 live births; California was second with of 30.7. However, the rate in Washington, D.C. was 233.4.

Despite two major Supreme Court decisions in 1973, *Doe* v. *Bolton* and *Roe* v. *Wade,* uniform abortion practices have not yet been implemented in all states. According to one study by Tietze and Murstein:

> Under severe political pressure from a well-organized and well-financed "right to life" movement, legislatures and various law enforcement officers in several states, as well as many hospital boards and hospital administrators, have taken a variety of actions designed to prevent, or at least limit or delay, implementation. Some of these actions have already been challenged and declared unconstitutional by the courts. At the same time, efforts were made in the Congress of the United States to initiate a

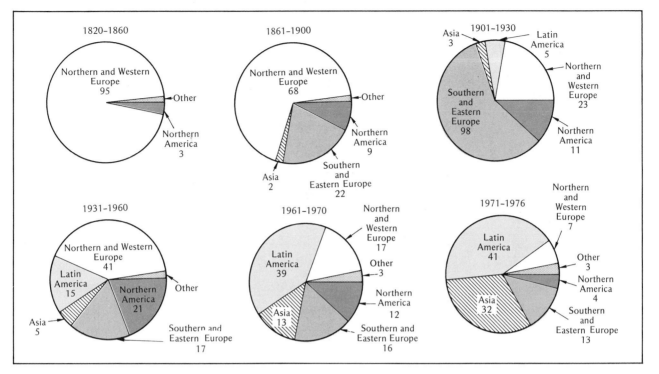

FIGURE 4–6 U.S. immigration rate by region of origin, 1820–1976. (Leon F. Bouvier with Henry S. Shryock, Harry W. Henderson, September, 1977, "International Migration: Yesterday, Today, and Tomorrow," in *Population Bulletin* 32, no. 4, pp. 24–25. Courtesy of the Population Reference Bureau, Inc., Washington, D.C.)

constitutional amendment that would nullify the decision of the Supreme Court. (1975, p. 7)

In recent years approximately 75 percent of all legal abortions have been performed on unmarried women, one-third of whom were teenagers. Almost 50 percent of all legal abortions were obtained by women who had no children and another 20 percent by those who had only one child. Since 1972 there has been a decrease in the percentage of abortions obtained by white women and an increase in the percentage obtained by nonwhite women.

The role of immigration

The United States has often been referred to as a nation of immigrants, and so it is. The origin of immigrants has shifted since 1820, as is shown in figure 4–6. Throughout the 19th century, immigrants came primarily from northern and western Europe, whereas immigrants in the first three decades of the 20th century

came mainly from southern and eastern Europe. Increased immigration from Latin America has also occurred during the present century, accounting for 41 percent of all immigrants from 1971 to 1976. Since 1900 immigration from Asia has increased from about 3 percent of the current total to 32 percent.

The distribution of aliens in 1976 in the United States is shown in figure 4–7. California, New York, Texas, and Florida are major entry points for immigrants, many of whom remain in those states. Areas with the fewest aliens are either low-income areas, such as some of the southern and Appalachian states, or relatively isolated areas, such as the upper Great Plains, the Rocky Mountain states, and Alaska.

Currently legal immigration in the United States averages around 400,000 annually and accounts for about 25 percent of the nation's annual population growth. However, not all immigration is legal.

Illegal Immigration. Illegal immigration is a subject of increasing concern to people in the United States, yet it is difficult to discuss because of its emotional impact and the lack of accurate information.

Illegal immigration results from the same conditions at places of origin and destination that stimulate legal immigration. People faced with unsatisfactory living conditions in their home countries may choose to

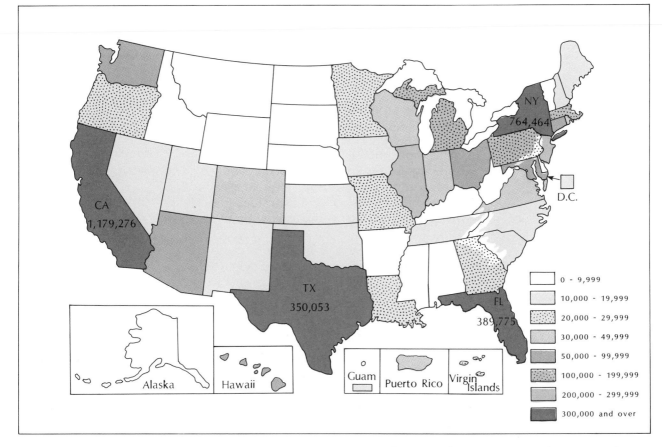

FIGURE 4–7 Alien address reports by state, 1976. (U.S. Dept. of Justice, Immigration, and Naturalization Service, *1976 Annual Report.* Washington, D.C., U.S. Government Printing Office, 1977, p. 26.)

illegally immigrate if legal immigration is impossible. Illegal immigration is especially likely if a nearby country offers the possibility of better jobs, higher incomes, and an improved quality of life.

Such is the situation for Mexicans looking northward the United States. Mexico's economy is struggling, while the rate of population growth remains over 3 percent annually. This population increase puts pressure on per capita rates of economic growth, housing, and health. At some point for many people the benefits of illegal immigration outweigh the risks, and so they cross the border.

As figure 4–8 shows, most apprehended illegals are from Mexico. Until recently most illegals entering from Mexico remained close to the border; now many more move inland. Also, their destinations have shifted more toward urban areas, whereas they used to remain primarily in rural areas; apparently, more jobs are available now in urban areas for illegals.

A variety of controversies surround the illegal alien question. It is debatable, for example, whether illegals displace Americans from jobs or whether they mainly fill menial jobs which would otherwise go unfilled. The costs of illegal immigration to the United States are also debatable. Some argue that illegals overburden social services and depress the economy, whereas others claim that illegals pay far more in taxes than they receive back in services. Without accurate data such debates must go unresolved, but it seems clear that illegal immigration is a problem and that the United States will continue its attempt to find solutions.

Internal migration and population redistribution

The United States is not only a nation of immigrants but also a nation of movers. Americans always seem to be on the move, and nearly one in five changes residence each year.

THE NEW COLOSSUS

by
Emma Lazarus

Not like the brazen giant of Greek fame,
With conquering limbs astride from land to land;
Here at our sea-washed, sunset gates shall stand
A mighty woman with a torch, whose flame
Is the imprisoned lightning, and her name
Mother of Exiles. From her beacon-hand
Glows world-wide welcome; her mild eyes command
The air-bridged harbor that twin cities frame.
"Keep ancient lands, your storied pomp!" cries she
With silent lips. "Give me your tired, your poor,
Your huddled masses yearning to breathe free,
The wretched refuse of your teeming shore.
Send these, the homeless, tempest-tost to me,
I lift my lamp beside the golden door!"

Emigrants in a waiting room, Ellis Island. (Library of Congress, Underwood & Underwood, 1907)

Ellis Island, New York. (Library of Congress, 1891)

Migration is a complex mechanism of response to socioeconomic changes. People move for a variety of reasons, but most move in an attempt to improve the quality of their lives. Economic motives, such as better jobs or higher salaries, are still important in deciding to migrate, though other motives, including the desire to escape the smog and congestion of cities, are becoming more important. Motives differ for different age groups, of course. For example, a young executive who is upwardly mobile would be likely to move for much different reasons than would a recently retired South Dakota couple who yearn for warmer winters.

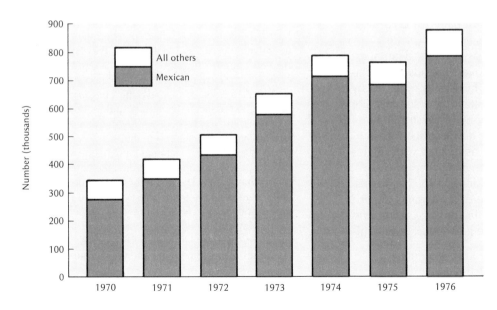

FIGURE 4–8 Illegal aliens apprehended in the United States, 1970–1976. (Leon F. Bouvier with Henry S. Shryock, Harry W. Henderson, September, 1977, ''International Migration: Yesterday, Today, and Tomorrow,'' in *Population Bulletin* 32, no. 4, p. 29. Courtesy of the Population Reference Bureau, Inc., Washington, D.C.)

Farm boy in Cimarron County, Oklahoma. (Library of Congress, Arthur Rothstein, 1936)

Too often we forget the difficulties associated with migration. Distance is an obvious obstacle because of the direct cost of moving. Moving a family of four from New York to Los Angeles is a costly venture and, at least for people who must pay their own moving expenses, such a decision is not easily made.

There are also social and psychological costs, especially with long-distance moves. Friends and relatives must be left behind. The familiar is replaced by the unfamiliar. Children must attend new schools. For many people, even today, moving is a disturbing and difficult experience and, in our desire to see the numbers and the evolving patterns associated with migration, we sometimes forget the migrants themselves.

However, someone occasionally catches for us, on film or in print, the essence of a migrant's experiences. So it is in the following passage from *The Grapes of Wrath,* describing the great "dust bowl" migration:

The cars of the migrant people crawled out of the side roads onto the great cross-country highway, and they took the migrant way to the West. In the daylight they scuttled like bugs to the westward; and as the dark caught them, they clustered like bugs near to shelter and to water. And because they were lonely and perplexed, because they had all come from a place of sadness and worry and defeat, and because they were all going to a new mysterious place, they huddled together; they talked together; they shared their lives, their food, and the things they hoped for in the new country. Thus it might be that one family camped near a spring, and another camped for the spring and for company, and a third because two families had pioneered the place and found it good. And when the sun went down, perhaps twenty families and twenty cars were there.

In the evening a strange thing happened: the twenty families became one family, the children were the children of all. The loss of home became one loss, and the golden time in the West was one dream. And it might be that a sick child threw despair into the hearts of twenty families, of a hundred people; that a birth there in a tent kept a hundred people quiet and awestruck through the night and filled a hundred people with the birth-joy in the morning. A family which the night before had been lost and fearful might search its goods to find a present for a new baby. In the evening, sitting about the fires, the twenty were one. They grew to be units of the camps, units of the evenings and the nights. A guitar unwrapped from a blanket and tuned—and the songs, which were all of the people, were sung in the nights. Men sang the words, and women hummed the tunes.

Every night a world created, complete with furniture—friends made and enemies established; a world complete with braggarts and with cowards, with quiet men, with humble men, with kindly men. Every night relationships that make a world, established; and every morning the world torn down like a circus.

At first the families were timid in the building and tumbling worlds, but gradually the technique of building worlds became their technique. Then leaders emerged, then laws were made, then codes came into being. And as the worlds moved westward they were more complete and better furnished, for their builders were more experienced in building them.

The families learned what rights must be observed—the right of privacy in the tent; the right to keep the past black hidden in the heart; the right to talk and to listen; the right to refuse help or to accept, to offer help or to decline it; the right of son to court and daughter to be courted; the right of the hungry to be fed; the rights of the pregnant and the sick to transcend all other rights.

And the families learned, although no one told them, what rights are monstrous and must be destroyed: the right to intrude upon privacy, the right to be noisy while the camp slept, the right of seduction or rape, the right of adultery and theft and murder. These rights were crushed, because the little worlds could not exist for even a night with such rights alive.

And as the worlds moved westward, rules became laws, although no one told the families. It is unlawful to foul near the camp; it is unlawful in any way to foul the drinking water; it is unlawful to eat good rich food near one who is hungry, unless he is asked to share.

And with the laws, the punishments—and there were only two—a quick and murderous fight or ostracism; and ostracism was the worst. For if one broke the laws his name and face went with him, and he had no place in any world, no matter where created.

In the worlds, social conduct became fixed and rigid, so that a man must say "Good morning" when asked for it, so that a man might have a willing girl if he stayed with her, if he fathered her children and protected them. But a man might not have one girl one night and another the next, for this would endanger the worlds. The families moved westward, and the technique of building the worlds improved so

that the people could be safe in their worlds; and the form was so fixed that a family acting in the rules knew it was safe in the rules.*

Not all migration involved deep changes in social structure and philosophy, of course. A person who moves from suburban Des Moines to suburban Omaha may hardly notice the change, whereas a person moving a much shorter distance, say from Watts to Beverly Hills, may find a totally different world. Thus, there is a social distance to be considered as well as the physical distance between places.

With some general notions about migration in mind, what recent trends do we see emerging in the 20th century? We have already mentioned the westward movement, which continues even today. However, two other major *migration streams* have been important in reshaping the population map of the United States. One was the movement, especially of Blacks, out of the South; the other was the continuous movement of people from the rural areas to the cities. A more recent trend is the movement into the suburbs. The first two trends, as we shall see, have persisted until recently. Suburbanization, of course, continues, though minor countercurrents have developed in some metropolitan areas.

The migration of Blacks. The migration of Blacks in the 20th century has been a major element of internal migration in the United States. Blacks were initially brought to the southern states, where they tended to remain. In 1900, 90 percent of the Blacks in the United States lived in the South, mainly in rural areas; by 1950, however, many had left the rural areas. The percentage of Blacks living in the South had dropped to 68 percent, and two-thirds of these lived in urban areas (Hart, 1960). Between 1950 and 1970 the Black population continued to urbanize, mainly because they continued to leave the rural South and move to metropolitan areas, especially in the Midwest and the Northeast.

Since 1970, however, the pattern of Black migration has been changing. Between March, 1975 and March, 1977, the Northeast experienced a net out-migration, in contrast with the net in-migration between 1960 and 1970. During the same period, in the north central region, the number of Blacks moving in was about the same as the number moving out, whereas the 1960–1970 period experienced a net immigration. Furthermore, the number of Blacks leaving the South was about equal to the number moving in, whereas previously more had left than entered. The West continues to have a net immigration of Blacks.

Most likely many Blacks moving into the South are return migrants, though we will not have sufficient data to substantiate this pattern until the 1980 census is tabulated. Incomes have risen more rapidly in the South than in the Northeast recently, and both Blacks and whites appear to be responding to regional inequalities in income-earning opportunities.

Movement from rural to urban areas. In 1900 the population of the United States was about 40 percent urban; by 1975 this had increased to 74 percent. Urbanization has been rapid and nationwide during the 20th century, with all areas converging toward a predominantly urban population.

Rural–urban migration and urbanization represent responses to the general transformation of the United States from a rural-agrarian to an urban-industrial society. In 1900 almost 40 percent of the labor force was employed in agriculture; today that figure has dropped below 5 percent.

Population redistribution since 1970

Despite the rural–urban redistribution of people which has continued throughout the 20th century in the United States, there has never been unanimous agreement that the cities, especially the large ones, were desirable places to live. Industrialization tended to concentrate people in cities for economic reasons. From an industry's viewpoint, urban locations often meant lower transportation and communication costs, easier access to service needs, and local markets for goods. From a worker's viewpoint, industrial concentration in urban areas meant more jobs and higher wages. However, today's industries are often more *footloose*, that is, they are less bound to particular locations because of transportation and communication costs. Figure 4–9 shows the recent overall trends of interregional migration. Two recent trends in migration patterns are the movement to the "Sunbelt" and the "Rural Renaissance."

The sunbelt. The **Sunbelt** states are those of the South and Southwest. Since 1970 there has been a dramatic shift of population away from states in the North Central and Northeast and toward the Sunbelt states.

Of the 13 million people added to the resident population of the United States between 1960 and 1970, 40 percent of the growth occurred in the states of California, Florida, and Texas. During the same period the Sunbelt states with the highest rates of growth were Nevada, Arizona, Florida, New Mexico, Hawaii, and Texas. Regional growth was highest in the West. Reductions in growth rates are occurring in many states in the Midwest and Northeast, and a few states—Pennsylvania, New York, and Rhode Island—actually lost population between 1970 and 1977.

People are increasingly moving away from the older areas of the North Central and Northeast states, partly in response to environmental preferences and partly as a result of aggressive economic development in states in both the Southeast and Southwest. Others are moving to the amenities of the Rocky Mountains and Pacific Northwest, especially as new energy development in these areas offer new employment opportunities.

The economic geography of the United States is also changing as capital expenditures rise in the Sunbelt states. If the movement of people continues, there will also be a shift of political power away from the Northeast.

The Rural Renaissance. The long-established trend toward rural–urban migration has undergone a surprising reversal since 1970. Perhaps for the first time in American history more people are leaving metropolitan areas than entering them. Some basic observations by Morrison and Wheeler included:

> Each year between 1970 and 1975, for every 100 people who moved to the metropolitan sector, 131 moved out. During the five years before, an average of only 94 moved out for every 100 who moved in.
>
> Many metropolitan areas, especially some of the largest ones (New York, Chicago, Philadelphia, Cleveland, Seattle, and Los Angeles, for example), stopped growing altogether.
>
> Conversely, three-fourths of all nonmetropolitan counties registered population gains from either natural increase or migration (or both), compared with only half in the 1960s and two-fifths in the 1950s. More significantly, net migration gains (more migrants moving in than out) occurred in nearly two-thirds of all nonmetropolitan counties compared with only one-fourth in the 1960s and one-tenth in the 1950s.
>
> Even nonmetropolitan areas that are far distant

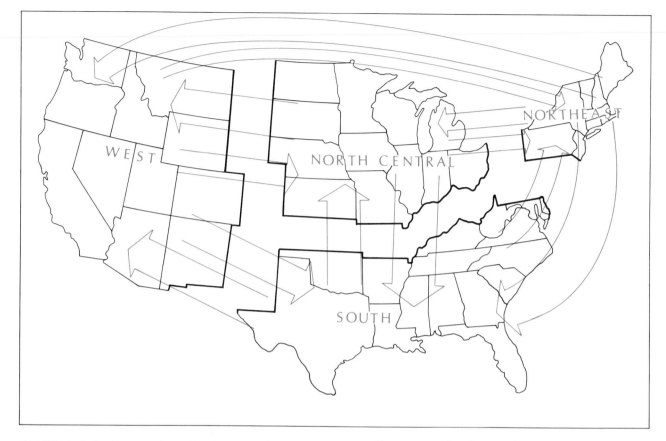

FIGURE 4–9 Region-to-region migration, March 1975 to March 1977. (U.S. Dept. of Commerce, Bureau of the Census, Current Population Reports, February, 1978, *Population Characteristics*, Series P-20, no. 320, cover page.)

from urban and metropolitan influence—the kinds of places that used to be regarded as "nowhere" in the 1950s— have been registering net migration gains instead of their once perennial losses. (1976, pp. 3–4)

Not all nonmetropolitan areas are equally pleased with the prospect of increased population growth and "rural urbanization." Conflicts arise between advocates of growth and those who seek to limit growth. Some small-town residents fear that growth will destroy the very features that make such areas attractive. They point to rising crime rates, increasing traffic congestion and even smog as inevitable results of small-town growth.

The sudden reversal of long-term urbanization in the United States caught many people, including demographers, by surprise. At first, many figured that most of the nonmetropolitan growth was just spillover from expanding metropolitan areas; however, nonmet-

ropolitan areas far from urban centers were also growing.

Spillover, of course, has been occurring for some time, but a new pattern of urbarnization seems at hand. Among its causes are: changes in communication and transportation technology have removed, or at least diminished, the need for urban concentration; and the expansion of highways allow easy access to urban areas. The growth of retirement and recreational communities has also contributed to nonmetropolitan growth.

Early retirement, coupled with increased benefits for retirees, frees an increasing number of people to choose a location based on place preferences rather than economic necessities. Wherever they go, services are required and growth occurs. Not only Florida and the Southwest but also the Ozarks, the Texas hill country, and the "Gold Country" in the western foothills of the Sierra Nevada are experiencing growth from influxes of retirees.

Migration differentials

Migrants do not characterize a random sample of the population of the United States; rather, they differ in various ways from persons who do not move. Thus, they have an impact on communities of origin and destination which is often greater than their numbers alone would suggest.

Age. One of the most commonly observed migration differentials is age. Amost universally migrants tend to be young, and this is true in the United States. The peak age group for migrants is 25–29 years, migration decreases rather quickly for older age groups. Between 1970 and 1975, 41.3 percent of all persons 5 years old and over moved, whereas 72.0 percent of those aged 25–29 years moved.

Race. For short distance moves, such as those within a county, Blacks are more likely to move than whites. On the other hand, whites have higher rates of intercounty and interstate migration than do Blacks.

Education. The probability of migration is influenced by the level of educational attainment. For intercounty and interstate movements college graduates are more likely to move than high school graduates, who are in turn more likely to move than are persons with only a grade school education.

POPULATION GROWTH AND ENVIRONMENT IN THE U. S.

Our purpose in this section is to provide a brief overview of a few salient aspects of the relationship between population growth and the environment, although the topic deserves a volume to itself.

Population, resources, and environment

Population growth undoubtedly impacts both resources and the environment, and it is safe to suggest that during the coming decades, the pressure we put on resources and the environment will depend on the size of the national population, the size of populations in local areas, consumption patterns of the people, and the ways in which goods and services are produced and consumed.

Most projections of economic growth in the United States over the next few decades, irrespective of population growth, suggest that the **Gross National Product (GNP)** —the total value of goods and services produced in one year—will be considerably larger than it is now. According to the U. S. Commission on Population Growth and the American Future:

> In short, total GNP, which is the principal source of the demand for resources and the production of pollutants, will become much larger than it is now. But if population should grow at the 3-child rate, GNP will grow far more than it will at the 2-child rate. (1972, p. 43)

Some implications of future population growth under both the 2- and 3-child rates are shown in table 4–1. Consider them as you look through the table, and ask youself some questions about which you prefer. How many people, for example, can one congressional representative adequately represent? It's no wonder that there are many advocates of no-growth, or at least slow growth. In one form or another, the growth syndrome manifests itself, first in one place, then in another. In the United States the combined influences of population and economic growth severely threaten the natural environment, as evidenced, for example, by smog and congestion in industrial cities and by surface mining for coal in the Appalachians and elsewhere.

Water. One example of a problem associated with population growth is the need for water. More growth requires more water and both create regional problems of geographic interest.

The map in figure 4–10 shows the expanding water deficit regions under an assumed 3-child per family growth rate to the year 2020. Note that, according to the map, much of the southwestern United States already is considered a water deficit region. However, it is also an area toward which people continue to move, as we saw in our discussion of the Sunbelt migration. In some cases, especially in Los Angeles, extreme measures have been taken to assure water supplies via water imports.

A growing population and expanding economic activities are likely to result in the eastward and northward expansion of the water deficit region over the decades ahead, and this expansion will be accelerated if population grows at the 3-child rate. Most likely, population growth will be more important than economic growth in creating further water resource problems—problems which will arise despite sizable investments in dams and other water projects. According to the U. S. Commission on Population Growth and the American Future:

TABLE 4–1 Comparison of life in the U.S. in 1974 with that for stable and growing populations in 2015

Characteristic	1974	2015 (stable)	2015 (growing)
Average children per family	2.1	2.1	3
Total population	214 million	275 million	322 million
Time to reach zero population growth	Depends on population plan and behavior; may never stabilize	Stabilized	Never; population would double to 650 million in 45 years
Age structure under 18 18–64 over 64: median age	75 million(35%) 118 million (55%) 21 million (10%) 28	77million (28%) 169 million (61%) 29 million (11%) 36	114 million (35%) 179 million (56%) 29 million (9%) 32
Dependency ratio (dependents are persons under 18 or over 65)	81 dependents per 100 workers	62 dependents per 100 workers	80 dependents per 100 workers
Urbanization	150 million (70%) living in urban areas	234 million (85%) living in urban areas unless population redistribution policies were successful	274 million (85%) living in urban areas
Average family income	$12,000	Greater than $20,000	Greater than $20,000
Estimated per capita income	$5600	$8800	$7700
Education		Fewer secondary and college students; all should be able to get better education than in 1974	45% more secondary and 30% more college students with only about 7% receiving better education than in 1974
Labor	35 million new workers per decade looking for jobs	35 million per decade	44 million between 2005 and 2015
Average congressional representation	One congressman to represent 490,000 people	One congressman to represent 630,000 people	One congressman to represent 740,000 people
Water supplies	Country as a whole has abundancy but supply short in some regions	Shortages in one-third of country	Shortages in more than one-half of country
Farmland	About 75% of high-quality farmland in use	All high-quality farmland in use	All high-quality farmland in use, plus 50 million acres of low-quality land
Recreation	Urban areas crowded; some national parks under heavy seasonal pressure	Great pressure on recreation areas but 30% less than that with 3-child family	Very heavy pressure on recreational areas

TABLE 4–1 *Continued.*

Characteristic	1974	2015 (stable)	2015 (growing)
Pollution	Amount of pollution and cost of control rising sharply	Control still expensive but reduced by 30 to 50%	Because of increased population, pollution not significantly better than 1974 levels; costs extremely high, perhaps prohibitively high.

Source: From *Living in the Environment: Concepts, Problems, and Alternatives* by G. Tyler Miller, Jr. © 1975 by Wadsworth Publishing Co., Inc., Belmont, CA 94002. Reprinted by permission of the publisher.

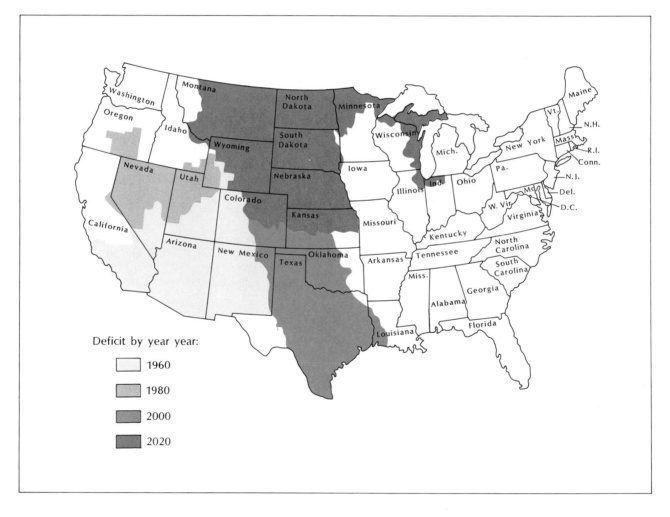

Deficit by year year:

☐ 1960
▨ 1980
▨ 2000
■ 2020

FIGURE 4–10 Water deficit regions. Estimates assume rapid economic growth, maximum development of water storage facilities, and tertiary treatment. (Ronald G. Ridker, "Future Water Needs and Supplies, with a Note on Land Use," in U.S. Commission on Population Growth and the American Future, 1972, *Population and the American Future*. Washington, D.C., U.S. Government Printing Office, p. 26.)

Sooner or later we will have to deal with water as a scarce resource. The sooner this is done, the fewer water crises will emerge in the years ahead. However, doing this will not be easy technically or politically—most water supplies are run by local governments. And few will like the austerity created by the need to conserve on something as fundamental as water. The rate of national population growth will largely determine how rapidly we must accomplish these changes. (1972, p. 47)

Risks and choices

American development has always involved risks and choices. However, it is likely that continued population growth will narrow the range of choices available and may even cause us to have to choose too hastily among alternatives or accept risks which otherwise would be unacceptable. Projects may be accepted, for example, before their social and ecological ramifications are clearly comprehended.

Pollution provides numerous examples. The socioeconomic consequences of urban pollution in various forms are not easily calculated. Increased energy production will generate environmental consequences of major proportions, whether by expanded strip-mining for coal, or more nuclear power plants, or both.

The United States can probably cope with continued population growth over the next half century,

but not without the risk of changes in lifestyle and living standards. As the U.S. Commission on Population Growth and the American Future aptly stated:

Population growth forces upon us slow but irreversible changes in life style. Imbedded in our traditions as to what constitutes the American way of life is freedom from public regulation—virtually free use of water; access to uncongested, unregulated roadways; freedom to do as we please with what we own; freedom from permits, licenses, fees, red tape, and bureaucrats; and freedom to fish, swim, and camp where and when we will. Clearly, we do not live this way now. Maybe we never did. But everything is relative. The population of 2020 may look back with envy on what, from their vantage point, appears to be our relatively unfettered way of life. (1972, p. 51)

Population policy in the U.S.

The United States still has not adopted an explicit policy for population growth or distribution, though other policies—for example, aid to depressed regions through the Economic Development Administration—often have some impact on population variables. There is increasing pressure on the government to control population processes directly, though agreement on the type of policy to be implemented is not likely to occur quickly.

Plan for stabilizing U.S. population

1. Base all programs on individual freedom of choice with the recognition that freedom can be exercised rationally and responsibly only when one is aware of the possible choices and their potential consequences.

2. Greatly extend voluntary programs to enable an individual of any age, sex, race, or economic status to control his or her own reproductive behavior based on individual conscience and needs. These programs would include greatly expanded education, women's rights, and voluntary and open access to abortion, sterilization, contraceptive devices, and counseling at no cost for those unable to pay.

3. Place special emphasis on reducing births among middle and upper class Americans, rather than focusing on the poor. This will do more to actually slow population growth and environmental disruption and will also decrease minority group concern over genocide.

4. Put a primary emphasis on eliminating poverty through annual income support for those unable to work and increased job training and opportunities for others.

5. Conduct crash research programs and selected pilot trials to determine what integrated array of incentives would be successful in decreasing family size without injustice to the poor and to children. Implement the appropriate incentive programs between 1980 and 1985 if stabilization goals are not being met.

6. Initiate crash research programs on improved contraceptives, basic reproductive biology, and motivational psychology for reduced family size, migration away from cities and living in a stabilized population.

7. Gradually reduce immigration to half of its present value by 1980 with no immigration of trained and skilled persons, who now make up about 50 percent of the immigrants each year. (This involves the United States in a brain drain that robs underdeveloped countries of their most valuable resource).

8. Carefully integrate population policies with those for use of resources, land use, energy use, and pollution control by creating a cabinet level Department of Population, Natural Resources, and Environment.   (Miller, 1975)

HISTORICAL GROWTH OF CANADA'S POPULATION

Like the United States, Canada has developed as a nation of immigrants. Before the coming of European settlers, Canada was a sparsely populated area inhabited only by small numbers of Eskimos and Indians. These early populations were further reduced in number as European settlement brought with it disease and war.

Population growth in the 17th century

Permanent European settlement of Canada began in 1608 when 28 French citizens arrived with Samuel de Champlain to found Quebec. However, as we see in figure 4–11, the total population of Canada decreased gradually until around the middle of the 17th century, when it began a gradual increase. Immigration from France made only a minimal impact on growth, because fewer than 10,000 persons came from France to Canada between 1608 and 1760 (Beaujot, 1978, p. 5).

Population growth in the 18th century

As figure 4–11 shows, Canada at the beginning of the 18th century had just about regained its population of a century earlier. Slow growth of the population characterized the 18th century up until its last quarter. In 1763 Canada was ceded to Great Britain, and within a decade the rate of population growth began to accel-

erate. High fertility and heavy immigration combined to produce more than a ten-fold increase in population between 1775 and 1861 (Hamelin, 1973, p. 90).

Population growth in the 19th century

During the 19th century, Canada's population grew from 535,000 to over 5.5 million. Between 1831 and 1841 the population increased by 45 percent, but between 1861 and 1896 the decennial growth rate dropped to around 10 percent. Several events combined to reduce growth rates: a dropoff in immigration, an increase in emigration, and a decline in the rate of natural increase (Weir, 1967).

CANADA'S POPULATION IN THE 20TH CENTURY

Data in table 4–2 show the influence of the components of growth from the last half of the 19th century until 1976. As the 20th century began, Canada's population map was showing the impact of westward expansion and an accompanying upward surge in the growth rate. Also, the ethnic composition was undergoing some alteration as Germans and others became more apparent among the new arrivals. During the 20th century, fertility and immigration have altered in response to changing socioeconomic conditions.

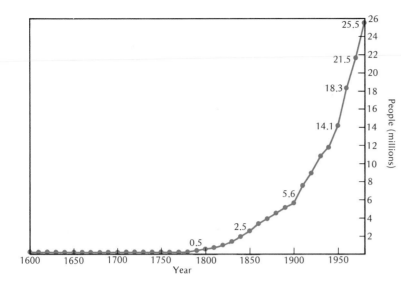

FIGURE 4–11 Canadian population, 1601–1981. (Louis-Edmond Hamelin, *Canada: A Geographical Perspective*. Copyright © 1973 by John Wiley & Sons Ltd., p. 90. Reprinted by permission of John Wiley & Sons Ltd.)

Fertility

In New France and among French Canadians until well into the 20th century, high fertility was legendary. Between 1760 and 1800 the Catholic population of Quebec had a crude birth rate of 60 (Henripin, 1972).

However, once fertility among French Canadians started downward, it did so with a vengence. In 1959 Quebec's crude birth rate was 28.3, as opposed to 27.4 for all Canadians; in 1976 the rates were down to 15.3 for Quebec and 15.9 for all of Canada.

TABLE 4–2 Components of Canadian population growth (in thousands)

Census year	Total population	Change since preceding census				
		Natural increase	Net migration	Ratio of natural increase to total growth	Ratio of net migration to total growth	Average annual growth rate
1851	2436	—	—	—	—	—
1861	3230	611	182	77.0	23.0	2.9%
1871	3698	610	−150	132.6	−32.6	1.3
1881	4325	690	− 54	108.5	− 8.5	1.6
1891	4833	654	−146	128.7	−28.7	1.1
1901	5371	668	−130	124.2	−24.2	1.1
1911	7207	1025	810	55.9	44.1	3.0
1921	8788	1270	311	80.3	19.7	2.0
1931	10,377	1360	230	85.5	14.5	1.7
1941	11,507	1222	− 92	108.1	− 8.1	1.0
1951	14,009	1972	169	92.1	7.9	1.7
1956	16,081	1473	598	71.1	28.9	2.8
1961	18,238	1675	482	77.7	22.3	2.5
1966	20,015	1518	259	85.4	14.6	1.9
1971	21,568	1090	463	70.2	29.8	1.5
1976	22,993	934	350	65.5	24.5	1.3

Sources: M. V. George, *Population Growth in Canada,* 1971 Census of Canada Profile Studies (Ottawa: Statistics Canada Catalogue No. 99–701, pp. 5 and 7); and Statistics Canada, *Estimates of Population for Canada and the Provinces, June 1, 1977* (Ottawa: Statistics Canada Catalogue No. 91–201, 1977).

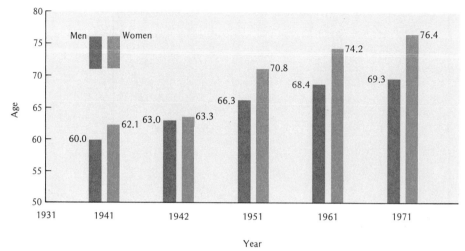

FIGURE 4–12 Canadian life expectancy at birth, 1931–1971. (M. V. George, 1976, *Population Growth in Canada,* 1971 Census of Canada Profile Studies. Ottawa, Statistics Canada Catalogue No. 99–701, p. 13.)

Fertility in Canada has closely followed the United States pattern in the 20th century, only at higher levels, at least until the mid-1970s. In both countries fertility declined slowly during the last half of the 19th century, then more quickly in the 1920s and 1930s, a decade in which crude birth rates reached all-time lows not equaled again until the 1970s. Between the 1930s and the 1970s, fertility increased to a peak around 1959 or 1960, then began a new decline toward current low levels. However, recent low crude birth rates may or may not prevail, depending on the specific reasons why women are currently having so few children. It is not yet clear whether they today are choosing to have smaller families or merely postponing births until later ages.

Mortality

The crude death rate reached 38 per thousand in Quebec between 1750 and 1760 and has never been as high since that decade; by 1867 the mortality of Catholics had dropped to 20.9, a 50 percent decrease from a century earlier (Kalbach and McVey, 1971, p. 44). By 1930 the crude death rate in Canada had dropped to 13 per thousand, and between 1930 and 1978 it fell by nearly 50 percent to only 7 per thousand. Obviously Canada, like the United States, experienced an epidemiological transition which greatly altered Canadian mortality throughout the 19th and into the 20th centuries.

Mortality declines have occurred for the entire Canadian population. However, male mortality has not only remained above female mortality, but it has also declined more slowly. The differential mortality experiences for the sexes shows that, on the average, life expectancy for females increased by 14.3 years between 1931 and 1971 while that for males increased by only 9.3 years (figure 4–12).

Infant mortality, the number of deaths to infants (ages 0 to 1 year) in a year per 1000 births in that same year, has fallen dramatically in the 20th century. In 1921 the rate was 102.1 infant deaths per 1000 live births; by 1978 it was down to only 14.

The role of immigration

Immigration has always played an important role in Canada's population dynamics; less well-known is the role of emigration during certain periods. Figure 4–13 shows the relationship between immigration and emigration since the middle of the 19th century. We see that net losses occurred during most of the last half of the 19th century and again during the depression years of the 1930s.

Since World War II net immigration has accounted for nearly 25 percent of Canada's population growth, and between 1966 and 1975 it accounted for 33 percent of the total increase in population (Barrett and Taylor, 1977, p. 16). In recent decades high immigration rates have been coupled with low fertility rates, making immigration a major contributor to overall population growth.

Canada's view of immigration has varied over the years, and immigration policies have been altered from time to time to reflect prevailing Canadians attitudes. Most recently, sparked by an economic slowdown dur-

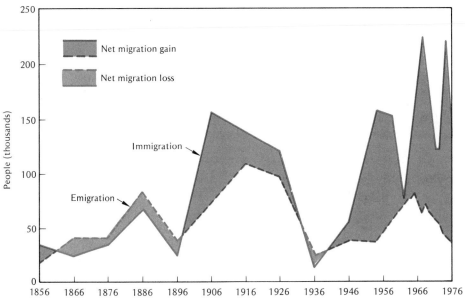

FIGURE 4–13 Canadian immigration and emigration, 1851–1976. (Roderic P. Beaujot, April, 1978, "Canada's Population: Growth and Dualism," in *Population Bulletin* 33, p. 17. Courtesy of the Population Reference Bureau, Inc., Washington, D.C.)

ing the 1970s, there has been opposition to maintaining high immigration levels.

Following a governmental review of immigration policy in the mid-1970s, the Canadian Parliament passed a new Immigration Act in August of 1977, which was implemented in April of 1978. The volume of immigration will be decreased by the new policy, probably to an annual immigration of fewer than 100,000. The new act also retains the nondiscriminatory criteria established in 1962, despite the fears of many Canadians that such a policy increases the potential for social unrest by allowing minority groups to settle in the country.

One especially geographic problem associated with Canadian immigration in recent years is the limited number of places in which most immigrants seek to reside. Over 50 percent of all immigrants between 1961 and 1971 went to Toronto, Montreal, and Vancouver. This concentration of immigrants has led to explosive situations, especially when large numbers of non-Europeans have congregated together. For example, immigrants from the Indian subcontinent have been the targets of recent hostility in both Vancouver and Toronto, partly because of their easy visibility.

Population distribution in Canada

Canada's 1971 census counted 21,568,311 people; however by 1978 that number had grown to an estimated 23,600,000. When compared to the total land area of approximately 3.8 million square miles, we find that Canada has a population density of 6.2 persons per square mile. However, as is readily apparent in figure 4–14, the Canadian people are primarily clustered in settlements along the southern border, especially in eastern Canada, reflecting the harsh physical environment as well as close economic ties with the United States. Over 60 percent of the total population lives in the provinces of Ontario and Quebec, mainly in their southern reaches. On the other hand, few people are found in the Yukon and the Northwest Territories.

Population policy in Canada

At least the following three variables are usually of central concern in any **population policy;** population size and rate of growth, population distribution, and population age-structure. Leaving immigration aside, Canada, like the United States has no national population policy; however, there is increasing pressure to establish one.

Some recommendations for the formulation of a Canadian population were suggested by the National Man and Resources Conference and are as follows:

1. Develop an explicit national population policy which would accommodate the growth inherent in the present population but allow for a leveling off of further growth by the year 2000.

2. Create an immigration policy consistent with this objective.

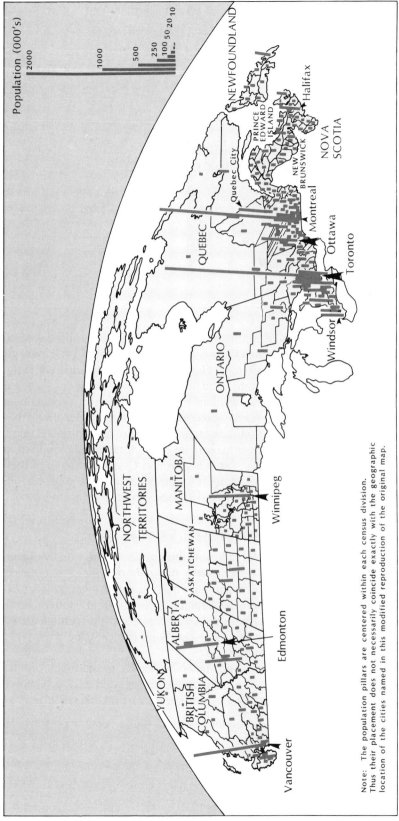

Population (000's)

2000
1000
500
250
100 50 20 10

Vancouver

YUKON

BRITISH COLUMBIA

NORTHWEST TERRITORIES

ALBERTA

Edmonton

SASKATCHEWAN

MANITOBA

Winnipeg

ONTARIO

QUEBEC

Quebec City

NEWFOUNDLAND

PRINCE EDWARD ISLAND

NEW BRUNSWICK

NOVA SCOTIA

Halifax

Montreal

Ottawa

Toronto

Windsor

Note: The population pillars are centered within each census division. Thus their placement does not necessarily coincide exactly with the geographic location of the cities named in this modified reproduction of the original map.

FIGURE 4–14 Canadian population distribution by census division, 1976. (Roderic P. Beaujot, April, 1978, "Canada's Population: Growth and Dualism," in *Population Bulletin* 33, p. 24. Courtesy of the Population Reference Bureau, Inc., Washington, D.C.)

3. Devote increased efforts and resources to education in the field of population and family planning.

4. Intensify their efforts at decentralizing and redistributing population in order to more clearly satisfy provincial and regional aspirations.

5. Recognize their global responsibilities by increasing aid in technical, capital and especially population programs.

6. Consult fully and openly with the people of Canada by means of public hearings, written submissions, and a national conference for the U.N.'s World Population Conference.

7. Recognize and respond to the fact that total impact on environment, resource consumption and social problems, is a result of a combination of population size and rates of consumption.

8. Establish a permanent independent agency to provide continuing policy advice, and promote research and public awareness of population problems (Barrett and Taylor, 1977, pp. 39–40).

Canadians are faced with a number of alternatives with respect to population policies, but the time to make their choices is now rather than later.

KEY TERMS

Forced migration
Urbanization
Population densities
Epidemiologic transition
Fertility trends
Immigration
Migration streams

Population redistribution
Sunbelt
Rural Renaissance
Migration differentials
Gross National Product (GNP)
Population policy

REFERENCES

Barrett, M. and Taylor, C. (1977), *Population and Canada, Social Problems in Canada*. Toronto: Guidance Center, Faculty of Education, University of Toronto.

Beaujot, R. P. (1978), "Canada's Population: Growth and Dualism," *Population Bulletin* 33, 1–47.

Billington, R. A. (1959), *The Westward Movement in the United States*. New York: Van Nostrand Reinhold Co.

Bouvier, L. with Shryock, H. S. and Henderson, H. W. (1977), "International Migration: Yesterday, Today, and Tomorrow," *Population Bulletin* 32, 1–42.

Hamelin, L. (1973), *Canada: A Geographical Perspective*, Storrie, M. C. and Jackson, C. I., trans. Toronto: Wiley Publishers of Canada Ltd.

Handlin, O. (1951), *The Uprooted*. New York: Grosset's Universal Library, Grosset & Dunlap.

Hart, J. F. (1960), "The Changing Distribution of the American Negro," *Annals of the Association of American Geographers* 50, 242–266.

Henripin, J. (1972), *Trends and Factors of Fertility in Canada*. Ottawa: Statistics Canada.

Kalbach, W. E. and McVey, W. W. (1971), *The Demographic Bases of Canadian Society*. Toronto: McGraw-Hill Co. of Canada Ltd.

Kitigawa, E. M. (1972), "Socioeconomic Differences in Mortality in the United States and Some Implications for Population Policy," in U. S. Commission on Population Growth and the American Future, *Demographic and Social Aspects of Population Growth*, Westoff, C. F. and Parke, R., (eds.), Vol. I of Commission research reports. Washington, D.C.: U. S. Government Printing Office.

Lanegran, D. A. (1973), "Where Is Everybody: A Geographer's View of the Population of the United States," in Lanegran, D. A. and Palm, R. (eds.), *An Invitation to Geography*. New York: McGraw-Hill Book Co.

Miller, G. T., Jr. (1975), *Living in the Environment: Concepts, Problems, and Alternatives*. Belmont, CA: Wadsworth Publishing Co, Inc.

Morrison, P. with Wheeler, J. P. (1976), "Rural Renaissance in America?" *Population Bulletin* 31, 1–26.

Omran, A. R. (1977), "Epidemiologic Transition in the U. S.: The Health Factor in Population Change," *Population Bulletin* 32, 1–42.

Paterson, J. H. (1975), *North America: A Geography of Canada and the United States*, 5th ed. New York: Oxford University Press.

Steinbeck, J. (1939), *The Grapes of Wrath.* New York: Viking Press.

Stone, L. O. and Siggner, A. J. (1974), *The Population of Canada: A Review of Recent Patterns and Trends.* Paris: Committee for International Cooperation in National Research in Demography.

Stone, L. O. and Marcean, D. (1977) *Canadian Population Trends and Public Policy Through the 1980s.* Montreal: McGill–Queen's University Press.

Taeuber, C. and Taeuber, I. B. (1958), *The Changing Population of the United States.* New York: John Wiley & Sons, Inc.

Taeuber, I. B. (1967), "Demographic Transitions and Population Problems in the United States," *Annals of the American Academy of Political and Social Science* 360, 131–140.

Tietze, C. and Murstein, M. (1975), "Induced Abortion: 1975 Factbook," in *Reports on Population/Family Planning,* No. 14, 2nd ed.

U. S. Commission on Population Growth and the American Future (1972), *Population and the American Future.* Washington, D.C.: U.S. Government Printing Office.

Weit, J. R. (1967), "Population Changes in Canada, 1867–1967," *The Canadian Geographer* 11, 197–215.

The total way of life of a specific group is generally referred to as their *culture*. In this section we discuss the attributes that define culture, as well as the more specific aspects of one's cultural heritage, such as race, religion, language, and political system. All of these elements of culture combine to form characteristic life styles and spatial patterns throughout the world. As geographers we are interested in the spatial patterns of cultural attributes as well as the imprint of culture upon the landscape.

The mosaic of culture 2

Basilica of the Sacre-Cour, Paris
(French Government Tourist Office)

5

Human reliance upon culture

The title of this section of our discussion of peoples, environments and places, *the mosaic of culture,* is an apt description of the essence of human geography. The concept of culture builds upon a foundation of the interrelationships and interdependence between the technological, social, economic, aesthetic, spiritual, and political aspects of human societies. Cultures are, in a real sense, a mosaic—that is, a collection of diverse parts which together form a coherent picture of the beliefs, attitudes, and activities of various human groups.

Human geographers are concerned with this mosaic of culture because the manner in which human beings use the earth and its resources and develop the locations for their activities is largely the result of a long-term evolutionary process associated with the development of the various cultures found on earth today.

In this chapter we consider the meaning of *culture* as well as the earth's surface as an expression of cultural activities. Our discussion must deal with both the material basis of culture and the process of cultural diffusion through space and time. The underlying factors in all of these issues is the role of culture in the development and growth of societies and the manner in which culture and the process of modernization have influenced human use of the earth.

THE CONCEPT AND DYNAMICS OF CULTURE

Jacob Bronowski has said that we, as human beings, are singular creatures. We have certain gifts making us unique among the other animals, so that we are not simply figures in the landscape but rather shapers of the landscape. We did not find a home on every continent, but instead have made our home on every continent and in nearly the total range of physical environments (1973, p. 19). Understanding why and how we shape the landscape as we do is understanding the dynamics of the evolution of human cultural systems.

Cultural systems in evolutionary perspective

When viewing a mosaic of painting, the observer is not seeing simply a random collection of colors but instead a purposeful design of organized bits of materials, and the same is true of culture.

The culture of a group, be it a small isolated society in central Brazil or the United States as a cultural region, is no mere haphazard collection of artifacts. Rather, it is the result of specific processes which react to the complex of human wants and interests. Culture defines, gives form to, and influences the locations of human activites. The complexity of cultural wants and interests, especially when concerned with how people use the earth, must be examined in a systematic manner, that is, as culture consisting of a collection of entities and the relationships between those entitites in space, time, and scale. Culture includes all the various elements that comprise a people's "way of life."

The manner in which the human geographer views the cultural system is analogous to the approach a skilled mechanic takes when considering an automobile. The mechanic is very much aware that the entirety of the automobile (the system) is a collection of entities (subsystems—engine, exhaust, transmission), with specific relationships between the subsystems. When a motorist brings an automobile to be repaired, the mechanic begins to intellectually dissect the automobile, knowing that the problem is with a subsystem, the engine for example. Certain inevitable repercussions result if a malfunction occurs in the engine, because unique activity in this subsystem generally has a predictable effect on the entire system. The mechanic can further define the problem as being in some subunit of the engine and, through this sytematic process, develop a schematic framework for analyzing how a change in even the most minute component would alter the entire system. What we have described is the systematic approach to problem analysis, a clearly defined hierarchical method for establishing the relationship of parts to the entire system.

Obviously a cultural system is not as specific and objective as an automobile, though the processes of dissecting and analyzing both systems are very similar. There are definite interrelated subsystems of a dynamic, and most probably modernizing, culture—the intellectual, political, economic, social, and psychological traits of human groups. One must be able to find the place of, and interrelationships between, various subsystems to understand a cultural system.

At this juncture two points must be made. First, it is important to note that the categorization of cultural subsystems is based on extremely broad and general divisions of the elements of human activity. Second, unlike the automobile, everything in life is not harmoniously adjusted to everything else; thus the elements of a cultural system have a high degree of autonomy. Prediction of the inevitability of events resulting from a change in one element of the cultural system is extremely difficult.

Two other elements make a systematic analysis of culture difficult, scale and location. In the study of culture, one of the most important questions to be asked is at what scale, or level of detail, should the investigation be undertaken: with the individual, the group, region, nation, or even the inhabitants of a continent. As larger areas and cultural groups are observed there is an attendant need to become more general; however, if the unit of observation is extremely restricted, then conclusions with broad applications are difficult to generate. The Pomo Indians of Northern California, for instance, had three major tribal subgroups within a range of 100 miles. Although they

were similar in many ways, enough major differences existed between the Pacific Coast, Russian River, and Clear Lake groups that each could be considered a separate cultural unit. Much of the variation between the three Pomo groups can be explained by differences in the physical environments of the subareas. The variable character of the earth as the home of humankind makes universal cultural comparisons extremely difficult.

Suppose we were to consider the cultural systems of primitive peoples in today's world. How could we come to any general conclusions about peoples from physical environments as different as those of the Arctic Eskimos, the Camayuras from tropical South America, or the Bushmen of the southern African deserts? Two fundamental schemes for dealing with the problems of scale and geographic diversity are to view cultures in either a holistic or an abstract sense, or to consider culture and modernization. These designs for studying culture are certainly not mutually exclusive. They build one upon the other, but each possesses sufficient basic differences so that we may consider each method both separately and as it relates to the others.

Holistic and abstract viewpoints. Those following a holistic approach to the study of culture often see the forest but not the trees. This philosophy emphasizes to the maximum extent possible that culture is a system unique to each people and place observed. The holists would consider each element of a cultural system solely within the context of that particular system; thus the Eskimos, the Camayuras, and the Bushmen of the Kalahari Desert would be viewed as distinct cultural systems.

The abstracter would simply abstract similar traits from each society and treat them as though the traits were the same regardless of societal differences. For example, the division of labor—the specific and separate tasks to be performed by the men, women and children of a group—would be compared and contrasted as components of a larger human cultural system. Geographers are both holists and abstracters. The holistic approach is the foundation of the classical approach to the study of people and their habitat, whereas the abstractive method is basic to the study of modernization and cultural evolution.

Modernization and cultural evaluation. Proponents of the holistic school of thought speak of **cultural relativity**—that is, each culture is specific to a particular group, and there is no way to evaluate the aspects of one culture relative to other cultures. There are others who contend, however, that when the dynamics of modernization are considered, the elements of various cultures can be examined for differences or similarities within the context of a society's process toward modernization. C. E. Black considers the process of modernization to be one by which evolving institutions adapt to the rapidly changing conditions resulting from the unprecedented increases in knowledge, permitting control over the environment, which accompanies the evolution of science (1966, p. 7). The extent to which people control the environment is certainly subject to question and debate. However, Black's basic premise—that our cultural institutions have evolved through the need to keep pace with the changes a developing technology brings to cultural systems—is a good measure with which to consider comparative cultural change. By examining the subsystems of a cultural system (the intellectual, political, economic, social and psychological components) in the perspective of technological change—especially developments in agriculture, urbanization and environmental modification—we can either abstract traits from various cultures for comparison or consider the changes for the entire culture.

Using our analogy of the automobile as a system to culture as a system, we can develop examples of the relationship between culture and modernization in a systematic framework. When plants and animals were domesticated by the people in the Tigris–Euphrates valley over 8000 years ago, the change in one subsystem (the economic component of culture, agriculture) eventually brought about massive changes in the social, political and intellectual components of the system which later led to the origins of Western cities. Substantial evidence indicates that the people of Southeast Asia domesticated plants and animals at about the same time, but the related impact on other components of the cultural system were far different. Thus modernization, in the form of the development of agriculture, had a vastly different impact on the cultural systems and institutions of Southeast Asia than on those of the Middle East, and we can trace the evolution of these differences in each cultural system over time.

In the contemporary world we can abstract traits from various cultures for comparison, for instance, the application of science to the betterment of our material life. If we examine the avilability of consumer goods

made possible by technological advances in electronics in the United States, Japan, and the Soviet Union, we find that the Americans and Japanese have far greater access to a particular item than their contemporaries in the Soviet Union; with equal access to technology, the difference in the Soviet pattern results from political and social factors, thus these elements of the system help explain the differences in a particular trait in each of the three nations.

Using modernization as an indicator of culture and a measure of cultural change elicits several questions. How does our own culture affect the way we see others; that is, how does our cultural system shape our perception of other peoples, environments, and resource use? How do the most dominant societies in the world today both contribute to and threaten our survival? How can we measure the impacts of the activities of our cultural groups on the earth, especially when considering feedback to the biosystems, organisms, populations, and ecosystems?

The remainder of this chapter examines cultures from both holistic and abstractive perspectives and considers some answers to the questions posed above. It is most important to remember that human culture results from the interaction between the various elements which form the broad categories of human activity. As these elements affect the interrelationships of subsystems, the manner in which human activities are located is shaped. Locations, then, are a function of cultural systems, greatly influenced by the physical environment, made spatially dynamic by the expansion of the human realm into harsh environments, and made temporally dynamic by the process of modernization. As with all geographical inquiry, we are dealing not with abstraction but location; thus we begin with the study of the places or origin of the world's major cultural systems, then move to the different spatial scales of cultural systems that geographers study.

THE SPATIAL EXPRESSION OF CULTURE

Cultural hearths

An understanding of culture and the dynamics of modernization is the key to the determination of how and why people have changed the face of the earth. Whether we consider culture from the holistic or ab-

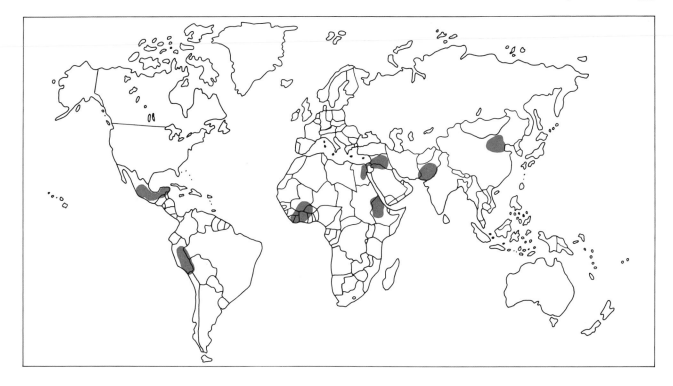

FIGURE 5–1 Cultural hearths.

stract orientations, we must determine the scale of our study. It may be that our investigation is of a local area as a unique *cultural landscape,* or of a much larger area as a *cultural region,* or on yet a larger scale, an entire continent as a *cultural realm.* Regardless, the point of origin for a study of culture, modernization, and human geography is often traced to the *cultural hearths* of the major cultural groups of the world.

A hearth is a fireside at the center of family life; this is an appropriate description for the cultural hearths of the world, the places from which the world's major cultural systems have evolved. The fireside is a particularly apt term since, as we shall see, it was only after the mastery of fire and the development of tools and systematic communication that cultural systems evolved.

The areas of origin of major cultural systems seem to share one common characteristic, a diverse physical environment. Consider the Old World cultural hearth, the Fertile Crescent of Mesopotamia, located in the Middle East in the valley between the Tigris and Euphrates Rivers (figure 5–1). This area is thought to be the place of origin of the initial development of the Western European, Mediterranean, and

North American cultural systems. In order to understand why this particular region is of such importance, we must consider both the *site,* the characteristics of the absolute or fixed location, and the *situation,* the location of a place relative to other places.

The characteristics of the Fertile Crescent include a diverse physical environment composed of major river valleys, the surrounding foothills, and the microenvironments found in the foothills. The variety of the physical microenvironments provided the area's inhabitants with the opportunity to observe a wide range of different plant and animal types and to focus on the characteristics of each as a possible source of food. The Tigris and Euphrates Rivers provided not only water but also a limited source of additional food, fish. A surplus of food was critical to the development of culture for, as Carl Sauer noted, cultural development rarely evolved where people lived in the shadow of famine.

Surely other areas had similar physical characteristics, so we must question why this area is singled out as the cultural hearth. This question can be answered through an analysis of the situation, or the location of one place relative to others, of the Fertile Crescent. The relative location of this area many thousands of years ago was at the center of the developing world. Ideas, information, and innovations in the use of tools, metals, and agricultural practices—all passed through this crossroad with the traders and nomadic peoples who routinely travelled through this region. It is important to note that the critical factor in a place becoming the point of origin of a cultural system is not found exclusively in the attributes of its geographical location, but rather, to a larger degree, in its location relative to other areas. The locations in which information and new technological developments were collected and from which they were disseminated became cultural hearths.

Major river valleys were often cultural hearths (figure 5–1). The Tigris–Euphrates valley in the Middle East, the Indus River valley of the Indian subcontinent, and the Huang Ho (Hwang Ho) valley of China were all major cultural hearths. In Africa and the Americas, the exact locations of the cultural hearths are more difficult to determine, partly because of the recency of necessary investigations. However, in Africa it appears that two areas were likely candidates: one in western Africa and the other in what is now Ethiopia (figure 5–1). In the New World the two major cultural hearths were located in the area of the Yucatan Peninsula of Mexico and the Andes Mountains of Peru.

Innovation and the diffusion of technology from cultural hearths are the first steps on the road to modernization. Before investigating the development of cultural systems and modernization, however, we need to examine the different geographical scales from which we view the earth as an expression of culture and cultural change.

The cultural landscape

The cultural landscape reflects the uses people make of the earth in providing food, shelter and defense. They were initially necessary to enhance chances of survival and later to create a "better life." Some view the cultural landscape as an artificial landscape built upon the natural environment which existed before humans had a shaping role. The character of the cultural landscape is reflected in the artifacts created by humans in their efforts to modify physical environments and fulfill their needs. For our purposes the cultural landscape is the most detailed case we will consider. A unique cultural landscape might be the product of the actions of members of a religious enclave, such as the Amish of Pennsylvania or the Hasidic Jews of Brooklyn.

The Hasidic Jews of Brooklyn provide a fascinating example of the manner in which a small cultural

system can be easily identified within an ethnically diverse American city. They began to settle what would become a 40-block enclave in Brooklyn shortly after the Second World War (Arden, 1975). Hasidic Jews, or the "pious ones," engage in strict and well-ordered religious practices. The majority of the men wear their hair long and have flowing beards to comply with a prohibition on cutting hair. They generally wear the traditional Eastern European Jewish dress of dark or black suits, wide-brimmed hats, and white shirts buttoned to the neck with no tie. In the shadow of the Manhattan skyscrapers, the Hasidic children learn Yiddish as the primary language, and the law against travel or work on the Sabbath and religious holidays is strictly enforced.

The food consumed by this cultural group is subject to the most rigorous Jewish dietary laws, so it must be prepared within the community. As a result, baking bread and slaughtering animals takes place within this area of Brooklyn. This unique cultural group, with its different customs, language, and religion, is a most interesting social enclave whose territory, as a reflection of their culture, forms an intriguing cultural landscape. It is one example of the great flexibility provided by the term *cultural landscape,* for it can be used to describe a single structure, its surrounding environs, or a larger group of peoples, places, or activities. In a philosophical sense the flexibility of the cultural landscape is somewhat different from the more traditional and rigid notion of the *cultural region* (Sauer, 1925.)

The cultural region

The term *region* is one of the most commonly used but least thought about words in our language. An almost infinite variety of regional patterns are found on the earth, defined by applying different criteria to sets of physical and/or cultural phenomena. Phrases referring to cultural or physical regions are a common part of our vocabulary: we refer to the Corn Belt, the Bible Belt, the Rocky Mountain Region, the Pacific Northwest, the South, the Big Ten, the Ivy League, or the Mormon cultural region. The question remains, however, what are we really describing when we refer to a *region?*

In one of the most famous works on the nature and meaning of regions, Derwent Whittlesay proposed several major elements essential to the study of regions (1956, p. 32). In order to say that an area of the earth is a *region,* one needs formal criteria and a systematic method of investigation with which to demonstrate that certain specific factors—people of a given race or re-

B *C*

A

The cultural landscape. (A) Downtown Singapore. (World Bank Photo by Edwin G. Huffman, 1975) (B) Growing rice in Dacca, Bangladesh. (World Bank Photo by Tomas Sennett, 1974) (C) The Pahlavi Dam in Iran. (World Bank Photo by Ray Witlin, 1972)

ligion, for instance—are related to each other in location and form some sort of cohesive unit. We must initially establish the criteria to judge what traits we will place in our region, for example, counties in the Western United States with a certain percentage of people of the Mormon religious faith, which we will want to include in the "Mormon cultural region." Then we must determine the characteristics of the units of observation (characteristics of counties, census tracts, and so on) in order to decide which units will be included in the region; the next task is to determine the core or central area and the boundaries of the region. The final task in the process of regionalization is the most difficult: is there a regional consciousness or group identity which comes from a sense of homogeneity among the people in the region?

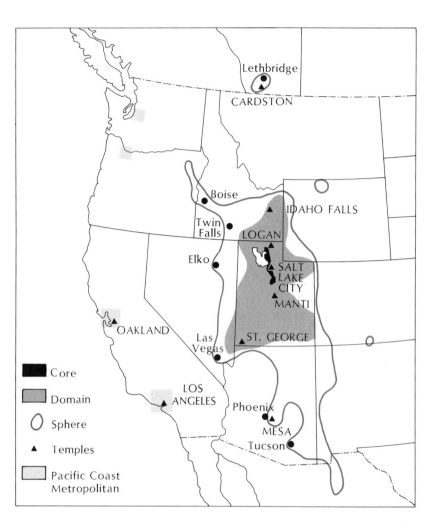

FIGURE 5–2 The Mormon cultural region. (Reproduced by permission from the *Annals* of the Association of American Geographers, Volume 55, 1965, D. W. Meinig.)

One group that scholars have found to exemplify this regional consciousness are the members of the Mormon religion (Meinig, 1965). The Mormons, members of the Church of Jesus Christ of Latter Day Saints, have a definite, highly cohesive subculture within the more general pattern of American life, a subculture to which all the elements of a cultural region apply (figure 5–2).

In categorizing the spatial aspects of cultural systems we have the highly flexible cultural landscape and the more precisely defined or ordered cultural region with which to work. The largest scale of the spatial expression of culture is the cultural realm.

The cultural realm

The cultural realm is composed of groups of peoples linked only through the broadest of criteria. At first glance the vast generalizations inherent in the division of the earth into such large subareas may seem to negate the value of organizing the world into cultural realms. There is, however, a great value in this scale of observation in that the spread of cultures through time and the emerging importance of cultural systems in the future may be demonstrated. Examination of the diffusion of the Western European or Occidental cultural realm between 1300 and 1800 does a great deal to demonstrate the pattern of the imposition of Western European cultures on the New World.

The expansion of cultural realms is also a touchstone for considering the accompanying **economic colonialism.** *Economic colonialism* refers to the practice of exploiting the resources of the area into which the colonizing culture entered, such as the case of drawing the material wealth of one land into the economy of another.

From the cultural hearths have come the cultural systems of the earth, which can be examined in a variety of geographical contexts. Two questions remain, however: What was the material basis for development in the cultural hearths? How did the diffusion of innovation and information circulation take place in order for modernization to occur?

THE MATERIAL BASIS OF CULTURE

In considering the development of cultural systems, finding a precise point of origin in time and space for each major system is nearly impossible. We can make some reasonable approximations about the locations; these are the cultural hearths. It is far more difficult to pinpoint the time, for the development of cultural systems was the result of long, evolutionary processes. The length of time involved in the piece-by-piece nature of the development of the material basis of culture cannot be overemphasized.

Although it is difficult to say precisely when any specific events occurred, these mose certainly were three fundamental components in the development of culture and the process of modernization. Often called the *tripod of culture,* they were fire, tools, and systematic communication.

Technology and environmental adaptation

The cornerstone of the origins of technology, and the resulting development of cultural systems which were to shape our world, was the capture and use of fire. Professor Carl Sauer argued that the first people to successfully use fire on a consistent basis must have lived in an area containing a fairly regular source of geothermal heat, for the repeated capture of fire from random occurences, such as lightning strikes or natural fires, was unlikely. The first people to master the retrieval and use of fire had a most powerful tool indeed: fire provided defense at night, extended the day somewhat, provided the fireside around which surely took place the exchange of ideas and information, offered a method for driving game and clearing land, and expanded the range of the human diet. The capture and use of fire also allowed human beings to expand their habitat into more difficult physical environments and became a device for refining the earliest tools.

The first application of technology to environmental alteration was probably through the use of fire to drive animals. Repeated and systematic burning by early humans may have created changes in some areas which allowed grasses and shrubs to replace trees as the primary vegetation type.

In reviewing Jacob Bronowski's statement, humankind is the animal that did not find but made its home on every continent—we can conclude that the capture of fire was the first step in this process.

The use of fire in the chemical sense—the process of combustion—has evolved through technological change. The march toward modernization can be categorized into the following three phases of combustion: the earliest form of energy from fire was burning or *charring* wood; developed at the time of the industrial revolution, *coking* used fire for the conversion of more energy than was possible from simple burning; and the combustion technique called *cracking* was the process of breaking down fossil fuels to produce combustion. Modernization, whether expressed in the capture and use of fire or the development of the wheel, is simply an evolutionary process of one advancement upon another and is always traceable to our earliest technological origins.

The second leg of the tripod of culture was the development of tools. Again, we look at this development in an evolutionary framework. Tools simply allow human beings greater power than muscle alone provides. The earliest tools were undoubtedly native materials, mainly rock and wood, and relatively uncrafted. The importance of the development of tools is underscored when we consider the terms generally applied to the early development of humankind. The earliest segments of human history are referred to, sequentially, as the Old Stone Age, the New Stone Age, and the Age of Metals, specifically, copper, bronze, and iron.

The first dramatic transition in human use of tools came when human beings ceased using only the unaltered materials provided by nature—such as the stick as a spear or club and the rock as a projectile—and began making tools to suit their needs. Chipping flint into a primitive hatchet blade, spearhead, or knife provided a much more serviceable and powerful tool than the unsculptured branch or rock. Fashioning of stone tools required great skill and patience and was perfected only after thousands of years of evolution. The users of the earliest crafted tools are said to have existed in the Old Stone Age, or Palaeolithic, a period tens of thousands of years before the birth of Christ. Toward the end of the Old Stone Age, toolmakers began to work with bone, ivory, and horn.

The New Stone Age, or Neolithic, approximately 10 thousand years ago, marked a period in which tools

Odessa, in western Texas. An oil refinery is located near a cattle-grazing area. (United Nations/Rick Grunbaum, 1974)

made from basic materials were greatly refined. Arrowheads of this period suggest that the bow had been invented and, since many of the arrowheads are polished, that grinding stones existed. The capture of fire, probably during the late Palaeolithic, and the power of tools allowed human groups to better adapt to their environment and to expand their range of dwelling places.

One example of environmental adaptation is found in the remains of the lake dwellers of Switzerland, who constructed huts on stilts and actually lived over the water. This unique style of settlement was made possible through the use of tools. People were able to expand the range of their environments, as is evidenced by the large "kitchen middens" or mounds of debris, left of settlers living along the coast of the Baltic Sea; this inhospitable environment would not have been suitable without fire to provide warmth. Artifacts from the New Stone Age are found throughout the Mediterranean area, Northern Europe, Northern Africa, Western Asia, and the New World. Considerable evidence suggests that the first transition to the use of metals for other than decorative or ceremonial purposes occurred in regions of the Mediterranean cultural hearth. This is an important point, for the move toward civilization and the take-off point for the rapidly spiralling process of modernization rests on the use of metals and complex tools.

The earliest metals used were probably the soft metals, gold, silver, tin and copper, because they could be easily shaped. The American Indian groups near Lake Superior were accomplished coppersmiths. Also, these metals are often found in a pure state; those found as ore are workable only with the application of great heat.

Among the first people to smelt ore were Egyptians, who worked metals mined in the Sinai Peninsula. The spread of copper tools from the Middle East through the Mediterranean into Western Europe 5000 years ago, gave rise to the Age of Metals. Problems with the use of soft metals, specifically copper which does not hold an edge well, led people to experiment for a stronger metal. It is difficult to say exactly what people, or when, discovered that mixing a small quantity of tin with copper made a much more useful alloy, but it probably took place near what is now Turkey, where tin and copper were found in close proximity nearly 5000 years ago.

The next major advancement in the development of tools was the use of iron, but it came much later in history. Iron was a rarity in the world of the Egyptians and the Greeks: a small quantity of iron was often the

Belo Horizonte, Brazil. This shovel at the Aguas Claras iron ore mine represents a complex tool. Note the use of the wheel, pulley, and level combined with an inanimate power source. (Thomas Sennett for World Bank, 1973)

prize in Greek athletic contests. The relative scarcity of iron is also reflected in the Torah, where bronze and copper are mentioned with great regularity, but iron receives only an occasional mention.

The final two advancements in the development of tool materials were steel and, finally, the very complex alloys, such as aluminum.

Innovation in toolmaking is a two stage process: development in the materials used to form tools occurs and development in the actual shaping of tools. If we consider the technological history of the basic tools—wheel, lever, wedge, and pulley—we find they are combined to form increasingly complex equipment as technology advances. Thus, we have better materials from which to work and more creative ways in which to arrange the basic tools to form complex tools or machines. However, this explains only a part of the development process, for without innovation in the power source to drive machines, complex tools would be of little use.

Prime movers. The ***prime mover*** is the most powerful driving force to which humans have access in any given age. The first and most basic prime mover, is of course, human muscle. This prime mover was used basically in conjunction with the tools available to human groups in the Old and New Stone Ages.

The second major prime mover was the combination of human and animal power, which coincided with the domestication of plants and animals some

8000 years ago. The use of draft animals enabled humans to greatly alter the environment. The combination of animal and plough, especially the plough with a metal blade, allowed people to farm in areas which would have been inhospitable to the agriculturalist with stick and stone tools and only muscle power. This time period, from 8000 to 6000 years ago, is a vitally important era in modernization; during this time humans first domesticated wild plants and animals. The animals provided a new power source and, with metals and the plough, humans could produce more food; consequently, they could develop a surplus. The surplus, in turn, was crucial to the rise of cities and the growth of the institutions from which modernization and cultural change evolved. This period marked the beginning of widespread environmental alteration.

The third in the series of prime movers was the power derived from moving air and water. Wind and water mills were used to grind cereal grains, and wind mills were used to pump water. The use of wind and water power meant that certain locations along a stream were more desirable places for settlement than others.

The manner in which resource availability fixes location can be observed when we consider the transition from wind and water power to the next prime mover, steam power. The generation of steam required coal burning and, because coal is bulky and difficult to transport, proximity to the coal fields became an important factor in the location of many activities. Steam

Bal, Pakistan. This farmer is opening an irrigation ditch to water the wheat field. (Kay Muldoon for World Bank and IDA, 1970)

The combination of human and animal power is illustrated by this Ethiopian agriculturalist. (Paul Conklin for IDA, 1969)

power became the dominant prime mover at the start of the 18th century and did not lose dominance to the use of fossil fuels until the first part of the 20th century.

Many suggest that one of the most pressing problems facing our world today is the question of what the next prime mover will be. In the late 1950s and 1960s the answer seemed clear, atomic power. However, the doubts and fears about nuclear energy raised during the 1970s cloud the question somewhat, especially in light of the nuclear accident at the Three Mile Island power plant near Harrisburg, Pennsylvania, in early 1979.

Communication. Technological development was a product of the control of fire, the development of tools, and the development of language. Humankind rose above the other animals because people had the ability to reason, and to store and build upon knowledge; thus, systems with which to exchange and record knowledge were critical to human survival and development. Depending on the human mind alone to store knowledge was unacceptable because ideas and innovations could be lost or reduced in value. A formal system of accumulation was of the greatest importance.

Organized communication did more than keep records; it provided a means of maintaining orderly relations with other people and allowed for precise communication over long distances. As human beings began to live in cities and large villages, communication provided the accounting system which regulated the agricultural surplus and later divided up the land. Some of the earliest artifacts found in the Fertile Crescent were harvest accounts, and some of the earliest maps, clay tablets found in Babylon, can best be described as real estate maps.

Great advances in communication undoubtedly came after the agricultural surplus allowed people to live in cities. In order for communication to develop, there must have been teachers and time for learning; neither enterprise could be undertaken if people spent all their time gathering food. The increase in knowledge was a major factor in the increase in human productivity, and modernization, the industrial revolution, and postindustrial society followed.

We can trace the history of communication by considering the manner in which information has been stored. Initially all information was kept in people's minds, then later inscribed on bits of bone or wood, or painted on the walls of caves. In the following centuries, new dimensions in the storage of communication were brought forth, and by the time of the first cities, some 6000 years ago, information was stored by knotted ropes, or on clay tablets and papyrus scrolls.

A development of singular importance in communication occurred in Europe during the 15th century, the introduction of movable type and printing. The Chinese were the first to print using movable type; however, a German printer, Johann Guttenburg, is generally credited with being the first to print on a large scale. Movable type allowed more rapid book production than the hand-copied manuscripts and with far fewer errors. Book production in the 15th century broke the hold on learning that the cost of hand-copied manuscripts had limited to the literate elite.

As printing technology became more advanced, the cost of books, pamphlets, and newspapers was reduced. The sheer volume of the printed word in our society has necessitated the new industry of information storage.

Fire, tools, and communication have given rise to the evolving cultural systems that satisfy human wants and needs. To obtain a perspective on the degree to which we actively use technology to change the earth, consider the following example: if we condense the history of the earth, believed to be 4.8 billion years, into one 365-day year, and if we say that the world began on January 1 at 12:00:01 A.M. and the present is December 31 at 11:59:59 P.M., then the time and date of our technological exploitation of the earth would begin on December 31 at 11:58 P.M., two minutes before midnight. In other words, we have been changing the environment on a large scale during only two minutes of our entire hypothetical year. One need only visualize the human use of the earth today in order to begin to understand the magnitude of change made possible through technological advance.

Although technology's impact on the environment is global, we have demonstrated that the elements of technology were drawn together in some generally defined cultural hearths early in human history. Questions remain, therefore, on the manner in which technology spread or diffused and the nature of the processes of technological development and environmental change.

Technological evolution and patterns of settlement

The application of technology to the production of food served the vitally important function of creating a surplus of agricultural products, which freed some members of human groups from the daily tasks of acquiring food. These people could then specialize in crafts, such as the metal working, basket weaving, and pottery; such specialization led to political control over areas larger than those controlled by extended families, and some figure of authority was needed to regulate the surplus. In the case of the Fertile Crescent, someone was needed to supervise such large-scale projects as irrigation.

The surplus of food made available through the first agricultural revolution caused the development of a specialized labor force, which, through a long evolutionary process, came to be located in the clusterings which became the first cities. The origin and evolution of cities provide us with examples of how technology allowed people to manipulate the physical environment to meet the needs of evolving cultural institutions.

Environmental change and the first cities.   Lewis Mumford referred to the development of urban form as *the natural history of urbanization* (1956, pp. 382–397). If we consider the city as a type of biological organism, we can understand how the city has created changes in the physical environment. Mumford felt that the city of 6000 years ago in Mesopotamia, the Fertile Crescent, and Egypt, maintained a symbiotic relationship with the surrounding countryside; that is, the dwellers of the city replaced as much as they extracted from the land. For example, city residents may have added such elements as nitrogen, phophorous, and potassium to the soils of the areas surrounding their cities; the accumulation and distribution of fertilizers essential for healthy, productive soil were not part of some deliberate plan, but were the result of the placement of human and animal wastes in fields near the city. The earliest cities were agricultural settlements which depended upon the surrounding territory for food. These were extremely localized entities because they could not exceed the limited capacity of the immediate area to provide food, water, fuel, and building materials. Surely some cities engaged in a limited amount of long distance trade, but these cities were decidedly in the

minority until the early stages of the Industrial Revolution. The reliance of the earliest cities on their surrounding territories meant that cities of the pre–Industrial Revolution era were generally limited in population size and in area, were relatively evenly spaced, and produced mostly organic wastes. This set of conditions meant that the city as a cultural institution had little impact on all but the surrounding ecosystems until the time of the Industrial Revolution. There were exceptions, of course. The leaders of the city of Rome imported grain from Africa and the Near East and even oysters from Great Britain, but such a case was indeed rare.

Growing populations forced cities to expand, ironically, into the very lands that once fed them, thereby creating a need for agriculturalists to expand the lands they worked. The cycle began: cities grew and created a demand for more food; as new technology and prime movers were applied to farming, a quantity of food was continually produced which surpassed demand and allowed for further urban growth; agricultural land was consumed by cities, so new lands were needed for agriculture. This did not mean that we had a world population living in cities. As late as 1930, only 20 percent of the world population resided in urban areas, whereas over 50 percent resided in urban areas in 1980. However, it did mean that more and more arable (useable) land had to be devoted to agriculture in order to feed both the agricultural and urban populations.

At the time of the first cities, the carrying capacity of the land was limited to only a few people. However, we are not implying a uniform or even distribution of people; rather, with their limited ability to produce and transport food, we are saying that the densest clusters of people would necessarily have been limited. Consider for a moment the modern metropolitan regions of the northeastern seaboard of the United States or the Los Angeles basin, where thousands of people are supported on a square mile of land. The carrying capacity of the land has obviously changed. The application of technology in food production, urban economies, and transportation means that large amounts of food can be transported to a given area. The New Yorker may eat Florida oranges, Washington apples, Kansas wheat, California lettuce and Idaho potatoes; we have created very specialized agricultural regions in the United States which concentrate on the production of only certain foods, which are then shipped to the major

A   B

Two methods of wheat production. (A) The Ghazvin Plain, Iran. (Ray Witlin for World Bank, 1972) (B) Saskatchewan, Canada, tractor–combine methods are necessary to feed large urban populations. (United Nations/Canadian Government Travel Bureau, 1975)

population centers. We may be able to support a great number of people per square mile in some places, but only at the expense of converting much of the remainder of the landscape into agricultural production. Thus, in order for cities to grow, there has been a continual demand for new technology in the production and the transportation of food stuffs.

Technology, industrialization, and urban growth.
At what point did we move from cities whose sizes were confined by the limits of the local countryside to the modern megalopolis? The answer lies mainly with the Industrial Revolution. The transition was made possible by the application of technological advances in tools and prime movers to accommodate growth in agricultural, urban, and economic systems.

Cultural systems, as we know, are collections of interrelated parts. As modernization occurred in the

cultures generated from the cultural hearths of the Fertile Crescent, the political, economic, social, intellectual, and psychological components of the cultural systems revolved around the city as the dominant feature of the landscape. In other cultures, the city remained a part of the landscape, not capturing and consuming the natural environment, but rather serving as administrative center for people working in greater harmony with the environment. The cities of the cultural realm originating in the Hwang Ho River basin exemplify this pattern. The relationship of specific cultural groups with nature, as we shall see, is evidenced by the artifacts of a culture including such phenomena as art works, gardens, literature, and architecture. The general trend toward modernization of the world's cultural groups is illustrated by Daniel B. Luten's "empty land, full land, poor folk, rich folk" thesis (1969).

Luten directed his remarks toward the United States specifically, but we can consider the general notion as a comment on the world situation. His basic premise is that the earliest human groups were poor people who came into an empty land; they were poor in the sense that they did not accumulate a great deal of material wealth and had little more than the food

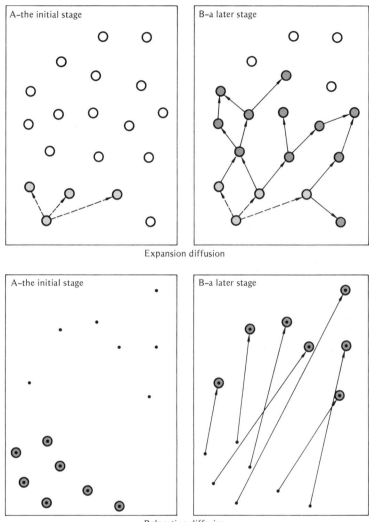

FIGURE 5–3 Expansion versus relocation diffusion. (Peter Gould, "Spatial Diffusion." Washington, D.C.: Association of American Geographers, *Resource Papers for College Geography*, No. 4, 1969, figures 1 and 4, p. 4. Reprinted by permission.)

necessary for survival. As they occupied the empty land, they altered the environment only around their cities. We have become a rich people and, as a world population, have more in terms of goods than at any other time in history, though our current riches are far from evenly distributed. We now live in what is becoming a relatively full land: one in which most of the most useful spaces are covered with the works of human activity. Technology and modernization have created the transition, but we have yet to clarify the method of the diffusion of technological advances from the cultural hearth of 8000 to 6000 years ago to our present state.

CULTURAL DIFFUSION AND CHANGE

Innovation and information diffusion

Diffusion is the process through which ideas and information spread over space and through time. There are two general categories of diffusion, the spread of information which took place before the electronic age in which radio, television, telephones, and newspapers become commonplace in much of the world, and diffusion which took place after the advent of the electronic age.

The basic concept of diffusion in the preelectronic era involved face-to-face communication. The printing press did not come into widespread use until the end of the 15th century, meaning that, for information to circulate, it had to be carried by the individual. Recall that the situation, or relative location, of the Fertile Crescent was of critical importance to the area's becoming a cultural hearth because virtually all the agents of diffusion travelled through it, so that it became a collection point for new ideas.

Information may be carried in several important ways. One process is **expansion diffusion,** in which a person who knows the idea tells another, who tells another, who tells another, and so on, with the result that over time a great many people know of the idea (figure 5–3). Such diffusion, being close to the person who knows the information, is of fundamental importance, as demonstrated by the diffusion of pasture improvement subsidies in Sweden between 1928 and 1933 (figure 5–4). There should be little surprise that those close to the "teller" learn of an innovation first because the probability of contact is greater. This type of diffusion can be modelled using probabilities and the **mean information field.** The mean information field essentially weights the chances of your knowing of an innovation if you are close to the source by giving certain numerical values to those places close to the teller (figure 5–5).

In this manner we can simulate the way in which information spreads. For example, we have a list of numbers between 0 and 9999 and assign these numbers to *cells* or areas around the teller, placing only a few numbers in each of the corner cells and many numbers in the cells closest to the teller. Then we put numbered slips of paper into a box and randomly select one number from the box. Obviously there is a greater probability that the number selected will be in a cell close to the teller (figure 5–4) (Gould, 1969). This process, called **Monte Carlo simulation,** provides a useful tool for estimating how information will diffuse (figures 5–6 and 5–7) (Gould 1969, as adapted from Hagerstrand, 1965).

A second form of diffusion is **relocation diffusion.** In this process those with the information actually move to a new area and carry the information with them. People moving from one urban region to another or migrating to a new country would represent relocation diffusion.

In what type of physical location would one most likely come in contact with information and new ideas in the preelectronic era? It would probably be a place to which migrants came (relocation diffusion) or a place along a trade or transportation route (expansion diffusion), so that your chances of being in contact with tellers would be enhanced. The city would fit both of these criteria because it was the collection area for ideas and innovations. Its dependence on human contact made diffusion a slow process during the preelectronic era because of the many barriers to diffusion.

Barriers to diffusion

The barriers to diffusion are not unlike the components which we have defined as the make-up of culture. The same political, economic, social, intellectual, and psychological factors which form the basis of cultural change can also, in a reciprocal sense, be elements which restrict the ability to change. Another element which belongs on this list is the physical barrier to diffusion; physical barriers were most important in the preelectronic world. For example a great desert, such as the Sahara of North Africa, acted to isolate people in the same manner as the vast oceans. The physical friction of distance was also a hindrance to diffusion; it is unlikely that innovation would be carried a long distance when travel was slow, dangerous, and difficult. The innovations developed in the Middle East, therefore, stayed basically in that region for thousands of years.

If a **network for diffusion** existed, then opportunity for the diffusion of innovations was greatly improved. For example, the Roman Empire provided such a network, and as a result, information and innovation spread throughout the Mediterranean region and into northern and western Europe as travellers passed from one Roman city to another. Similarly, improvements in sea transportation in the so called "age of discovery" led to the introduction of European cultures into the New World. The introduction of one culture into a new area through the process of diffusion is referred to as *acculturation.*

The process of acculturation

Acculturation is the interaction between two human groups in which the cultural system of one group is

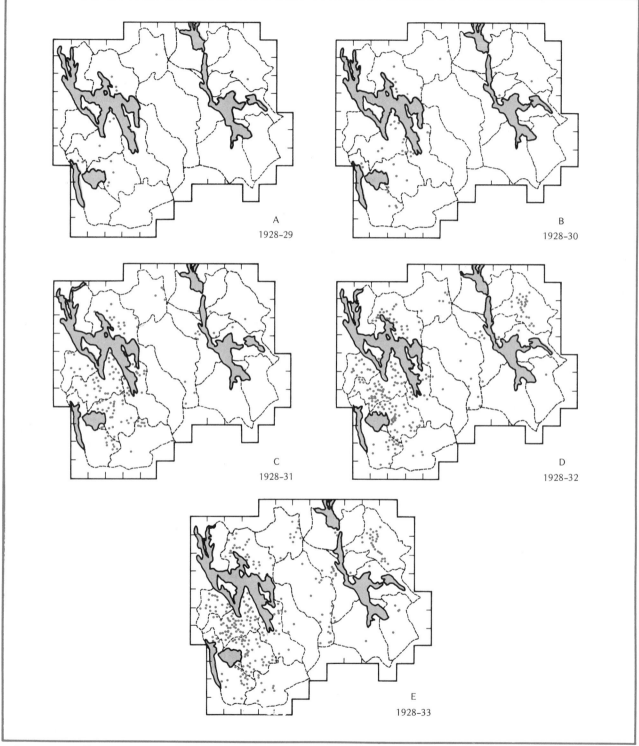

FIGURE 5–4 Diffusion of pasture improvement subsidies 1928–1933. (Peter Gould, "Spatial Diffusion." Washington, D.C.: Association of American Geographers, *Resource Papers for College Geography*, No. 4, 1969, figure 33a-e, p. 27. Reprinted by permission.)

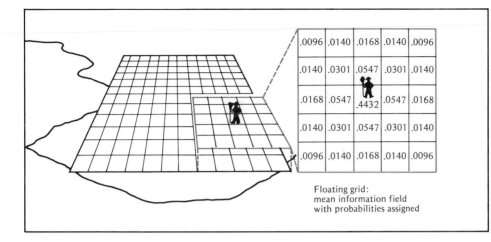

Floating grid:
mean information field
with probabilities assigned

0–95	96–235	236–403	404–543	544–639
640–779	780–1080	1081–1627	1628–1928	1929–2068
2069–2236	2237–2783	2784–7214	7215–7761	7762–7929
7930–8069	8070–8370	8371–8917	8918–9218	9219–9358
9359–9454	9455–9594	9595–9762	9763–9902	9903–9999

Accumulated intervals for mean information field

FIGURE 5–5 Mean information field and Monte Carlo simulation. (Peter Gould, "Spatial Diffusion." Washington, D.C.: Association of American Geographers, *Resource Papers for College Geography*, No. 4, 1969, figures 37 and 38, p. 30. Reprinted by permission.)

drastically changed by the actions of the other group. Diffusion during the age in which the nations of western Europe embarked upon exploration of the New World led to the Spanish and Portuguese becoming dominant over the indigenous groups in South America, and the Spanish, English, and French introduced drastic changes in the lives of the people of early North America.

The process of acculturation is one in which cultures with a strong technological base tend to dominate the culture of the receiving group. The history of acculturation throughout the world has been exploitative, and dominant groups have tended to draw the wealth of the receiving group into the dominant economy.

While the process of acculturation is a mainly one-sided affair, there is often some reciprocal effect,

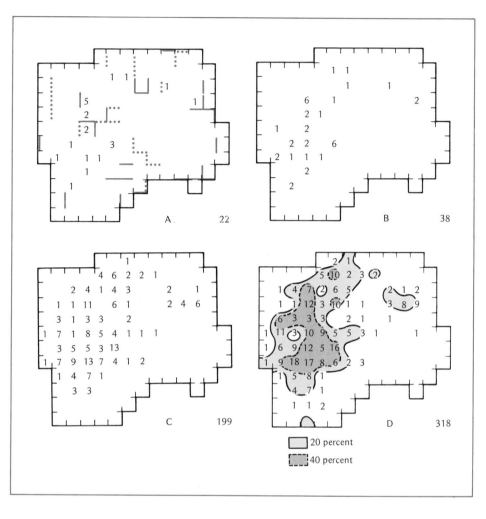

FIGURE 5–6 Simulation of pasture diffusion subsidy. (Peter Gould, "Spatial Diffusion." Washington, D.C.: Association of American Geographers, *Resource Papers for College Geography*, No. 4, 1969, figure 42a-d, p. 36. Reprinted by permission.)

as when crops and food types of the receiving culture are introduced into the homeland of the dominant culture. This occurred when Europeans, after beginning to colonize the New World, introduced various new crops to Europe. Soon tobacco, maize, and some root crops became important additions to the European economy. The process of acculturation tends to accelerate modernization, though at times the process produces disharmony in the receiving culture.

Modernization: The costs and conflicts

Acculturation can be viewed as a process which is simultaneously creative and destructive; modernization may be viewed in the same light. The major differences between the two processes are that acculturation is through introduction while modernization, at least in its truest sense, is through evolution.

Acculturation is often more localized in extent and more violent in nature than modernization. One basic misconception about the occurrence of acculturation is that the differences between the donor and recipient cultures are vast. Yet the Incas of Peru were extremely advanced prior to contact with Europeans in the early part of the 16th century. The Incan people produced a food surplus sufficient to require a complex administrative bureaucracy and a large labor force, which constructed a superb highway system and great cities in the most inhospitable terrain. The bridges built by Incan architects are still considered masterpieces. Many people worked in craft industries, and a complex record-keeping system was devised, based on the Quipa or knotted string. During the first quarter of the 16th century, the Spanish made repeated contact with the Incan people and eventually plundered the Incan

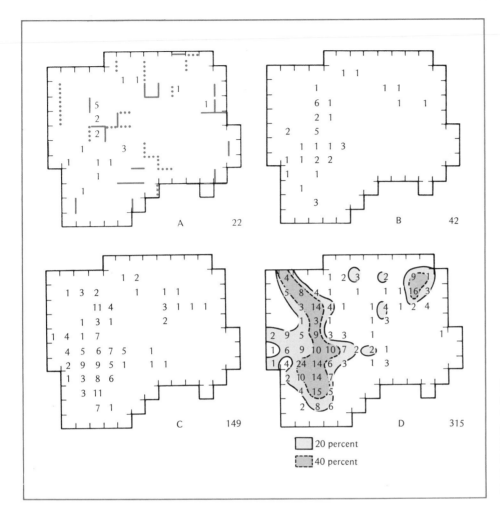

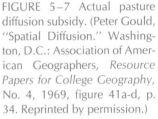

FIGURE 5–7 Actual pasture diffusion subsidy. (Peter Gould, "Spatial Diffusion." Washington, D.C.: Association of American Geographers, *Resource Papers for College Geography*, No. 4, 1969, figure 41a-d, p. 34. Reprinted by permission.)

civilization in search of gold. The Spanish were victorious because they brought the artifacts of war created through a technological process far different than that of the isolated Incan nation and the notion that certain metals were precious, not shared by the Incas. In the span of one quarter of a century, the acculturation process was so complete that the Spanish dominated every phase of Incan life.

For a more contemporary example of this phenomenon, we can consider Japan before and after World War II. The widespread introduction of the American cultural system into postwar Japan created an immediate and dramatic impact on the Japanese cultural system, which rapidly came to resemble the American cultural make-up in many ways.

Modernization is change through evolution on a wider scale and generally implies a longer and perhaps more subtle process of the diffusion of ideas and information. While the process of modernization holds the hope of utopian societies, the results have more often been social turmoil and violence on an even global level. Many blame the emergence of the negative on the fact that so often new ideas overrun age-old principles and that human needs are often less important than national aims. This is also true of the environment, for modernization could bring a high quality physical environment but far more often produces environmental despoilment. A large part of this discrepancy can be explained by the attitude that various human groups hold towards nature, a topic we will explore in the following chapter. One of the measures of both acculturation, in the specific instance, and modernization, in general, is reflected in the art and architecture of different cultures found at various times and places.

THE LANDSCAPE AS A CULTURAL MAP

Art

The art of any given age tells us a great deal about the state of a cultural system. The artist may depict a town in ruins with crumbling walls and fearful inhabitants; such is often the case at times of great conflict. The disorganization of society may be portrayed, as during the early part of the Middle Ages, by the characterization in art works of fearsome beasts and cataclysmic happenings.

In many cases the vision of nature held by a school of artists is a reflection on cultural attitudes toward nature. Does the artist attempt to represent nature as being in perfect order, to capture on canvas nature as it appears to the eye, or to picture nature in the abstraction of a purely symbolic landscape? It also may be the case that art work reflects a nature which is too perfect, like the landscapes painted by Leonardo da Vinci. One comparison of attitudes toward nature as reflected in art is found in the consistent representation of the compatibility between nature and human culture often found in Chinese art and the great variance in relative harmony existing between nature and culture in European art. The process of turning the landscape into art is indeed a fascinating endeavor and does much to illustrate the attitudes toward the environment held by various cultures at differing points in the modernization process. The development and design of gardens is yet another display of cultural perception; however, this manifestation is drawn on the actual landscape.

Gardens

Gardening on a wide scale apparently originated during the rise of civilization in the Mediterranean area. The first gardens were both functional, providing shade and agricultural products, and aesthetically pleasing; in the Mediterranean region orchards and vineyards provided shade, fragrance and fruit. The size of the garden was largely the result of the constraints of land and water, which of course, is much the case today.

During the period in which the Egyptian civilization dominated the Mediterranean, gardens began to take on a much more regular and geometric form. The Egyptians began to import exotic plants from long distances for their gardens, and flowers were used in great abundance in social and religious practices. The Greeks opted for more natural settings, with native vegetation and irregular shape, whereas the Romans followed more in the Egyptian tradition.

Perhaps the most impressive age in the evolution of gardens in western civilization was during the Renaissance. This era provides us many examples of gardens as manifestations of the cultural view of the natural environment. The magnificent gardens of the Palace of Versailles near Paris, France, are works of percision and geometric design. In contrasting these with Chinese gardens, it is apparent that the latter are in as "natural" a state as the Versailles gardens are in a regulated one. The Versailles gardens are modelled to bring nature into better harmony with human design; many believe this illustrates the Western cultural attitude that the natural environment is to be subjected to human needs and wants. The Chinese gardens are also viewed as a symbolic expression of how the Eastern cultural groups perceive humankind and the natural environment as existing in a symbiotic relationship, for nature is altered only slightly. If this symbolization is correct, the point of origin for such attitudes may be found in the character of the respective cultures as expressed in urban form and function.

The Eastern European city was the focus of activity for all the cultural subsystems, hence ties with the land were somewhat broken as people and institutions became more urbanized. In the Asian cultural system cities served as trade and administrative centers, but the society was basically rural. Thus, we can speculate that the rural and urban orientation of the respective cultural systems was reflected in the attitudes of people's relationship with nature as expressed in their gardens (Semple, 1931).

Architecture

A consideration of architecture and modernization involves two basic elements. The first concern is for the stage of modernization in a given era, ranging between the most primitive of times and the present. At issue here would be such factors as the number of people freed from agricultural pursuits to work elsewhere, the level of technological skill available to the architect, and the availability of sophisticated tools and powerful prime movers. An important point to keep in mind in this historical context is the number as well as the types of structures. The massive pyramids of Egypt and the

Housing types in an African village—Bobo-Dioulasso, Upper Volta. (United Nations, 1967)

Colosseum of Rome are examples of monumental building projects done by people in times long past, but remember that a great deal of the collective skill and economic resource of the respective nations went into these projects. As cultural systems evolved, building projects became more widespread and had greater impact on the environment.

The second element in the analysis of architecture, culture, and modernization is the consideration of the actual architectural monuments. There are four basic components in such an analysis: the spatial composition of the structure; the builders' treatment of mass and surface; the treatment of light, color, and other optical effects; and the relation of design to social function (Frankl, 1968). As geographers studying human activities, we are concerned both with the structures themselves and with the historical context of the monument as an expression of the manner in which people perceive the environment and modify the surface of the earth.

The nature of shelter

If we investigate the most basic architectural need of human beings, shelter, the geographic influences on architecture are clearly visible (Rapoport, 1969). One of the most critical factors in the type of shelter is climate. This is not to say that climate is the sole determinant of what is built, but undoubtedly it was of great importance, especially to early humans.

When we consider the two factors important in our review of architecture—the era and the characteristics of the structure—then technology, building materials, and the values of the cultural system are of great importance. The structures of the winter Arctic Eskimo, for example, are built from the most abundant native material, ice, because of the environmental constraints. The use of locally found materials in construction is true of all cultures, whether current or past, which do not possess the technological ability to transport materials over long distances. It has been pro-

Contemporary ceremonial building and urban settlement in Africa—(A) Dassouri, Upper Volta and (B) Bellville, South Africa. (United Nations, 1967)

posed that one factor influencing the early trade and interaction from the cultural hearth of the Fertile Crescent was the need to secure scarce materials for building. The destruction of lands to provide materials for construction and fuel was a concern early in human history, as reflected by the writings of Plato and Confucius.

Clearly physical factors were not the sole determinant of what was constructed in a given place by a particular people, because the entirety of the subsystems of the cultural system must be taken into account. The psychological and social elements of cultural systems, for instance, would most likely be responsible for the relatively elaborate construction of buildings for

A

(A) The Transamerican Pyramid in San Francisco. (B) The Marin Civic Center, California. (Christopher Exline)

B

use in ceremonial activities, while the living quarters of the masses of people were but the most basic of shelters.

Technological development eventually freed builders from the constraints of local materials. Architectural innovations, from the column and the arch through the development of the elevator in the past 100 years, when combined with the progression from the use of wood and stone to the use of concrete and metals as building materials, expanded the range of what can be done in building. Structures are also reflective of environmental attitudes. One need only consider the architectural history of America in the 20th century to find many examples of this phenomenon.

In the late part of the 20th century there has been a demand for structures, whether single houses or huge buildings, which are unique in appearance and in harmony with the environment. This uniqueness in appearance is not possible in most instances, as evidenced by most American suburbs, but concern for the environmental aspects of building is developing in many regions of the United States. Examples of this trend are found in attempts to bring landscaping into harmony with the local climatic conditions through the use of low maintenance (using vegetation requiring little water) designs and home insulation to preserve energy.

In larger building projects the difference in attitudes toward construction has shifted from size to uniqueness as the most important attribute. The TransAmerica Pyramid in San Francisco is evidence of this, as is the Marin County Civic Center located just north of San Francisco in San Rafael, California.

The Marin County Civic Center: A case in point.   The Civic Center for Marin County, California, was designed by Frank Lloyd Wright and constructed during the 1960s. This structure has been referred to as one of the most beautiful and spectacular public buildings in the world. The Civic Center is more than 1500 feet in length and has enough floor space to qualify as a major structure. Wright designed the building with nature in mind and the entire complex blends subtly into the countryside. Notice how a part of the building emerges from one low hill and seems to gently flow to the other low hill in a series of graceful arches, which accentuate the pattern of the local topography (Chapin, 1969). The building is a brownish color to match the color of the grasses which surround it, and the roof is a sky blue. It is admittedly a unique structure, but the concept of building in harmony with the landscape is beginning to be applied throughout the United States (McHarg, 1971). Some Americans may be shifting from the attitude that bigger is better to one in which an increasing concern with environmental and esthetic considerations is predominant.

LOOKING TOWARD THE FUTURE

We have described the emergence of cultural systems in this chapter. Modernization is a product of a technological development which places great demands on the earth and its resources. The major cultures of the world today result from the manner in which their respective political, economic, social, intellectual, and psychological subsystems have adjusted to innovations and the pressures created by other cultural groups. The material basis of the world's current cultural subgroups evolved along with technology based initially on advances in the use of fire, tools, and communication. It would seem that the degree to which a society became urbanized was fundamentally responsible for the rapidity of modernization; we cited the differences between European and Asian cities as examples of this process. The ability to come in contact with new ideas and information made the cultural systems of Western Europe and North America economically dominant in current world society. It is at this point that we pose the question, where do we go from here?

Our discussion of cultural realms and development issues may serve us at this juncture. There are a growing number of scholars from various academic fields who believe that we will have to form a global society in order to maintain economic and social stability. Members in this global society will undoubtedly be cultural groups and, with the growing solidarity of people of like ethnic backgrounds, will be based upon cultural realms. Instead of a few cultural realms dominating the modernization process, which has historically been the case, it may be that all cultural realms will have significant impact on a world in which a growing population brings demands for global specialization. The world of the future will not know the historical constraints of diffusion of innovation and information circulation that existed in the preelectronic world, so that the era of domination of the world's resources by a few cultural systems may be rapidly coming to a close.

In this chapter we have presented a broad overview of the material basis of culture, modernization, and cultural systems. In the following chapters we will discuss several of the cultural subsystems in greater detail. The first specific components of culture we will focus on are race and religion.

KEY TERMS

Cultural relativity
Cultural landscape
Cultural region
Cultural realm
Cultural hearths
Site
Situation
Economic colonialism
Tripod of culture

Charring
Coking
Cracking
Expansion diffusion
Mean information field
Monte Carlo simulation
Relocation diffusion
Network for diffusion
Acculturation

REFERENCES

Arden, H. (1975), "The Pious Ones," *National Geographic* 148, No. 2, 276–298.

Black, C. E. (1966), *The Dynamics of Modernization.* New York: Harper & Row, Publishers, Inc.

Bronowski, J. (1973), *The Ascent of Man.* Boston: Little, Brown & Co.

Chapin, W. (1969), *The Suburbs of San Francisco.* San Francisco: Chronicle Books.

Frankl, P. (1968), *Principles of Architectural History.* Cambridge: M.I.T. Press.

Gould, P. (1969), *Spatial Diffusion,* Resource Paper No. 4. Washington, D.C.: Association of American Geographers.

Hagerstrand, T. (1965), "Aspects of the Spatial Structure of Social Communication and the Diffusion of Information," *Regional Science Association Papers* 16.

Luten, D. (1969), "Empty Land, Full Land, Poor Folk, Rich Folk," *Yearbook* 31 of the Association of Pacific Coast Geographers, 79–89.

McHarg, I. (1971), *Design with Nature.* Garden City, NY: Doubleday & Co., Inc.

Meinig, D. (1965), "The Mormon Cultural Region," *Annals of the Association of American Geographers* 55, No. 2, 191–220.

Mumford, L. (1956), "The Natural History of Urbanization," in Thomas, W. (ed.), *Man's Role in Changing the Face of the Earth.* Chicago: University of Chicago Press, 382–397.

Rapoport, A. (1969), *House Form and Culture.* Englewood Cliffs, NJ: Prentice–Hall, Inc.

Semple, E. (1931), *The Geography of the Mediterranean Region.* New York: Holt, Rinehart & Winston.

Sauer, C. O. (1925), *The Morphology of Landscape.* Berkeley: Publications in Geography, University of California, Vol. 2, No. 2.

Whittlesey, D. (1954), "The Regional Concept and the Regional Method," in James, P. and Jones, C. (eds.), *American Geography: Inventory and Prospect.* Syracuse, NY: Syracuse University Press, 19–69.

6

Elements of the cultural system: Race and religion

In the previous chapter we considered the fundamental nature of cultural systems. In this chapter the concepts of race, religion and the environment are explored. Our investigation will include a discussion of race and culture, the physical differences between human groups, and racial conflict.

In our examination of human geography and religion, we will develop a distinction between the geography of religions and religious geography. We will also consider the interrelationships between religion, politics, and social change in developing nations.

The lesson of the last chapter should not be forgotten when considering the remainder of the mosaic of culture: what may seem to be isolated parts of the total system of human culture are actually interrelated and constantly interacting.

THE CONCEPT OF RACE

Race and culture

The concept of race is extremely complex. Human beings are from one *species,* and the term used to describe the subunits of that species is race. The question that has been debated throughout human history is, how different in reality are the subgroups of our species?

Historically, theorists have considered races as simple distributions of different types of people—people who somehow came to exist in a wide variety of physical environments. It was the development of a theory, *natural selection,* and a method of scientific study, *genetics,* that allowed complex analysis of the differences between peoples of the earth.

The theory of natural selection suggests that those with attributes allowing adaptation to the physical environment would prosper, while those who could not adapt would fail (Banton and Harwood, 1975). Attendant to this theory was the notion that great diversity exists among the people of a single group, just as diversity exists between groups. The proof needed to support these contentions came from the science of genetics.

Genetics is the branch of biology that deals with heredity and the variation in the features and constitution of groups of plants and animals. The basis of genetics is the analysis of the genes of plants and animals. Genes are the units appearing at various points on the chromosomes through which heredity characteristics are transmitted and determined. Genetic traits that are predominant are referred to as *dominant,* and those that are less influential are *recessive.* There are many who suggest that the major biological differences in humans are the result of *clines,* or gradients of change in a measurable genetic characteristic. Currently clinal analysis is the basis of the contemporary study of human groups.

Skin color is perhaps the most noticeable example of differences in people related to location. Moving poleward from the equator, we find a rather dramatic transition in skin color, from dark at the equator to light in the high latitudes. However, as Banton and Harwood noted, there are clines for characteristics which are far less apparent (1975, pp. 56–66); for example, the frequency of occurrence of blood type B increases as we move from west to east across Europe and into Asia. Less than 5 percent of the Spanish population has type B blood, whereas in France the percentage rises above 5 percent, and in Germany it rises to nearly 10 percent. Moving further eastward the percentage rises to 15 percent in Western Russia and, finally, to a peak of 25 percent in Central Asia. From there the percentage begins to drop as we move on toward the Pacific.

Several factors may help account for this pattern, natural selection and migration being two of the most important. If natural selection is the cause of the phenomenon, then we could also assume that physical characteristics of various parts of the earth act to select against the ill-adapted (Banton and Harwood, 1975, pp. 60–66). This would explain the relationship between dark skin and intense sunlight, for dark skin would aid in protecting the body from the adverse effects of strong sunlight. There are also concordant and discordant factors to consider before conclusions can be drawn. A concordant relationship is one in which there appears to be a correlation between factors; for example, as the color of the skin darkens, the percentage of people with black hair increases. A discordant relationship is a case in which features that would be assumed to be related do not correlate. Discordant patterns make the study of race an extremely complex undertaking. It is currently believed that clinal analysis will prove that the human subgroups are separated only by a matter of degrees. What then accounts for the differences in the various groups?

We must understand something of both the biological and cultural evolution of humankind to be able to study the spatial organization of cultural groups. Certain groups—most with some unique physical characteristics, such as dark skin in the tropics or the epicanthic eye fold in areas of bright sunlight—are associated respectfully with certain cultural hearths. However, just as advanced technological development did not spring from one particular hearth because its specific location (site) had greater attributes than others, it also did not result from any superior characteristics of that biological subgroup. Most researchers now agree that technological development resulted from the relative location (situation) of the cultural hearth.

An aspect of natural selection which is often ignored is that it occurs in a number of forms. We have mentioned the development of specialized abilities

which allow only the most genetically able to survive; another fundamentally important aspect of biological survival is *plasticity,* or the ability to adapt to change. The most viable animals possess a genetic make-up which suits the environment but also can adapt to change. The changes in human diets associated with modernization demonstrate this adaptation. Fire was the first step in expanding the range of the diet. This was followed by the domestication of plants and animals, the global exchange of Old World–New World foods, the widespread exchange of all manner of food made possible by modern transportation, and finally chemical manipulation of our foods. Comparing the diet of the earliest humans with that of the typical American demonstrates our evolution from a very basic dietary regime, in a chemical sense, to one which is very complex. We have demonstrated a high degree of plasticity, which gives humankind more flexibility for adjusting to environmental change. These adjustments can be made through the plasticity inherent in the human species or through genetic *mutation.*

Mutation is the process through which an organism's genetic composition changes through a slight chemical change in the genes. Mutations appear to be random and spontaneous events which occur very slowly through time. This slow process provides human beings with the phenotypic variability which allows for survival as the environment takes new form.

Cultural systems and modernization come into play at this point. As people developed the basis of culture, they were able to overcome the limits of the physical constraints inherent in relying solely upon the ability of the human body for power. People were able to expand the range of their activities, and human groups were forced to adapt through plasticity and mutation to new environments. People moving to remote regions also were influenced by a process known as *genetic drift.* If a population were isolated, whether by physical or social restrictions, then eventually the dominant genetic characteristics of those people would begin to predominate, and societies of very similar traits would evolve. Evidence suggests that the strict rules prohibiting intermarriage between Hindu castes over a period of many centuries has lead to significant genetic differences between some castes (Banton, *et al.,* 1975, p. 74).

The factors accounting for the various subgroups found on the earth are, then, associated with environmental (natural) selection—the clinal differences between groups.

The human race. (A) Thailand. (M. Bolotsky for World Bank, 1967) (B) Ecuador. (Larry Daughters for World Bank Group, 1971) (C) Tangier. (World Bank Photo by Bill and Christine Graham, 1973) (D) Kenya. (Ivan Massar of Black Star for World Bank, 1960) (E) India. (World Bank Photo by Ray Whitlin, 1977) (F) Malaysia. (Tomas Sennett for World Bank, 1970)

Human groups of the earth

We have discussed four of the factors which might be used to explain the development of the various racial groups of the earth: heredity, environment, mutation, and natural selection. The extent to which any single factor or combination of factors plays a part in the development of human groups is difficult to determine. In any event, these four processes have determined the major racial subgroups of the earth today, the Caucasoid, the Mongoloid, and the Negroid groups (Boas, 1940).

If we attach the names of various cultural groups, as defined by national origin, to these three classifications, the physical differences in body type become readily apparent. If we visualize a person from China, for example, we would most probably think of someone with the epicanthic eye fold, slight of build, and with little body hair. The residents of Nigeria in Western Africa would have dark skin, black hair, and varying body types; someone from Ireland may have very light skin, light hair, and blue eyes.

There are two problems with this type of generalization. First, we have assumed a more or less pure or nonmixed racial stock, which exists on a rather limited scale in reality. The mixing of three major racial types occurred, for example, when Europeans began to colonize South America and the Caribbean (Boas, 1940). In addition to the fact that an absolutely "pure" racial stock is difficult to find, there are also subgroups within the major racial groups. Although clinal analysis

is the main focus of study today, early discussions of race were concerned almost solely with body type. In one of the pioneer works on the races of Europe, for instance, William Ripley recognized three fundamental subgroups (1899): the Mediterraneans, with long heads and dark features; the Alpine group, characterized by light complexions, short heads, and brunette hair; and the Nordic type, with blond hair and long features. Regardless of the method of analysis, racial intermixing and subgroups created by the genetic processes of heredity, mutation, and selection make it difficult to specifically delineate racial groups.

The diffusion and interweaving of the major racial groups of the earth has not been without difficulty; tension and hostility have existed in most places where members of various racial groups have had to coexist. It is a simple matter to say that a problem exists because of "racial differences;" the truth, however, is more often found in the elements of our cultural subsystems—in social, psychological, political, historical, or economic factors—with the color of one's skin being simply a convenient label. The notion of racial inferiority is clearly without foundation. The levels of technology of various human groups, as we have mentioned, result from relative location and cultural systems rather than the biological attributes of any specific groups. However, throughout history the physical characteristics of human racial groups have been used to set human beings apart politically, economically, and socially.

CASE STUDY:
South Africa: A study in conflict

The initial white settlement in the southernmost part of Africa occurred in 1652. Although there had been some previous contact with Portuguese sailors along the coastal areas, the introduction of the Dutch East India Company in 1652 initiated prolonged white contact. Although slavery was long a way of life among Black African groups, Pierre van den Berghe notes that South Africa did not become an entrenched interracial slave society until as late as 1834 —the same year that slavery was abolished throughout the British Empire. This is not to say that the enslavement of the African population did not occur in South Africa from the time of the earliest permanent European settlement. Slavery was a critical aspect of life; however, race was not the initial means of social stratification, as suggested in the following comment:

> The early slave situation gave rise to the first type of race relations which
> I have called "paternalistic," and to an ideological current which has mistakenly

been termed "Cape Liberalism." According to existing evidence race or colour did not immediately become a primary criterion of stratification, but rather Christianity conferred by baptism, and the status of slave or free man. Early cases of legal marriage between Dutchmen and baptized women of colour support that fact.

Within a generation or so colour had become the primary index of status. (van den Berghe, 1970, p. 14)

Let us recall our earlier notion that the physical features of a group are simply used as a classification device. From van den Berghe's statement, we see that the basis of social stratification, a type of bias, is found in religion and economics as well as skin color. However, by the end of the 17th century, South African social stratification had become based solely on race, and a system of social organization was firmly established. It should be noted that this process occurred to the greatest degree on the coastal areas in which European settlement was most firmly established.

As European settlement became more strongly entrenched on the Cape, the social distance between white and black groups rapidly increased. Social principles, which were to become laws, were established and aided in fostering of social inequity (Silvert, 1967). Some slaves were forbidden to wear shoes, and a complex system of rank according to age and sex, slave or master, evolved, which perpetuated the notion of white superiority and black inferiority (Marquard, 1962).

This system remains a part of South Africa today and has caused that nation to become a **plural society,** one in which interface, but not intermixing, between major cultural systems exists. The European components of this plural society are the Dutch—or their cultural derivative, the *Afrikaner* —and the English. Add to this the influence exerted by Asians, several smaller groups of French- and German-speaking peoples, and an extensive Jewish community. The non-European component of the population are the *coloureds,* those of mixed ancestry, and the *Africans.* If we consider these groups in light of historical, economic, and sociopolitical processes, we have a perspective from which to view the problems in South Africa today. The difficulties faced by South Africans are further compounded by the existence of a cultural mélange exemplified by the multilingualism of diverse groups —for instance, the English, Afrikaners, Zulu, and Xhosa. While there is some conflict between the Afrikaners and the English, the major confrontation is between the whites, the coloureds, and the Africans.

Ngubane views this situation as a conflict of minds—specifically, the clash of issues resulting from the attempts of one group to expand their range of liberties while another group attempts to reject that expansion (1971). Ngubane further observes that, throughout the centuries of white dominance in South Africa, Black South Africans evolved a *syncretic culture,* one that attempts to combine different beliefs. Through the evolution of traditions, institutions, and norms of thought and behavior, this cultural evolution has been responsible for Black South Africans' acquiring an identity as a cultural group. The source of conflict in South Africa today is found in the denial of the basic human rights of this cultural group.

Black and white spectators in a segregated sports stadium—Zoo Lake Recreation Park, Johannesburg, South Africa. (United Nations/Contact)

In order to counter the Black Africans' demands for liberties, the white-dominated government established a policy of **apartheid,** or specific discrimination and geographical segregation of the races. Prior to the official policy of apartheid, regulation against nonwhites was formidable. Laws were passed, such as the Mines and Works Act in 1911, which prohibited skilled Black African labor in mines, and the Native Land Act in 1913, which prohibited Africans from buying or renting land in most areas. The Civilized Labor Policy instituted in 1924 stated that poor whites were to take the place of Africans in even unskilled jobs (Brown, 1968).

By 1948 Blacks were needed in the urban labor force and migrated to cities in great numbers. In order for whites to control this population, acts such as the Bantu Authorities Act (classifying urban Blacks as aliens) and Group Areas Act (moving nonwhite households into restricted areas in rural regions) served to separate the urban-employed from their families for long periods of time. These and many similar acts left the nonwhite South Africans with no rights or freedom of expression.

Even with such stringent regulations, Black Africans were seen as a social and economic threat to the whites, so the Population Registration Act was passed in 1950, fixing the "race" of each person forever. This law forbad any integration of the South African people whatsoever. If one even "looked" nonwhite, that person was subject to regulations affecting nonwhites (Brown, 1968).

By the early 1950s apartheid as an official governmental policy was considered by many whites to be the way of life in South Africa. However, in 1952 the African National Congress, an organization of mostly Blacks, opened a campaign of passive resistance against discriminatory laws. The white government responded with the Criminal Law Amendment Act of 1953 which made even the most minor infraction committed by a nonwhite into a major criminal offense.

Black Africans protested many of these laws as well as the system of passes which were required of all nonwhites in order to travel or obtain employment. Inspired by the Pan-African Congress, a relatively militant organization fighting for Black freedom, protests and government reprisals continued. In 1960 in Sharpeville, a protest led to governmental forces killing 67 Africans and wounding nearly 200 others. The nonwhite people responded by rioting, and the government countered by passing the Unlawful Organizations Act, banning nonwhite political organizations. The saga of apartheid, apartness, is replete with many more examples of injustice and inequity than we have shown in this overview of the racial conflict in South Africa.

Apartheid continues to this day. The policy means that Blacks and coloureds have no chance for a share in most of the activities taking place around them (figure 6 – 4). A nonwhite child will have little chance for an education and virtually no chance to obtain employment at a fair wage unless dramatic changes occur.

Why this type of discrimination? We have stated that it is the result of many processes which gave rise to the whites' "need" for Black subjugation, including the economics of cheap labor and the politics of minority control. These processes over time have led to an attitude often called "the white man's burden," as noted in the following comment:

> As carriers of a "higher civilization" the whites cast themselves into the role of the stern but just master who has to look after the welfare of his childish and backward servants.

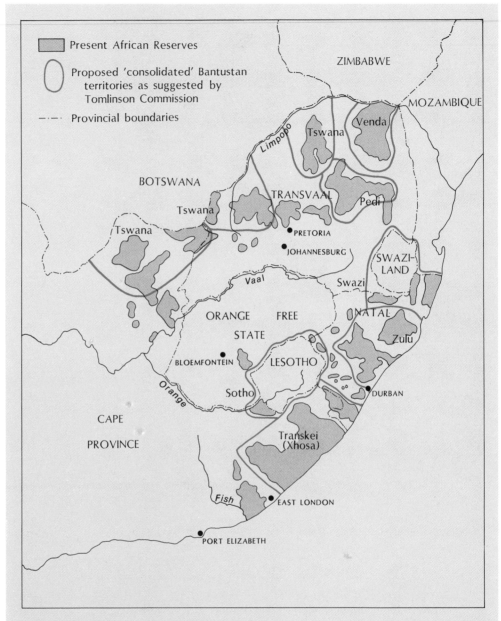

FIGURE 6–1 The Apartheid Plan. African "reserves" were established to remove nonwhites from the mainstream of political and economic life. Often the man works in the city while his family remains on the reserve. (J. Cope, 1967, *South Africa*. New York, Praeger Publishers, Inc., p. 43.)

The "white man's burden" attitude is a useful rationalization of European dominance, because the benevolent aspect of paternalism appears to reconcile despotism with justice . . . . Paternalism has transformed the reality of the "Black man's burden" into the myth of the "white man's burden." The master — servant relationship is considered by the majority of whites as the

A coloured family living near Cape Town. These children may well ask
what the future holds for them. (United Nations/K. Muldoon, 1970)

> ideal and only relationship between Europeans and non-Europeans and
> successive governments have basically aimed at extending and preserving that
> model at the national level. (van den Berghe, 1967, p. 111)

The most obvious fallacy in this attitude is the concept of an inferior race. Skin
color is quite obviously not a measure of the abilities or worth of an individual
or group. Site, situation, and the degree of modernization, and not individual
biological characteristics of the individuals, are the determinants of the level
of technology of a group.

The world community is appalled at the practices of the South African
government, yet little real action is taken by either the Black African nations
or other world governments. The reasons for this inaction can be traced, using
our systems approach, to several basic factors. There is a natural reluctance
for governments to interfere in the internal policy of other governments; any

nation crying out with indignation is subject to having its own internal policies examined. There are also military and economic considerations; the political unit of South Africa is located in a strategic military position. South Africa also supplies much of the world's diamonds, gold, and plutonium, and many nations are reluctant to interfere with a major source of these materials. Further, South Africa is important to the economy of the entire African continent, supplying many goods and services needed by "Black Africa" for modernization. Economic needs often tend to override concerns for social equity.

The dilemma of the racial policy of the government of South Africa continues. One can only speculate what changes may occur. One thing is fairly certain: with increasing expectations of dominated groups, confrontation and stress will continue (Thompson and Butler, 1975).

RELIGION AND THE LANDSCAPE

We have seen how skin color has been used as the basis of social segregation; the same is true of religion. European Jews have experienced persecution throughout much of European history; Catholic immigrants to the United States in the 19th and 20th centuries were subject to discrimination as well, and this list could go on. Our purpose here is not to discuss the intermixing of religion and politics which led to such problems in the past, but rather to explore the contribution of various religions to the cultural mosaic which forms our landscape.

Religious geography and the geography of religions

This discussion of human geography and religion will focus on four areas:

    the geography of selected world religions

    religious geography

    specific religious groups in the United States and Canada

    religion as a factor in economic development and modernization.

Although the first two topics listed, the **geography of religions** and **religious geography,** may seem to be basically the same, there is an important distinction: the *geography of religions* implies the origins and diffusion of religious systems, whereas *religious geography* is more a study of the specific imprint which a religious practice leaves on the local landscape.

Throughout our discussion of religion and human geography, three questions should be considered (Glacken, 1972): How does the landscape provide a record of religious systems? What is the impact of religious practice on ecological systems? How does religion, as a subsystem of cultural systems, interact with the remaining subsystems to influence the human use of the earth?

The geography of religions. *Religion* may be defined as a system of belief in a divine or superhuman power and the performing of rituals associated with that belief. *Religion* is also referred to as a code of ethics and a philosophy. Within the broad scope allowed by these definitions, one can find all manner and type of beliefs, methods of worship and extents to which religious practice dominates other types of social and economic activities. We will explore a representative cross section of the world's religions, focusing on the questions posed at the beginning of this discussion.

How did religion originate? This is a most puzzling and interesting question. It is also a concern of some importance, for many scholars have linked the rise of organized religion and the rise of technology.

Lewis Browne echoes the sentiments of a vast number of scholars by putting the development of religion into a step wise perspective (1941). The earliest religions were most likely associated with "magic," as primitive people attempted to explain why events occurred. At some point in prehistory people began to hope that, through ritual, they could influence the happenings in the world around them. This was undoubtedly tied to environmental events, for it would be logical to try to create a positive relationship with the spirit which provided the resources for food production.

As prehistoric peoples evolved and as fire, tools, and communication developed, the importance of religion began to increase. Technological development, religious practice, and the rise of the earliest cities have been linked together by a wide range of scholars. In *The City in History,* Lewis Mumford attaches great importance to religion and the gathering of people for ceremony, and describes religious practice as one of the cornerstones of the development of cities (1962). Early religious systems were not only responsible for bringing people together but also for regulation of activities.

In most ancient civilizations organized religion was an important part of daily life; the customs, fears, and taboos associated with religion dominated activity. The Druids or "wise ones" of the Celts, for instance, were looked upon for advice on nearly every issue of importance; the same was true in Egyptian animal worship and in the reverence for Greek gods. In modern civilizations as well, religion is obviously an important force in decision making.

The major religions of today's world originated in the Middle East, India, and China. The belief systems originating and diffusing from the Middle East were Judaism, Christianity, and Mohammedanism, or Islam. The Indian subcontinent was the founding place of Brahmanism, Jainism, Buddhism, and Hinduism. People from the Chinese cultural hearth have contributed two important religions or philosophies, Confucianism and Taoism. The origin and diffusion of the world's major religions makes an interesting geographical study.

The origins of the world's major religions.   The oldest of the Middle Eastern religions is Judaism. The Hebrews of four thousand years ago were primarily nomadic herdsmen in the Arabian Desert. Their religion was probably animism or the worship of mountains, heavenly bodies, and so on (Levner, 1976). The Jews trace formal evolution of their religion to Abraham, the first patriarch. The covenant which inspired Abraham was repeated to Isaac and Jacob, who eventually settled in Egypt. The Jews in Egypt grew in number from a small group into a substantial element of the population. The history of the Jews in Egypt is one of a people deprived, oppressed, and finally enslaved.

The Jews were led from enslavement by Moses in the most far-reaching event in Jewish history, the exodus. Moses led them into the Sinai. One of the successors of Moses, David, conquered Jerusalem and made it the eternal city of the Jews.

The religion of the Hebrew people was not the result of some instant revolution, but rather a slow evolutionary process; Judaism was a firmly entrenched part of the cultural system of the Middle East by the time of Roman domination. The conflict between the Jewish belief in a Messiah and the Roman demands of worship and allegiance to the emperor was a constant source of political turmoil. It was at this time that Jesus of Nazareth became an important religious leader.

The doctrine espoused by Jesus inspired a following from which a new religion was to develop. This religion grew in importance following the death of Jesus and eventually spread to all parts of the globe. Jesus was considered to be the Christ, or Anointed One, by his disciples and followers. Based on the events of Jesus' life and a firm conviction in his Resurrection after death, those who believed that Jesus was the Christ went on to win converts to Christianity.

As we shall see in the case of almost all major religions, the process of the diffusion of a particular faith is slow and difficult. One major religion that was a relative latecomer to world cultural systems, but diffused rapidly, was Islam.

> The religion of Islam is one of the outstanding phenomena of history. Within a century of the death of its founder, the Muslim Empire stretched from Southern France through Spain, North Africa, the Levant and Central Asia to the confines of China. (Anderson, 1976, p. 91)

The founder of the Islamic religion, Mohammed, was born about A.D. 570 in Mecca. In his early adulthood Mohammed began to formulate a religous doctrine which may have been influenced by both Christianity and Judaism.

Mohammed, the Praised One, whose given name was actually Ubu'l-Kassim, was an orphan with little education. He had an opportunity to see much of the Middle Eastern world as a camel driver in caravans. At the age of 25 he married a woman, Khudija, who provided him with financial security, and by his 40th year he was said to have experienced revelations about the one true God. It is not possible to detail the evolution of the Islamic religion here; suffice it to say that Mohammed established a way of life which included daily prayer, abstinence from pork and alcohol, a number of religious holidays, and a strong desire to carry the Islamic religion throughout the world (McCasland, 1969).

Upon the death of Mohammed it was not clear who his successor would be, and the resulting turmoil divided the members of the Islamic religion into several major subunits. This becomes an important consideration since the Islamic people view church and state as one. To this day, the national policy of Islamic states is strongly affected by the particular sect in power.

Two major religions of non–Middle Eastern origin may be used as examples of the remaining major religions of the world. Hinduism is one of the most unique of the world's religions. It has no founder, but grew gradually over a period of nearly 5000 years, absorbing and assimilating all the religions and cultural movements of India. Professor Bruce Nicholls observes that Hinduism selects elements from many religions, beliefs, and cultural systems, and adapts them. The Hindu looks for fundamental truths and sees no distinction between religion and the total cultural system (1976, p. 137).

The Hindu is concerned with *Karma;* Karma is, in a sense, a moral law of cause and effect. In essence, Karma is the product of a person's deeds—good works produce positive rewards, undesirable activity brings negative response. Hinduism is fascinating in that the emphasis is on Karma and the eternal soul of the individual rather than the relationship of the soul with God. The belief that the soul remains immortal and that it is found in plants and animals as well as humans has a major impact on cultural systems influenced by Hindu peoples. The soul is in a neverending state of change; therefore, all forms of life must be protected. The avoidance of animal flesh in the diet is an example of this protection of all life.

The Hindu religion originated in India and has diffused to much of Indonesia and Eastern Africa (figure 6–2). Another major religion originating in India was Buddhism. Buddhism predates Christianity by about 600 years, and unlike Christianity which diffused westward, Buddhism diffused eastward. Like most other religions, Buddhism is not simply one homogeneous entity but rather a conglomeration of a wide variety of doctrines and practices (McCasland, 1969).

The name Buddha, the Enlightened One, was given to Siddhartha Gautama, who was born near Nepal about 536 B.C. Unlike Christ or Mohammed, Siddhartha Gautama was thought to have grown up in relative luxury. His religious awakening came during prolonged meditation. It is reported that he meditated beneath a fig tree, which became known as the *Bo* or *tree of wisdom;* that is of great interest when we consider religious geography (Taylor *et al.,* 1976, p. 171).

Gautama developed a basic code of living built upon "Four Truths" or philosophical principles. There was also incorporated into this philosophy an "Eightfold Path," or code of conduct, which guided followers into a lifestyle deemed morally and spiritually proper.

The common factor found in all of these religions is that disciples carried the teachings of their particular faith from a point of origin into new lands. This diffusion and the impacts of religious practice on ecological systems are the particular concerns of the geographer.

The diffusion of the world's major religions.   In considering the diffusion of religion, we may call upon the principles of spatial diffusion examined in the preceding chapter. Religious belief diffused from nodal areas along specific paths, basically trade routes. We are obviously dealing with the preelectronic era; therefore, the processes of expansion diffusion and relocation diffusion are of major importance.

Judaism's diffusion was supported by the forced relocation of Jews at various times in history. The case of the Jews is interesting, for there was a great reverse migration back to their area of origin following the creation of the political state of Israel after World War II.

Unlike the sporadic relocation diffusion of Judaism, Christianity spread in waves through a process of expansion diffusion. Christianity was embraced by many in the Roman Empire in the final era of Roman dominance. Roman adoption or at least tolerance of the fledgling religion allowed Christianity to diffuse along the established network of Roman roads and cities. It became strongly interwoven with political leadership, a relationship that carried over into the age of contact between the Old and New Worlds. One of the missions of nearly every voyage of discovery was to bring Christianity to the people of distant lands. Thus, Christianity established an especially strong foothold in South and Central America, and the organized church became a major factor in the march toward modernization in the New World.

Like Christianity and Judaism, Buddhism and Hinduism spread through expansion and the relocation of religious believers. The paths of diffusion of Buddhism and Hinduism were mainly trade routes. In each

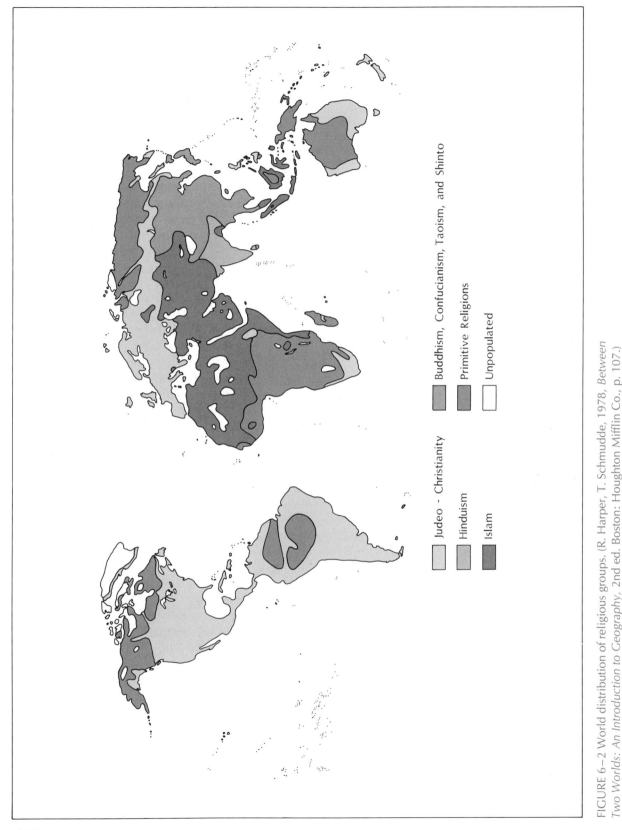

FIGURE 6–2 World distribution of religious groups. (R. Harper, T. Schmudde, 1978, *Between Two Worlds: An Introduction to Geography*, 2nd ed. Boston: Houghton Mifflin Co., p. 107.)

Judeo - Christianity

Hinduism

Islam

Buddhism, Confucianism, Taoism, and Shinto

Primitive Religions

Unpopulated

of these four major religions, the tellers and receivers of information were initially part of a passive process. As some religions grew in political and economic strength, the method of conversion became more aggressive. One of the world's major religions, however, incorporates this type of forced diffusion into its philosophical base.

In the Islamic religion is the duty of *Jihad,* or Holy War; theoretically, all adult male Muslims are charged with the responsibility of serving in the religious war. The Islamic world is divided into two groups, ''Dar al-Islam, where Islam reigns supreme, and Dar al-Harb (the Abode of War), where the rule of Islam should be extended, if necessary, by war'' (Anderson, 1976, p. 121). The diffusion of the world's major religions was not without impact on ecological systems and the landscape. The land records the effects of religion in many different ways.

Religious geography

The study of religious geography is concerned with specific positive and negative expressions of religious practice on the landscape. We will focus our discussion of religious geography on an overview of these basic topics: the church as a structure, land-use patterns, the distribution of plants and animals, names on the land, food and work taboos and sacred space, and ecological systems (Glacken, 1967 and 1972; Sopher, 1967; Ewing, 1975).

Mountains have probably played a more important role in geography and religion than any other landform. The Japanese thought of mountains as resting places for the dead. The Greeks perceived them as the places where gods resided. In many other cultures the mountain was a place of contact between the diety and the person on earth; Moses received the Ten Commandments on a mountain.

The sacred nature of some mountains could have great influence on land-use patterns. Mountains that were sacred places were not to be disturbed by human activity; in other cases the mountain was seen as the axis which connected earth to the upper world, thus it was a desirable place for settlement. Mountains are an example of the manner in which natural features become part of the religious landscape. In the same vein, churches serve as examples of human activity and religious space. The religious landscape, as seen through the perception of church structure, differs widely throughout the world.

The introduction of a church into an area which was relatively unsettled brought on many changes in local ecological systems. In the 5th century St. Benedict advised his followers to seek nonurban places and establish monasteries. To provide food for these institutions, the local landscape was converted to agricultural use. Monasteries attracted other people who, in turn, settled, acting to expand urbanization into rural Europe. Religion at times inspires unique land use patterns which attempt to create, on the earth, a model reflective of the spiritual world.

The Dogon people of Africa have organized the arrangement of their agricultural fields to be in harmony with the religious philosophy of their culture (figure 6–3).

> The country of the Dogon has been organized as far as possible in accordance with the principle that the world developed in spiral form. In theory, the central point of development is formed by three ritual fields, assigned to three of the mythical ancestors and to the three fundamental cults. When layed out, they mark out a world in miniature on which the gradual establishment of man takes place. (Griqule and Dieterlen, 1954, p. 94; as quoted in Sopher, 1967, p. 31)

To the Dogon people cosmic or spiritual harmony is in the spiral pattern. Many Asians attempt to model the earth in order to achieve a spiritual good in a different manner.

In many parts of Asia, the practice of Fung-Shui has been an important element in locational decisions. The underlying principle of Fung-Shui is that water is the blood and breath of the earth and that virtue accumulates in mountains. The ideal location, therefore, is one that is based upon a consideration of the flow of air and water (Glacken, 1972). The currents of moving air and water represent good. If the site selected for a residence or grave location is at the bend of a stream or at the base of a mountain, the flow of air and/or water will be restricted and positive values will accumulate (figure 6–4). A long straight river or a valley through which the wind flows freely are not suitable sites. The nature of this pattern is often reflected in Asian Gardens.

The distribution of plants and animals can also be a reflection of religious activity. We have mentioned that Gautama meditated beneath the Bo tree (a

Religious structures. (A) Notre Dame, Paris. (French Government Tourist Office) (B) Inner courtyard of the main pagoda, Rangoon, Burma. (United Nations, 1960) (C) Angkor, Cambodia. (United Nations, 1960) (D) Mexican cathedral. (World Bank Photo by Edwin G. Huffman, 1968)

fig tree) referred to as the *tree of wisdom*. Through studying the location of the Bo tree, it is possible to trace the migration of Buddhists from northern India as far as Japan since the migrating Buddhists carried the Bo tree with them. Sopher notes that the white iris flower was dispersed all over the Middle East because of its use in Muslim graveside practice (Sopher, 1967, p. 36).

The use of wine in both Jewish and Christian ceremonies was largely responsible for grapes being grown beyond the Mediterranean realm. Christians carried the grape into Western Europe and eventually

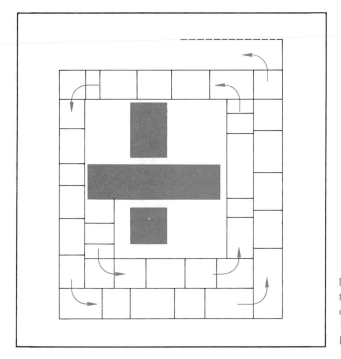

FIGURE 6–3 Dogon cosmic field pattern illustrates the counterclockwise spiral extension of cultivated land around three original fields. (David E. Sopher, *Geography of Religions,* © 1967, p. 31. Reprinted by permission of Prentice-Hall, Inc., Englewood Cliffs, NJ.)

to the New World. A number of the Spanish missions which dotted the coastal area of California produced wine. The large California wine industry of today owes its start to the introduction of grape vines by religious leaders nearly two hundred years ago.

California provides another example of the interrelationship between geography and religion. If one were to take a trip up the California coast from San Diego to Santa Rosa, one would pass the following towns: Los Angeles, Santa Barbara, Santa Maria, San Luis Obispo, San Jose, San Mateo, San Francisco, and San Rafael. In many countries of the world, religion has played an important part in contributing place names.

California is only one example in the United States. By studying an atlas of your particular region, you may determine the distribution of place names with a religious origin. The names of places are interesting; however, the most important question is whether or not there is an historical pattern to such names. In our California example, Spanish Catholic missionaries founded towns from south to north as they explored the California coast. The coastal towns were named for Saints (the prefix *San* or *Santa*), but as one moves inland, the pattern of place names changes completely since the Spanish did little to colonize the interior of the state. Does this type of historical pattern of place name locations exist in your region?

Turning our attention to ecosystems, we find the use or avoidance of certain foods has a strong influence. Religions which prohibit the consumption of pork, such as Judaism or Islam, may result in few pigs being found in an area. In most economies hog-raising is a very beneficial activity; hogs provide food, fertilizer, and in some cases a cash return, yet require small investments of capital or energy. In addition, pigs occupy little space, have no special food demands, and every part from bristles to tail can be used. In Spain and Portugal the pig is an inexpensive and plentiful supply of food. Across the Strait of Gibraltar, in a similar physical environment, there are virtually no pigs because the people of the Atlas Mountains practice the Islamic religion (Sopher, 1967, p. 36). Sopher notes the importance such a food taboo can play in an ecosystem.

> . . . Muslim Malays no longer keep pigs. Agriculture in Chinese villages in Malaya is characterized by the intensive cultivation of vegetables, in which pigs play an integral role: vegetable mash and other wastes are fed to pigs, which are raised for human food, while returning fertility to the soil in the form of manure. This successful tropical ecosystem is absent in adjacent Malay villages. (1967, p. 36)

Pigs are absent from the Malay villages because of a religious restriction on eating or handling pork. The

Conceptual model

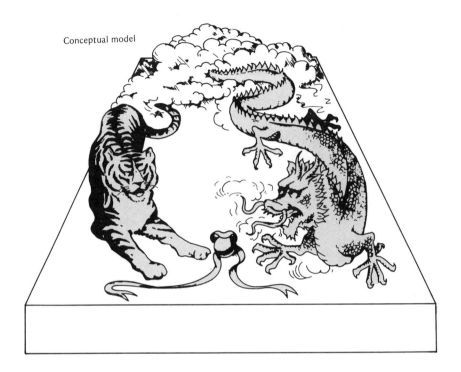

Topographical model

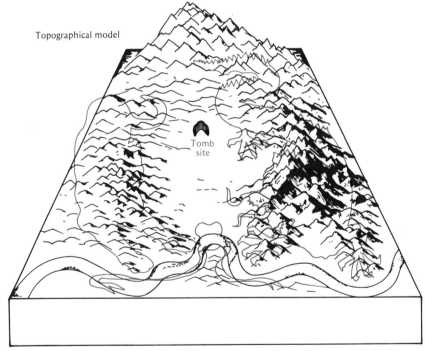

FIGURE 6–4 Conceptual and topographic models of an ideal *Feng Shui* site. (Reproduced by permission from the *Annals* of the Association of American Geographers, Volume 64, 1974, p. 509, figure 2, D.C.Y. Lai.)

Chinese in this area have a considerable ecological and economic advantage over the Malays.

The final element in the discussion of religious geography is pilgrim circulation, or journey to a place of religious significance. The most famous religious pilgrimage is perhaps the journey of people of the Islamic faith to Mecca, referred to as the *jajj*.

Islamic people have been journeying to Mecca for more than thirteen centuries. In times past one walked or rode in slow-moving caravans or ships, but today airplane loads of people land at Jidda for the short trip to Mecca. In 1972, for example, well over 1 million people made the pilgrimage. The trip to Mecca has strong religious meaning and is to be undertaken at least once in a Muslim's lifetime.

Mecca is the focus of such activity for it was the birthplace of Mohammed. In contemporary times, the pilgrimage brings wealth and prestige to the city; historically, the pilgrimage provided the opportunity for the diffusion of ideas and information.

The geographer may view the religious subunit of a cultural system in many ways. We have presented an overview of culture, religion, and ecosystems for the world's major religions. We may also consider religion as a catalyst which fosters change.

Socioeconomic change and religion

Religion has been important in political change, whether violent or lawful, throughout history. The complex interrelationship between government and religion is beyond the scope of this volume. We can, however, attempt to summarize the general ways in which church and state interact.

Benson finds six types of interaction between government and religion (1960, pp. 662–665):

1. Government is looked to for protecting religious freedom.
2. Government serves a protective function for those holding the views of the religious minority. Government is called upon to prevent the dominant religion from attempting to forcibly convert the minority groups.
3. Government may operate the church for the people.
4. Religious groups may attempt to influence governmental activity.
5. Religion may have a formative influence on the young of a nation.
6. Religion is called upon by government to aid in national problems. In time of war for example the interaction between religion and government increases.

Nearly all of these six factors apply to many modern world nations where religion is recognized. The exceptions are that (1) in most communist countries, religion is not explicitly recognized by the state, and (2) the majority of political states do not directly operate the church.

The degree to which the church is influential in national policy varies considerably throughout the world. In much of Latin America, for instance, the church exerts tremendous influence on national government. Through political activity, the Catholic Church in Latin America has acted to reduce the impact of various methods of population control. The influence of the Catholic Church on this issue is by no means confined to Latin America, as indicated by the lobbying efforts of the church against abortion in Asia, Western Europe, and the United States. It would be misleading to present the equation as simply "Catholic-dominated country equals specific policy on birth control;" we know from our study of cultural systems that no issue is that fundamental. But the role of the Catholic Church in population control policy cannot be denied.

In still another example of the interaction between church and state, the Catholic Church is active at the grass roots level in land reform in Latin America. There is increasing evidence that during the past several years local priests have been urging the peasant population to strive for political and economic reform. There are some who claim that a desire for a more uniform distribution of the wealth resulting from the economic process ties the action of a religious group with the philosophy of Karl Marx. The ironic aspect of the link between Marx, religion, and social change lies in the Marxian perception of religion. Marx believed that all culture was the product of self-interest and technology. Religion was viewed as an economic pawn in the conflict between capitalist and workers (Benson, 1960).

In Latin America the Marxian philosophical principles of equality in the political, social, legal, and economic realms are often used as a model. People in Latin America are becoming more aware of the inequity and injustice in the existing political structures. In this situation the seeming equity provided by the philosophy of Marx is an attractive alternative.

The vehicle which may bring about change lies in the institution of the church. In the Latin American Jesuit Journal, *Mensaje,* this proposition was stated: "We must therefore re-establish a political regime, a legal, social and economic order which effectively achieves the 'common good,' the good of all, even though we sacrifice certain 'particular' goods" (Smith, 1971, p. 257). The "pawn of the capitalist" may indeed be the factor which creates political redefinition.

Once again the intricacy, interdependence, and even ironic interaction between the elements of cultural systems become apparent.

Race and religion are important aspects of the mosaic of culture. These two components of culture provide us with an insight to the manner in which individual elements of cultural systems can influence the trend toward modernization of the entire system. The following two chapters, dealing with language and politics, respectively, offer additional insights into the impact that specific aspects of cultural systems have on the overall process of modernization.

KEY TERMS

Species
Natural selection
Genetics
Dominant
Recessive
Clines
Plasticity

Mutation
Genetic drift
Plural society
Syncretic culture
Apartheid
Geography of religions
Religious geography

REFERENCES

Anderson, N. (1976), *World's Religion.* Grand Rapids, MI: Wm. B. Eerdmans Publishing Co.

Baker, J. (1974), *Race.* New York: Oxford University Press.

Banton, M. and Harwood, J. (1975), *The Race Concept.* New York: Praeger Publishers, Inc.

Benson, P. (1960), *Race in Contemporary Culture.* New York: Harper & Row, Publishers, Inc.

Boas, F. (1940), *Race, Language and Culture.* New York: Free Press.

Brown, D. (1968), *Against the World.* New York: Doubleday & Co., Inc.

Browne, L. (1941), *This Believing World.* New York: Macmillan, Inc.

Crowley, W. (1978), "Old Order Amish Settlement," *Annals of the Association of American Geographers* 68, No. 2, 249–259.

Ewing, S. (1975), *Man, Religion and the Environment.* Dubuque, IA: Kendall/Hunt Publishing Co.

Gheddo, P. (1970), *The Cross and the Bo Tree.* New York: Sheed and Ward.

Glacken, C. (1967), *Traces on the Rhodian Shore.* Berkeley: University of California Press.

Glacken, C. (1972), Information based on a lecture series presented at the University of California, Berkeley.

Horrell, M. (1972), *A Survey of Race Relations in South Africa.* Berkeley: University of California Press.

Levner, H. (1950), "Judaism," in Anderson, N. (ed.), *World's Religions.* Grand Rapids, MI: Wm. B. Eerdmans Publishing Co., 49–90.

Marquard, L. (1962), *The Peoples and Policies of South Africa.* London: Oxford University Press.

McCasland, S., et al. (1969), *Religions of the World.* New York: Random House, Inc.

Mumford, L. (1961), *The City in History: Its Origins, Its Transformations, and Its Prospects.* New York: Harcourt Brace Jovanovich, Inc.

Ngubane, J. (1971), "South Africa Race Crisis: A Conflict of Minds," in Adams, H. (ed.), *South Africa: Sociological Perspectives.* New York: Oxford University Press.

Nicholls, B. (1976), "Hinduism," in Anderson, N. (ed.), *World's Religions.* Grand Rapids, MI: Wm. B. Eerdmans Publishing Co.

Ripley, W. (1899), *The Races of Europe: A Sociological Study.* New York: Appleton-Century-Crofts.

Silvert, K. (1967), *Expectant Peoples.* New York: Vintage Books/Random House, Inc.

Smith, D. (1971), *Religion, Politics and Social Change in the Third World.* New York: Free Press.

Sopher, D. (1967), *Geography of Religions.* Englewood Cliffs, NJ: Prentice–Hall, Inc.

Taylor, D. and Offner, C. B. (1976), "Buddhism," in Anderson, N. (ed.), *World's Religions.* Grand Rapids, MI: Wm. B. Eerdmans Publishing Co.

Thompson, L. and Butler, J. (eds.) (1975), *Change in Contemporary South Africa.* Berkeley: University of California Press.

van den Berghe, P. (1967), *South Africa.* Berkeley: University of California Press.

7

Language patterns

General agreement exists among those who have studied speech and language patterns that the origin of language is obscured in antiquity. The origin and use of language developed in conjunction with the cultural evolution of early human societies. Language is both a necessary condition for, and an integral part of, culture. It may even be the major characteristic of culture.

All human beings, according to both archaeological and documentary records, have had languages. Societies in all levels of cultural development have developed languages—some of them simple in structure and others more complex. Languages have been one of humankind's first cultural inventions; they are necessary in order to acquire as well as to transmit other important cultural traits.

Language is such a central and important part of our life that we often overlook its importance. Human cultural achievements have resulted primarily from two things, tools and speech. These two developments have enabled people to control their environment and thus increase their numbers as well as the area under their control. Substantial evidence indicates that considerably more languages existed in the past than do today. Before the advent of modern communication and transportation facilities, each isolated cultural group had its own language; as transportation and communication improved, the number of languages diminished.

Languages, like people, change over time, and in many ways, changes in a language are analogous to changes in a person. Looking in the mirror every day, it is difficult to see changes that are occurring because they are so gradual. In order to notice these small, imperceptible changes we must use a larger time frame. Language changes occur over centuries instead of days or years.

LANGUAGE AND EVOLUTION

The concept of **evolution** has been an important aspect of many disciplines, including the biological/physical sciences as well as the social sciences and humanities. Although Darwin has received most of the credit for articulating the concept of evolution, **linguists** and others who studied languages accepted the idea of the evolution of languages before Darwin's classic analysis of biological evolution. Darwin's principal achievement was the establishment of the idea that differences among species were the result of gradual changes over time, **transformism,** and not an original creative act, **creationism.** The idea was not originally conceived by Darwin, but he solidified the concept through careful study and gathering of data.

In linguistic science, creationist theory was generally accepted until the turn of the 19th century. The creationist view of the development of language is exemplified by the Biblical account of the Tower of Babel, where all languages were created at the same time. The origin of language diversity was thus associated with the Biblical event.

The genetic theory of language evolution preceded the general acceptance of transformism in biol-

Charles Darwin. (Library of Congress)

1840

1881

1854

ogy. Transformationalist theory in both language and biology are associated with a dynamic process of growth and developmental change. The model of evolution is that of a branching tree and is sometimes referred to as branching evolution. Transformism in both biology and language is a slow process. Changes can, however, occur more rapidly in language evolution. Old people can sometimes observe language changes in their lifetime. New words or phrases are added to a language, and other expressions are deleted: not too long ago people rode in "rumble seats" and listened to the "wireless." Written records over several centuries can be used to trace changes within a language.

There are several parallels between the evolution of languages and the evolution of species. In both cases geographic isolation leads to the development of several forms. Variations occur; some are perpetuated while others disappear. The metaphor of a branching tree works for evolution of both species and languages; each are spread over wide areas after initial development and differentiation. Unlike the evolution of species, however, one language will succeed another not because it is more advanced or better adapted to an area, but rather because of the economic, cultural, or military superiority of its speakers. For example, both

English- and Spanish-speaking peoples have been major colonial powers in recent world history, and today we can find English or Spanish as the secondary, if not primary language of many nations.

Language change

Many factors are associated with language changes. The changes may be relatively simple, such as the addition of a new word or the change in meaning of a word already in use, or they may involve more complex grammatical structures. In either case, linguistic changes cannot be separated from the sociocultural milieu in which they occur (Wagner, 1958, p. 96). Geographic factors are important aspects of linguistic change and assimilation. Many languages have borrowed words from neighboring languages, and these word distributions are clues to other geographical connections. For example, many English words have been borrowed from Greek, Latin, French, or the Germanic languages, and the use and meaning of these words reflect the culture from which they were borrowed.

Languages are not static. The speed and tempo of language changes are variable and are the result of many factors. An analysis of English over the past sev-

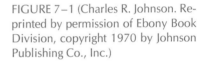

FIGURE 7–1 (Charles R. Johnson. Reprinted by permission of Ebony Book Division, copyright 1970 by Johnson Publishing Co., Inc.)

eral centuries illustrates the dynamic nature of language.

> The English of the King James Bible or Shakespeare is unlike the English of today. The fourteenth-century English of Chaucer is intelligible to us only if we use a glossary. The ninth-century English of King Alfred the Great, of which we have contemporary manuscript records, seems to us like a foreign language; if we could meet English speakers of that time, we would not understand their speech, or they ours.
> (Bloomfield, 1933, p. 281)

Language changes usually do not affect the fundamental structure. Several principal types of language changes have been outlined by Joyce Hertzler in his study of the sociology of language (1965, p. 144). The addition of new words for new experiences or aspects of culture is one method of language change. These new words could be invented, borrowed from another language, or could be built from words already in the vocabulary: *smoke* and *fog* are combined for *smog*, and *fourteen nights* is shortened to *fortnight.*

A second method of language change is through shifts in the meaning of words. Such shifts may involve applying new meanings to old words or extending the meaning of a word to be more inclusive; for example, the English word *meat* originally applied to all food, but now it specifically refers to flesh of other animals.

Replacement or loss of words is a third method of language change; words may be replaced or dropped from the vocabulary because they no longer have cultural relevance (figure 7–1). The final method of language change involves phonetic, grammatical, or spelling changes in words. For example, although Shakespeare's works are constantly being reprinted, the newer versions have changed much of his original spelling.

Of the many factors which cause linguistic changes, the primary ones are ***sociocultural*** in nature. According to Hertzler, "In the main, it is societal and cultural developments, social conditions, social requirements, social influences and pressures, emanating from within and without the given language community, that mold the spoken and written language" (1965, p. 150). The factors that induce or retard change can be divided into three general categories: external factors associated with contacts with other languages or cultures, internal factors requiring adjustments in language patterns, and factors related to the basic conservatism of language.

Few cultural groups in today's world are completely isolated. Contacts, whether incidental or deliberate, are made between cultural groups, and so they influence each other. Spatial interaction in the form of migration has had a great influence on language patterns. In newly settled areas, migrants generally name things or places according to their former cultural experience; for example, in the eastern United States we find such place names as Worcester, Cambridge, Northampton, and Ipswich—names also found in England. Small groups of immigrants, although usually assimilated by the dominant culture, have impacted language change to a certain degree by adding words or expressions. Foreign travel and tourism are other forms of spatial interaction that have been instrumental in promoting language change.

Territorial occupation and the subjugation of one cultural group by another has often been a method of imposing language changes. Colonialism, which frequently followed conquest, influenced the colonizer's language as well as the language of the indigenous population. In some cases—English in India is a classic example—the language of the invader or colonizer was not accepted by the masses, but it was adopted by most of the business and government elite.

Slavery has also been a method of language change. The introduction of over 15 million Black slaves into the Western hemisphere has greatly changed the language patterns of those areas. Slaves must learn the language of their enslavers, but they also have an influence on the dominant language.

A final type of external influence on language change is associated with cultural interchanges. They can involve the exchange of people, books, journals, or other cultural features. Since World War II nations have engaged in an organized effort to voluntarily exchange ideas as well as people.

The second general category of factors that induce or retard change are internal cultural factors. Demographic changes within language communities or in contacting societies are associated with linguistic changes. The composition of a population relative to age or sex, as well as the spatial mobility of a population, can have linguistic implications. Many new words or phrases, such as the *population explosion, birth control,* or *in-migration,* are the result of demographic variables.

Institutional changes within a society can also have important linguistic consequences. The advent of science and modern technology has brought with it a host of new words. Political and social changes have likewise introduced new words and changed meanings of existing words; the *Cold War* and the *Moonies* are examples of such changes. Of course *stagflation,*

which seems little understood by economists, is a recent addition to the economists' vocabulary.

Although language changes are relatively common, they occur over extended periods of time. The nature of language dictates that language changes occur more slowly than do changes in the political or social realm. A "language revolution" is not as common an occurrence as a political or social revolution. Physical and social isolation are also important factors retarding language change. Physical isolation has historically played an important role in language isolation; for example, the language of the Basques has changed little over the past several centuries principally because of their isolated position in the Pyranees Mountains.

Tradition also retards language change; a language has a literature, and that literature is based on or contributes to a tradition. People tend to fear strange situations and thus are resistant to change. For some cultural and political groups, language is a badge of group identity and solidarity, and such strong attachments may retard change: the use of French in Quebec serves to maintain the identity of French Canadians.

In summary, the speed of linguistic change is a function of the balance between the factors promoting change and those retarding change. In general, the speed of change is greater in times of political and social turmoil. In the last 50 years the volume and rate of linguistic change have been greater than in any previous 50-year period. Furthermore, because of rapid developments in global communication systems, linguistic changes will probably continue to occur more rapidly.

GENERAL FUNCTIONS OF LANGUAGE

The general population is unaware of the importance and function of language, but culture continually develops through the transmission of accumulated experiences by language. Language is at the root of cultural change, because it is the vehicle by which other cultural events can take place. Although literature is primarily the creation of the intellectual elite and the aristocrats, language is a product of the masses. Because everyone speaks, everyone contributes to language. Parents pass it on to their children, teachers transmit it to their students, and leaders command followers

Graffiti on 118th Street in Manhattan. (United Nations/John Robaton, 1970)

through it. Without language it would have been impossible to create such architectural wonders as the pyramids of Egypt or the great gothic cathedrals of Europe. Language is important to cooperation, and without it, we could not transfer the thoughts or ideas necessary for collective action.

It is difficult to conjure an image of the world without language. Perhaps the best way to appreciate its value is to travel to a foreign land and experience a different language. If we cannot speak or communicate effectively, it is difficult to do much of anything else. In a discussion on the indispensability of language, Mario Pei said:

> Although language is the transmitter of thought, it is not enough to grant it a niche among the humanities and leave it there to serve as a tool of literature and philosophy. Although it has numerous physical manifestations, it is not enough to relegate it among the physical sciences and describe it as a branch of physics, physiology, or anthropology. Although it is one of the most refined products of the mind, it is not enough to view it as a mere psychological activity. Language is the sum of all these things, and something more. It is the conveyor, interpreter, and shaper of man's social doings. It is all-pervasive. It enters into, influences, and is in turn influenced by every form of human activity without exception. Its functions are as numerous as the fields in which human ingenuity operates. (1965, p. 201)

If the curse of Babel were to suddenly fall upon us, there would be frustration and chaos. Unable to communicate, whether through the spoken or written medium, societies would disintegrate.

Language as perception and thinking

Language is an important aspect of all mental processes. It is a major determinant of how we look at and perceive our environment. It tells us what is important and what is not. The first thing we do is look at things or people, then we name them, and only then can we really begin to know them. Language is thus an important tool in the conceptualization process, because we use it in the construction of reality and in the conceptualization of experiences. Ideas take form through language and, according to Colin Cherry, "The only way to pin down a thought before it can slip away . . . is to jump on it with both verbal feet, to pin it down with language" (1957, pp. 76–77).

Language is related to culture like a map is related to the area it represents. Through the use of symbols, a map represents some portion of reality, but cannot and does not represent every aspect of a particular area. Items of relevance to our particular purpose are presented on the map. The language of a people is really a map of their culture. The words in a language are symbols that represent, locate, and to some degree, explain what a culture is like. In general, the culture with a more complex language can be more easily understood once the language is understood. In a similar vein, possessing very detailed maps of a region would be more useful than a sketchy map in understanding that region.

Language: Adjusting to space and time

Space and time can be conceptualized only through language, and any particular location in either space or time can be designated only by language. The designation or defining of space takes place through symbols. It is necessary to have boundaries, markers, units of measurement, direction, and distance in order to conceptualize space. According to Joyce Hertzler, "language makes it possible for men to control space, to use it, maintain contacts in it, and conduct all manner of enterprises across it" (1965, p. 54).

All animals, except humans, live only in the present. Humans can live simultaneously in the past, present, and future. Language enables us to do this; we can use the past accumulation of knowledge to accommodate the present, as well as to plan for the future. Language is an important tool in the accumulation of knowledge and in the transmission of culture across both space and time.

LANGUAGE AS A SOCIAL INSTITUTION

Any society that functions effectively must have an interrelated network of **social institutions;** they are the basis for the operation, regulation, and maintenance of society. The principal sectors of society—education,

religion, politics, economics, science, technology, communication—are all institutionalized.

A social institution has several characteristics or constituent parts (Hertzler, 1965, p. 70). First of all, a social institution has a group of rules or norms that governs the behavior of its members. Second, these rules are reflected in specific roles or forms of behavior followed by people in different social positions. Third, these rules are sanctioned by the society through its system of social rules or laws. Finally, conformity with the rules is aided by social organizations and procedures. The characteristics of social institutions are the bases of the social order and transmit as well as preserve the society's culture.

Although most institutions overlap and are thus functionally interrelated, none could exist without language. Language is one of the most important, if not the most important, social institution; it is a prerequisite for all other institutional development. There must be some initial and preliminary level of language development in order for other institutions to function properly. Also, they cannot be transmitted across time or space—or reorganized—without language.

Language is like other social institutions in that it has a set of uniform and universal symbols which become rules or norms. Language also helps to produce a standardized set of behavior. Unlike other institutions, however, language is perhaps more fixed and has less freedom. People are also unaware of how language regulates their lives and everyday activities; although members of most societies are constantly discussing rules associated with other social institutions, there is little, if any, criticism of language as a social institution.

Names as culture records

One fundamental function of any language is the process of naming. Names are durable records of the past and give us important insights into past cultural evolution.

One important naming function is the naming of places. **Toponymy,** the study of place names, provides important insights into a culture. One significant aspect of place names is that they can outline the historical evolution of a place. Early settlers in an area usually named important physical or environmental features after familiar features or objects from their area of origin. For example, the word *new* is frequently used in conjunction with place names, and such places as New York, New England, or New Orleans have names that reflect nostalgia for a place. Sometimes place names indicate reverence for great people associated with a cultural group, such as *Washington, Pittsburgh,* or *Bolivia*. Place names frequently indicate the onsite resources of a region *(Gold Hill, Coal Valley)* or notable animals or plants *(Goose Lake, Deer Park, Sunflower Valley)*. The American Indian heritage of the United States is reflected in place names; roughly half of the states in the United States have names derived from Indian names. Similarly, the southwestern United States is full of names indicative of the Spanish heritage, including *Los Angeles* and *Sierra Nevada*.

Changes in the political climate in an area can bring about changes in place names: *New Amsterdam* became *New York* and *St. Petersburg* became *Leningrad*. Place names have such an important role in American culture that the Department of the Interior has a special bureau to deal solely with them.

Personal or family names are another important aspect of the cultural record. In early cultures it was common for a person to be named after an animal *(Little Bear, Lone Eagle)*, and with the advent of the Christian faith, many people were given Biblical names. English surnames are generally derived from four places: after personal names *(Peterson, Williamson)*, after the name of the locality of one's ancestors *(Woods, Banks, Ford)*, after the occupation of an ancestor *(Cook, Weaver, Taylor)*, and after a physical or personality attribute of an ancestor *(Longfellow, Goodman)*. Tracing the evolution of family names may also point out another type of major social upheaval, conquest. As one culture invaded and conquered the territory of another a great influx of new family names usually occurred.

Demographic changes, particularly those associated with in-migration, can readily be seen in personal and family names. A quick glance through the telephone directory will help delineate the ethnic make-up of a community. If we could assemble a time series of telephone directories for a particular city, we could easily trace the influx of people from different ethnic backgrounds. A related aspect of this change would be the Americanization of foreign names, which also could be traced through a comparative analysis of telephone directories.

Black American speech patterns

The relationship between speech patterns and ethnicity or race has always been an emotionally charged issue. Because the dominant speech characteristics were those of the white population, Black speech patterns were frequently attributed to some inherent mental or physical characteristic. This racist view, although thoroughly discredited by linguists, is still held by a surprising number of Americans. Therefore, those who wanted to propagate a racist viewpoint insisted upon the inherent deficiency of Black people, whereas those who wanted to emphasize the potential of the Black population tried to minimize the differences between white and Black speech patterns.

In the past fifteen years considerable research has been done on the origin and development of the nonstandard English spoken by some segments of the Black population, called **Black English vernacular** or **BEV** (figure 7–2). There is still much controversy over whether a Black speech pattern exists. The term *Black English vernacular* (usually refers to the relatively uniform speech patterns of Black youth in most regions of the United States, particularly in urban areas, although many Blacks don't exhibit these speech characteristics and some whites do. Also, in the South there is a greater overlap of Blacks and whites, and any BEV characteristic can be found among almost all whites. In some aspects the regional speech patterns of the South are being diffused to northern cities and are now considered class or ethnic patterns.

What are the characteristics of Black speech patterns? Where did they come from? These are important questions, and definite answers have not been forthcoming. In a nutshell, BEV, or *Black dialect* as it is sometimes called, had its origin as an Africanized form of English developed out of the cultural milieu of Black Africans brought to the New World as slaves. Early slaves brought to America probably spoke a variety of African languages. They initially developed a **pidgin,** a language for communication with whites. As time passed this pidgin became a common language for slaves and eventually evolved into a **creole.** This language, which was never formally taught in schools, involved the substitution of English words for West African words, although the basic language pattern remained West African. In essence, slaves attempted to mix the sounds and words of English, their new language, into the basic speech patterns of their native tongue. The problem was compounded by the fact that the slaves had many different native tongues, and in order for slaves to communicate with each other, they spoke in this English-African language.

As new generations of slaves were born in the New World, the native African languages became extinct, and the English pidgin and creole varieties became more dominant. Unfortunately, we have only

FIGURE 7–2 (Courtesy of Morrie Turner.)

scanty records of the language changes that took place during this time. Thus, in the early periods of slavery Blacks relied heavily on their pidgin language, but as time passed many began to take on what Langston Hughes has called "the ways of white folks," including their culture, customs, religion, and, most importantly, their language.

However, some resistence by Blacks to many white cultural attributes, including language, remained. There was a "double consciousness," as W.E.B. DuBois called it, or a "push–pull" syndrome: on one hand Blacks were pushing toward white culture, yet on the other hand they tried to pull away from it.

> The dynamics of push–pull can help to illuminate the complex sociolinguistic situation that continues to exist in Black America. That is, while some blacks speak very Black English, there are others who speak very White English, and still others who are competent in both linguistic systems. Historically, black speech has been demanded of those who wish to retain close affinities with the black community . . . . On the other hand, White America has insisted upon White English as the price of admission into its economic and social mainstream. (Smitherman, 1977, p. 12)

In summary, the very survival of early Black Americans depended upon their ability to communicate with the white world (a *push*). Yet, on the other hand, the slavery and general oppression of Blacks associated with white English speakers created a desire for Blacks to have their own language (a *pull*). All languages change over time, and the Black English spoken two hundred years ago, like the white English of two hundred years ago, is very different today.

Origins of Black English. The words and concepts of Black English are primarily derived from four traditions: West African languages, servitude and oppression, music, and the traditional Black church (Smitherman, 1977, p. 43). Many common English words have a West African origin, including *tote, gorilla, el-*

ephant, banana, and *cola.* The oppression of Blacks contributed to their need to code or disguise English from whites. Slaves had to communicate in English and therefore devised ways to disguise the real meaning of their conversation. For example, although many Negro spirituals appeared to deal with other-worldly matters, they really had this-worldly meanings. The train in "this train is bound for Glory" was not an other-worldly train but referred to the "freedom train" of the Underground Railroad.

Music provides a third source for Black speech patterns. In his *Dictionary of Afro-American Slang,* Clarence Major identified music as the paramount influence. He argued that, "more than any other aspect of this experience the language of the black musician has had the greatest total effect on the informal language Americans speak" (Major, 1970, p. 27).

Because of the tremendous influence of the traditional Black church on Black culture, many semantic concepts and expressions have a religious base. The popular concept of "soul" came directly from the Black religious experience, as did the "sister, brother" forms of address. Whichever of the four traditions a particular phrase or word can be traced to, it is important to realize that Black semantics has a historical evolution that can be traced from early slave times to today.

An important aspect of Black American speech patterns is the dichotomy found within the Black community regarding what "proper" English should be. On the one hand are those who feel Black speech is just as functional as white speech in communicating meanings; others, however, feel people should use "correct English." This push–pull dichotomy is illustrated below in the dialogue between Jesse B. Simple and his girlfriend, Joyce, in Langston Hughes's play *Simply Heavenly.**

---

*Langston Hughes, "Simply Heavenly," in *Five Plays,* ed. by Webster Smalley. Bloomington: Indiana University Press, 1963, 143–145.

Simple:	What're you doing with all those timetables and travel books, baby?
Joyce:	Just in case we ever should get married, maybe I'm picking out a place to spend our honeymoon—Niagara Falls, the Grand Canyon, Plymouth Rock . . .
Simple:	I don't want to spend no honeymoon on no rock. These books is pretty, but baby, we ain't ready to travel yet.
Joyce:	We can dream, can't we?
Simple:	Niagara Falls makes a might lot of noise falling down. I likes to sleep on holidays.
Joyce:	Oh, Jess! Then how about the far West? Were you ever at the Grand Canyon?
Simple:	I were. Fact is, I was also at Niagara Falls, after I were at Grand Canyon.
Joyce:	I do not wish to criticize your grammar, Mr. Simple, but as long as you have been around New York, I wonder why you continue to say, I were, and at other times, I was?
Simple:	Because sometimes I were, and sometimes I was, baby. I was at Niagara Falls and I were at the Grand Canyon—since that were in the far distant past when I were a coachboy on the Santa Fe. I was more recently at Niagara Falls.
Joyce:	I see. But you never were "I were."! There is no "were." In the past tense, there is only "I was." The verb to be is declined, "I am, I was, I have been."
Simple:	Joyce, baby, don't be so touchous about it. Do you want me to talk like Edward R. Murrow?

Joyce: No! But when we go to formals I hate to hear you saying, for example, "I taken" instead of "I took." Why do colored people say, "I taken," so much?

Simple: Because we are taken—taken until we are undertaken, and, Joyce, baby, funerals is high!

Joyce: Funerals *are* high.

Simple: Joyce, what difference do it make?

Joyce: Jess! What difference *does* it make? Does is correct English.

Simple: And do ain't?

Joyce: Isn't—not ain't.

Simple: Woman, don't tell me ain't ain't in the dictionary.

Joyce: But it ain't—I mean—it isn't correct.

Simple: Joyce, I gives less than a small damn! What if it aren't?

Baby, you ain't mad with me, is you? Because I know you know what I mean when I say, "I is"—or "I are" or "was" or whatever it be. Listen, Joyce, honey please. (He sings)

When I say "I were" believe me.
When I say "I was" believe me, too—
Because I were, and was, and I *am*
Deep in love with you.

If I say "You took" or "taken,"
Just believe I have been taken, too,
Because I were, and am, and I *is*
Taken by you.

If it *is* or it *ain't* well stated,
And it *ain't* or it *aren't* said right,
My love still must be rated
A love that don't fade over night.

When I say "I am" believe me.
When I say "I is" believe me, too—
Because I were, and was, and I *is*
Deep in love with you.

Damn if I ain't!

Joyce: A small damn?

Joyce's and Simple's two distinctly different attitudes reflect the ongoing push–pull dynamic in the historical evolution of Black Americans. The attitudes they symbolize can not only be found in Black Americans as a group but can also be found in most Black individuals.

DISTRIBUTION OF LANGUAGES

Many factors are related to the current distribution of various languages. The separation and distinction of languages is a function of both cultural and physical environmental factors. Groups of people separated or isolated by rivers, forests, deserts, or mountains generally have developed different languages. If separate and distinct languages have not evolved under these circumstances, then **regional dialects** usually develop.

A relatively uniform language that has developed in a particular region is referred to as a **standard language.** It is an institutionalized language with a uniform vocabulary, syntax, pronunciation, and meaning. It is not necessarily a superior speech pattern, and it

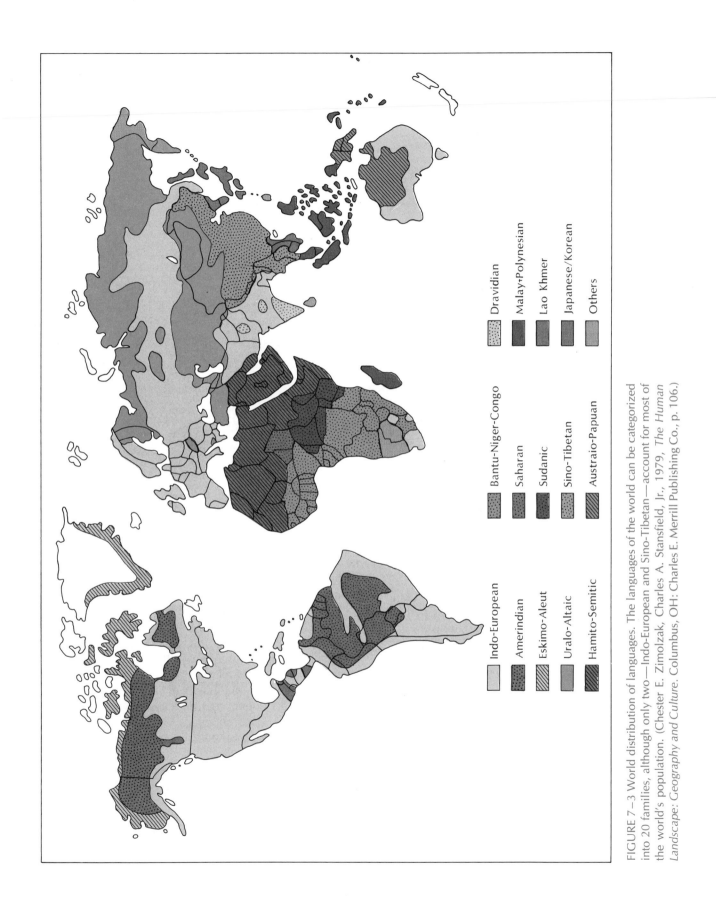

FIGURE 7–3 World distribution of languages. The languages of the world can be categorized into 20 families, although only two—Indo-European and Sino-Tibetan—account for most of the world's population. (Chester E. Zimolzak, Charles A. Stansfield, Jr., 1979, *The Human Landscape: Geography and Culture.* Columbus, OH: Charles E. Merrill Publishing Co., p. 106.)

Indo-European

Amerindian

Eskimo-Aleut

Uralo-Altaic

Hamito-Semitic

Bantu-Niger-Congo

Saharan

Sudanic

Sino-Tibetan

Austraio-Papuan

Dravidian

Malay-Polynesian

Lao Khmer

Japanese/Korean

Others

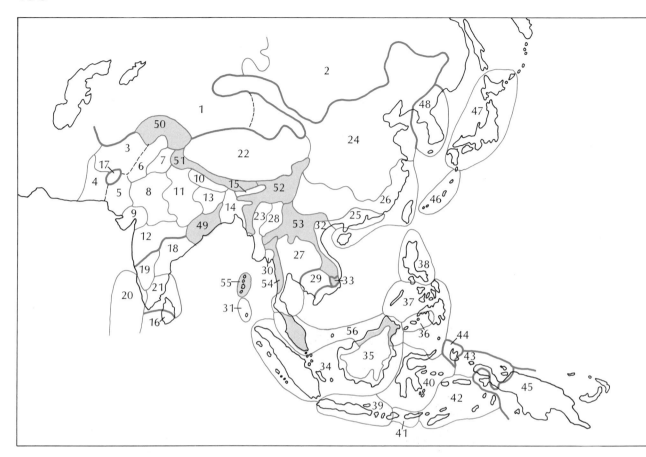

FIGURE 7−4 Major Asian languages; see legend at right. (J. E. Spencer, William Thomas, *Asia, East by South,* 2nd ed. Copyright © 1971 by John Wiley & Sons, Inc., p. 22. Reprinted by permission of John Wiley & Sons, Inc.)

probably evolved from a favored dialect; perhaps it was once the language of an elite and powerful class. The rules for the standard language are taught to foreigners, and the language is generally set out in dictionaries and textbooks. Standard languages, as all others, are constantly changing.

Linguists and linguistic geographers estimate that there are anywhere from 2500 to 4000 separate and distinct languages, not including dialects. Over 1000 languages have been identified for the Indians of the Western Hemisphere, although most are only spoken by a few hundred to a few thousand people. Africa alone presently has over 800 distinct languages. We are not sure of the exact number of languages for several reasons. First, we have limited information about many isolated areas of the world, and information concerning language patterns in these areas is either scanty or nonexistent. Second, it is sometimes difficult to distinguish between separate languages and different dialects of the same language. Third, it is difficult to accurately define the boundaries of language areas; language regions do not always coincide with political boundaries. For example, four distinct languages are spoken in Switzerland, a closely knit political entity. Finally, languages are constantly changing, adding to the difficulty of definition.

Although a multiplicity of languages exist, from a political, economic, and military viewpoint probably fewer than 100 are important. Of these perhaps 13 can be considered major languages (figure 7−3). Most have from 50 to 800 million speakers, whereas others have far less than one million speakers. The 12 languages with over 50 million speakers, in order of importance relative to speakers and usage, are English, Chinese, the languages of India, Russian, Spanish, Malay and Indonesian languages, German, Japanese, Arabic, Portuguese, French, and Italian.

Altaic family
Turkish branch
    1. Turkish languages
Mongol branch
    2. Mongol languages

Indo-European family
Iranian branch
    3. Pashto (Afghan)
    4. Balushi
Indo-Aryan branch
    5. Sindhi
    6. Lahnda
    7. Punjabi
    8. Rajasthani
    9. Gujarati
    10. Nepalese (Gurkha)
    11. Hindustani (Hindi)
    12. Marathi
    13. Bihari
    14. Bengali
    15. Assamese
    16. Singhalese
Dardic branch, to which belong Persian and other languages spoken north and west of Persia

Dravidian family
    17. Brahui
    18. Telegu
    19. Kanarese
    20. Malayalam
    21. Tamil

Sino-Tibetan family
Tibeto-Burman branch
    22. Tibetan
    23. Burmese
Sino-Siamese branch

24. "Peking" Chinese
    (Northern Mandarin)
25. "Canton" Chinese (Cantonese)
26. Mixed Chinese languages
27. Tai
28. Shan

Austro-Asiatic family (relations very unclear)
Mon-Khmer branch
    29. Khmer (Cambodian, etc.)
    30. Mon
    31. Nicobarese
    32. Vietnamese branch (relationship debatable)
Remnant languages
Several languages belong here, but they no longer dominate regions and are not shown on the map. Many are not yet adequately studied and classified.

Austronesian family
Indonesian branch (Malay)
    33. Cham
    34. Sumatran Malay
    35. Bornea "Dyak"
    36. Mindanao "Moro"
    37. Visayan
    38. Tagalog, Ilocano, Bicol, and others
    39. Javanese
    40. Celebes
    41. Soemba
    42. Timor-Ceram
    43. West New Guinea

Papuan family (poorly studied; relations unclear)
    44. Halmahera
    45. New Guinea

Composite languages (mixed linguistic patterns)
    46. Ryukyu (Indo-European, Sino-Tibetan, and Austronesian families?)
    47. Japanese (Indo-European, Sino-Tibetan, and Austronesian families?)
    48. Korean (Altaic, Indo-European, Sino-Tibetan, Austronesian, and ? familes)

Regions of multiple languages
    49. Munda—Oriya—Kurukh (Austro-Asiatic, Indo-European, and Dravidian families)
    50. Turkish—Tibetan—Dardic (Altaic, Indo-European, and Sino-Tibetan families)
    51. Indo-European and Sino-Tibetan mixtures.
    52. Chinese—Tibetan—Tai—Mon—Khmer—tribal (Sino-Tibetan family)
    53. Chinese—Vietnamese—Tai—Shan—Karen—Remnant languages of Austro-Asiatic family
    54. Burmese—Karen—Mon—Tai
    55. Andamanese—Burmese—Indo-European and Dravidian families
    56. Malay—Chinese—"Indian"

Metropolitan city areas and other local areas of the Orient possess highly mixed language patterns in such small areas that they cannot be shown on a map.

The distribution of these languages varies widely. In some instances, like Spanish and Portuguese, the number of speakers found in the homeland of the language is exceeded by the number of speakers in former colonies. In other cases, like Russian, the language is primarily restricted to one area.

English is the most widely used of all contemporary languages; as a native or colonial language it covers over one-fifth of the earth's land area. It is a second language for many people and is quite readily understood by many more. Furthermore, it is the leading commercial and scientific–technical language of the world; more material has been printed in English than in any other language.

The North Mandarin dialect, the national tongue of the People's Republic of China, is spoken by approximately two-thirds of the Chinese population; the remainder speak one of the nine major dialects or one of the many minor dialects. Next to the North Mandarin dialect, Cantonese ranks second in number of speakers, most of whom live in southern China. It is the dialect most frequently spoken by Chinese in the United States. Most Chinese-speaking people are confined within the boundaries of China.

The languages of India include many separate, distinct languages, as well as dialects (figure 7–4). The 1951 Indian census estimated 845 languages and dialects. The official language of India, spoken by the largest number of Indians, is Hindi; the second leading language is Bengali. Although there are over 200 separate languages spoken in India, more than 90 percent of the population indicated that their mother tongue was one of the 15 primary languages.

Russian is spoken in an area that covers one-sixth of the earth's land surface. Although it is the binding tongue of the Soviet Union, it is the native language of only approximately 65 percent of the population; therefore, it is a second language for many Soviets. Those who don't speak Russian as their native tongue speak one or more of 145 different languages, including the Georgian of Stalin, Ukranian of southern Russia, or a variety of Turkic languages. Russian is becoming increasingly more important as a scientific–technical language.

Only one-fourth of the world's Spanish-speaking people live in Spain. The remaining three-fourths are found in Latin America.

The Malay or Indonesian family of languages are spoken throughout Southeast Asia. They consist of approximately 200 different languages, with Japanese and Malay being the leading tongues.

The Japanese language is primarily concentrated in the Japanese archipelago, though smaller numbers of speakers can be found in Korea and the nearby areas of the Asiatic continent. Arabic is spoken throughout the Muslim area of the Middle East, including northern Africa. Portuguese is of course the mother tongue of Portugual, but the largest number of speakers are found in Brazil, where it is the official language. It is also spoken in former Portuguese colonies in Africa, Asia, and the Pacific.

German is another leading language, and it is primarily restricted to Germany, Austria, and Switzerland. German speakers are also found in the nations of central and eastern Europe, as well as in the lands of German immigration, including the United States, Brazil, Chile, Uruguay, and Argentina.

The final major languages are French and Italian. French is almost as widespread throughout the world as English, although there are far fewer speakers. Besides being the language of France, it is also one of the official languages of Switzerland, Canada and Belgium, and it is spoken by many educated people throughout Europe. It is the official language of both Haiti and Guadelupe in the Western Hemisphere, and is also a widely read cultural language. Italian, besides being the mother tongue of Italy, is spoken in the former Italian colonies and is used by many emigrant groups of Italian origin in the Western Hemisphere.

It is important to note that the distribution patterns of languages, as previously outlined, is only an approximation. Because of the intermixing of languages and dialects, as well as the problems of definition, it is difficult to determine exact speech patterns for the entire world.

Bilingualism

For most Americans there is little probability of being fluent in more than one language, so we usually think of most people as speaking only one language. However, it is essential for many people in the world to speak more than one language. This is true for most people in Europe, Asia, Africa, and Latin America. We need only look north to Canada to see the importance of speaking two languages. Of course, in some parts of the United States people commonly speak two languages. The Puerto Rican ghettos of New York City and areas with high concentrations of Mexican-Americans in the southwestern United States are examples of the importance of *bilingualism* in America. We can also look at many American Indians as having at least two languages. In the past, due to large numbers of immigrants entering the country, being fluent in more than one language was not uncommon.

There is some controversy among linguists as the exact nature of bilingualism. It means having the ability to use two different languages, but some argue that it means having equal ability, whereas others believe bilinguals are generally more competent in one language than the other. Most bilinguals, however, belong primarily to one speech community and have only a partial facility with the second language. For many, bilingualism means having a primary language along with a secondary language, which is considered a *lingua franca,* one used among people of different tongues as a language of communication. For example, English is a *lingua franca* for many people in India and is used by Indians as a language for trade and commerce. English is also a *lingua franca* for some ethnic groups in the United States, although the native tongue is commonly spoken at home.

KEY TERMS

Evolution
Linguists
Transformism
Creationism
Sociocultural
Social institutions
Toponymy

Black English vernacular (BEV)
Pidgin
Creole
Regional dialect
Standard language
Bilingualism
Lingua franca

REFERENCES

Bloomfield, L. (1933), *Language*. New York: Henry Holt & Co.

Cherry, C. (1957), *On Human Communication: A Review, A Survey, and A Criticism*. New York: John Wiley & Sons, Inc., with Technological Press of Massachusetts Institute of Technology.

Hertzler, J. (1965), *A Sociology of Language*. New York: Random House, Inc.

Hughes, L. (1968), "Simple Heavenly," in Smalley, W. (ed.), *Five Plays*. Bloomington, IN: Indiana University Press.

Major, C. (1970), *Dictionary of Afro-American Slang*. New York: International Publishers Co., Inc.

Pei, M. (1965), *The Story of Language*. New York: J. B. Lippincott Co.

Smitherman, G. (1977), *Talkin and Testifyin: The Language of Black America*. Boston: Houghton Mifflin Co.

Wagner, P. L. (1958), "Remarks on the Geography of Language," *Geographical Review* 48, 86–97.

8

Politics and nation-states

Political geography has long been considered an essential part of human geography. It is perhaps the most *human* aspect of geography because it is concerned with the weaknesses, strengths, and ambitions of people. These human characteristics are reflected in the way people organize the earth's surface into political units.

This chapter is concerned with the political organization of the earth's surface. The first section deals with how political territory is organized and the nature of the processes that keep political units together. The second section discusses the evolution of the concepts of boundary and frontier and applies these concepts to the modern world. The final section analyzes the history of the colonization process, as well as modern day neo-colonialism. The chapter ends with a discussion of supranationalism and its role in solving international problems, specifically the problem of environmental degradation.

THE NATION-STATE

All states have a territorial base; that is, they are politically organized areas with a spatial identity and a population. The physical limits of this territorial base are defined by political boundaries, and when crossing a boundary, one has entered a state. A *state* also has several other attributes. Whatever the form of its government, the state claims **internal sovereignty,** defined by C. F. Strong as "the supremacy of a person or body of persons in the state over the individual or association

of individuals within the area of its jurisdiction" (1966, p. 7). The state also claims sovereignty in international relations; state governments reserve the right to make treaties and other agreements with other states.

In everyday conversations we often emphasize different characteristics of states. For example, we emphasize the spatial or territorial aspect of a state when we talk about crossing a boundary line or border; yet when we talk about paying taxes to "the state," we are emphasizing its governmental aspect.

The term *state* is often used interchangeably with **nation.** In a strict geopolitical sense, however, these two terms are not interchangeable. A "nation" does not necessarily have a territorial base, but it always has a social or cultural base. There is a sense of social cohesion and a complex of social attitudes and ideas that distinguish one nation from others, and some states are inhabited by two or more nations; Cyprus, with its distinct Turkish and Greek nations, is a good example. A state that is a stable political structure usually corresponds closely with a nation and is actually the political expression of the nation.

The term **nation-state** is used to distinguish states, such as Japan and Denmark, with populations of a common language and tradition. Few modern states, based on this definition, would qualify as nation-states. However, most states are striving to attain common characteristics by minimizing their cultural differences and maximizing interaction between diverse groups. Most states have this common objective, although they often differ in the means employed to achieve it. Political geographer Richard Hartshorne emphasized the importance of national cohesion for the successful integration of a nation-state.

> Any state, to become well established, must present to the populations of its areal parts a distinct *raison d'être*, its justification for existence as an areal unit separate from the neighboring state-areas . . . . The problem is to construct a *raison d'être* that will enlist the loyalty of regional groups having different associations and ideals. (1940)

Centrifugal and centripetal forces

The cohesive nature of a state is a function of the forces that tend to disrupt cohesion counterbalanced by the forces that pull a state together and strengthen it. The disruptive or weakening forces, called **centrifugal forces,** can result from either the physical or cultural characteristics of the state. The physical attributes of a state—size, shape, and topography—can be divisive by, for example, hindering transportation and communication. Perhaps even more divisive are the cultural factors, such as religion and language; for example, the French language, spoken primarily in Quebec, has become a centrifugal force in Canada. Minority groups within a state, particularly those powerful and organized like tribal groups, can cause tremendous internal stresses. Tribalism may well be the most divisive of the cultural centrifugal forces; when people in a state feel a greater loyalty to a tribe than to the state, problems can ensue, such as the tribal conflict during the Biafran War in Nigeria in the mid-1960s. Intertribal conflict can virtually destroy a state.

Centripetal forces counteract the centrifugal forces and tend to unify a state. No state will last long if the centripetal forces are weaker than the centrifugal forces. There must therefore be strong centripetal forces that bind together a state, and the principal centripetal force, as outlined earlier by Hartshorne, is the unifying idea or *raison d'etre,* the reason for existing.

Morphology: Size and shape

The boundaries of a state give it a specific size and shape, which have important consequences in its political and administrative organization. Currently there are approximately 146 sovereign states, which range in size from the Soviet Union with 22,402,200 square kilometers (8.5 million square miles) to the Vatican City, less than one quarter of a square mile. Thus, the largest

state is approximately two million times larger than the smallest state, with the average size being 1,040,000 square kilometers. Approximately one-half of the states are between 25,000 and 250,000 square kilometers (figure 8–1).

Another aspect of the size of a state is the number of people under its jurisdiction and the density of this population. A large land area like Antarctica cannot be considered a state because it lacks a permanent resident population. Population size and density have important military and strategic ramifications. For example, states with large populations can amass large numbers of soldiers and, barring nuclear warfare, gain advantages because of the sheer weight of numbers. Population size has other advantages, particularly in the industrial organization of a state. In a study dealing with the economic consequences of the size of nations, E. A. G. Robinson stated:

> There are certain industries or groups of industries which are ordinarily found in larger countries and not found in smaller countries . . . . The dividing line seems ordinarily to come between 10 and 15 million of population, though it is not difficult to find exceptions. (1960, p. xvii)

Several states, small in both area and population, have reached a high stage of economic development. Switzerland and Denmark are obvious examples. In some instances smallness has its advantages; smaller states may have more homogeneous populations and closer internal ties, which often facilitate the social decisions necessary to attain more rapid economic growth.

Another important aspect of a state is its shape. According to most political geographers, the ideal shape of a state is a circle. A circular state, with an evenly distributed population and a capital city in the center, would have all parts equally accessible, assuming some uniform transport system. Any deviation from circularity presents certain problems.

The political geographer Harm de Blij divided states into five different categories (figure 8–2). He defined the **elongated** or **attenuated state** as a state that is at least six times as long as its average width. Included in this category would be the states of Chile, Norway, Sweden, Italy, Panama, Gambia, Togo, and Malawi. Elongation has both advantages and disadvantages. On the one hand an elongated state may be part of several climatic and physiographic regions, thus giving it a physical diversity that might be useful for economic reasons. On the other hand an elongated state

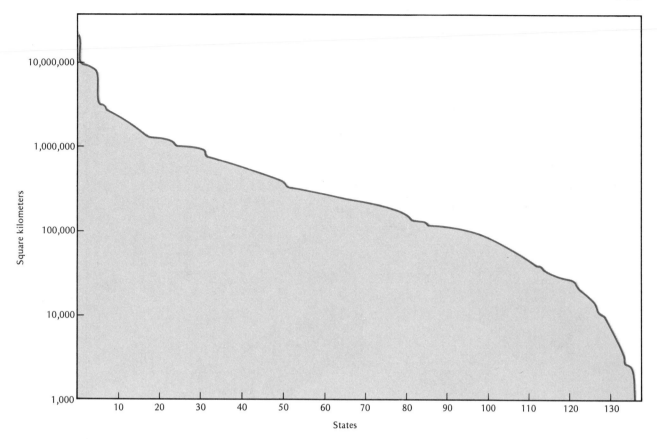

FIGURE 8–1 Areas of states. (Norman J. G. Pounds, 1972, *Political Geography,* 2nd ed. New York, McGraw-Hill Book Co., p. 34.)

may, because of distance, have transportation and communication problems.

The compact form is the most efficient form for a state. Because all boundary areas of a **compact state** are theoretically the same distance from the center, certain advantages accrue. One obvious advantage is that, because the boundary of a compact state is the shortest possible in regard to the area enclosed, military defense of this boundary is easier. Because the compact state has no peninsulas or other protruding appendages, communication and transportation should be more efficient, which in turn makes it easier to administer and control. These advantages, however, do not pertain to a compact state that has many physiographic divisions or one that may have its capital city or core area located on the periphery.

The **prorupt state** is similar to the compact state, but it has an extension of its territory in the form of a corridor or peninsula leading away from the compact portion of the state. These states often face the same

internal problems of communication and transportation that are found in the elongated state. Unfortunately, added problems arise because many times the extension or proruption is very important for political, strategic, or economic reasons.

The **fragmented** or **divided state,** consisting of two or more individual parts separated by land or international water, has many obvious problems. One requirement for the smooth functioning of a state is for that state to have an uninterrupted territory; the internal cohesion of a state is strained and governmental control can be made ineffective if large distances separate fragments of the state. In the past, the classic example of a fragmented state was Pakistan with its east and west segments. However, it was exactly this fragmentation that led to the evolution of the state of Bangladesh and the dissolution of the former fragmented state of Pakistan. Furthermore, the selection of a capital city can exacerbate the problems of fragmentation. Deciding which fragment will contain the capital city and administrative center can lead to considerable friction and long-lasting jealousies which may jeopardize political and economic stability.

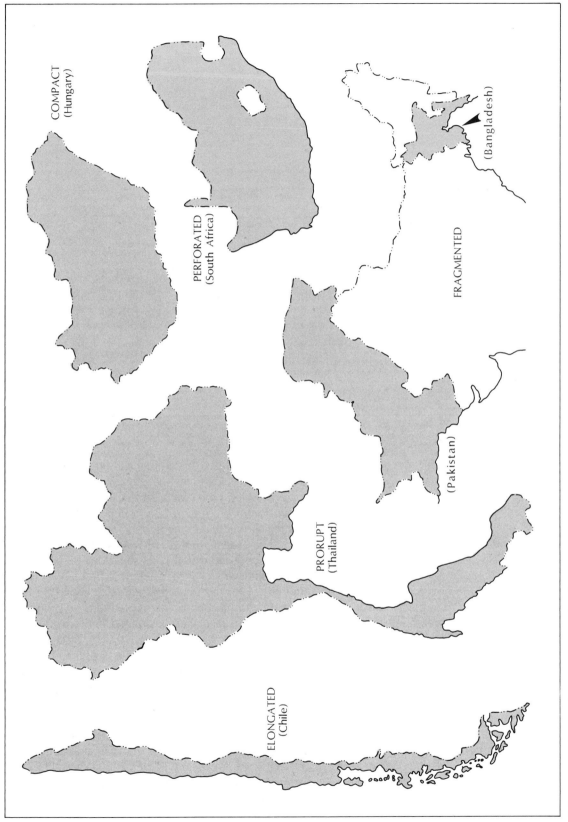

COMPACT
(Hungary)

PERFORATED
(South Africa)

FRAGMENTED

(Bangladesh)

(Pakistan)

PRORUPT
(Thailand)

ELONGATED
(Chile)

FIGURE 8–2 Shapes of states. (Harm J. de Blij, *Systematic Political Geography*. Copyright © 1967 by John Wiley & Sons, Inc., p. 43. Reprinted by permission of John Wiley & Sons, Inc.)

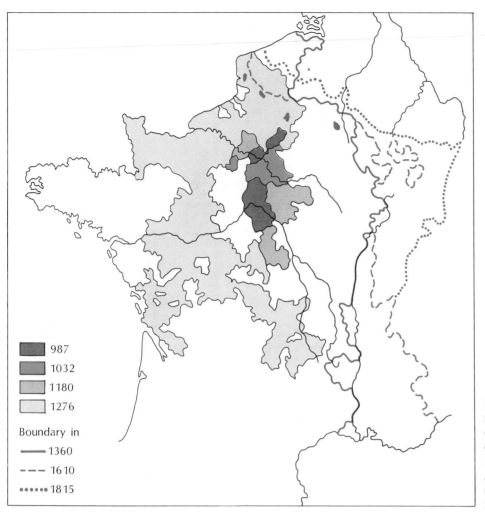

987
1032
1180
1276

Boundary in
——— 1360
– – – 1610
•••••• 1815

FIGURE 8–3 Territorial expansion of royal authority from the core area of France. (Reproduced by permission from the *Annals* of the Association of American Geographers, Volume 54, 1964, N. J. G. Pounds, S. S. Ball.)

Some states are completely surrounded by the territory of another state. Such political entities are called **perforated states,** and access is one of their obvious problems: the only way to reach them is to cross the territory, either land or air space, of another state. The state that surrounds the perforated state can have considerable control over it.

Not all states fit into one of de Blij's shape categories. Some states have more than one shape characteristic, although usually one characteristic is predominant. For example, Italy and Chile are elongated states, but they are also fragmented because some of their islands are outside their territorial waters. In both cases, however, the elongation aspect is much more critical to their social and political functions. Similarly, France could be considered a compact state, even though it has a fragmented aspect associated with the island of Corsica. However, the compact nature of

France has played a much more important role in its evolution and survival than has the existence of the island of Corsica.

Core areas and capital cities

The development of a state is a slow evolutionary process that usually grows out of a *core area.* The core area has been defined by Derwent Whittlesey as "the area in which or about which a state originates" (1939, p. 597). It is a basic element of the state system and usually includes that part of the state which has the highest population density, the most developed transportation and communication system, and the highest degree of urbanization. Furthermore, it is probably more richly endowed with natural resources than other areas of the state. In most instances the capital city is also located in the core area, thus the administrative

Brasilia, Brazil. This sculpture in the modern capital was inaugurated on April 21, 1960. (United Nations/J. Frank, 1975)

and political aspects of a state are usually controlled from there.

Although the attributes of a core area can be outlined, they are difficult to operationally define. It is easy to understand the relationship of population density to the core area, but a dense population for one state may not be for another. Likewise, the development of a transport and communication system will vary depending upon the general level of economic development. A good transport system for a state like Bolivia may not be a good system for France. We must, therefore, look at the total economic and social system within a given state in order to define its core area.

In most states the location of the core area has remained constant and its domain has expanded from this nucleus through the process of accretion, as illustrated by the classic case of the state of France. From Roman times onward, settlement in France was centered around the Paris basin (figure 8–3), and the outlying provinces were tied closely to the Paris region. Today France is still a highly centralized state, though it has adopted a policy designed to discourage concentration in the Paris basin.

Although most states have developed around a single core area, some have evolved from more than one nucleus. In some cases multiple core areas came

from differing cultural traditions, but in others there were no conflicting cultural groups. Examples of the latter include the several coastal core areas of Brazil and Australia which, despite a certain amount of rivalry, have evolved from essentially the same cultural tradition. An example of the former is Canada, which developed two distinctly different core areas, the English province of Ontario and the French province of Quebec, based on differing cultural traditions. Even in states with a relatively uniform cultural tradition, friction can occur between the core area and the surrounding regions. Many people outside the core area may resent the power held there and, conversely, those who live in the core area may develop a patronizing attitude toward those outside its boundaries.

Like core areas, **capital cities** have evolved and changed over time. Ordinarily the capital city is both a part and a reflection of the core area. They are frequently sources of national pride and objects of considerable monetary investment. Some states have put large amounts of money into the development of a new capital, as was the case of Brasilia, which was built primarily to draw people to the interior of Brazil.

A capital city serves several important functions. Primarily it is the cultural center of the state and binds the state together. It is the home of the chief of state

Tokyo, Japan. The appearance of this metropolis is constantly changing. (Embassy of Japan, 1976)

and the seat of government, and operates as the "control center." A capital city is usually an international city with foreign embassies and the headquarters of foreign business concerns, as well as the headquarters of many national firms or organizations. Many religious "seats of power," from a national standpoint, are also located in the capital city. The boundaries for many Christian ecclesiastical jurisdictions are the same as the political boundaries for the state, and therefore, the seat of religious power is also in the capital city.

Capital cities have been classified according to several schemes, but perhaps the most widely used scheme is the morphological one developed by Harm de Blij, who grouped capital cities into three categories: permanent capitals, introduced capitals, and divided capitals (1967, p. 411). Permanent capitals are those which have evolved over an extended time period and currently are political, cultural, and economic centers; examples include Rome, Paris, London, Athens, To-

kyo, and Mexico City. The introduced capital is one replacing a former capital to perform new and different functions, including the desire of a state to focus attention upon certain places or problem areas. Building a new capital is thus a mechanism to accomplish such tasks. Capital cities included in this category would be Canberra, Brasilia, Washington, Lagos, Islamabad, and Madrid. The final type is the divided capital in which the functions of the capital city are shared by two urban areas. One example is the Netherlands, where the titular capital and residence of the monarch is in Amsterdam, but the legislative center is located in The Hague. A similar situation occurs in Bolivia, where the legal capital and seat of the judicial system is in Sucre, but the much larger city of La Paz is the home of the legislature and all governmental offices.

FRONTIERS AND BOUNDARIES

For a long time geographers have been concerned with the definition and evolution of frontiers and bounda-

Canberra, Australia. The site for the new Parliament House on Capital Hill. (Australian Information Service, 1979)

ries. At the present time the **boundary** *line* is an agreed upon demarcation line marking the limits of the jurisdictions of two different political authorities. Although a boundary appears as a thin line on a map, it is actually formed by the intersection of a vertical plane with the earth's surface (figure 8–4). This plane extends deep below the surface and is an important aspect in determining who owns subsurface ore deposits; it also extends into the air and is therefore an important factor in determining a country's airspace.

Unlike the boundary line, the **frontier** is a *zone,* and in many cases a boundary line may be drawn within a frontier zone. The frontier frequently preceeds the actual demarcation of a boundary line. There are two principal types of frontiers: *settlement frontiers* separate the developed and less developed areas with-

in a single political jurisdiction, whereas *political frontiers* separate individual political jurisdictions or states.

Political geographers have had problems distinguishing between frontiers and boundaries. However, some common differences have been agreed upon. First, the frontier is *outer-oriented,* meaning that its principal focus is directed toward outlying areas. Frontier regions of nation-states often develop interests quite different from those of their central governments. The boundary, however, is *inner-oriented* and is created and maintained by a central government. Second, the frontier acts as an integrating force and as a zone of transition between different social, economic, or political groups. On the other hand, a boundary acts as a separating factor impeding the contact between peoples. A boundary line is a fixed obstacle that keeps people apart rather than bringing them together. According to political geographer J. R. V. Prescott, there are two aspects of boundary and frontier studies of interest to geographers:

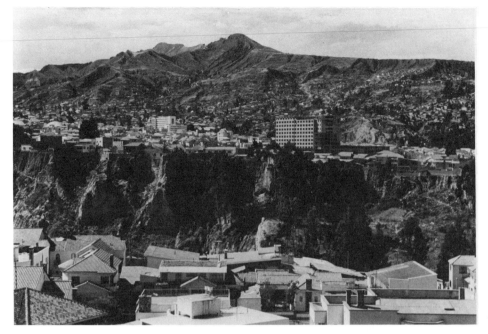

La Paz, Bolivia. (United Nations/Rothstein, 1973)

First, the position and character of any boundary or frontier is the result of the interaction of many factors, some of which are geographical and best studied by geographers. Second, once any boundary or frontier is established it is capable of influencing the landscape of which it is a part and the development and policies of the separated states. (1967, pp. 25–29)

The concept of a boundary has changed over time, and these changes are a function of what Stephen B. Jones has called "their geographical and historical milieu" (1959, p. 241). With increasing populations and more elaborate political systems, it became essential to establish more precise boundaries. In early tribal societies the exact demarcation of a boundary line was unnecessary. The area between tribes, generally called a *no-man's land,* was a zone or frontier region claimed by neither tribe, but through which people from each tribe would occasionally pass. Although many tribal societies were separated by such zones, there is evidence that some tribes had achieved a high degree of precision in establishing boundaries.

The Chinese and Roman empires had more sophisticated ideas about boundaries than did earlier tribal societies. Although China did not have formal international boundaries until modern times, early Chinese civilizations did conceive the idea of precise limits to their civilization. The Great Wall of China, which stretches across northern China for over 1500 miles, is dramatic evidence that early Chinese cultures

thought of separating what was Chinese from what was not. Similarly the Romans were also cognizant of geographic limits to their empire. They established a European boundary along the line of the Rhine and Danube rivers, which was supplemented in places with banks and walls.

Although ancient concepts of boundaries and sovereignty in China and Rome were similar to present day notions, the advent of the Middle Ages and the associated feudal societies brought about a change. The sovereignty of people over territory was replaced by the sovereignty of people over people. Thus, in the feudal system kings were not interested in establishing boundaries but with their authority over people. One well-known feature of the political geography of medieval Europe was that feudalism produced a patchwork political map (figure 8–5) resulting in the decentralized nature of feudal society. The development of the nation-state, however, brought about the demise of the patchwork feudal system.

Stages of boundary evolution

A new boundary under most conditions is determined through a series of stages. The first stage is an ***allocation*** process—a general agreement between two or more political entities on the division of a specific territory. It involves a general description of the core areas of the political entities and an attempt to roughly de-

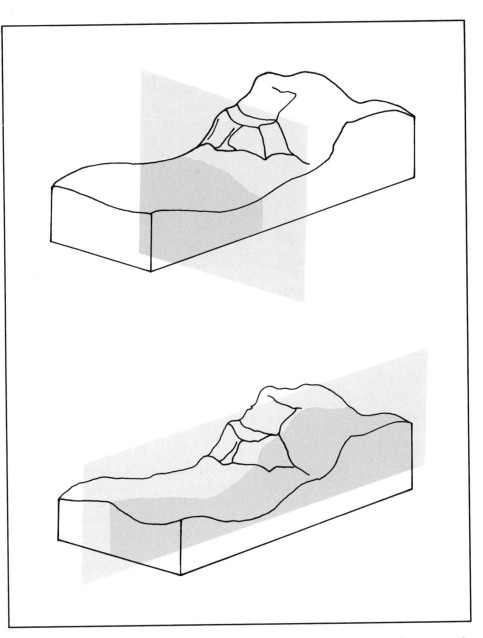

FIGURE 8–4 Boundary line between surface and air.

cide a dividing line in the ill-defined region between core areas. Usually this dividing line, or boundary line, is an arbitrarily selected parallel of latitude or meridian of longitude, though it can be a line connecting certain prominent physical features like mountain peaks. In many cases it is difficult to exactly delineate the boundary on the ground.

The second stage in the evolution of boundaries is the *delimitation* process. In some cases the delimitation of an area or boundary follows closely behind the allocation process, though sometimes it may not occur for some time. The length of time usually de-

pends upon the number of inhabitants or the economic worth of the region. Delimitation involves the actual definition of a boundary in a treaty or agreement.

Demarcation is the final stage in the evolution of boundaries and involves the precise marking of the boundary on the ground with walls, concrete pillars, fences or other physical features.

Boundary classification systems

Several schemes have been proposed for the classification of boundaries. One of these schemes, devel-

The Pataling section of the Great Wall of China. Pataling is the outpost of Chuyungkuan. (United Nations/T. Chen, 1974)

oped by Richard Hartshorne and called a *genetic classification,* involved relating the origin of a boundary to the cultural landscape through which the boundary is drawn. This system includes boundaries that were determined before any settlement took place in an area, those drawn during the settlement and cultural evolution of an area, and those determined after settlement and cultural development had occurred. Boundaries that were allocated and delimited before significant settlement in an area are called *antecedent boundaries.* In most cases these were determined at a time when the area was of little economic consequence and had few settlements. A good example of an antecedent boundary is that between the United States and Canada, west of the Great Lakes (figure 8–6). This boundary was allocated and delimited at a time when, except for trappers and Indians, few people inhabited the area. A boundary that was drawn in an area that was completely uninhabited is referred to as a *pioneer boundary,* and is a form of antecedent boundary.

A second type, called a *subsequent boundary,* was used to define a boundary that was made during the settlement and cultural evolution of a region. These boundaries conform to the cultural divisions of an area and generally separate peoples of different religious, linguistic, or ethnic origins. Several boundaries in Europe fall into this category, as does the religiously determined India–Pakistan border (figure 8–6).

Superimposed boundaries are a third category and include boundaries established after the cultural development of an area but do not conform to ethnic or cultural characteristics. In some cases these boundaries are unrelated to the cultural milieu and are the result of arbitrary decisions made by distant powers who waged war in an area (figure 8–6). Colonial powers were noted for drawing boundary lines irrespective of cultural similarities or differences. *Truce lines* are another form of superimposed boundaries. The boundary between Belgium and the Netherlands is such a truce line, as is the boundary between North and South Korea.

A boundary that has been abandoned for political purposes is another type of boundary and is referred to as a *relic boundary.* Although these boundaries no longer have political significance and do not appear on maps, they still, in some areas, are recognizable on the landscape (figure 8–6). They can sometimes be traced by looking at changes in field patterns, as with the former Polish–German boundary, or the architectural style of homes and public buildings, as in the industrial region of Upper Silesia and the former Russo-German border.

A second type of general boundary classification scheme is referred to as a *morphological classification.* This system is based upon conspicuous physical features of the landscape. A quick glance at any political map of the world will point out that many boundaries are not straight geometrical lines but follow a zigzag pattern; this pattern is usually related to a physical feature like a mountain range or a river. Although these physical features seem easy to delimit on a map, their actual demarcation on the ground is often quite diffi-

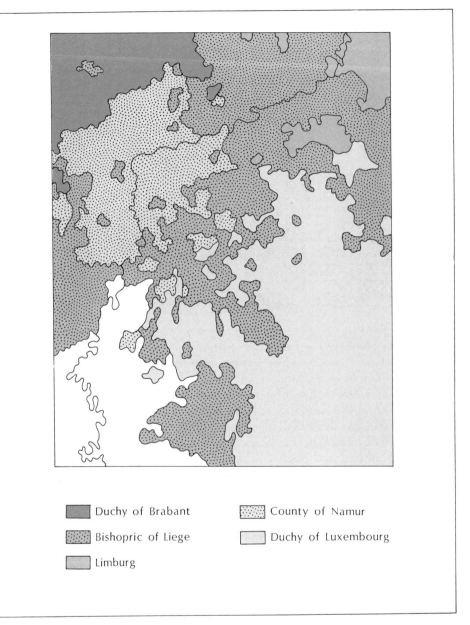

Duchy of Brabant   County of Namur

Bishopric of Liege   Duchy of Luxembourg

Limburg

FIGURE 8–5 Feudal boundaries in the Low Countries, ca. 1300. (Norman J. G. Pounds, 1972, *Political Geography*, 2nd ed. New York, McGraw-Hill Book Co., p. 69.)

cult. Morphological or "natural" boundaries can be grouped into three categories: those following a ridge crest or line of hills or mountains, those following the line of a river, canal, or lake, and those running through swamps, marshes, deserts, or forests.

Mountain ranges seem ideal candidates for boundary lines. In many instances mountain ranges separate differing cultural groups and act as barriers to military adventures. However, a more detailed geographic study of mountain boundaries points out some

serious problems. Although mountain ranges act as cultural divides and separate some major cultural groups, there are many mountain ranges which include small cultural regions with societies that have adapted both socially and physically to mountain life; therefore, any boundary drawn through a mountainous area will inevitably break up societies unless the area is totally uninhabited. A good example of controversy generated by a boundary line along a mountain range is the case of the Chile–Argentine border. The original

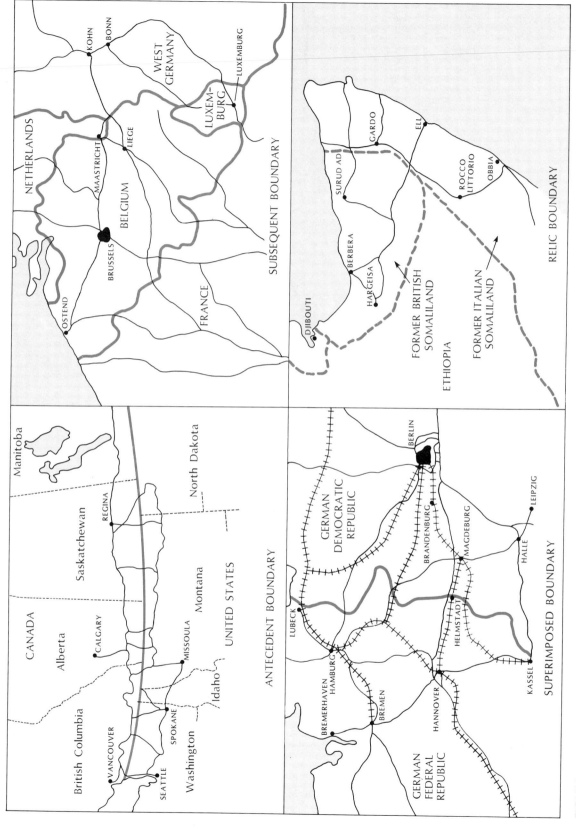

FIGURE 8–6 Types of boundaries. (Harm J. de Blij, *Systematic Political Geography.* Copyright © 1967 by John Wiley & Sons, Inc., p. 246. Reprinted by permission of John Wiley & Sons, Inc.)

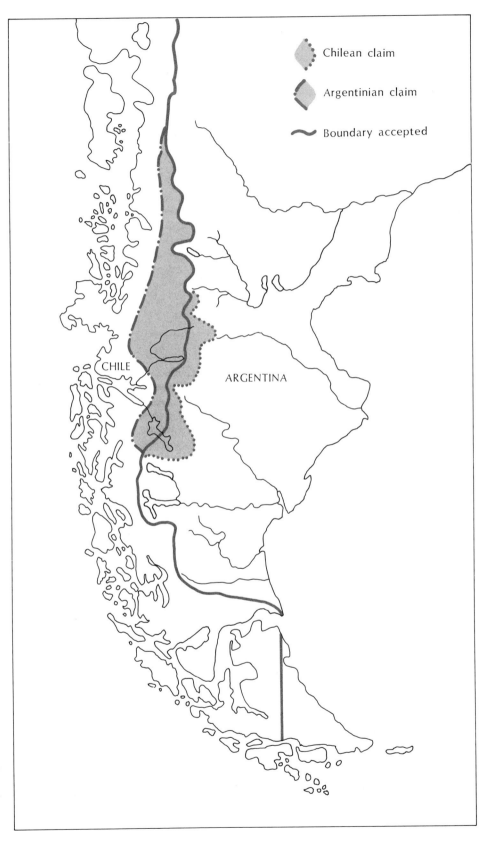

FIGURE 8–7 Chilean–Argentinian boundary dispute. (Norman J. G. Pounds, 1972, *Political Geography,* 2nd ed. New York, McGraw-Hill Book Co., p. 88.)

154

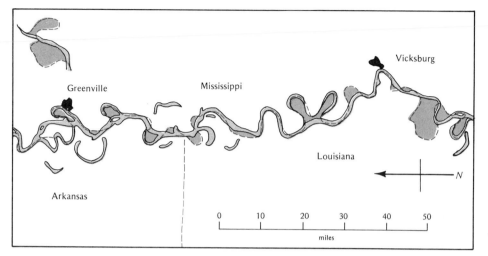

FIGURE 8–8 Portions of Arkansas, Louisiana, and Mississippi involved in boundary shifts along the Mississippi River. (Norman J. G. Pounds, 1972, *Political Geography*, 2nd ed. New York, McGraw-Hill Book Co., p. 81.)

boundary line, based on the Andean mountain range (figure 8–7), was hotly disputed for many years. Sir Thomas H. Holdrich, in a study of this boundary problem, said the dispute

> raged for half a century with a vigor which was all the more intense in that the actual basis of it was always obscure—either buried in the universal ignorance which prevailed as to the physical conditions of the districts concerned, or enveloped in a cloud of conjecture when those districts were but half explored. (1904, p. 2)

Although the Andes Mountains were the basis for the boundary, detailed studies revealed that there was no distinct crest line. The final boundary line, adopted in 1902, was a compromise position commemorated with the Christ of the Andes statue, erected where the boundary crossed Uspallata Pass.

Rivers, canals, and lakes are commonly used in drawing boundary lines; they are usually easier to define than mountain ranges. Although rivers can act as divides, they frequently are areas of increased interaction as societies focus around river valleys for water use, trade, and transportation. In many instances large river basins are centers of social and economic interaction, and their divisive function is overcome by increased interaction.

It may appear at first glance that rivers, lakes, and canals form very precise delimitation and demarcation areas. However, waterways also have width, and deciding the exact location of a boundary line can be difficult. River boundaries may take on several forms. The boundary may coincide with one of the banks; it may follow the windings of the navigable channel

(thalweg); or it may be placed along the median line. The use of one bank as opposed to the other is fraught with practical problems, giving one political entity the unfair advantage of control over the water supply and transportation. Following the navigable channel can also create problems, particularly as river courses change over time. A good example is illustrated by the changes in the channel of the Mississippi river due to cutoffs (figure 8–8), creating boundary problems between the states of Arkansas, Louisiana, and Mississippi.

No less confusing is a boundary that follows the median line of a waterway. It is essential, with this type of boundary, to know and agree upon the exact location of the banks of the river. If the banks change, which occurs frequently in areas prone to flooding, problems ensue. Another problem with using the median line is that the navigable channel can swing from one side of the river to the other, repeatedly crossing the boundary line. The median line is normally used to delimit political jurisdictions in a lake, as is the case of the United States–Canada border through the Great Lakes (figure 8–9).

The final category of natural boundaries includes swamps, marshes, deserts, and forests, which are irregular and have few inhabitants. Historically, they have been frontiers between population regions and have served as barriers to cultural diffusion.

A final type of boundary line is the geometric boundary, usually used where clearly defined physical features were absent or where the areas to be considered were of little economic value. In most instances, the boundary lines were drawn along parallels or me-

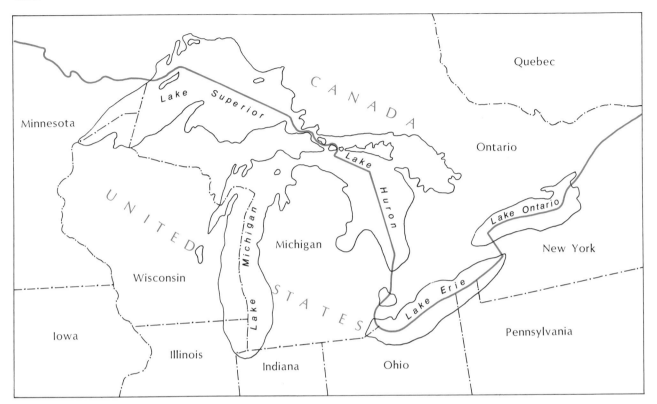

FIGURE 8–9 International boundaries in the Great Lakes.

ridians, and in some cases compass arcs were used. Much of Africa was delimited in this fashion at the Berlin Conference in 1884–85. In some areas of Africa, like the Sahara where there were few permanent settlements, there was a justification for delimiting the boundaries. However, in many other areas of Africa geometrical boundaries correspond to neither physical nor cultural characteristics. Most of the state boundaries in the United States are geometrical boundaries (figure 8–10), although rivers, lakes, and mountain ranges were often used.

In summary, boundaries are drawn for a variety of political, economic, social, and strategic reasons. Determining what type of boundary is best depends upon the nature of the people and the physical characteristics of the area.

Maritime boundaries and territorial waters

Our discussion of boundaries has been primarily concerned with sovereignty over land. However, another important aspect of the territorial system is sovereignty over the sea. Unlike a boundary on the land surface, which usually involves only two political entities, a maritime boundary involves the relationship of one state to all other states. At the present time only 27 nations are considered land-locked, having no direct access to the sea (figure 8–11).

The importance of a maritime boundary depends on a variety of factors. Some nations are economically dependent on off-shore fishing banks; others are concerned with mineral resources found off-shore on the continental shelf. For other nations, their maritime boundaries may have little economic or political meaning.

All maritime boundaries are geometrical in nature, and their delimitation and demarcation have created many problems. Unlike boundaries on land, there are few permanent or static features on which to base a maritime boundary. Coastlines are constantly changing. A shoreline is rarely straight enough to measure from, and the location of the shoreline relative to high or low tide changes twice a day. Indentations in the shoreline, such as bays and estuaries, can create further problems of boundary definition.

Recent decades have seen an increasing interest in the delimitation and nature of maritime boundaries

 Rivers

.... Mountains

——— Geometrical lines

FIGURE 8–10 Types of boundaries in the United States.

(Glassner, 1978, p. 7). This increased interest has been the result of several factors:

1. The rapid rate of decolonization during the 1960s created many new nation-states that wanted to partake in the development of international law and to exploit natural resources off their coasts.

2. The assessment of the value of large amounts of manganese nodules found on the continental shelves, valued in the trillions of dollars, was first understood and publicized in the early 1960s, and many nations realized their economic potential.

3. Rapidly growing populations, as well as new fishing technology, resulted in an increased demand for and harvest of fish.

4. Some species of fish were brought to the brink of extinction, and some nations felt something had to be done about this problem.

5. The superpowers were developing powerful nuclear devices that could be placed on the sea floor and were capable of destroying everyone.

6. The oil spill of the Torrey Canyon in 1967 pointed out the worldwide environmental dangers of new technology and the threat to the ocean's ecosystem.

7. International cooperative scientific ventures, like the International Indian Ocean Expedition (1959–65) and the International Geophysical Year (1957–58), pointed out the value of joint scientific ventures.

8. The realization of the vast wealth of the continental shelf led to more nations' changing their jurisdiction over certain offshore zones.

The territorial waters of nation-states have been divided into several offshore zones whose number and width have changed over time. In a recent analysis of these areas, Martin Glassner defined several zones of national jurisdiction (figure 8–12). The most important zone is the **territorial sea,** whose outer edge is the legal boundary of the state. Long the subject of controversy, the territorial sea serves many important functions—most importantly, the defense of the state. A state has the right to exclude or search vessels that enter its territorial sea, enabling it to control smuggling activities. Territorial seas have also been an important aspect of fisheries protection because states maintain the exclusive right to fish in them; in recent years a number of states have increased the size of their terri-

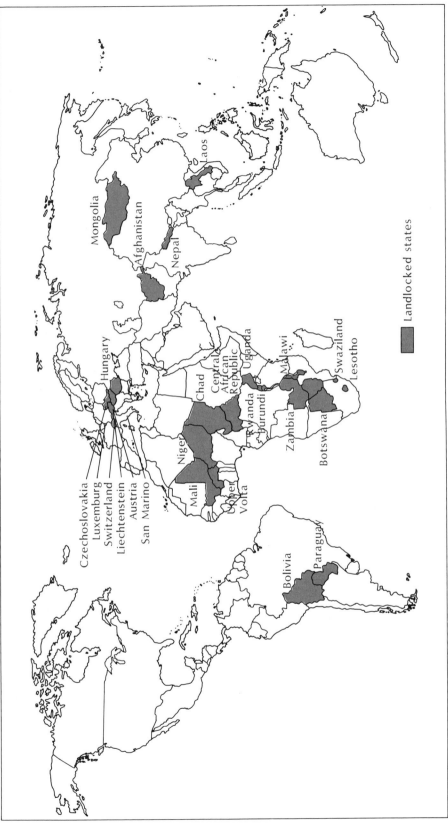

FIGURE 8–11 Land-locked states. (Martin Ira Glassner, March-April, 1978, "The Law of the Sea," in *Focus* 28, p. 22, New York.)

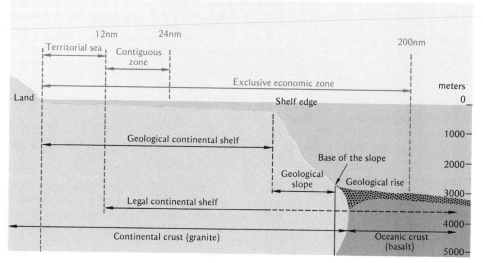

FIGURE 8–12 Zones of national jurisdiction. (Martin Ira Glassner, March-April, 1978, "The Law of the Sea," in *Focus* 28, p. 15, New York.)

torial seas in order to extend their exclusive fishing rights. The territorial sea is less important, from most nations' viewpoints, with respect to pollution and sanitation, though recent events like the Torrey Canyon oil spill have led to more rigorous control.

The width of the territorial sea has always been a subject of controversy. Although it was never accepted as universal international law, the three-nautical-mile limit was observed by many states, at least until recently. The three-mile limit was originally based on the assumption that this was as far "as a cannon could throw a shot" (McFee, 1950, p. 139). Many nations have extended the three-mile limit to twelve miles, and a few have claimed sovereignty up to 200 miles.

A second offshore zone is called the **contiguous zone,** which generally extends from 12 to 24 nautical miles, although its width can vary from one state to another. A state does not have complete sovereignty in this zone, but it generally has the right to intercept and search vessels suspected of smuggling and may extend its control of fisheries and mining rights.

A third zone, called the **exclusive economic zone (EEZ),** extends from the shoreline to 200 nautical miles. According to the Third United Nations Conference on the Law of the Sea (UNCLOS III), within the exclusive economic area, a coastal state has many powers, including

> Sovereign rights for the purpose of exploring and exploiting, conserving and managing the natural resources, whether living or nonliving, of the sea-bed and subsoil and the superadjacent waters, and with regard to other activities for the economic exploitation and exploration of the zone, such as the production of energy from the water, currents, or

winds; the establishment and use of artificial islands, installations, and structures; marine scientific research; the preservation of the marine environment; and other rights and duties provided for in the present Convention. (Glassner, 1978, p. 14)

Extension of national jurisdiction to as far as 200 miles has created several problems. Foremost among them is that the extension has essentially subtracted resources from the common heritage of humankind and placed them in the hands of a few countries. Those that will gain the most are already relatively wealthy—the United States, Australia, Indonesia, New Zealand, Canada, the Soviet Union, Japan, Brazil, Mexico, and Chile. There is also the danger that, if these countries gain control over the resources of the EEZ, they will eventually claim sovereignty over the area.

The final and outermost zone, outside any national jurisdiction, is the **high seas.** Most oceans are included in this zone. Freedom of the seas in this zone also includes the right to fly over it and lay cables across it. This is the only part of the earth's surface that cannot be claimed by any political entity.

Buffer zones and shatter belts

The purpose of the frontier was to separate competing power centers, but as time passed most frontier areas were divided up among them. However, some areas are still located between major power blocks. Such areas have been called **buffer zones** or **shatter belts,** and are defined as

> small political units located between large nations. They survive because they separate states that would

otherwise be powerful neighbors and because the attempt to conquer them would be met, not by the relatively weak resistance of the buffer, but by the much stronger opposition of the other neighbors. (Spykman, 1942, p. 436)

The buffer zone is not a recent phenomenon; some have emerged over an extended period of time, and others have been artificially created. Some buffer zones were created by colonial powers. Thailand, for example, was a buffer separating the competing British and French colonial empires in Asia. Iran (Persia) and Afghanistan served as buffer states between the British territory and Russia. The buffer zone thus acts as a frontier of a higher order, keeping competing powers apart.

Boundaries and behavior

Boundaries often affect the behavior of people living nearby, as well as those who live farther away. In general, the greater the social, political, and economic differences from one side of the boundary to the other, the greater the influence this boundary will have on behavior. Differences are most pronounced with international borders, although in some instances there are great differences between states or other smaller political subdivisions.

The United States–Canada boundary is relatively easy to cross, and there are few major cultural, language, and socioeconomic differences. In many ways, crossing this border is very similar to going from one state to another. Crossing the United States–Mexico border, however, is usually a much different situation. The cultural landscape, particularly the buildings, streets, and field patterns, look significantly different. Perhaps the most obvious difference is the language change, and many people who cross this boundary are immediately aware of the fact that they are in a foreign country. This feeling is especially prevalent among the Anglo community, whereas those of Hispanic origin do not perceive so great a change.

COLONIALISM, NEOCOLONIALISM AND SUPRANATIONALISM

Colonialism

Early records show that throughout human history nations or groups of people have occupied the territory of other nations. This rule of a group of people by a foreign state or power is called **colonialism.** The importance of colonialism in today's world is not in the amount of territory under control, which amounts to only four percent of the land surface (figure 8–13), but in the legacy of former colonial control. Although colonialism is no longer of direct political importance, its imprint on former colonies is evident.

The eradication of colonialism, as well as the general acceptance that it is wrong, has been a rather recent event. Fenner Brockway, in a study of the evolution of colonialism, stated,

Indeed, only since Woodrow Wilson's affirmation of self-determination at the end of the First World War has the right of peoples to govern themselves been internationally accepted, and only since the Second World War has the imposed occupation of the territories of others—the essence of colonialism—been generally adjudged wrong in practice. (1973, p. 13)

Although colonialism is primarily associated with the European nations and their overseas colonies, its historical development dates back to ancient times. The original motivation behind colonial expansion was primarily related to the search for a more habitable land, including a better climate and more natural resources. In the New World the Inca Empire was the result of colonial expansion, whereas in the old world the Roman Empire was well known for its subjugation of people in Europe, Africa, and the Middle East. However, colonial activity reached its peak during the 17th century.

The realization that the earth was not flat and the search for a westward route to India led to European expansion and colonization of much of the world. Colonization was an effective method of spreading the culture and economic system of Europe throughout the world. At one time more than half of the land surface of the world was under European control, including all of Latin America, most of Africa, much of Asia, and part of North America. The length of time that areas were under colonial control varied, with much of Latin America under European domination for centuries, whereas African colonization occurred within the last hundred years.

The motives behind colonization varied over space and time, though authorities generally agree that the principal motive, particularly for the great increase in colonization during the 18th and 19th centuries,

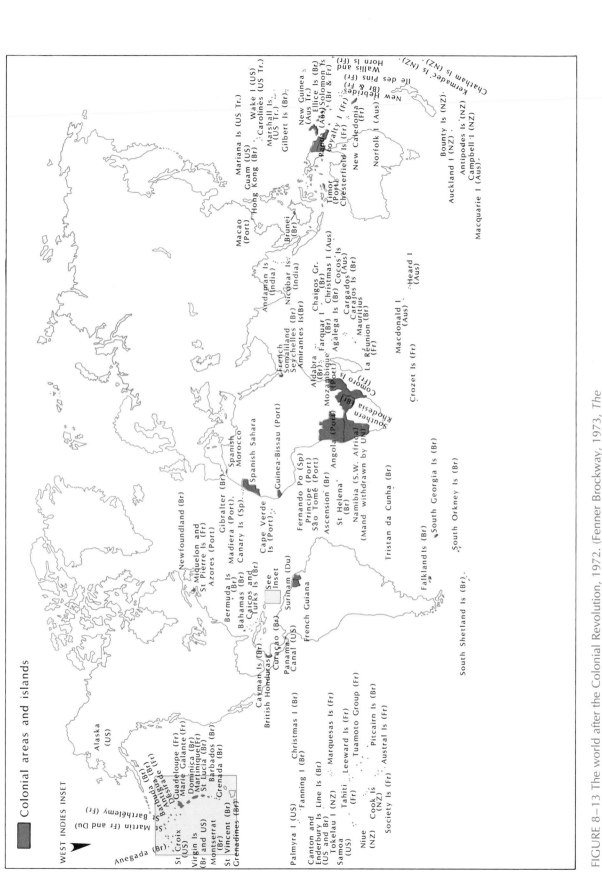

FIGURE 8–13 The world after the Colonial Revolution, 1972. (Fenner Brockway, 1973, *The Colonial Revolution*. New York, St. Martin's Press, cover-inside.)

was economic gain. The spread of mercantilism, the need for cheap labor, and greed were important aspects of European colonization. The rivalry and competition among European powers was reflected in their quest for overseas territory. It is interesting to note that many of these early attempts at colonial control did not involve direct control by the European governments, but rather by commercial interests, such as the East India Company or the British South Africa Company. Eventually this mercantile control did lead to direct government intervention and acquisition of territory.

Other motives were often involved. Prestige and power were associated with the acquisition and control of overseas territory, therefore encouraging European nations to expand their colonial holdings. Military adventurism and the ambition of some ruling elites were also reasons for expanding colonial empires, as were cultural expansion and domination, particularly the effort by some European powers to "convert the heathens" of distant lands to Christianity. In many cases economic and cultural domination went hand-in-hand.

The 20th century has seen a dramatic decline in the number of colonial powers and the amount of territory under colonial control. The total amount of the earth's land area under colonial administration has declined from 36 percent in 1900 to 5 percent in 1969 (table 8–1). A significant decline has occurred since 1945, with the independence of most of the African nations (figure 8–14). The end of large-scale colonialism since 1945 has been the result of three factors: colonialism came to be viewed by many as unjust; nationalist feelings and demands for self-government increased in Africa and Asia; and former colonial powers had been weakened by World War II and were in no condition, either economically or politically, to resume their former role.

Colonialism has both good and bad effects. Positive changes include the economic development which occurred in some colonies. Many dedicated teachers, missionaries, doctors, technicians, and civil servants were involved with increasing the living standards of colonial people. Public health techniques introduced by the European powers led to the control or

TABLE 8–1 Areas administered by the former imperial powers

Imperial power	Area in square miles[a]					
	1900	1920	1945	1958	1960	1969
Australia	—	183,557[b]	183,557[b]	183,557[b]	183,557	178,270
Belgium	905,144	926,054[b]	926,054[b]	926,054[b]	20,910[b]	—
Denmark	879,672	839,782	839,782	839,782	839,782	839,782
France	4,587,085	4,662,895[b]	4,587,083[b]	4,586,889[b]	3,722,249	22,407
Germany	1,231,513	—	—	—	—	—
Italy	245,882	926,084	926,084	198,018[c]	—	—
Japan	—	86,074[c]	86,074[c]	—	—	—
Netherlands	2,048,626	2,048,626	2,048,626	215,027	215,027	371
New Zealand	—	1125[b]	1125[b]	1125[b]	1125[b]	1125[b]
Norway	—	23,951	21,216	24,216	24,216	24,216
Portugal	808,253	808,253	808,253	806,735	806,735	800,304[d]
South Africa	—	318,016[d]	318,016[d]	318,016[d]	318,016[d]	318,016
Spain	132,425	132,425	132,425	114,164	114,164	102,688
United Kingdom	8,964,571	5,322,614[b]	3,970,618[b]	2,882,951[b]	2,509,689[b]	184,820
United States	342,203	116,538	968	1797[e]	1797[e]	1797[e]
Total	20,145,373	16,372,043	14,828,667	11,074,115	8,732,676	2,473,796
Percentage of land area	36	30	26	19	16	5

[a]Antarctica is excluded from this table, but Greenland is included.
[b]Includes trusteeship territory.
[c]Trusteeship territories.
[d]Mandated territory under the League of Nations; South Africa has not accepted the trusteeship.
[e]Includes trusteeship territory but excludes Puerto Rico.
Source: Norman G. Pounds, *Political Geography*, 2nd ed. (New York: McGraw-Hill Book Co., 1972, p. 364).

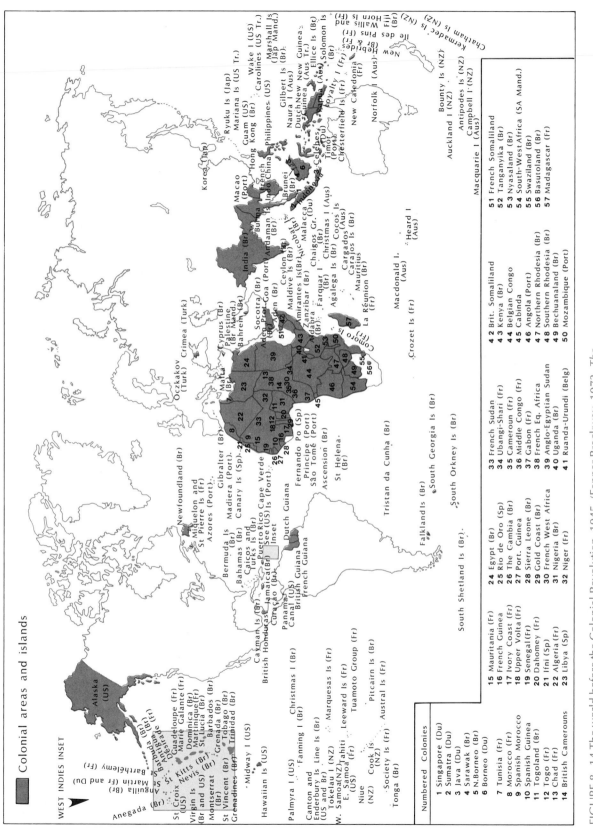

FIGURE 8–14 The world before the Colonial Revolution, 1945. (Fenner Brockway, 1973, *The Colonial Revolution*. New York, St. Martin's Press, cover-inside.)

Colonial areas and islands

WEST INDIES INSET

Anegada (Br)
Anguilla (Br)
St Croix (US)
Virgin Is (Br and US)
Montserrat (Br)
St Vincent (Br)
Grenadines (Br)
St Barthélemy (Fr)
St Martin (Fr and Du)
St Barthélemy (Br)
St Kitts (Br)
Nevis (Br)
St Lucia (Fr)
Dominica (Br)
Marie Galante (Fr)
Guadeloupe (Fr)
Désirade
Martinique (Fr)
Barbados (Br)
Grenada (Br)
Tobago (Br)
Trinidad (Br)

Alaska (US)

Midway (US)
Hawaiian Is (US)
Palmyra I (US)
Fanning I (Br)
Christmas I (Br)
Canton and Enderbury Is Line Is (Br) (US and Br)
Tokelau I (NZ)
W. Samoa (NZ)
E. Samoa (US)
Tahiti (Fr)
Marquesas Is (Fr)
Leeward Is (Fr)
Tuamoto Group (Fr)
Niue (NZ)
Cook Is (NZ)
Society Is (Fr)
Austral Is (Fr)
Tonga (Br)
Pitcairn Is (Br)

Bermuda Is (Br)
Madiera (Port.)
Canary Is (Sp)
Cape Verde Is (Port)
Bahamas (Br)
Caicos and Turks Is (Br)
Cayman Is (Br)
British Honduras
Jamaica (Br)
Curaçao (Br)
Puerto Rico (US)
See US) Inset
Panama Canal (US)
British Guiana
Dutch Guiana
French Guiana

Newfoundland (Br)
Miquelon and St Pierre Is (Fr)
Azores (Port.)
Gibralter (Br)

Fernando Po (Sp)
Principe (Port)
São Tomé (Port)
Ascension (Br)
St Helena (Br)
Tristan da Cunha (Br)
Falkland Is (Br)
South Georgia Is (Br)
South Orkney Is (Br)
South Shetland Is (Br.)

Oczkakov (Turk)
Crimea (Turk)
Cyprus (Br)
Palestine (Br Mand.)
Bahrein (Br)
Malta (Br)
Socotra (Br)
Aden Prot. (Br)
Goa (Port)
Aden (Br)
Maldive (Br)
Ceylon (Br)
Andaman Is (Br)
Malacca
Nicobar Is (Br)
Amirantes Is (Br)
Zanzibar (Br)
Chagos Gr. (Br)
Christmas I (Aus)
Cocos Is (Br)
Farquar I (Br)
Agalega Is (Br)
Cargados Carajos (Br)
Mauritius (Br)
La Réunion (Fr)
Comoro Is (Fr)
Crozet Is (Fr)
Heard I (Aus)
Macdonald I. (Aus)

India (Br)
Burma (Br)
Macao (Port)
Korea (Jap)
Ryuku Is (Jap)
Hong Kong (Br)
French Indo-China (Fr)
Philippines (US)
Mariana Is (US Tr.)
Guam (US)
Wake I (US)
Caroline Is (US Tr.)
Marshall Is (US Tr.)
Brunei (Br)
Sumatra
Celebes (Du)
Timor (Port)
Gilbert Is (Br)
Nauru I (Aus)
New Guinea
Dutch New Guinea (Du)
French New Guinea (Fr)
Ellice Is (Br)
Solomon Is (Br)
Ile des Pins (Fr)
Loyalty I (Fr)
New Hebrides (Br & Fr)
New Caledonia (Fr)
Chesterfield Is (Fr)
Walis and Horn Is (Fr)
Norfolk I (Aus)
Fiji (Br)
Kermadec Is (NZ)
Chatham Is (NZ)
Auckland I (NZ)
Bounty Is (NZ)
Antipodes Is (NZ)
Campbell I (NZ)
Macquarie I (Aus)

Numbered Colonies

1 Singapore (Du)
2 Sumatra (Du)
3 Java (Du)
4 Sarawak (Br)
5 N.Borneo (Br)
6 Borneo (Du)
7 Tunisia (Fr)
8 Morocco (Fr)
9 Spanish Morocco
10 Spanish Guinea
11 Togoland (Br)
12 Togo (Fr)
13 Chad (Fr)
14 British Camerouns

15 Mauritania (Fr)
16 French Guinea
17 Ivory Coast (Fr)
18 Upper Volta (Fr)
19 Senegal (Fr)
20 Dahomey (Fr)
21 Ifni (Sp)
22 Algeria (Fr)
23 Libya (Sp)
24 Egypt (Br)
25 Rio de Oro (Sp)
26 The Gambia (Br)
27 Port. Guinea
28 Sierra Leone (Br)
29 Gold Coast (Br)
30 French West Africa
31 Nigeria (Br)
32 Libya (Sp)

33 French Sudan
34 Ubangi-Shari (Fr)
35 Cameroun (Fr)
36 Middle Congo (Fr)
37 Gabon (Fr)
38 French Eq. Africa
39 Anglo-Egyptian Sudan
40 Uganda (Br)
41 Ruanda-Urundi (Belg)

42 Brit. Somaliland
43 Kenya (Br)
44 Belgian Congo
45 Cabinda
46 Angola (Port)
47 Northern Rhodesia (Br)
48 Southern Rhodesia (Br)
49 Bechuanaland (Br)
50 Mozambique (Port)
51 French Somaliland
52 Tanganyika (Br)
53 Nyasaland (Br)
54 South-West Africa (SA Mand.)
55 Swaziland (Br)
56 Basutoland (Br)
57 Madagascar (Fr)

eradication of many lethal diseases. The introduction of modern industry and agriculture, as well as the development of roads and railroads were important economic assets to some colonies after independence. Political control by European powers ended many local tribal wars, thus uniting the people of the colony—often against the "common enemy," the colonists.

Trying to balance the good and bad of colonialism is a difficult task. The natural resources and people of colonies were exploited; this eventually led to nationalist feelings that brought about the downfall of colonialism.

Neocolonialism

With the passing of colonial empires, a new form of colonialism, **neocolonialism,** has evolved. The term *neocolonialism* is a misnomer: it does not refer to a new form of political control, as the term may suggest, but rather to the development and maintenance of military, cultural, or economic control over a state after it has achieved sovereignty. *Military neocolonialism* refers to the military dependence of former colonial states. These relatively new states rely upon the western and Soviet Bloc nations, as well as the Chinese, for military assistance, and therefore are tied to the states that supply them with arms. The dependence of former colonies on economic assistance from wealthy states is referred to as *economic neocolonialism.* The wealthy states, primarily those of Europe and the United States, have vast investments throughout the world and thus have great influence on the economic decisions made in former colonies. The third type of neocolonialism, *cultural neocolonialism,* refers primarily to the dominance of European culture in formerly occupied territory. This cultural dominance was a result of the strong hold colonial powers had on the formal education system. Many leaders of the newly independent states were educated in European schools, and many of the children of the current ruling elites are educated in the United States or Europe. Neocolonialism is a much more subtle form of control, and thus it is more difficult to identify and analyze.

Supranationalism and the United Nations

It is evident that the principal means of organizing people into political groups has been through the development of the state. Economic interdependence among states, along with the development of modern transportation and communication systems, has highlighted the common interests of states throughout the world. These common interests have led to both conflict and cooperation in international affairs.

The organization of states into supranational groups has generally taken two forms. Some of the multistate organizations have a regional character and include groups or blocks of nations with a common regional interest, whether military or economic. Many times such organizations, like the Organization for European Economic Cooperation, have a common economic interest and organize to further their economic development; in other instances regional groups are primarily cultural organizations, such as the Arab League or the Organization of American States.

The second group of multistate organizations are those whose function is to further worldwide cooperation and development. The first effort to this end was the League of Nations, primarily formed to discourage aggressive war and obtain collective security for its members. It was an outgrowth of World War I, and its principal weakness was that it didn't have the support of all the powerful states, particularly the United States.

The League lost all its political influence after the outbreak of World War II and was officially terminated in 1946 with the development of the United Nations. The United Nations based many of its founding principles and practices on the earlier concepts of the League, but the United Nations, unlike the League, had the support of the major world powers, including the United States. In many ways the significant accomplishments of the United Nations have been made by its subsidiary organizations, like the Food and Agricultural Organization (FAO), the World Health Organization (WHO), and the International Monetary Fund (IMF). In addition to this work the United Nations provides a forum for mediating international disputes, and the states of the world have been willing to give up some sovereignty in the interest of international cooperation.

Environmental degradation: an international problem

The impact of people on the physical environment in the 20th century has been greater than in the previous three billion years. Modernization and industrialization, especially the development of nuclear energy, have provided the means of drastically changing the biosphere. Unfortunately, political institutions have

The Parthenon Acropolis, Athens. (United Nations, 1965)

not developed or evolved at the same pace as our ability to degrade the environment; in essence, we have outmoded political institutions trying to deal with environmental problems.

Environmental degradation is an international phenomenon. Many internationally famous structures, like the Coliseum in Rome, the Parthenon in Greece, and the Lincoln Memorial in Washington, are falling apart because of deteriorating environmental conditions. These structures are slowly being eaten away by acid pollution in the air or shaken to pieces by the rumble of heavy trucks and vehicular traffic. Even more fragile than these human-made structures are the earth's natural systems. Throughout the world species of animals are becoming extinct, oceans are being polluted, and the air we breathe is becoming contaminated. The pollutants, particularly those in the air and water, do not respect international boundaries; it will take an international effort to solve the problem.

A strange dichotomy exists between the developing and the developed nations in this regard. Most of the developing nations do not want any form of international control on pollution; they feel it will interfere with their economic and industrial development. Pollution control costs money and, with a lack of capital anyway, the developing nations do not want to invest their scarce capital in pollution abatement. On the other hand, the developed nations, like the United States and the Soviet Union, support some form of international regulation of pollution activities.

Policies to deal with international pollution can be set at two general levels, external and internal. External policies are related to areas outside national boundaries; whether on the regional or global scale, pollution control will involve international cooperation and regulation. Internal policies refer to the regulation of local problems which have international implications; for example, policies related to overpopulation or depletion of natural resources. Although there is general agreement that environmental management is a task for all nations, and a new framework of international environmental law should be devised, there is no agreement past these general principles. When it comes to the specific rules and the institutions to enforce them, most states and international bodies are floundering.

Environmental disruption in the United States and the Soviet Union.

Many people in the United States believe that pollution is a by-product of the capitalist system and that capitalism and private greed are the root causes of environmental disruption in the United States. Although it might be true that most private businesses have only a marginal concern for the environment, private ownership is not the only reason for environmental degradation. Environmental problems in the Soviet Union, to the surprise of many radical critics of United States capitalism, are very much the same as those in the United States. State ownership of production does not automatically insure a clean environment. We might assume that the public good is more carefully guarded in a socialist country than in the United States, but a comparison of pollution in both countries shows little difference.

Water pollution and its associated fish kills and dead lakes and rivers are found in both countries. The air in Russian cities is polluted, even though they have far fewer cars than American cities. The sensitivity of government bureaucrats to environmental problems in the Soviet Union is not much different than that of the American entrepreneur or bureaucrat.

There are several reasons for this lack of environmental concern in a state-owned, centrally planned economy like that of the Soviet Union. First of all, like economists in the United States, Russian economic planners cannot calculate the social costs of pollution. The Russians regard both air and water as free goods, and if they are free, there is little concern for what happens to them. Another reason is the nature of the government bureaucracy: as in the United States, there are no clear lines of authority, and several government agencies may be concerned with the same issue. Also, in many instances, the fines for polluting are small so that it is often cheaper to pollute. Increasing industrialization and modernization in the Soviet Union has caused a correspondent rise in the amount of plastics

and other goods that are difficult to dispose of or recycle.

Some of the reasons for pollution in the Soviet Union are peculiar to their social and economic system (Goldman, 1970, p. 40). First, government bureaucrats are evaluated on their ability to increase production and economic growth, and the added expense associated with pollution controls or conservation methods can decrease production. Second, industrialization is relatively recent in the Soviet Union, and production is held paramount. Third, unlike the United States, there are no large groups of private property owners who will defend environmental issues. Fourth, the power of the state is so great that one-sided growth can be encouraged. For example, in the early 1960s Krushchev decided that the Soviet Union needed a large chemical industry and ordered mass construction of chemical plants. In their haste to build a chemical industry, the state planners neglected their disruptive effects on the environment.

The nature of pollution in the Soviet system was perhaps best outlined in Marshall Goldman's book *The Spoils of Progress: Pollution in the Soviet Union*.

> In sum, based on Soviet experience, there is no reason to believe that state ownership of the means of production will necessarily guarantee the elimination of environmental disruption. Industrialization, urbanization, and technological change gave rise to environmental upheavals that so far no society has been able to harness completely. While state ownership of a country's productive resources may eliminate some forms of environmental disruption, it also exacerbates rather than ameliorates other forms. Were the United States and its form of government to vanish from the earth, the world would still have to contend with the Soviet supersonic transport and the degradation of Lake Baikal. (1972, p. 7)

Clearly, environmental degradation transcends the type of political system. Modernization's emphasis on increased production creates stresses between production needs and ecological realities, and perhaps only through international organizations will we be able to adequately balance world production with ecological necessity. Natural systems can be altered, perhaps even destroyed, but at the very least we must understand the consequences.

KEY TERMS

State
Internal sovereignty

Nation
Nation-state

Centrifugal forces
Centripetal forces
Raison d'être
Elongated or attenuated state
Compact state
Prorupt state
Fragmented or divided state
Perforated state
Core area
Capital city
Boundary
Frontier
Allocation
Delimitation
Demarcation

Genetic classification
Antecedent boundary
Subsequent boundary
Superimposed boundary
Relic boundary
Morphological classification
Genetic boundary
Territorial sea
Contiguous zone
Exclusive economic zone (EEZ)
High seas
Buffer zone
Shatter belt
Colonialism
Neocolonialism

REFERENCES

Brunn, S. D. (1974), *Geography and Politics in America.* New York: Harper & Row, Publishers, Inc.

Brockway, F. (1973) *The Colonial Revolution.* New York: St. Martin's Press, Inc.

de Blij, H. J. (1967), *Systematic Political Geography.* New York: John Wiley & Sons, Inc.

Glassner, M. I. (1978), "The Law of the Sea," *Focus* 28, No. 4, March–April.

Goldman, M. I. (1970), "The Convergence of Environmental Disruption," *Science* 170, October 2, 27–42.

Goldman, M. I. (1972), *The Spoils of Progress: Environmental Pollution in the Soviet Union.* Cambridge: M.I.T. Press.

Hartshorne, R. (1936), "Suggestions on the Terminology of Political Boundaries," *Annals of the Association of American Geographers* 26, 56–57.

Hartshorne, R. (1940), "The Concepts of 'Raison d'Etre' and 'Maturity' of States: Illustrated from the Mid-Danube Area," *Annals of the Association of American Geographers* 30, 59–60.

Holdrich, T. H. (1904), *The Countries of the King's Award.* London: Macmillan and Co., Ltd.

Jones, S. B. (1959), "Boundary Concepts in the Setting of Place and Time," *Annals of the Association of American Geographers* 49, 241–255.

McFee, W. (1950), *The Law of the Sea.* Philadelphia: J. B. Lippincott Co.

Prescott, J. R. V. (1967), *The Geography of Frontiers and Boundaries.* Chicago: Aldine Publishing Co.

Robinson, E. A. G. (1942), *The Economic Consequences of the Size of Nations.* London: Macmillan and Co., Ltd.

Spykman, N. J. (1942), "Frontiers, Security and International Organization," *Geographical Review* 32, 436–447.

Strong, C. G. (1966), *Modern Political Constitutions,* 7th ed. London: Sidgwick & Jackson.

Whittlesey, D. (1939), *The Earth and the State.* New York: Henry Holt & Co., Inc.

In order to meet the needs of the world's growing population, we must learn to use the earth's resources wisely. Because resources and wealth are unevenly distributed throughout the world, it is important to understand resources in relation to the modernization process. Although resource development can be an important element in the modernization process, it can also have detrimental effects.

In this section we discuss the relationship between natural resources, economic development, and environmental degradation. Natural resources are important to the economic development process; however, we must be careful that resource development does not lead to environmental degradation.

In chapter 9 we discuss types of natural resources and methods of measuring and estimating resource availability. A geographic survey of major natural resources is presented, along with a discussion of conflicts associated with resource development. A discussion of modernization and economic development is presented in chapter 10; this discussion relates economic development to cultural processes and spatial organization. The final chapter in this section outlines the nature of ecosystems and the means by which they become polluted. A discussion of environmental hazards is also included.

Resources, environment, and development 3

Belo Horizonte, Brazil
(Tomas Sennett for World Bank, 1973)

9

Natural resources: The basis for economic development

RECOGNIZING NATURAL RESOURCES

Resources are the foundation of wealth and power because people are material-using animals. Everything we use, from the food we eat to keep us alive to the objects we manufacture, comes from substances found on this planet. Our concern over resources, however, is nothing new. Throughout history people have wondered where tomorrow's bread would come from. The hunger for land, water, and mineral supplies is as old as the ages.

No consensus exists, however, on the exact meaning of the term **resource;** many popular misconceptions do exist. One common misconception identifies resources as only tangible things or substances. Of course, substances can function as resources and play an important role as such, but there are many less tangible resources, like knowledge, wise policies, or social harmony. This preoccupation with resources as tangible phenomena in nature creates the false impression that resources are fixed or static. In his classic study Erich W. Zimmermann defined resources as

> living phenomena, expanding and contracting in
> response to human effort and behavior . . . . To a
> large extent, they are man's own creation. Man's own
> wisdom is his premier resource—the key resource
> that unlocks the universe . . . . The word "resource"
> does not refer to a thing or a substance but to a
> function which a thing or a substance may perform.
> (1951, p. 7)

Resources are an expression or reflection of human appraisal, and without people, there would be no resources. Resources are not static, but expand and contract in response to human needs and human actions.

Resource creation and destruction

Resources are the result of human culture; the materials of the physical environment become resources only when they fulfill a human want or need. "Natural" resources, therefore, exist only in conjunction with human culture. According to Zimmermann (figure 9–1), human culture forges further into the realm of nature, converting more and more **neutral stuff** into resources.

Because resources are a creation of human culture, they can be destroyed by human culture. A good example of **resource creation and destruction** is the development of rubber in the Amazon basin of Brazil. For many centuries rubber had been familiar to the people of the western hemisphere, but little could be done with it until Charles Goodyear developed vulcanization in 1839. As a result, rubber could be used to satisfy human needs, and many manufactured articles made of vulcanized rubber began to appear on world markets. The worldwide demand for rubber products determined the process by which neutral stuff in the Amazon basin could be converted into a rubber resource. According to Zimmermann, this complex resource-creating setup was composed of many parts, including "invention and technology, business enterprise, market demand, labor, capital

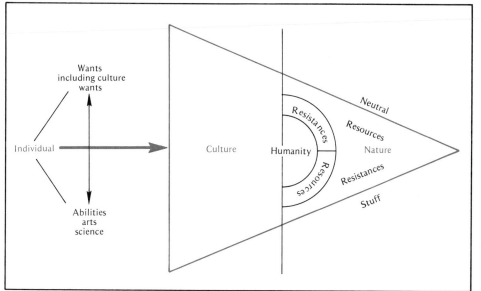

FIGURE 9–1 Meaning and nature of resources. (Erich W. Zimmerman, 1946, *Some Economic Aspects of Postwar Inter-American Relations*. Univ. of Texas, Institute of Latin-American Studies.)

equipment, the social and political institutions governing international trade and regulating human relationships both intranationally and internationally'' (1951, p. 14).

The case of rubber in Brazil is not an isolated incident; the same story could be told over and over again in different parts of the world with different resources. Resource creation, therefore, stems from the interaction of natural and cultural processes.

The process can also be reversed. Modern science and technology can not only create the needs and wants that make neutral stuff into resources, but can also destroy these resources, turning them back into neutral stuff. The case of Brazilian rubber is once again a good example. As the internal combustion engine and the automobile became an important part of world technology, a tremendous demand for cheap rubber tires developed. Geneticists developed new strains of rubber trees, which were much more productive than the indigenous varieties of the Brazilian jungle. These new varieties of rubber trees were cultivated in plantations primarily in Ceylon (Sri Lanka), Indonesia, and the Malay peninsula. Rubber plantations could produce more rubber at cheaper prices than the wild trees in the Amazon basin. Eventually Brazilian rubber was squeezed out of the world market and the rubber resources of the Amazon basin were little more than a memory. Ironically, even the rubber plantations eventually were hurt by the development of synthetic rubber.

Types of natural resources

As we have mentioned, defining a natural resource can be a very complex matter. On the broadest scale we have defined a natural resource as something available from the physical environment which meets human needs. This definition may seem simple, but consider the question, What are human needs? We know that cultural systems and environmental perception have much to do with the definition of a resource. The level of technology of a given people is the primary factor in the determination of importance of various resources.

The pre-Columbian Indians of the American southwest had no real use nor means of recovering the fossil fuels which lay beneath their land. Does this mean that the fossil fuels were not a resource? There are vast oil shale formations in Colorado, Utah, and Wyoming. Many predict that one day we will mine and process most of the oil shale, but there is currently only marginal use. Does this mean that oil shale is not yet a resource? We see once again the importance of the cultural perspective in both space and time. The same consideration is important when we discuss the types of resources, resource availability, and the present distribution of resources.

The two basic types of resources are **renewable** and **nonrenewable** resources. The nature of resource renewability is simply a question of whether or not the resource in question can be readily renewed or reproduced. A forest is a renewable resource because most varieties of trees grow rapidly (relative to the replacement time of other resources). Fossil fuels and minerals, such as gold, silver, or copper, obviously do not renew themselves, thus once extracted from the earth and consumed, they are not replaced. Many minerals can be recycled, of course, as evidenced by the collection of aluminum cans.

We can add another term to our discussion of renewable and nonrenewable resources, the concept of **recoverability.** Recoverability is similar to the notion of renewability in that it refers to the length of time involved in the replenishment and viability of the resource. Fossil fuels and minerals have essentially no recoverability; that is, once used the resource will not recover to its original condition (Luten, 1972). Forests are variable in recoverability. A forest of pine trees, especially Monterey Pine, will recover rapidly after the original forest has been cut. Forests of trees important for commercial lumbering operations, such as the Ponderosa Pine, recover relatively rapidly. Human influence, such as replanting a forest after trees have been removed and reforesting in such a way that the young trees receive optimum growing conditions, hasten recoverability. The Redwood forests of coastal California and Oregon recover extremely slowly regardless of human influence.

Water as a resource may recover very quickly. A rapidly flowing river will recover once pollution sources are eliminated; but a large lake with little inflow and outflow may take thousands of years to recover. Animals also demonstrate a variable nature in recoverability. The California Condor, or any one of a number of the great whales, replenish their population very slowly. If the population of one of these types of animals decreases, the species may not survive because their recoverability is a slow process. If the population of many microscopic organisms was reduced to just a handful of individuals, in a matter of hours, the populations would climb rapidly. The questions we must deal with are whether or not a resource is renewable and, if it is, what is the recoverability rate.

There are other concepts to consider within the major categories of land, water, mineral, and energy resources: stretchability, flexibility, and vulnerability. (Luten, 1972).

Stretchability is a term given to the ability of the resource to produce greater yields as the result of more efficient methods of resource manipulation. For example, we may increase the production from farmlands through the use of chemical fertilizers. The question

and attendant problems of resource definition appear again at this point. There is a certain amount of land on the earth, and of this surface, only a portion is suitable for agriculture. If we increase the amount of land in agricultural use, is this not an example of resource stretchability? The answer is yes, and we will view any exploitation of a natural resource which produces greater yield as stretching the resource.

Greater returns of products from fossil fuels can be accomplished in many ways. At the most basic level, fluids are pumped into some oil fields in an attempt to force all possible crude oil out of the ground. In the processing stage, research is currently focused on substances which might be mixed with gasoline to stretch the amount of fuel produced from each barrel of crude oil. Attempts by automobile manufacturers to produce vehicles with better fuel mileage are another example of the stretchability of fossil fuels.

Perhaps one of the most discussed potential sources of fossil fuels is oil shale. This particular type of rock material can be processed mainly through the use of extreme heat to precipitate the oil material from this unique sedimentary rock. The stretchability of this source of fossil fuel is great. The present level of technology produces only about 25 gallons of crude oil per ton of quality grade shale. Researchers believe that significantly more crude will be produced per ton of shale as technology in this area progresses. The search for methods of yielding greater returns from fossil fuels results from increases in demand for this resource.

Demand is generally referred to as the need or desire for a resource. We will add to that definition the concept of **flexibility** as being a measure of the ability to find adequate substitutions for a resource to satisfy demand. Basically, we are asking how flexible a resource is, given a particular cultural system. The flexibility of farmland illustrates this principle. In the United States we have a great flexibility in demand for farmland. Large tracts of this part of the American resource base are removed from production every year as a result of urban sprawl. Agriculturalists continue to produce greater amounts of food, however, because they are able to stretch the returns from the remaining land. In Southeast Asia the demand for agricultural land is very inflexible. If significant amounts of agricultural lands were changed from that particular land use, the overall production of food would most likely decline.

Fossil fuels are very inflexible. We have no widely used substitute for this resource. Forests, on the other hand, are highly flexible, since many substitutes

Gas station in Liberia. (Pamela Johnson for World Bank, 1968)

for wood can be found. It should be noted that the concept of flexibility is used in reference to the current level of technology and style of life found in world societies. Many argue that great economic investment in energy resources could produce many substitutes for fossil fuels, but no major technological breakthroughs are on the horizon. However, petroleum shortages and high prices are stimulating increased research efforts. In order to maintain current societal status, great quantities of fossil fuels must be consumed, and without realistic substitutes available, we maintain that the fossil fuel resource is very inflexible.

Vulnerability is a measure of how susceptible the resource is to destruction. Land is a highly vulnerable resource. Agricultural land converted to urban or suburban uses is removed from the food producing resource base. Wilderness as a resource of both ecological and aesthetic importance is highly vulnerable. The impact of human activity on wilderness areas changes the character and basic value of the resource. The problems of perception of resources and resource utilization are culminated in the issues of wilderness land use and conservation. Anyone who has recently visited Yosemite Valley knows something of the human impact on the visual and aesthetic qualities of natural environments.

Resource vulnerability. Hawkes has summarized the basic elements in the conflict of how to use the land through his discussion of Gifford Pinchot, a famous forester, and John Muir, the mountaineer (1960). Pinchot is characterized as representative of those having a utilitarian perception of the wilderness and resources in general. The ***utilitarian viewpoint*** is fundamentally that resources are to be used and should serve the general economy.

Muir is perhaps most famous for his writings about the Sierra Nevada of California and Nevada. Near the turn of the 20th century Muir inspired the founding of the Sierra Club, an organization originally devoted to resource preservation in California, and which continues to be a powerful voice for the environment. Muir represented the **preservationist movement** in Hawkes' dichotomy.

Eighty years ago the main confrontation between preservationists and utilitarians was over the use of forest lands (Hawkes, 1960). There followed a series of conflicts over petroleum, soil erosion following the dust bowl years, and water and wildlife management. There seem to have been shifts in public attitudes toward resources, with utilitarian concerns dominating prior to the Second World War. In the years following World War II, the preservationists seem to have been the strongest group. In the last years of the decade of the 1970s, utilitarian arguments seem to be gaining in popularity. The battle over the Alaskan Pipeline was fought along utilitarian and conservationist lines. Those favoring resource utilization finally were able to dominate this issue.

Questions of the best use of lands where strip mining and agriculture compete, and the future of wilderness areas, will be discussed later in this chapter. Resource vulnerability, stretchability, and renewability must all be considered when we estimate resource availability.

Measuring and estimating resource availability

You have undoubtedly heard or read that the world will deplete its supply of coal or oil within a given number of years. These estimates are made for nearly every individual country and obviously for the earth as a whole. One fact which will not escape the attentive reader is that the amount of time remaining before resource depletion takes place varies remarkably. Why the difficulty in estimating **resource availability?**

Consider for a moment the complexities involved in every aspect of cultural systems. The economic, political, historical, social, and psychological factors that make so many issues difficult to deal with are also involved in estimating resources. Combine these factors with some of the difficulty inherent in defining resources, assessing the perception of resources, and the continuous reappraisal of existing resources, and it is not difficult to imagine why there is such a wide range of estimates of future resources. Figure 9–2 illustrates the projections that were made for the period between 1960 and 2000. Since we are near the midpoint of that

time span, we should consider the factors originally used to make these estimates and discuss events which have acted to influence actual consumption and availability.

In making projections for future resource needs, Landsberg considered the following factors: populations; gross national product; individual, government, and business investment; and advances in technology (1964). Estimating population, as we have seen, is a difficult proposition; the baby boom following World War II produced a sharp upward deviation in actual population as compared with population estimates. Likewise, the present decline in population growth rates in Anglo-America and Western Europe was not foreseen in long-range estimates. Planning based on the extrapolation of short-term trends is a hazardous business.

Population is the essential element in the estimation of resource consumption and subsequent needs. Obviously a population exhibiting a growth pattern will demand more natural resources. The habits of cultural groups are equally as important as pure numbers of people; a person born and raised in India, for example, will generally consume far less than the average citizen of the United States. Population and cultural systems, as well as the economic subsystem and modernization, must all be considered in estimating for the future.

The principle measure of the economic activity of a nation is the total range of goods and services produced in the nation. In the United States we use a measure referred to as the gross national product (GNP). In many nations, however, an accurate reflection of all production is impossible to calculate. The trend toward modernization can be used as an estimator in these countries.

A high gross economic output reflects a need for the consumption of resources. This is a generalization, of course, but it is difficult to argue that more goods and services can be produced without some increased input of raw materials. The resources which drive the economic output of our world society come from the land, water, and minerals of the earth and are processed by the use of energy. Future estimates of need are based upon the rate of growth in the use of basic natural resources. In the United States, for example, the consumption of electrical energy was growing by 8 percent per year during the 1970s. This means that as a nation the United States will nearly double its con-

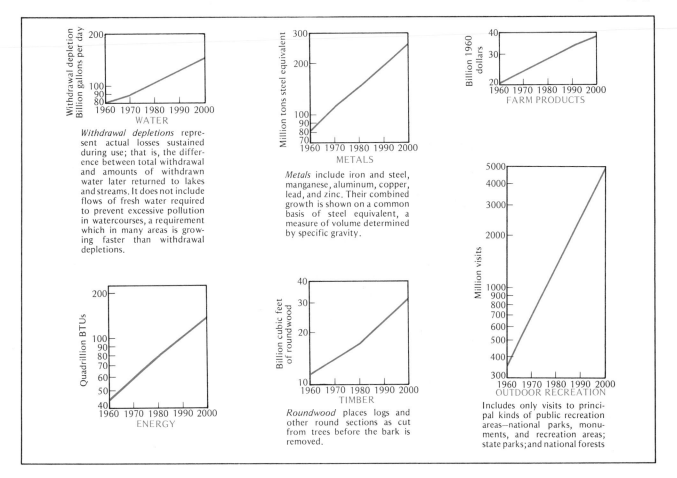

FIGURE 9–2 Growing U.S. need for natural resource goods and services. These projections reflect current trends in population, gross national product, technological progress, and other key factors. (Hans Landsberg, 1964, *Natural Resources for U.S. Growth.* Baltimore, MD, The Johns Hopkins Univ. Press, p. 14.)

sumption of electrical energy every eight and one-half years.

Based upon exponential growth rates in the consumption of fossil fuels, Hubbard estimated that a child born in 1935 would live to see 80 percent of the petroleum in the United States consumed (1969). He further predicted that, within the life span of a child born in 1973, 80 percent of the world's petroleum reserve would be consumed. Nothing takes into account possible new discoveries of petroleum, innovative technology which may stretch the resource, or a change in lifestyle in favor of conservation; this not a severe crit-

icism, because estimates of future resource availability are perhaps more accurately made excluding these three factors. It is more responsible to be conservative in future estimates than to promise a cornucopia of long-term resources which may or may not exist. Two other aspects of prediction of resource availability which must be considered are the issues of quality versus quantity and the costs of providing resources.

Landsberg cites individual spending, governmental spending, and business investment as major factors in future resource availability. If the costs of urban sprawl became so high that consumer demand diminishes, perhaps sprawl would be reduced and agriculturally productive land preserved. If U.S. gasoline prices rise to two or three dollars per gallon, it is possible that consumption of petroleum would be reduced.

In virtually all studies dealing with the availability of resources, the cost input is a major factor. As the price of energy increases, more money is expended for

Bauxite plant near Spaulding, Jamaica. (United Nations/King, 1973)

obtaining resources. If the nations of the world are willing and able to divert much of their economic output into resources, especially energy, then resources will continue to be available for some time. However, there may be limits. Gas prices have risen phenomenally in some parts of Europe. The days when the economic cost of obtaining and processing resources was very small are a part of history. The term *economic cost* may be used to describe one aspect of meeting future resource needs. However, there are other costs— social costs—that must be considered as well.

The quality of the environment and the quantity of resources produced often are in conflict. For example, the production of oil shale, as well as coal, often requires extensive strip mining. Increasing the world's food supply through sea-harvesting poses the potential for the loss of some species of sea animals. These are only a few examples of the dichotomy between environment and economy. When estimates of future resources are given, regardless of the source, we should question the economic and environmental costs of resource production. It could be claimed that, with enough money and monumental environmental sacrifice, the world production of coal would be virtually infinite, but this is an unrealistic estimate. In the assessment of resource availability we must consider the anticipated needs for the future, the environmental and economic costs of production, and population factors.

The interrelations between these components of the question offer the opportunity for a systems approach to problem analysis.

Estimates of the need for, and cost of, fossil fuels made during the early 1960s by Landsberg and others have proven generally inaccurate, mainly because of unforeseen events which are impossible to work into an equation. The systems dynamics of economics, politics, new developments in technology, and the discovery of new resources make long-range predicting difficult. For example, who could have forecast in 1960 that, by the mid-1970s, those Middle Eastern nations who control so much of the world's oil reserves would, through economic and cultural solidarity, be able to dictate a policy of great impact on virtually every nation? The rise of OPEC (Organization of Petroleum Exporting Countries) has literally altered the distribution of wealth in a short time as "petro dollars" have accumulated at unprecedented rates since 1973. In 1979 a change in the political leadership in one nation, Iran, led, through interaction of cultural systems, to a number of economic consequences, especially in the United States. In 1979 the new government restricted the export of oil, and gas prices rose rapidly in the United States. These are representative of the types of events which influence resource availability, and of costs which often go unrecognized when estimating future availability. We can, however, examine a few

Highway network to access new areas and move agricultural products in the State of Parana, Brazil. (Tomas Sennett for World Bank, 1973)

broad generalizations of existing world resources which influence the analysis of the resource base.

THE MATERIAL BASIS OF DEVELOPMENT

No simple relationship exists between economic growth and natural resources. Many areas of the world are endowed with a variety of natural resources, yet they are relatively poor (India, China, parts of Africa). On the other hand, nations like Japan or Switzerland have a paucity of natural resources yet a high level of development. According to geographer Norton Ginsburg, the important questions to ask are, "How important are natural resources in the course of economic development, and what relationships do they bear to other factors which enter into the developmental complex?" (1957, p. 197). In its broadest sense, the resource base would include all the material phenomena of nature, including land, air, sea, and the nonmaterial quality of location or situation.

If all things were equal *(ceteris paribus),* the larger and more varied the resource base of a particular state, the greater the likelihood that it would modernize or develop. Ginsburg offered several preliminary ideas concerning the relationship between natural resources and economic growth (1957, p. 212).

1. An ample supply and diversity of natural resources is a major advantage to a country attempting to modernize.

2. Although it is not necessarily critical to have natural resources within the political boundaries of a country, those resources must be accessible. This means facilities must be available to transport those resources.

3. An easily exportable natural resource can be the source of wealth for capital accumulation. Large quantities of a natural resource such as oil can provide enormous amounts of development capital.

4. Even if abundant natural resources are available, they cannot determine the kinds of uses, if any, to which they will be put.

5. The particular stage of development of a country will be an important factor in resource use. Natural resources play an especially important role in the early stages of the development

Kawasaki Steel Corporation's Chiba Works, Tokyo. (Kawasaki Steel Corporation, 1965)

process because they can supply capital necessary for the acceleration of economic growth.

6. Natural resources, although important, do not play as crucial a role in the developed nations because these wealthier nations have larger supplies of skilled labor, capital, technology, and development experience.

7. Any economic development program of a comprehensive nature must begin with a sophisticated inventory of the resource base.

Though Ginsburg's ideas may seem appropriate, we might argue that they represent neither necessary nor sufficient conditions for economic development and modernization in the 1980s. Abundant resources in poor countries have often been controlled by rich countries, thus hindering development. On the other hand, Japan has modernized with a minimum of natural resources. Services are increasingly important and require less than manufacturing in terms of natural resources. Look, for example, at the importance of banking in the Swiss economy. Furthermore, the relation-

ship today between rich and poor countries restrains development, as does rapid population growth.

Natural resources and economic development: The case of Japan

Perhaps more than any other modern nation, Japan's rise to international prominence illustrates the interrelationship between resource availability and economic development. The beginning of modern Japanese development can be traced back to the fall of the Shogunate and the restoration of the Emperor in 1867. Prior to this time Japan was a nation virtually isolated from the rest of the world.

By most objective standards of resource endowment, Japan would be classified as a nation with a paucity of resources. Less than 20 percent of its total land area is arable; soil fertility is high in some areas, but overall it is not exceptional; and, though it contains a variety of mineral resources, most are in small quantities and have little commerical value. At the fall of the Shogunate, Japan had a population of approximately

35 million which had remained unchanged for a number of years. Also, at the time of the Meiji Restoration, Japan was using its resource base at a level appropriate for its technological development. How then was Japan able to dramatically increase its economic base and become a world power in a relatively short period of time?

Most analysts agree that the initial source of capital came from within the country. Foreign investments, although important in some areas, were very small. The internal resource base was the source of capital, which was used to fuel productivity increases. Small investments in sericulture enabled Japan to displace China as the world's principal supplier of silk. Also, investments in agriculture increased productivity in that sector, and the government, through forced savings techniques of taxation, transferred capital from agriculture to other productive sectors of the economy.

It was primarily the textile industry, initially silk and later cotton, that permitted rapid economic growth. The textile industry was developed through the application of already available technology to the production process. The resultant increase in production helped supply the capital to initiate the Japanese program of heavy-industry expansion. The development of heavy industry was initially financed internally but later was aided by foreign investment. Japan is thus a successful example of a nation using its limited resource endowment, in conjunction with improved technology, to supply the capital to finance further development.

RESOURCES: A GEOGRAPHIC SURVEY OF MAJOR CATEGORIES

Land

Land as a resource may be assessed in many ways. The basic determinants of what makes land a resource are found in the composition of soil and in environmental conditions. Soils provide the home for bacteria, fungi, and a variety of other organisms; they are comprised of organic materials and inorganic components, such as weathered rock particles, along with water and gases, mainly oxygen and nitrogen. The organic and inorganic elements are acted upon by sunlight, water, plant and animal communities, and human activities, with the product of this process being a particular type of soil.

The surface of the earth is roughly 30 percent land area, only some of which is suitable for agriculture; the rest is too wet, too dry, too warm, or too cold, or too acidic or alkaline, too rocky or sandy, or covered with urban settlements. Further, of the soils in production, only a small percentage are in intensive use. Areas of great agricultural productivity are generally limited to certain physical locations—river valleys, areas of volcanic soil, intensively irrigated rice lands, or in the prairie (chernozemic) soil regions, where extensive cultivation is common.

Forests are another land-based natural resource, providing such things as fuel, lumber, paper, wildlife habitats, and recreation. We have discussed forests as a renewable resource. Anyone who has travelled in regions noted for forest industries has probably seen reforestation. In most industrialized nations, even with reforestation, large expanses of forests have already disappeared. Deforestation is also occurring rapidly in developing countries. In Brazil, for example, a program is underway to clear tropical forest in order to provide new agricultural lands. The cutting of tropical forests, a frequently proposed source of new farm lands, presents several environmental problems. First, once trees are removed the ground is directly exposed to water from the constant tropical rain, leading to accelerated erosion and leaching. Leaching is the process by which the minerals and nutrients in the soil are washed out of the top layers of soil by the action of moving water. In the natural tropical ecosystem, the leached minerals and nutrients are constantly being replaced, but if forests are removed, massive amounts of chemical fertilizers must be added, increasing the cost of farming.

A second problem with this type of forest removal is that a very complex ecosystem is replaced by a simple one. A tropical ecosystem may have hundreds of types of plants and animals in a small area, whereas an agricultural ecosystem would have only a small variety of plants and animals in a given area. If a pest or plant disease moves through an area in which the ecosystem has beem simplified to this extent, widespread damage results. By sheer strength of numbers, a complex ecosystem will absorb this damage, whereas a simple ecosystem may be destroyed. The potato blight of the mid 1800s in Ireland is an example of the devastation which may occur when a simple ecosystem is overcome by disease; it resulted in the death by starvation of thousands and the migration of thousands more to North America.

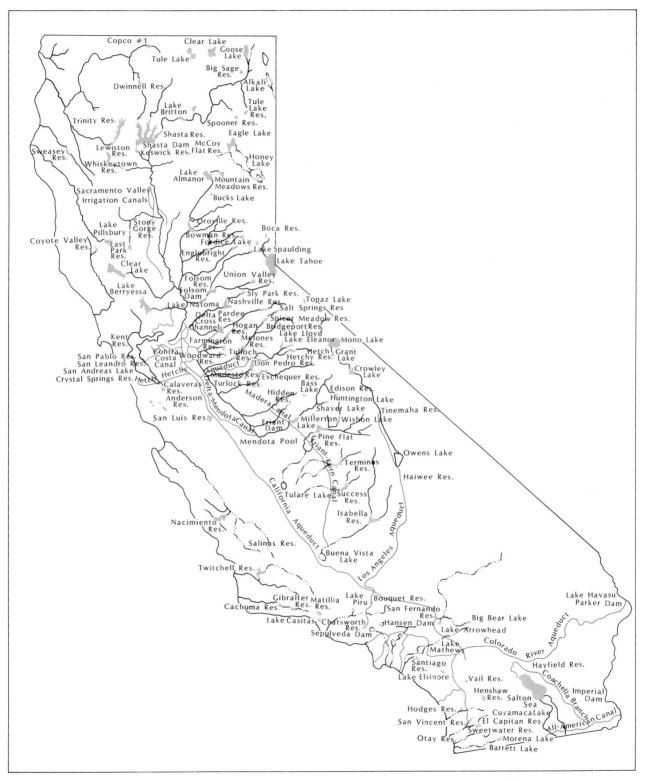

FIGURE 9–3 California water projects. (R. Durrenberger, 1972, *Patterns on the Land,* 4th ed. Palo Alto, CA, Mayfield Publishing Co./National Press Books, p. 73.)

Laying water pipes to a home site, Sao Paulo, Brazil. (Tomas Sennett for World Bank, 1973)

Water

Water is a renewable resource in both an absolute sense, as in the hydrologic cycle, and in a relative sense, as in a polluted stream being cleaned of pollutants. The stretchable nature of the resource is evident by the vast number of water quality standards which exist. Water is principally used by people for industrial activity (46 percent in the United States), irrigation (46 percent) and municipal uses (8 percent) (Luten, 1972). Water as a renewable resource is not consumed but can be polluted until it is virtually useless. Pollution has been a factor of human use of the earth for nearly as long as there have been settlements. Accounts of almost every water-based city in history describe waste materials being dumped into water systems. The prob-

lem became especially acute during the Industrial Revolution, as suggested in the following comment:

> And sprinklings of water a little cooled the main streets and the shops but the mills, and the courts and alleys, baked at a fierce heat. *Down by the river that was black and thick with dye,* some Coke town boys who were large—a rare sight there—rowed a crazy boat, *which made a spumous tract upon the water as it jogged along, every drop of the oar stirred up vile smells.* (Dickens, 1854; as quoted in Salter, 1971, pp. 217–218. Emphasis added.)

In the modern era pollution continues to be a problem. A myriad of federal, state and local laws to curb water pollution have been passed in recent years, both in the United States and elsewhere.

Development of energy resources often acts to pollute water systems. The chemical residue from strip mining adds a pollutant to the water of surrounding streams. Water discharge from nuclear power plants creates thermal, or heat, pollution.

In the contemporary urban world, a frequent problem is the lack of water resources at specific urban sites. Los Angeles is a prime example, where water to serve the needs of the metropolitan area must be imported from great distances (figure 9–3). The lesson to be learned from Los Angeles might be that resource availability should govern the growth and ultimately the size of urban areas, but growth patterns do not follow such a rational plan. One of the fastest growing areas in the United States is the urban corridor along the Front Range of the Colorado Rockies from Ft. Collins in the north to Colorado Springs in the south, where vast quantities of water must be imported.

Water policy in much of the world seems to equate progress with growth and growth with the provision of water, almost regardless of economic or environmental cost. Water is so inexpensive and has traditionally been in such great supply that conservation has never seemed like a real necessity. However, this may not be the case in the future; conservation may become a more attractive alternative to continual expansion of the resource base.

CASE STUDY:
The California drought of 1976 – 77

Severe drought conditions existed in the Western United States during 1976 and 1977. California in general and Marin County in particular were especially adversely affected by the lack of precipitation.

Marin County receives most of its water from reservoir systems located in the foothills along the Pacific Ocean. During the drought period the normal pattern of Pacific storms was disrupted for two consecutive winters. Marin County has a Mediterranean type of climate which typically features a summer drought. The lack of rainfall in the winters meant that this particular area, with a population of over 200,000, had no new water added to its reservoirs for several years. The only immediate answer was water conservation.

The local water district began an immediate campaign to inform residents of the magnitude of the problem. A great many attempts were made to conserve water on a voluntary basis, which were somewhat successful; however, the water shortage became so acute that rationing was needed. An allocation of water for each resident in the house was assigned. The rationing system was designed to cut water use to approximately 40 percent of the consumption levels of the previous years. Each household was given a specific number of gallons per day; this amount was translated into cubic feet for a two month period (table 9–1). People in Marin County learned to read the water meters at their homes and could easily calculate the rate of their consumption.

There were no exceptions to the rationing plan. This, coupled with the nature of the resource shortage — the residents obviously knew these were drought conditions — prompted community action on a broad scale. Special newspaper issues were devoted to water saving tips. Bumper stickers appeared urging conservation. All conceivable manner of water saving devices were sold in stores. The main topic of conservation became how to cope with the drought. A number of lists comparing normal water use and conservative use were widely distributed (table 9–2).

TABLE 9–1 Water allotments for single-family and duplex homes during the California drought

No. of permanent residents in household	Gallons per day for each resident	Gallons per day for household	Cubic feet for 2-month period per household
1	49	49	400
2	43	86	700
3	41	123	1000
4	37	148	1200
5	34	170	1400
7	32	224	1800

TABLE 9–2 "How to save water": an example of guidelines issued during the California drought

Activity	Normal use	Conservation use
Shower	Water running 25 gallons	Wet down, soap up, rinse off 4 gallons
Brushing teeth	Tap running 10 gallons	Wet brush, rinse briefly 0.5 gallon
Tub bath	Full 36 gallons	Minimal water level 10 to 12 gallons
Shaving	Tap running 20 gallons	Fill basin 1 gallon
Dishwashing	Tap running 30 gallons	Wash & rinse in dishpans or sink 5 gallons
Automatic dishwasher	Full cycle 16 gallons	Short cycle 7 gallons
Washing hands	Tap running 2 gallons	Fill basin 1 gallon
Toilet flushing	Depending on tank size 5 to 7 gallons	Using tank displacement bottles 4 to 6 gallons
Washing machine	Full cycle, top water level 60 gallons	Short cycle, minimal water level 27 gallons
Outdoor watering	Average hose 10 gallons per minute	Lowest priority Eliminate

An esprit de corps developed in Marin County, because the nature of the problem was quite clear and everyone was involved equally. Marin County residents actually brought consumption below the ration level. At one point residents were averaging a use of only 23.3 gallons per person per day for *all* purposes; table 9 – 2 shows that, through normal household activities, 23 gallons of water could be consumed very quickly. The extent to which Marin County residents conserved can be brought into sharper focus if you calculate the water usage of your household for a period of time and compare that with an allotment of 23.3 gallons per person per day.

The only immediate detrimental impact of the water conservation effort was that some ornamental vegetation (lawns, some shrubs, and so on) did badly without constant watering. A lawn brown from lack of water became something of a status symbol. This example illustrates that conservation of some resources is possible with minimal change in lifestyle. One resource, which people in most parts of the world are being urged to conserve, is energy, though so far results have been rather poor.

Energy

Energy is perhaps the most complex of all resources. It may be defined simply as the ability to do work; although we speak of energy in a wide range of contexts, we are essentially describing the ability to perform some task. It may be said that one has little energy on a particular day, or that energy is obtained from the burning of coal, or that energy is potential, kinetic, or latent in nature. All of these concepts involve generating force to do work. Our concern with energy is in the realm of the broad overview of major energy sources in the world. Energy as a resource is nonrenewable, with the exception of solar, wind, and tidal energy (Luten, 1972). There are seven basic steps in utilizing energy: 1 discovery, 2 harvest, 3 transport, 4 storage, 5 conversion, 6 use, and 7 waste disposal (Luten, 1971, p. 109).

Discovery and *harvest* have become increasingly more efficient through technological innovation. It is possible to estimate where energy might be obtained from the earth through satellite imagery, a vast improvement over previous forms of analysis. Oil can now be pumped from wells over 10,000 feet deep. The techniques becoming common now are far more expensive than those of the past.

How much energy resource remains to be discovered? We have detailed the problems inherent in attempting to estimate such things earlier in this chapter. Suffice it to say that there are undoubtedly large quantities of energy resources which are yet to be harvested (figure 9–4).

Transport is the process which follows discovery and harvest. Large electrical wires transport electrical energy from a point of generation to places a great distance away. Oil is moved by pipeline, ship, rail, truck, and most recently, supertanker (figure 9–5). Natural gas may move through pipelines, and coal may be transported through slurry pipelines (coal through a pipeline propelled by moving water), or by truck, train, or sometime ship.

Storage of most major resources from which we obtain energy is often not difficult, but once a material has been converted to energy, storage becomes a more challenging problem.

Conversion is the term given to the use of a material to generate energy. Coal or fuel oil is burned to generate electrical energy. The problems in storing electrical energy come from the "free" nature of this source of energy. Electrical energy cannot be placed in piles or storage tanks, so it must be essentially *used* as generated. Demand for electrical energy is greatest in the early evening, declines at night, then begins a gradual climb in the early morning to its evening peak. If large-scale storage of electricity were possible, peak usage could be more efficiently handled.

When a resource is converted to form an energy source, a question of efficiency is involved. If coal or oil is burned to generate other types of energy, much of the potential energy held in oil or coal is lost as waste heat. One way in which energy resources may be stretched in the future is in minimizing this loss.

The final stage in our process of energy utilization is the *disposal of waste material*. In most cases waste material is heat. Energy generated by nuclear power produces heat, which is either released into the environment through cooling (evaporation) towers or discharged into water systems (figure 9–6). The by-product of using uranium for fuel is a radioactive waste which can be harmful for many thousands of years. Until adequate methods of nuclear waste disposal are found, this potential source of energy may not be fully utilized.

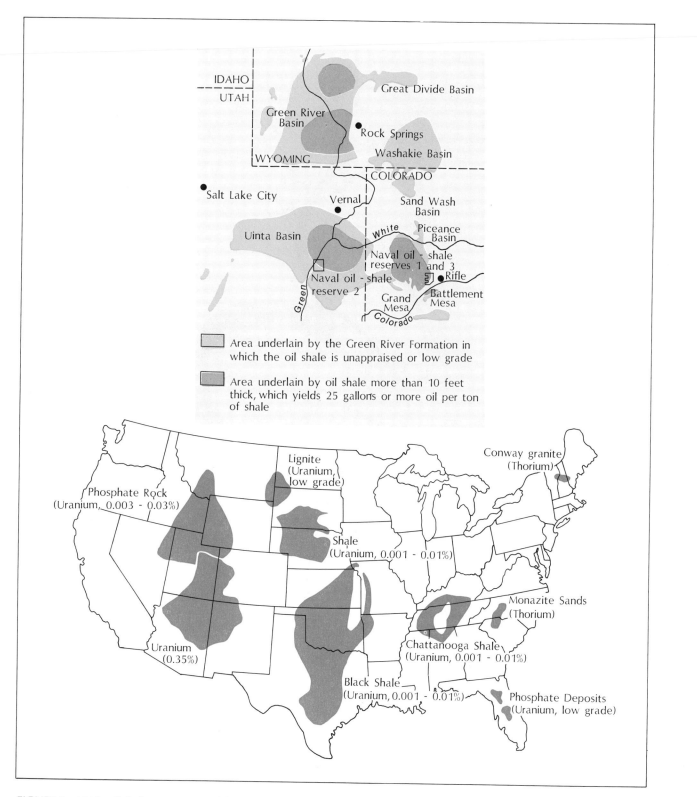

FIGURE 9–4 U.S. oil shale, uranium, and thorium deposits. (M. King Hubbert, 1956, "Nuclear Energy and Fossill Fuels," in *Drilling and Production Practice*. Dallas, TX, American Petroleum Institute, p. 23.)

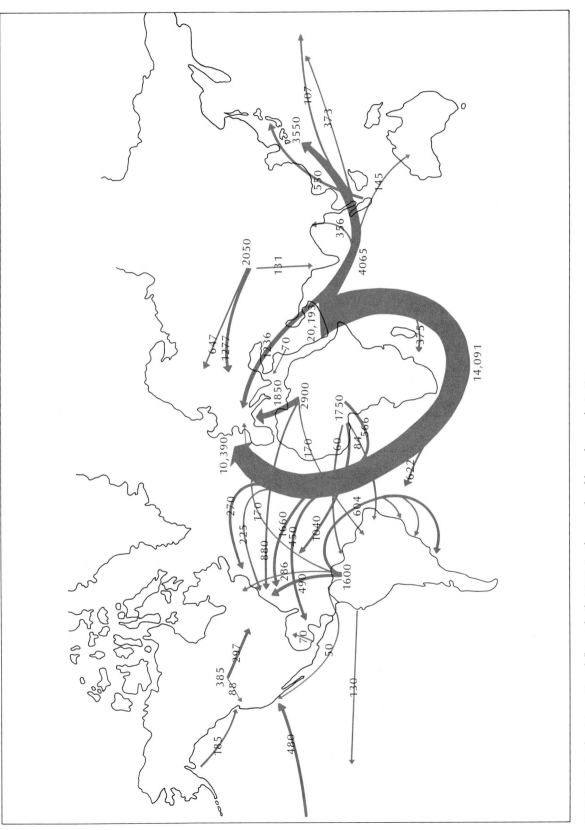

FIGURE 9–5 The international flow of oil, 1976 (in thousands of barrels per day). (*International Petroleum Encyclopedia*. Tulsa, OK, Petroleum Publishing Co., 1977.)

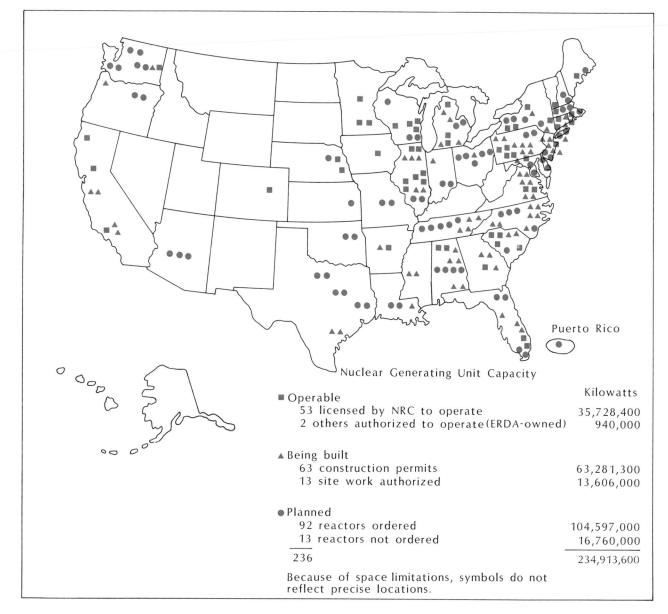

Nuclear Generating Unit Capacity

	Kilowatts
■ Operable	
53 licensed by NRC to operate	35,728,400
2 others authorized to operate (ERDA-owned)	940,000
▲ Being built	
63 construction permits	63,281,300
13 site work authorized	13,606,000
● Planned	
92 reactors ordered	104,597,000
13 reactors not ordered	16,760,000
236	234,913,600

Because of space limitations, symbols do not reflect precise locations.

FIGURE 9–6 Nuclear generating capacity, 1976. (From *Man, Energy, Society* by Earl Cook. W. H. Freeman and Co. Copyright © 1976.)

Disposal of waste products from energy production illustrates one of the basic conflicts produced by modernization. It is essential to generate more energy, but as this occurs, so does environmental deterioration.

RESOURCE CONFLICTS

Because natural resource policy decisions are made in conjunction with economic, social, and political factors, it is inevitable that conflicts will arise (Leonardo

Scholars, 1975, p. 71). For example, a decision to exploit one resource at the expense of another could lead to conflicts at the local, national, or international level.

The increased demand for both food and energy contains the seeds of several conflicts: (a) more ocean fisheries are threatened by the potential for massive spills which accompanies oil companies' reliance on oceanic transport; (b) strip-mining high-sulfur coal in Illinois, Indiana, and Iowa will disrupt farmlands that supply much of the nation's and, for that matter, the world's supply of corn, wheat, and soybeans; and (c) strip-mining in the western United States will destroy land valuable for wheat production and grazing. The

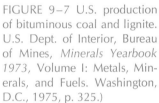

FIGURE 9–7 U.S. production of bituminous coal and lignite. U.S. Dept. of Interior, Bureau of Mines, *Minerals Yearbook 1973*, Volume I: Metals, Minerals, and Fuels. Washington, D.C., 1975, p. 325.)

use of one resource that is desperately needed by one group of people can therefore preempt the use of another resource needed equally badly by another group.

Oceanic transport and marine fisheries. The impact of oil pollution on marine fisheries is already widespread, and the increased demand for crude oil will most certainly add to the problem. People in the oil industry argue that increased reliance on supertankers will decrease the probability of an oil spill because there will be fewer tankers. However, supertankers contain much more oil—on the average, five times as much as a traditional tanker—and present the possibility of much larger oil spills. At any rate, increased reliance on supertankers will certainly increase the total volume of oil shipped via oceanic transport.

The exact impact of oil spills on marine life varies according to the type of organism and its habitat. Oil spills are more detrimental to marine life in inshore areas, such as estuaries, than in the open ocean, because they are important for spawning, shelter, and juvenile rearing for more than two-thirds of the food-fish (Longwood, 1972, p. 40).

The coal—wheat conflict. An increasing demand for energy resources in the United States, brought about by a growing and more affluent population, will

lead to a concomitant increase in mining activities in the final quarter of the 20th century. The United States has abundant supplies of coal, which is likely to be of major importance in America'a future energy policy (Tregarthen, et al., 1978, p. 351). Of concern to many planners are the land-use implications and conflicts associated with increased production of coal, especially the increasing percentage and the changing spatial pattern of production from strip mines (figure 9–7). Every state in the United States has at one time experienced some form of surface mining, although the largest reserves of strippable coal are found in the Appalachian region, the Midwest, and just east of the Rocky Mountains in Montana, Wyoming, Colorado, and North Dakota (figure 9–8).

Current estimates are that, of all the land that has been disturbed by strip-mining, more than half has not been reclaimed. Fortunately, most of the land affected in recent years has been reclaimed, but the difinition of reclamation is simply that local, state, or federal laws were complied with in whatever effort was undertaken. Although small experimental plots can be made to grow almost anything, there is little evidence to show that agricultural lands in the United States can be restored to their former productivity. Even if they could, the cost involved would most likely be prohibitive.

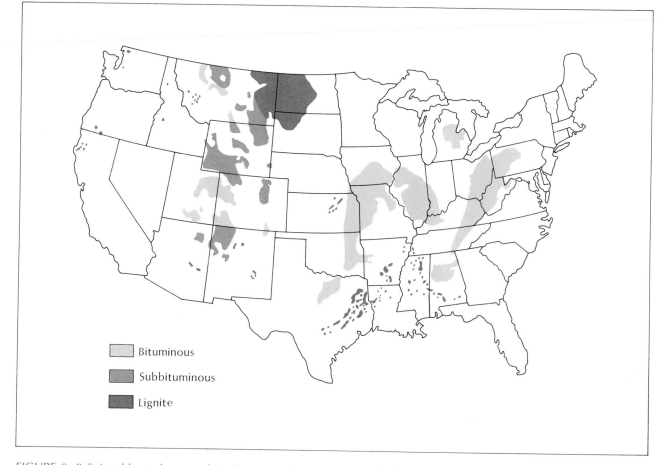

FIGURE 9–8 Strippable coal reserved in the conterminous United States. (T. D. Tregarthen, R. P. Larkin, G. L. Peters, July, 1978, "Mining, Markets, and Land Use," in the *Geographical Review* 68, No. 3; New York, American Geographical Society, p. 354. As modified from U.S. Dept. of Interior, Bureau of Mines, 1971, *Strippable Reserves of Bituminous Coal and Lignite in the United States,* Information Circular 8531, Washington, D.C., p. 19.)

Much of the land where strippable coal is found is presently used for cropland (figure 9–9). Large areas of primary wheat land—where wheat is at least 30 percent of planted crop acreage, and in most cases is at least 45 percent—overlie strippable beds of bituminous, subbituminous, and lignite coal in eastern Montana; secondary wheat lands—with wheat at less than 30 percent of planted crop acreage—overlie strippable coal in south central Illinois (U.S.D.A., 1971, p. 3-6). These two states are already encountering difficulty because of the land use conflicts associated with wheat and coal development.

Estimates are that, by the time the lignite and low-sulfur coal reserves are depleted in Montana, about 800,000 acres will have been strip-mined. The coal in Montana is primarily found in the eastern part of the state (figure 9–9), and approximately 85 percent of that land is pasture, cropland, or range. According to the United States Geological Survey, part of the coal lies under a piece of the Northern Plains spring wheat region, one of the nation's prime wheat-producing areas.

Like Montana, Illinois has a similar land-use conflict. Illinois is one of the oldest and largest coal-producing states in the nation. The principal crops grown in Illinois are corn and soybeans, although it also ranks high in wheat production. Some of the better wheat lands found in the state, as well as areas that are large producers of soybeans and corn, lie over strippable coal reserves (figure 9–10).

It is difficult to assess the exact parameters of this land-use conflict. According to a study by the Leonardo Scholars:

With the increasingly delicate balance of world food supplies and the rising significance of food-stuffs as

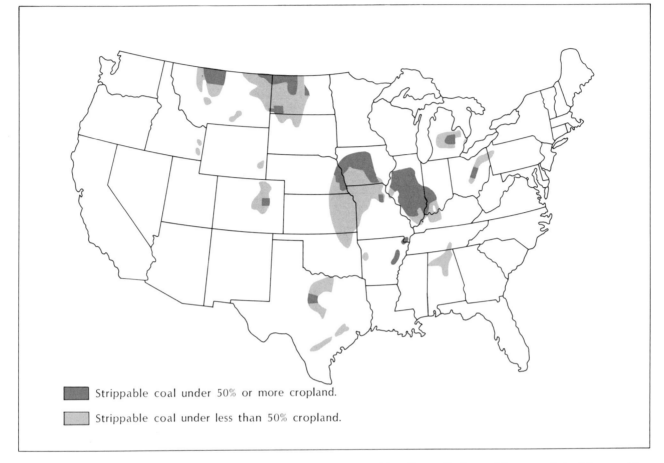

Strippable coal under 50% or more cropland.

Strippable coal under less than 50% cropland.

FIGURE 9–9 Cropland overlaying coal. (U.S.D.A. Economic Research Service, 1971, *Commercial Wheat Production,* Publication No. 480. And U.S. Dept. of Interior, Bureau of Mines, 1971, *Strippable Reserves of Bituminous Coal and Lignite in the United States,* Information Circular 8531, Washington, D.C., p. 19.)

export commodities for the United States, a number of unpredictable variables could affect the picture immensely. One could be a greater reliance upon coal than foreseen. . . .

Another variable is the relative productivity of land lying over coal fields. Some of the world's most productive land and most favorable climatic conditions occur in the Midwest. (1975, p. 80)

A Faustian bargain

An unexpected shortage in an important natural resource or energy supply can lead to short-sighted resource policy decisions with possibly long-lasting, re-grettable effects. Perhaps this type of decision-making is excusable under conditions of stress; however, they are inexcusable when there is sufficient lead time for more thoughtful policies.

The use of any resource involves a trade-off or payment, even at the most basic level. For example, a boy who wants to get an apple from the upper branches of a tree must "pay" for that apple in several ways.

First, he will make a very real payment on the spot in the form of energy he expends in climbing the tree. Second, he will take risks. One might be that of falling out of the tree. Another might be that from his vantage point on the ground he cannot be sure that the apple does not contain a worm. If the boy actually acquired the apple and ate it with satisfaction, we can assume that the expenditure of energy and risk-taking were worth it. (Leonardo Scholars, 1975, p. 60).

We could not know if the energy and risk involved were worth it until after the boy had climbed the tree

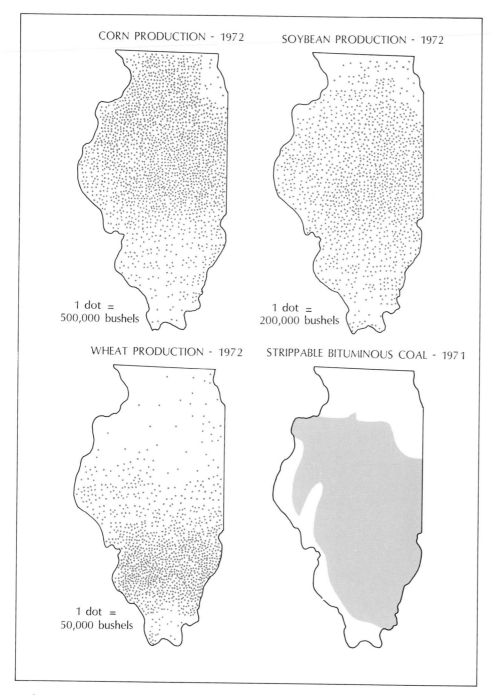

CORN PRODUCTION - 1972

SOYBEAN PRODUCTION - 1972

1 dot = 500,000 bushels

1 dot = 200,000 bushels

WHEAT PRODUCTION - 1972

STRIPPABLE BITUMINOUS COAL - 1971

1 dot = 50,000 bushels

FIGURE 9–10 Croplands and strippable coal reserves in Illinois. (*Illinois Agricultural Statistics, 1973 Summary*, Illinois Crop Report Service Bulletin 73–1, Springfield, 1973, p. 12. And U.S. Dept. of Interior, Bureau of Mines, 1971, *Strippable Reserves of Bituminous Coal and Lignite in the United States*, Information Circular 8531, Washington, D.C., p. 19.)

and eaten the apple. Therefore, only through hindsight can we determine if the boy profited from his efforts.

Unfortunately, not all the risks and trade-offs associated with resource exploitation and use are so clear-cut. In the totality of resource use, the boy becomes our global society, and the apple, losing its ex-

act definition, becomes a nebulous concept such as a "high living standard" or a "pristine environment." The price or payment made for the use of the resource is also obscured. Part of the payment, a polluted environment, may be delayed until later generations. Detrimental side effects may be an accepted consequence of resource exploitation or may have been unforeseen at the time of resource development.

The development of nuclear power highlights several important resource development issues. Most of the environmental costs associated with the development of nuclear power are natural science problems dealing with potential cost of a tangible nature. There are, however, intangible costs; these were outlined by Alvin Weinberg, Director of the Oak Ridge National Laboratory, in his article, "Social Institutions and Nuclear Energy" (1972).

According to Weinberg, the development of nuclear power had far-reaching social implications and was a direct threat to a cherished western value, individual freedom. He called it a **Faustian bargain** in which future societies would pay dearly for an inexhaustable source of energy, much like the bargain in the familiar German legend in which Faust sold his soul to the Devil in exchange for temporal influence and power.

> We nuclear people have made a Faustian bargain with society. On the other hand we offer—in the catalytic nuclear burner [the breeder reactor]—an inexhaustible source of energy. . . . But the price that we demand of society for this magical energy source is both a vigilance and a longevity of our social institutions that we are quite unaccustomed to. . . .

> We make two demands. The first. . .is that we exercise in nuclear technology the very best techniques and that we use people of high expertise and purpose. . . . The second demand is less clear, and I hope it may prove to be unnecessary. This is the demand for longevity in human institutions. We have relatively little problem dealing with [nuclear] wastes if we can assume always that there will be intelligent people around to cope with eventualities we have not thought of.

Finally, Weinberg asked:

> Is mankind prepared to exert the eternal vigilance needed to ensure proper and safe operation of its nuclear energy situation? This admittedly is a significant commitment that we ask of society. (pp. 33–34)

Social institutions must therefore watch over the dangerous lifespan of radioactive wastes which could be around for over 200,000 years, yet human institutions have endured for only a few thousand years. The nuclear power issue is a dramatic example of the Faustian bargain because the magnitude of time associated with the disposal of nuclear wastes is clear. There are, however, many other "bargains" where the true nature of the future payment is questionable.

KEY TERMS

Resource
Neutral stuff
Resource creation and destruction
Renewable resource
Nonrenewable resource
Recoverability
Stretchability
Flexibility

Vulnerability
Utilitarian viewpoint
Preservationist movement
Resource availability
Energy
Resource conflicts
Faustian bargain

REFERENCES

Cook, E. (1976), *Man, Energy, Society.* San Francisco: W. H. Freeman & Co.

Cook, E. (1977), *Energy: The Ultimate Resource.* Washington, D.C.: Association of American Geographers, Resource Paper No. 77–4.

Dickens, C. (1854), "Coke Town," *The Old Curiousity Shop, Hard Times and The Holy Tree Inn,* as quoted in Salter, C. (1971), *The Cultural Landscape.* Belmont, CA: Wadsworth Publishing Co., Inc.

Ginsburg, N. (1957), "Natural Resources and Economic Development," *Annals of the Association of American Geographers* 47, No. 3, 197–212.

Hawkes, H. (1960), "The Paradoxes of the Conservation Movement," *Bulletin of the University of Utah* 51.

Hubbard, M. (1969), "Energy Resources," in *Resources and Man: National Academy of Sciences—National Research Council, Report of Committee on Resources and Man*. San Francisco: W. H. Freeman & Co., 157–242.

Landsberg, H. (1964), *Natural Resources for U.S. Growth*. Baltimore, MD: Johns Hopkins University Press.

The Leonardo Scholars (1975), *Resources and Decisions*. North Scituate, MA: Duxbury Press/Wadsworth Publishing Co., Inc.

Longwood, W. (1972), *The Darkening Land*. New York: Simon & Schuster, Inc.

Luten, D. B. (1971), "The Economic Geography of Energy," in *Energy and Power*. San Francisco: W. H. Freeman & Co., 109–120.

Luten, D. B. (1972), Based on a series of lectures given in Berkeley, California, and San Diego, California, in 1972 and 1973.

Tregarthen, T. D., Larkin, R. P., and Peters, G. L. (1978), "Mining, Markets, and Land Use," *The Geographical Review* 68, No. 3, 351–358.

U.S. Dept. of Agriculture (1971), *Commercial Wheat Production*. Economic Research Service Bulletin ERS 480, September.

Weinberg, A. W. (1972), "Social Institutions and Nuclear Energy," *Science* 177, 27–34.

Zimmerman, E. W. (1951), *World Resources and Industries*, rev. ed. New York: Harper & Bros., Publishers.

10

The road toward modernization

Each night millions of children go to bed with a persistent gnawing hunger that saps their tired bodies of life and assures that they will never fully develop their physical and mental potentials. In the world's poorest nations, millions live near the physical margins that separate the living from the dead. It is obvious, even to the most casual observer, that the world's wealth is not equally distributed among the many nations—there are rich and poor nations and, within them, rich and poor people. However, despite this obvious gap, we are left with only an imperfect knowledge of the causes and consequences of wide disparities in living standards among nations.

MODERNIZATION AND DEVELOPMENT

Definitions

The United Nations designated the 1960s as the "Decade of Development," yet there were not great advances in the quality of life for most people in countries of the Third World. However, some lessons were learned about the needs of poor countries and about methods for understanding and improving their condition.

In the 1960s textbooks defined **economic development** as purely economic and emphasized increases in income per capita above all else. The essential ingredients for economic development were thought to be capital formation and technical progress. Economists were prone to overlook or disregard the social

and cultural diversity of the poor countries and to treat them as if they were relatively homogeneous.

In 1970 Dudley Seers, then Director of the Institute of Development Studies at the University of Sussex in England, argued that the complex nature of development problems was becoming increasingly apparent. He pointed out that the use of one aggregate measure of well-being was no longer viable and that perpetuating its use suggested a desire to avoid confronting development problems in a responsible way (1969). He emphasized the need to understand poverty, unemployment and inequality in the broader context of opportunities for fulfillment of human potential. More than just an increase in income is necessary, he argued, if the quality of life in the poor countries is to be improved.

During the 1970s social scientists increasingly questioned the values of models of economic development which ignored the cultural and historical context within which the world's nations had been divided into "haves" and "have-nots." According to Anthony de Souza and Philip Porter,

> A new spirit is emerging in the underdeveloped world, one of frustration, anger, and a changed evaluation of the political and economic conditions in which people find themselves. The gap between rich and poor countries, as measured by production and consumption, is widening, just as it is within most rich countries between wealthy and poor people. Political and economic thinkers in underdeveloped countries have given increasing attention to the historical processes which have brought their countries to their present condition. They see the

process as part of a worldwide network of intrusion by the rich countries into the poor, of neoimperialist penetration which forecloses most opportunities for development because of the hold foreign interests have on trade and investment. (1974, p. 2)

Though what we could call a "Western perspective" on economic development still dominates the social science literature throughout most of the developed world, we see a rising tide of literature asserting a Third World perspective. We provide a discussion of both perspectives, though we may be accused of giving them unequal weight.

Measuring development

The most commonly used measure of the overall economic performance of a nation is the **Gross National Product (GNP):** the total value of goods and services produced in one year. Of course, in order to make comparisons among countries of different population sizes, it is necessary to standardize for size variations by using GNP per capita. Figure 10–1 provides us with a useful view of material well-being in the world despite some of the criticisms which are made toward using this measure.

Among the criticisms are at least the following: (a) GNP per capita tells us nothing of how income is actually distributed within a country; (b) GNP is difficult to calculate for centrally planned economies; and (c) in poor countries many products never enter a marketplace at all, hence are not counted as part of GNP. However, GNP is a starting point in measuring international disparities in income, though we should use it cautiously.

Two other indicators of the level of economic development have been used occasionally. One is energy consumption per capita; the other is the percent of the labor force employed in agriculture. Both tend to be related to GNP per capita and both have been similarly criticized.

We could construct a long list of characteristics of developing societies to which most social scientists would probably nod agreement. Besides low income per capita, we could add other economic attributes such as a low volume of trade per capita, poor housing, inadequate credit facilities, deficient diets, and small amounts of capital per worker. Furthermore, we could add such noneconomic characteristics as high birth rates, high infant mortality rates, high illiteracy rates,

inferior status of women, and crude technology (Leibenstein, 1957, pp. 40–41). However, not all developing countries exhibit the same set of attributes. We cannot easily generalize about countries as diverse as Brazil or China, on the one hand, and Malawi or Kuwait, on the other.

In recent years some geographers have suggested that we should consider the quality of life as a central concept to be measured by such quantitative indicators as per capita GNP, and by such nonquantitative indicators as satisfaction or happiness. However, the application of a quality of life concept is not without its pitfalls and conceptual difficulties. Wilbur Zelinsky has gone so far as to argue the unlikelihood that social scientists will ever find a good measurable definition of quality of life (1976, p. 8). Hopefully progress will be made toward better and more meaningful ways of measuring the quality of life and its variations from place to place. However, in the interim we must move on, using what measures are available.

DEVELOPMENT AND MODERNIZATION IN A CULTURAL CONTEXT

Though we can find some basic agreement among social scientists on the characteristics of developed and developing societies, the causes and consequences of development are keenly debated, and agreement is unlikely. Economic changes occur within the larger milieu of cultural transformation and cannot be clearly understood in isolation from characteristics of other peoples and places.

Social scientists have tried to explain economic development from different disciplinary perspectives. Their results are often narrow and leave us with numerous unanswered questions and unsolved problems, especially the major one of how to improve the lot of people whose fate it was to be born to peasant parents in a poor country.

Tribal and peasant societies

Tribal societies are virtually closed systems which function with neither connections with, nor an understanding of, modern industrial societies. Individuals behave according to well-defined traditional patterns. Because such social groups are relatively inflexible,

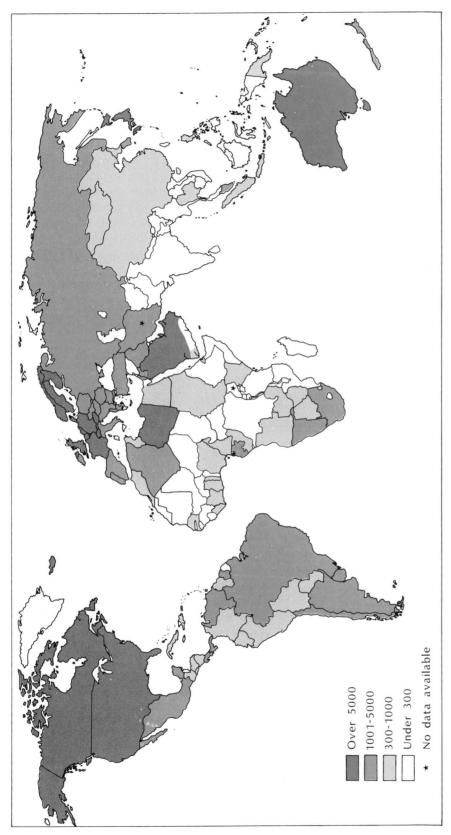

FIGURE 10–1 GNP per capita, 1980 (in U.S. dollars). (Data from the *1980 World Population Data Sheet.* Courtesy of the Population Reference Bureau, Inc., Washington D.C.)

Over 5000

1001-5000

300-1000

Under 300

★ No data available

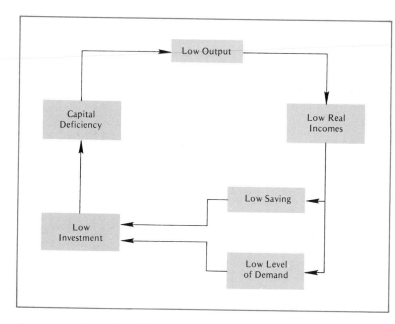

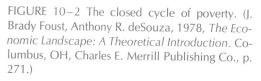

FIGURE 10–2 The closed cycle of poverty. (J. Brady Foust, Anthony R. deSouza, 1978, *The Economic Landscape: A Theoretical Introduction.* Columbus, OH, Charles E. Merrill Publishing Co., p. 271.)

they are quite vulnerable to pressure exerted by more complex cultures.

Though peasant societies are in many ways more aware of outside societies and more flexible in their ability to deal with more complex societies, they still have many behavior patterns in common with tribal societies. Economic life in both is often controlled by cultural traditions which allocate scarce resources to various ceremonial activities rather than to what western development economists would see more fitting, such as investment in capital goods to increase low levels of productivity.

Modernization

We could discuss the cultural context of development at length, but instead we wish to consider another term, *modernization,* which carries with it an awareness that economic development does not occur in isolation from sweeping changes in the cultural fabric of transforming societies. As we saw in chapter 4, modernization is a broad term used to describe all the various changes that occur as a society is transformed from traditional to modern. Black (1967) suggested that modernization could be discussed in terms of the following categories of human activity: intellectual, political, economic, social, and psychological.

Much of the literature on modernization has tended to treat modern and traditional cultures as opposite ends of a single spectrum. Hope and progress are embedded in the idea of modernization, as is the

feeling that Western culture has invented most of the good things associated with modernization. Too often Western social scientists, in their zeal for embracing whatever is currently in vogue, are guilty of forgetting the richness of such traditional cultures as those of China and India. Modernization becomes a symbol of good, and traditional connotes something bad, or at least backward or less desirable.

Economic theories of development

For the most part, western economists have tried to use their models and methods, or modified versions of them, to explain the development process in developing countries. One economic view of **underdevelopment** is that developing countries are caught in a closed cycle of low output, low income, low savings, and low investment, as show in figure 10–2. Another view is that initially all countries were about equal in their levels of economic development, and what we now need to understand is what allowed some countries to escape the "low-level equilibrium trap" and how others can be helped to escape it.

Rostow and the stages of economic growth. W. W. Rostow, an economic historian, suggested that the transition from a traditional to a modern economic society occurs in an orderly fashion as the country passes through a series of *stages of economic growth.* Rostow was aware of the complexities of modernization, as well as the difficulty of generalizing about the development experiences of diverse economic and political systems, and was aware that his stages of growth were somewhat arbitrary. However, these five stages provide one useful way of viewing modernization.

1. The traditional society. Science and modern technology are absent, productivity levels are low, and a large proportion of the population is employed in agriculture. Conservatism and opposition to change are inherent features of the social structure, and political power is usually regional rather than national.

2. The preconditions for take-off. In this stage the transition toward modernization is underway, as changes overcome some obstacles to sustained economic growth. The society begins to perceive some of the benefits of modernization. Entrepreneurs become apparent in the private sector, banks appear to facilitate credit and exchange, and exogenous factors encourage new investment in transportation, communications, and raw materials. The creation of a coherent national state was viewed by Rostow as a necessity during this stage.

3. The take-off. This crucial third stage, according to Rostow, is one in which various impediments to sustained growth are overcome. Growth becomes the normal condition, and economic progress dominates society. The rates of savings and investment increase from 5 percent to over 10 percent of national income, some rapid expansion occurs in selected manufacturing sectors, and profits stimulate further investment. New techniques appear in both manufacturing and agriculture as innovation is encouraged.

4. The drive to maturity. Investment runs at 10 to 20 percent of national income, new techniques continually alter the structure of the economy, and the country enters the international economy. Growth becomes less concentrated in such industries as coal, iron, and steel, and spreads more into newer industries, including chemicals and electronics.

5. The age of high mass-consumption. In this stage major manufacturing sectors shift to the production of consumer durable goods as high incomes create a demand for them. Urbanization increases as does the proportion of the population working in skilled manufacturing jobs. Societies become increasingly concerned with income distribution and welfare. This stage has been reached by the United States, Canada, Japan and Western Europe, and the Soviet Union seems on the verge of entering it.

Rostow's model has been both praised and damned. Economists especially have criticized the fuzziness of definitions and the difficulties of precisely identifying the various stages. It assumes that all countries were once underdeveloped and that some have moved through a unilineal transformation into modern, developed economies, whereas others have remained behind.

A Third-World view. The last thought above has provoked considerable oppositon from many social scientists in the developing countries; they argue that *underdeveloped* refers not to some initial state, but rather results from imperialism (de Souza and Porter, 1974, p. 2).

Andre Frank, in one of several essays on the nature of underdevelopment, stated,

> It is generally held that economic development occurs in a succession of capitalist stages and that today's underdeveloped countries are still in a stage, sometimes depicted as an original stage of history, through which the now developed countries passed long ago. Yet even a modest acquaintance with history shows that underdevelopment is not original or traditional and that neither the past nor the present of the underdeveloped countries resembles in any important respect the past of the now developed countries. The now developed countries were never *under*developed, though they may have been *un*developed. (1972, p. 3)

Frank viewed current developing countries as a product of both historical and current economic interactions between themselves and the now developed metropolitan countries. Furthermore, he argued that this was a necessary concomitant of an international capitalist system and that development of the developing countries would be possible only independent of the diffusion of various attributes from the developed countries. He argued that "underdevelopment was and still is generated by the very same historical process which also generated economic development: the development of capitalism itself" (1972, p. 9).

Szentes, after considering Rostow and his critics, concluded, "it is rather obvious that economic underdevelopment can neither be satisfactorily explained by internal factors nor can it be seen as a natural stage in the general process of growth" (1971, p. 99). Like Frank, Szentes viewed underdevelopment as a result of the economic development process.

Colonialism is often associated with the process of underdevelopment because of the control it allowed the metropolitan, developed countries to exert over the underdeveloped countries. Nowhere, perhaps, is there a better example than the plantation system. The plantation is basically an economic system designed to produce agricultural products, usually with the help of unskilled labor. The ratio of laborers to managers is high, and production usually focuses on a single cash crop, mainly for export to the developed countries. Central authority determines the way plantations will operate as well as the social behavior of those who live and work on them. Plantations function as parts of a broader economic system, controlled by industrial countries, in which they are dependent on the markets of the industrial countries. So we again find dependence associated with underdevelopment. Because of this historical experience, people in plantation societies often lack the initiative and vision to carry out necessary changes (Beckford, 1972).

Critics of the Third World view of underdevelopment and its causes, including colonialism and exploitation, point to these causes as scapegoats. They point out the positive changes brought about under colonial control and the economic development of some colonies. However, we need to try to evaluate these views, as well as the views of western economists, if we are to understand the great contrasts in well-being which exist among countries, and if we are ever to provide ways of improving the lives of those who live in the poorer countries.

SPATIAL ORGANIZATION AND DEVELOPMENT

Geographers have focused on various aspects of the relationship between economic development and the spatial structure of economic activities, but especially important themes have been related to transportation development, diffusion, and growth centers. Some of these deserve more detailed treatment.

Transport development

In early geographic studies of development, Rostow's influence was often apparent, especially his notion that development occurred in a series of stages. One example is a model of transport development suggested by Taaffe, Morrill and Gould. Their model, based on studies of transport development in various developing countries, showed a series of stages in the development of a transportation network (figure 10–3). At the outset they assumed an underdeveloped region with an unexplored interior into which a transport system would

penetrate from the coastal zone. Reasons for establishing a transport link to the interior include mineral exploitation, agricultural exports, and connection with an interior area of military or political control (1963, p. 506).

The model suggests a sequential expansion of the **transport network** interrelated with an expanding and developing urban system. In the earliest stage (*Stage A*), there are only a few small ports. Then (*Stage B*) two cities are established in the interior (I_1 and I_2) and are connected by "penetration lines" to two ports, which thus benefit from increased trade and growth. In *Stage C* feeder routes develop, and new urban centers emerge along established routes as the urban system further expands. With still more time, new interconnections begin to develop (*Stage D*) and gradually lead to a completely interconnected network of urban places (*Stage E*). Finally "Main Streets" develop in *Stage F*.

Many studies have suggested that the development of an integrated transportation system was closely related to modernization. Furthermore, several studies have shown a considerable similarity between the model described by Taaffe, Morrill and Gould and the actual development of land transportation systems in developing countries, especially those developed under colonialism. For example, Alan Gilbert (1974), in a geographic study of Latin American economic development, found that the pattern of rail development in some areas closely followed the Taaffe, Morrill and Gould model. In Ecuador, Gilbert noted that the first and primary railroad was built to connect the port city of Guayaquil to the inland capital, Quito, and to Cuenca. Similarly, according to Gilbert, Peruvian railways were extended inland from the ports of Mollendo and Callao, in the latter case to inland mining centers. Chilean rail development followed a similar pattern. For the most part, however, Gilbert points out that the limited economic development in western South America resulted in the railway network's not reaching a further integrated pattern (figure 10–4).

The spatial impress of modernization

Toward the end of the 1960s, stimulated by a search for explanations of spatial patterns of economic development and modernization, and coupled with the geographic use of a wide variety of statistical techniques, a "geography of modernization" emerged (de Souza and Porter, 1974). At this point geographers were approaching the methods of other social scientists in

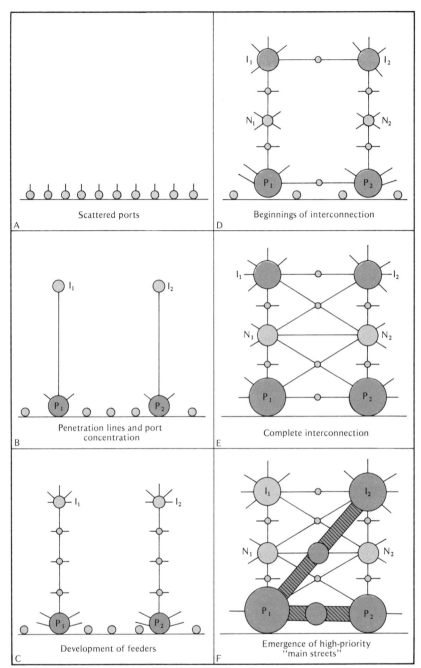

FIGURE 10-3 The ideal-typical sequence of transport development. (E. J. Taaffe, R. L. Morrill, P. R. Gould, October, 1973, "Transport Expansion in Underdeveloped Countries," in the *Geographical Review* 53, p. 504, with the permission of the American Geographical Society.)

studying the modernization process. Among geographers, Peter Gould was a major force in focusing attention on modernization as a process of spatial diffusion and on the spatial pattern of modernization in developing countries (1964). Several geographers followed Gould's suggestions in their studies of modernization. Their approaches have been quantitative and have mainly selected variables related to urbanization, social characteristics, communications, and transportation.

Central to studies of the geography of modernization is a descriptive view of spatial variations in the degrees of development, as illustrated by Gould's study of modernization in Tanzania (1970). Gould found that levels of modernization usually dropped rapidly away from the towns. The Tanzanian "modernization surface" for each time period showed a clear pattern of

Nigerian workers lift and pack railroad track near Gombe. (John Moss of Black Star for World Bank, 1961)

regional inequality, with core areas which were developed and peripheral areas which had not benefitted from modernization.

Another study of geography of modernization was done in Kenya by Edward Soja (1968). After providing a detailed historical picture of Kenya, especially of the population and the development of transportation and communications networks, Soja moved to an analysis of the spatial pattern of modernization using statistical techniques. He employed a total of 25 variables to measure the following general sets of characteristics: demographic, education, communications and transport, connectivity with Nairobi, economic development, and political development. The most important result of the statistical analysis was what Soja labeled the "development factor." Closely related were the communications variables; Soja argued that this lends support to the idea that diffusion and communications developments play a central role in modernization.

The spatial pattern of the development factor in Kenya, as with Gould's Tanzanian study, showed a marked pattern of regional inequality. The highest levels of development occur in areas like Nairobi, whereas the least developed areas tend to be located in relatively isolated peripheral areas.

Thus, spatial patterns of development tend to show patterns of regional inequality, in which core areas are well-developed and peripheral areas are poorly developed. Changes in modernization patterns over time strongly suggest that modernization diffuses outward from centers and downward through the urban hierarchy.

The core – periphery model and polarized development

The perspective provided by a ***core–periphery model*** (sometimes referred to as *heartland–hinterland*) may be used at various scales, from international to local or regional. Regardless of areal extent, the model suggests that we can divide an area into a center and a periphery, or a heartland and a hinterland. At different scales the concept of a core and a periphery remains valid. For example, a nation–state can be divided into a dominant core area and a peripheral area (or areas). Similarly, within a subnational region, we can still identify a core and periphery. Thus, we end up with cores and peripheries within cores and peripheries as we slide from the international scale to the local scale.

At any scale there are linkages and interactions between the core and the periphery, and there are processes operating in the directions of both reducing and increasing core–periphery differences. According to the Marxist interpretation, the core appropriates for its own development the surplus of the periphery (Foust and de Souza, 1978, p. 288).

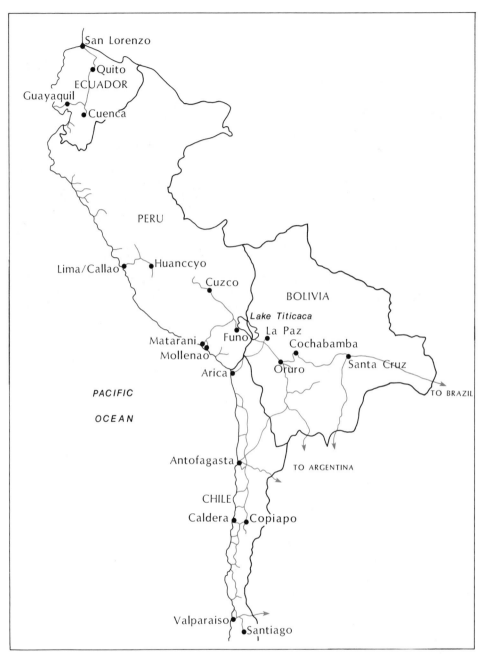

FIGURE 10–4 Railway network of Ecuador, Peru, Bolivia, and Chile, 1974. (A. Gilbert, 1974, *Latin American Development: A Geographical Perspective*. London, Penguin Books Ltd., p. 184.)

The core–periphery model has been formulated in various ways by different social scientists. Among them are Gunnar Myrdal and John Friedmann.

Myrdal's model. Reacting to various equilibrium-type models of economic development, Myrdal sug-

gested that, in a free economy, particular changes in one part of the economic system or the space–economy did not necessarily set in motion "countervailing changes" to restore equilibrium (1957). Rather, he suggested that, once changes were set in motion, they would follow a pattern of **circular**

A pay telephone station at Azezo near Gondar, Ethiopia. (Kay Muldoon for World Bank, 1969)

and cummulative causation. For example, if for some reason one region within a country began to experience accelerated economic growth, possibly as the result of a decision to locate a new industry there, then that area would be more attractive to investors, would attract more investment, and would experience even more economic growth, quite possibly at the expense of growth elsewhere in the country. Thus, Myrdal suggested a process of **polarized development** leading to the concentration of economic development in a core region, which would attract investment and labor from the periphery via the circular and cumulative causation mechanism.

In Myrdal's view, once economic growth had been initiated in a specific area, that area would act as an economic magnet, drawing inflows of capital, labor, and commodities from the surrounding peripheral region. These flows from the periphery result in backwash effects as the periphery loses skilled workers and investment capital to the core. Poorer health services and educational facilities in the periphery are further backwash effects. Thus, backwash effects, operating through various forms of spatial interaction, increase the differentiation between core regions and peripheral regions.

However, Myrdal recognized that there may also be benefits from the core to the periphery. These ben-efits, or *spread effects,* include the stimulation of demand for the products of the periphery, especially agricultural and mineral products.

Myrdal assumed a free economy with no government intervention. Under those conditions, he argued that polarized development would occur and that backwash effects would tend to be stronger than spread effects. Thus, he felt that the only way to move in the direction of regional equality would be government intervention.

Friedmann's model. John Friedmann has long been an advocate of center–periphery models and the concept of polarized development. Rather than one model, Friedmann's ideas have evolved over time such that he has developed a series of closely related models. His central concern has been the relationship between spatial patterns of urban-economic systems and corresponding stages of economic growth. Two examples should clearly illustrate both his concern and the direction of his evolving conceptual view of space economy.

An early view of an evolving national space economy appeared in 1966 and was based to considerable extent on the relationship between urbanization and economic growth in North America (figure 10–5). In this simplified schema, Friedmann suggested four

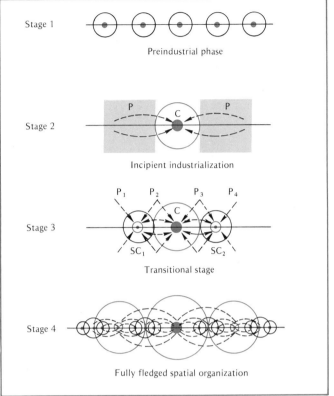

stages in which, as economic growth proceeds, the spatial economy becomes increasingly more complex, as well as more closely interrelated.

In the *Preindustrial Phase,* the space economy is composed of small, scattered, and independent urban centers. The system is poorly integrated and lacks a significant potential for economic growth.

During *Incipient Industrialization,* a primate city develops, shown by *C,* which begins to control and exploit the surrounding region or periphery, showh by *P.* Development of the primate city starts the movement of people from the periphery to the center similar to Myrdal's backwash effects.

Friedmann viewed the third stage, the *Transitional Stage,* as one within which the primate city moved toward industrial maturity. Though the primate city continues to dominate the region, its influence is not so overpowering, and other cities, shown by SC_1 and SC_2, increase in size and influence. Thus, the urban system is becoming better defined as a hierarchy of urban centers. In the periphery underdeveloped areas remain, as shown by P_1, P_2, P_3, and P_4.

In the last stage, *Fully Fledged Spatial Organization,* an integrated national urban hierachy is attained.

In 1973, Friedmann developed the process of polarized growth more fully, emphasizing the role of innovation and diffusion in the development of spatial systems. He suggests a theory of polarized development based on the following broad areas of concern: development as innovation; the conditions of innovation; innovation, power, and authority in spatial systems; authority–dependency relations in a spatial system; and polarized development in a hierarchy of spatial systems.

Friedmann suggested that core regions could be found in a series of spatial systems in a "nested hierarchy." The scales of such systems, he suggested, were world, multination region, nation, subnational region, and province. He viewed the diffusion of innovations from the core to the periphery as controlling growth of the developing urban system and the nature of the relationship between core and periphery. Thus, the diffusion of innovations affected economic and social characteristics in both the heartland and the hinterland. Theoretically the core region could ultimately expand to occupy the entire inhabited portion of the earth's surface, completely removing even the last vestiges of peripheral or backward areas, though such an outcome appears unlikely, at least in the foreseeable future.

CASE STUDY:
Modernizing the Masai
Emmett George

The world's cattlemen are conservatives and their lifestyle is difficult to change. The cowboy of the old American southwest, the Karamojong in Uganda, the Somali herdsman in northern Kenya, and the Masai of Tanzania and Kenya share a contempt for farming and other stationary occupations.

For the 125,000 residents of Masailand, a 54,000 square mile strip in northern Tanzania that inches over the border into Kenya, tradition means tending the herds and searching for grazing lands and water.

Historically, the Masai roamed as far north as Mount Kenya, as far south as Mount Kilimanjaro, to the shores of Lake Victoria on the west, and east to the beaches of the Indian Ocean.

On the range, their cattle must now compete with other aggressive grazers. Herds of goats and donkeys display an uncanny ability to survive in arid lands.

Civilization also threatens the Masai's livestock-raising traditions. Grazing lands are diminishing and a few Masai are farming two- or three-acre shambas, or gardens, to produce food for their families.

In recent years, the Masai have limited their migration at the urging of the Tanzanian government, which introduced programs to limit the Masai to areas with enough grass and water to support their herds.

The Masai are suspicious of strangers. Women cover their face with their forearm to avoid having their picture taken. The elders stomp boldly forward to challenge any outsiders who approach the boma, the Masai family compound.

Rongaltaika Boma, named for an official who supervises it, is perched on a slope with dried yellow grasses and volcanic rock fragments. A six-foot high circle of stiff brush keeps cattle in and intruders out.

Two teenage boys appear at the opening to the boma as a group of AID officials approach. They smile and run to summon their elders. The women huddle silently in a corner holding babies that cry at the sight of strangers. The first elder appears. The AID group is escorted to a rest hut outside the boma for a meeting. The elder is joined by the two boys. Names are known but not said in introductions.

The elder is willing to discuss the newly-completed all-weather road built with U.S. drought funds. "We use it to drive our cattle to the market, and to take our sick to the hospital. It is a help to us."

Masai problems vary only slightly from boma to boma. The primary concern is the welfare of the animals. A Masai's wealth and social status is measured by the number of animals he owns.

Small dams and wells provide water for cattle in Masailand—part of the government's national livestock development program assisted by AID. (USAID Mission/Tanzania)

"It's been raining and there are a lot of mosquitoes and disease [malaria]. We are worried about the goats. Many of them have diarrhea and several have died. We can't tell why this is happening, but the cattle are OK and the donkeys never get sick."

Israel Ole Karyongi is one of the 25 Masai who have received a college education. After primary school in Tanzania, he studied at Egerton College in Kenya and later at the New Mexico State University in the U.S., where he earned a bachelor's degree in animal husbandry. After further study at New Mexico State, he returned home last year to become acting regional livestock development officer.

Karyongi has few of the traditional scarations—the slitted and stretched ear lobes that characterize the Masai. Western ideas have influenced his lifestyle. He and his wife, Pewinah, and their three chidren no longer live in the boma. But, he says, the Masai have a way of reminding their own about their origin and traditions.

"The elders tell you 'Don't forget home.' They are constantly reminding the young of their customs. When I return home, I still have to follow the customs closely."

USAID officials work with the Masai and the Tanzania and Kenya governments to promote better land use, build roads and develop reliable water supplies and centralized services. (USAID Mission/Dar es Salaama)

Karyongi has spotted change in Masailand and a greater willingness to accept government development projects.

"Every time I go back I find more and more progress. The progress is slow but there is more development than in the past. The people are building better houses and more are going to school. They are beginning to follow more modern methods of cattle-raising than they were 10 years ago. They are even selling more of their livestock to buy goods and food."

A big change, he says, is that the Masai are now willing to let their children attend school. They days when the government went into the boma and forcibly took children for school have passed. There is now little resistance except to education for girls, who often come home for the holidays and are not allowed to return to school. Like most African societies, Masai culture is male-dominated.

"They are even slowly changing their eating habits and combining rice and wheat with their corn flour. Practically everyone wants tea in the mornings." Traditionally, the Masai lived almost exclusively on dried meat and milk. About 10 cows were always kept in milk to feed the boma.

"People said that the Masai always drank blood from the cattle. But that is not so. Blood was taken during times of famine when there was no milk and little water. Blood is full of protein. It helped them survive. They used it to make soup. This practice is going out. It never was the sole diet of the Masai."

Masai women shop for necessities at a small store near Arusha. The AID-built drought relief road provides the Masai with access to markets, schools and clinics. (Emmett George/AID)

The scarcity of prime grazing lands in Tanzania is forcing the government to impose limits on land use and herd size. "You have to do a very big selling job to get people to limit the size of their herds," Karyongi says.

"Another problem is that most people won't settle down so they can benefit from the projects. The land is very dry and they feel they must keep moving to feed the herds." To halt migration, the government's village settlement program has been designed to settle people in areas that will support them.

"We don't move that much anymore," Karyongi observes. "The government has given the Masai a lot of things like schools and dispensaries. The people have better diets and are wearing better clothing. So it is in their interest to stay near these facilities."

A mystique still surrounds the Masai's reputation as a warrior tribe. This reputation stems from their cattle-raiding days and made them virtually unapproachable. Karyongi feels that much of the Masai reputation is undeserved.

"We were very brave during times of war, but I don't accept that we are hostile. We are just very brave people. The whole problem centered around cattle and fighting over grazing rights.

"About 25,000 Masai lived on the Kenya side of the border. They would just cross borders and have to fight with other tribes."

Colby Hatfield, of Denver, Colorado, who has a doctorate from Catholic University in Washington, D.C., has spent years researching the agricultural people near Lake Victoria. Since 1973, Hatfield has been fascinated by Masai culture.

Masai society is structured into a hierarchy of elders and warrior groups. Age sets all relationships. For example, boys are circumcised at 12 to 14, and the newly-circumcised comprise one age group while the "morani," or warrior, stage reflects yet another group. The elders are also divided into age categories.

"Theoretically there is no control of animals or political power until a young man becomes an elder," Hatfield explains.

"Masai women remain as children for life, having no formal power of their own. They are wards of the husband. But informally a woman's power can be tremendous, derived from power vested in her son. She serves as custodian of her son's animals in the event he is not of age. When there's a marriage, she gets animals from her husband and son-in-law. She is always vying with relatives to build the animal herds of her son. She also has direct influence over her son because she is constantly promoting his interests.

"On the whole, Masai women don't work quite as hard as most agricultural women in Africa. They do about as much as the men. The herd boys are the hardest workers. They always have to be prepared to defend their animals from others."

The morani's responsibility varies, but he is generally entrusted with dipping the animals, digging wells, and defending the boma, Hatfield says.

Hatfield corrects another misconception about the Masai. "They don't give every animal a name. Unlike some pastoral societies, they name only special steers. Important human relationships are defined through cattle names. For example, a gift of a goat indicates friendship while a heifer ranks ahead of a goat. A nickname given an animal may have more meaning because it defines a relationship." The Masai refer to each other by names given to animals received as gifts from friends or relatives.

AID has provided $3.6 million in assistance to the Masai, enabling them to learn modern animal husbandry, new range management, marketing, and disease control. The project also helps the Tanzania Livestock Marketing Company establish and operate primary and secondary markets, develop and plan stock routes, and construct holding pens. In addition, ranching associations have been formed, six centers for veterinary services have opened, and 136 miles of access roads have been built.

The AID project is part of a national effort to build a commercial cattle industry.

A land use survey determined grazing patterns and the amount of grass and water available on the different pastures. The government can now advise the Masai on the location of water-holes and forage. A two-season grazing plan has been introduced, establishing certain pastures to be used for dry-season grazing and others for wet-season grazing. AID support also helped the government field three well-digging crews. $250,000 was provided for 12 tractors, two motorized graders, two drilling machines, and trucks plus spare parts, creating employment for six mechanics and 15 helpers.

Bob Booth, AID water resource manager for the project, says the need for reliable water sources cannot be over-emphasized in Masailand. Booth supervises the construction of small dams and wells.

The Masai are willing to have smaller sources of water for the livestock, but they are more secure with larger ones because small dams often do not stand up during the rainy seasons. There is little forage, so when it rains the run-off is great.

"There are no major springs in Masailand. Drillers have gone down as far as 2,000 feet without hitting water. This area really needs 600 million gallons of water." The goal is to have at least one permanent source of water for each of the 22 ranching associations being planned.

Reprinted from *Agenda* 1, no. 3 (March, 1978), pp. 13 – 16.

PEOPLE, ENVIRONMENT AND DEVELOPMENT

Economic growth and development have been almost universally accepted as "good." People everywhere want better lives for themselves and for their children, and for most it has been easy to believe that "more is better." Yet, as we have already seen, the benefits of economic growth and development have not been evenly distributed around the globe; there are still rich and poor nations, as there are rich and poor regions within nations.

However, sustained global economic growth is not without problems. Only in recent years have we heard an emerging voice which, at the very least, warns us to beware of an ecological pricetag associated with economic growth.

Ecology and development

During the 1970s many social scientists began to see signals indicative of mounting pressures on the earth's major biological systems and energy resources—pressures generated by a combination of population growth and economic growth. The growing conflict between economists and ecologists will not be quickly resolved, though it should continue to generate needed research efforts. According to Lester Brown, a noted agricultural economist, economists are not used to considering the importance of biological systems

(1978, p. 6). Brown argued that this lack of ecological awareness has affected economic analysis and policy-making in detrimental ways during the 1970s.

An ecological view. People depend on four major biological systems for food and numerous industrial raw materials. In an earlier chapter we saw that, even in ancient times, humans were prone to greatly modify natural ecosystems for their own benefit. Futhermore, we saw that humankind's control over the environment increased dramatically as the agricultural revolution and then the Industrial Revolution unfolded. So why all the sudden fuss about ecology and growth?

One answer begins with magnitude. Earth is home for a growing population already in excess of 4 billion. Each person has needs and wants which must be provided, at least in part, by exploiting the environment; in other words, the world economy rests on a biological foundation. It is the stress appearing in portions of this biological foundation that has many people concerned about the earth's ecological future.

Oceanic fisheries, for example, are a major source of protein and, at least until recently, we have assumed that we could always rely on the ocean's abundance of fish. Between 1950 and 1970 the world fish catch more than tripled, from 21 to 70 million tons annually. However, since 1970 the annual catch has remained around 65 to 70 million tons, despite newer technologies and the best efforts of the world's fishing fleets. Hopes for increasing the yield of oceanic fisher-

Asphalt plant 12 miles north of Bogota, Columbia. (United Nations/John Littlewood, 1974)

ies are clouded, as overfishing of certain species and areas, coupled with the rising tide of pollutants daily dumped into the ocean, threaten both the variety and abundance of marine life.

Most marine life is found along the continental coasts, as are most of our ocean-bound waste products, including chemical effluents, petroleum, automobile exhaust products, and detergents. Industrial and agricultural wastes, along with sewage from our great cities, make many ocean areas nearly uninhabitable for some species. For example, industrial wastes have nearly destroyed the oyster beds in New Jersey's Raritan Bay. **Minimata disease,** caused by high concentrations of methyl mercury in human body tissue, is another example. The disease is named after a tiny Japanese fishing village where several hundred people became ill. Once the disease had been identified, the mercury was traced to the effluence of a large chemical plant, which dumped its wastes into Minimata Bay. Other examples abound, and oceanic pollution is becoming global in scale.

Similar horror stories abound for our other major biological systems—forests, grasslands, and croplands. Accelerated deforestation is common in many areas. Forests are essential sources of lumber and firewood, and population growth increases the demand for both. Forests are also cleared in attempts to provide more farmland. Both population growth and economic growth place increasing demands on the earth's grasslands where overgrazing is already a common problem. In turn, cities and highways continue to consume cropland in many areas, including the United States, while accelerated erosion and desertification claim valuable cropland in other areas. The encroachment of deserts has been especially well-documented in West Africa.

We could go to other environmental consequences of economic growth and development as well. The production of minerals for industry and the provision of energy for the insatiable appetites of the industrialized nations often create havoc within the environment. For example, the legacy left behind after an area's coal has been strip-mined is often a dreary and desolate landscape devoid of beauty.

An ecomonic view. Economists are willing to admit that any technology employed is going to disturb the environment, but they are quick to point out that people derive benefits from the application of technology. Walter W. Heller, President Kennedy's economic advisor, once aptly commented,

> In starkest terms, the ecologist confronts us with an environmental imperative that requires an end to economic growth—or a sharp curtailment of it—as the price of biological survival. In contrast, the economist counters with a socioeconomic imperative

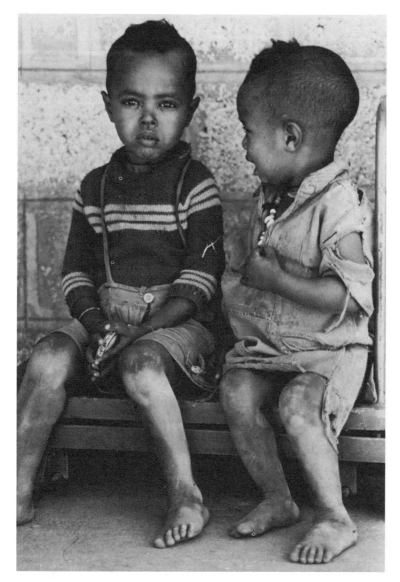

Farm children in the Debre Zeit area of Ethiopia. (World Bank Photo by Ray Witlin, 1975)

that requires the continuation of growth as the price of social survival. (1971, p. 14)

Economists do not collectively applaud the destruction of earth's natural environment. Rather, they think in terms of **trade-offs** and employ cost–benefit analysis in the allocation of natural resources. It is necessary, they argue, to seek a balance between economic growth and environmental degradation, between ecology and technology (1971).

In order to stop the often ugly and detrimental practices of modern industry, we will be confronted with costs, most of which ultimately will be borne by the consumer. For example, an industry producing steel from iron ore is found to be a major source of air pollution. It can curb that pollution by the addition of expensive antipollution equipment. However, the additional equipment represents a new cost, and in all likelihood, the company will, in turn, charge the customer more for its product. Thus, one of the obvious problems with providing a cleaner environment is likely to be increased inflation, a problem which received worldwide attention in the 1970s. Thus, at least in the foreseeable future, most nations will continue to deal with trade-offs, though changing values may alter the costs and benefits of specific projects.

CHILDREN AND THE FUTURE

Approximately one-third of the world's over 4 billion people are children under the age of 15. Most of them, some 80 percent, live in the developing regions, and in many countries they account for almost half of the population. These children are the means by which human society perpetuates itself; they are the legacy of its past and present, as well as the bridge to its future.

Most of today's children will be parents by the year 2000, and if recent projections hold, there will be about 1.93 billion children in the year 2000. This figure is roughly one-third larger than the number of children in 1975. About 57 percent of the children, 1.093 billion, will live in Asia; 346 million, or 18 percent, in Africa. Latin America will have 12 percent, or 226 million; and Oceania 9.6 million, less than 1 percent. The U.S.S.R. will have 4 percent of the total, some 74 million, while the combined totals of Europe, Canada, and the United States will be 181 million, only 9 percent of the world's population under 15 years of age (McHale, McHale, & Streatfield, 1979, p. 41).

The kind of world these children know will be primarily determined by the decisions that we make today. In the short term, the next 10 or 20 years, several measures could be taken to alleviate child poverty and deprivation:

1. Wipe out severe child malnutrition and reduce general malnutrition to more moderate proportions by food supplement programs.
2. Reduce infant mortality in the developing world to 50 or less per 1,000 live births compared to 113 at present.
3. Increase life expectancy in the developing regions to 65 years or more, against 56 at present.
4. Provide immunization for all children against the common diseases of childhood.
5. Ensure that all children and their families have access to a clean and convenient supply of water—and adequate sanitation.
6. Increase the supply of minimally decent shelter for families. (McHale, et al., 1979, p. 42)

These measures are certainly attainable in the next one or two decades, and at a relatively low cost. In the long run, however, solving children's problems will be inexorably intertwined with the global problems of poverty and inequity. According to Soedjatmoko,

> Our success or failure in dealing with the needs of the child, especially among the poorest part of the population, will determine whether or not, in the poor countries in the world, we will have a permanent underclass of second-rate citizens, who never had the chance and may never have the chance to fully develop their human potential, constituting a mass of human beings stunted in their physical, mental, psychological and social development. (1978), p. 2)

KEY TERMS

Economic development
Gross National Product (GNP)
Modernization
Underdevelopment
Stages of economic growth
Transport network

Core–periphery model
Circular or cumulative causation
Polarized development
Minimata disease
Trade-offs

REFERENCES

Beckford, G. L. (1972), *Persistent Poverty: Underdevelopment in Plantation Economies of the Third World.* New York: Oxford University Press.

Black, C. E. (1967), *The Dynamics of Modernization: A Study in Comparative History.* New York: Harper & Row, Publishers, Inc.

Brown, L. (1978), *The Global Economic Prospect: New Sources of Economic Stress,* Worldwatch Paper No. 20. Washington, D.C.: Worldwatch Institute.

deSouza, A. R. and Porter, P. W. (1974), *The Underdevelopment and Modernization of the Third World.* Washington, D.C.: Association of American Geographers,

Commission on College Geography, Resource Paper No. 28.

Foust, J. B. and deSouza, A. R. (1978), *The Economic Landscape: A Theoretical Introduction.* Columbus, OH: Charles E. Merrill Publishing Co.

Frank, A. G. (1972), "The Development of Underdevelopment," in Cockroft, J. D., Frank, A. G. and Johnson, D. L. (eds.), *Dependence and Underdevelopment: Latin America's Political Economy.* Garden City, NY: Anchor Press/Doubleday & Co., Inc.

Gilbert, A. (1974), *Latin American Development: A Geographical Perspective.* Baltimore, MD: Penguin Books/Viking Penguin, Inc.

Gould, P. (1964), "A Note on Research into the Diffusion of Development," *Journal of Modern African Studies* 2, 123–125.

Gould, P. (1970), "Tanzania 1920-63: The Spatial Impress of the Modernization Process," *World Politics* 22, 149–170.

Heller, W. W. (1971), "Economic Growth and Ecology—An Economist's View," *Monthly Labor Review* 94, 14–21.

Leibenstein, H. (1957), *Economic Backwardness and Economic Growth.* New York: John Wiley & Sons, Inc.

McHale, M. C., McHale, J., and Streatfield, G. F. (1979), "World of Children," *Population Bulletin* 33, No. 6.

Myrdal, G. (1957), *Economic Theory and Underdeveloped Regions.* London: Duckworth, Ltd.

Seers, D. (1969), "Challenges to Development Theories and Strategies," presented at the 11th World Conference of the Society for International Development, New Delhi, India, November 14–17. Reprinted by the Agricultural Development Council, September 1970, as "The Meaning of Development."

Soedjatmoko (April 1978), "The Child in Development Planning," presented at the 24th Reunion of National Committees of UNICEF, Brussels, Belgium.

Rostow, W. W. (1971), *The Stages of Economic Growth: A Non-Communist Manifesto,* 2nd ed. Cambridge, MA: Cambridge University Press.

Soja, E. W. (1968), *The Geography of Modernization in Kenya: A Spatial Analysis of Social, Economic, and Political Change,* Syracuse Geographical Series No. 2. Syracuse, NY: Syracuse University Press.

Szentes, T. (1971), *The Political Economy of Underdevelopment.* Budapest, Hungary: Akademiai Kiado.

Taaffe, E. J., Morrill, R. L., and Gould, P. R. (1963), "Transport Expansion in Underdeveloped Countries: A Comparative Analysis," *Geographical Review* 67, 503–529.

Zelinsky, W. (1976), "Quality of Life: An Inquiry into Its Utility for Geographers," *Geographical Survey* 5, 8–11.

11

People, technology, and the environment

It becomes more obvious each day that human beings are having a greater and greater influence on the environment. Although the interaction between people and the environment is quite complex, some basic principles underlie the human–environment system. Those principles are outlined in this chapter and are related to the problem of environmental pollution. The natural environment can present many hazards to humans, and the nature and magnitude of these hazards are discussed. The final section of this chapter deals with the interaction between people, technology and the environment.

THE NATURE OF ECOSYSTEMS

In the past decade scientists have become increasingly aware of the interaction between people and the environment. The science of **ecology,** which deals with the interaction between plants, animals, and the physical/biological environment, is recognized throughout the world. The word *ecology* was originally proposed by the zoologist Reiter in 1885 and was derived from two Greek words: *oikos* means dwelling place or home, and *logos* means a study or discourse. A simple definition was coined by another zoologist, Ernst Haeckel, in 1869, in which he defined ecology as the study of the reciprocal relationships between organisms and their environment.

The term **biosphere** is often used by geographers and other environmental scientists to describe that part of the earth where life exists. That is, the envelope of

life that encompasses the earth, from the deep trenches of the ocean floor to the upper levels of the atmosphere. Within this envelope, however, most life exists between 600 feet below and 20,000 feet above sea level. People share the earth's space with an enormous variety of other living things, both plants and animals. The exact number of species of organisms is impossible to pinpoint, but most estimates are of at least 10 million. The population of plants, animals, and microorganisms make up what biologists refer to as a **biological community.**

An awareness of the interrelationships among the physical and biological aspects of an environment has led ecologists to recognize the **ecosystem** (short for *ecological system*) as a natural unit in the study of landscapes. The term was first used in the 1930s, but it was not until the 1960s that it achieved prominence. An ecosystem consists of two basic components: an **abiotic** or nonliving component and a **biotic** or living component. Two classes of abiotic factors determine the basic characteristics of an ecosystem. One includes such physical features as temperature, light, water, rainfall, and climate. The second class is chemical in nature and primarily deals with the availability of nutrients; these factors determine the tolerance range within which a given species or biological community can survive (figure 11–1).

The biotic component of an ecosystem consists of producer organisms, consumer organisms, and decomposer organisms. Producer organisms include plants and bacteria that have the capability of synthe-

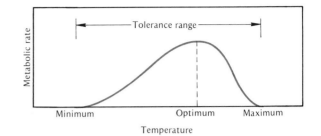

FIGURE 11–1 Tolerance range—temperature response curve for a typical animal. (Reprinted with permission of Macmillan Publishing Co., Inc. from *Natural Ecosystems* by W. B. Clapham, Jr., p. 59. Copyright © 1973 by W. B. Clapham, Jr.)

sizing organic compounds, taking abiotic or inorganic material and manufacturing organic material. All green plants would be included in this category, and they are, obviously, necessary for human survival. Consumer organisms include animals which either directly or indirectly use the organic materials produced by plants. The final biotic component, decomposer organisms, include fungi and bacteria, which degrade organic compounds; that is, they break down the complex organic materials of dead plants and animals into a form that can be absorbed by green plants. Although ecosystems are extremely complex and involve a wide variety of life forms, almost all of the biotic components can be classified as either producers, consumers, or decomposers (figure 11–2).

Energy paths and trophic structure

Energy is an essential component in the efficient functioning of an ecosystem. The sources of energy are important, as is the way energy is transformed into living organisms. The way an ecosystem is organized to maximize the use of energy is referred to as the *trophic structure* of the ecosystem. The trophic structure is the mechanism that binds together the different population groups in an ecosystem. Ecologists are concerned about both the methods by which energy enters the ecosystem and the ways it is transformed throughout the system.

The sun is the ultimate source of energy for all life processes. It supplies the equivalent of 684 billion tons of coal each day. Much of this energy, however, is reflected from clouds or dust particles and scattered back out into space.

The trophic structure of an ecosystem determines the pathways through which energy is funneled. This structure is composed of several separate groups of organisms that obtain food in the same general way. Each of these groups is called a *trophic level.* Thus all animals that obtain energy by eating grass, such as grass-

hoppers, cattle, or meadow mice, would be included in the same trophic level. Most trophic structures have from 3 to 6 trophic levels through which organic materials and energy flow. A very simple trophic structure (figure 11–3) would include grass → cattle → humans. Sometimes referred to as a *food chain,* this simple mechanism is very efficient in producing a large amount of living organisms per unit area *(biomass)* for a small amount of energy input. The longer the food chain, the greater the loss of energy between trophic levels. Therefore, shorter food chains are more efficient and can produce more biomass per given unit of energy input.

A more generalized model of a trophic structure (figure 11–4) depicts four trophic levels: autotroph, herbivore, primary carnivore, and secondary carnivore. The first level, an autotroph, includes organisms that can fix energy from inorganic sources into organic molecules; that is, except for a few bacteria that obtain energy from inorganic chemicals, they can take sunlight and convert it into biomass. The autotrophic level consists primarily of green plants. These plants are, in turn, consumed by organisms on the second trophic level, the herbivores. Herbivores are a very important trophic level because virtually all the energy utilized by animals passes from plants to animals via plant consumption by herbivores. Carnivores are animals that consume other animals. Primary carnivores are animals that eat herbivores, and secondary carnivores are animals whose main source of food is primary carnivores.

The nature of these relationships within the trophic structure is easily illustrated by the food chain for an Arctic terrestrial ecosystem (figure 11–5). Ecologists like to work arctic regions because of the relatively simple nature of their ecosystems. The autotroph or primary producer level is represented by lichens, which are a complex of plants primarily consisting of algae and fungi. These lichens are the main source of food for the herbivores—the caribou, snowshoe hares,

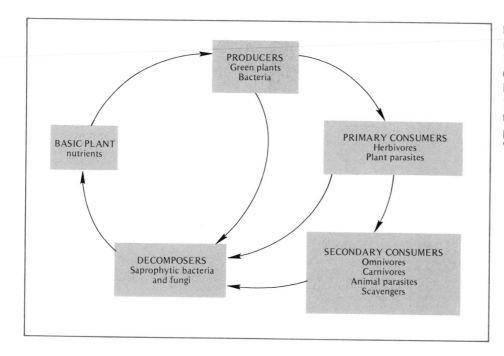

FIGURE 11–2 Basic components of an ecosystem. (From *Ecology and the Quality of Our Environment,* 2nd ed. by Charles H. Southwick, p. 108. © 1976 by Litton Educational Publishing, Inc. Reprinted by permission of D. Van Nostrand Co.)

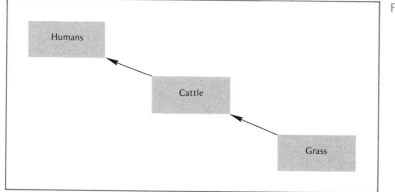

FIGURE 11–3 Simple trophic structure.

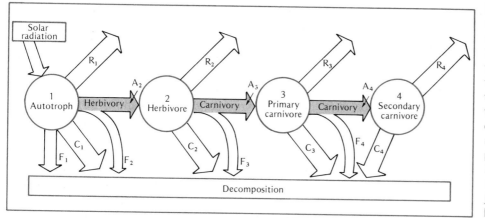

FIGURE 11–4 Grazing food chain, showing energy input and loss at each trophic level. The components of energy transfer are *A,* assimilation of food by the organisms at the trophic level, and energy loss through *F,* feces and other excretion, *C,* decay, and *R,* respiration. (Reprinted with permission of Macmillan Publishing Co., Inc. from *Natural Ecosystems* by W. B. Clapham, Jr., p. 27. Copyright © 1973 by W. B. Clapham, Jr.)

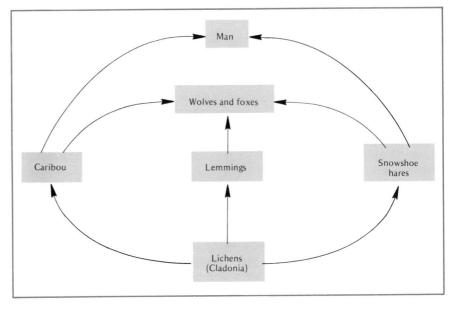

FIGURE 11–5 Simplified food chain of an Arctic terrestrial ecosystem. (From *Ecology and the Quality of Our Environment*, 2nd ed. by Charles H. Southwick, p. 138. © 1976 by Litton Educational Publishing, Inc. Reprinted by permission of D. Van Nostrand Co.)

and lemmings—which are in turn food sources for the primary carnivores—wolves, foxes, and people. Obviously, other plants and animals are present, though they all fit into this relatively simple trophic structure. Trophic structures, therefore, are simple in arctic areas and become more complex with progression through temperate regions to the equatorial tropics.

People and ecosystems

People have been a major influence on the world's ecosystems. The complexity of an ecosystem is related to its stability. Ecosystems that have relatively simple trophic structures are generally more vulnerable to change than are those with more complex structures. For example, in the simple Arctic ecosystem previously outlined, lichens are crucial. If lichen production were either impaired or destroyed, the whole system would collapse because the herbivores and carnivores directly or indirectly depend upon lichens. In more complex ecosystems, such as the tropical rain forest, however, alternate food sources are available, so the loss of one species does not necessarily mean the entire ecosystem will collapse.

It is difficult to predict the effect of human activity on natural ecosystems. People are, of course, part of the environment, while at the same time they can have a tremendous impact on that environment. Commenting on the relationship of people to ecosystems, Clapham said,

Despite the effectiveness with which he has barricaded himself behind centrally heated walls in sterile urban and suburban ghettos, man still depends on the food produced through photosysthesis for his source of energy and mineral nutrients. He moves through, reproduces in, and expends his waste products into the environment just like any other species on the face of the earth. As long as this is the case, the survival of human populations depends on the ability of ecosystems to meet these needs. When the fitness of an ecosystem becomes so low as to make this impossible, the populations inhabiting that ecosystem are in an extremely precarious position. (1973, p. 233)

One important impact that people have had on ecosystems is simplification. Agricultural activities diminish trophic levels, reducing them to their simplest terms. When farmers plowed the prairies, they eliminated many different species of native grasses and herbs and replaced them with single crops like wheat or corn. Although single crop agriculture greatly increases the production and efficiency of plant production, it also increases the probability of ecological disaster. For example, a pure stand of wheat could be totally decimated by the sudden invasion of a pathogen like wheat rust or an herbivore like grasshoppers. Similarly, animal populations may also be simplified by human activities.

People frequently ridicule ecologists by asking why we need so many different kinds of plants or animals. Who cares if a few of them become extinct? It is difficult to answer such a question in specific terms; however, an answer lies in the general principles involved with the complexity and diversity of ecosystems. Although there may not be an apparent, immediate impact by the extinction of a particular species, the ecosystem is somewhat impaired and becomes more vulnerable to ecologic instability. If the extinct species is part of a simple ecosystem, the impact may be catastrophic. A minor change in one part of the ecosystem may have major consequences for other parts of the system. This is the reason ecologists argue for the preservation of diversity; they believe that the stability of ecosystems may depend upon it.

An interesting analogy was offered by Clapham in the final paragraph of his book on ecosystems:

> There is an old technique used in coal mines of taking a caged canary into the mine, because canaries are much more sensitive to toxic mine gases than men are. When the canary dies, it is time for the miners to leave. The analogue between the coal mine and the biosphere is clear: Man lives in a tiny portion of the total solar system, and he shares it with many other organisms spread through many interconnected ecosystems. We know much about how natural ecosystems operate and how they are interconnected. We also know that the fitness of many ecosystems is deteriorating at an alarming rate. The symptoms of this deterioration, the fish-kills, the bird-deaths, the increasing algal blooms, the replacement of high-quality fish by coarse fish are all analogues to the death of the canaries in the coal mines. But the miner can get out of the mine. Man cannot leave the biosphere. (1973, p. 237)

POLLUTION AND ECOSYSTEMS

Geographers are concerned with the interaction between people and ecosystems; this interaction is particularly significant if it results in a polluted environment. According to the President's Science Advisory Committee, **pollution** is "the unfavorable alteration of our surroundings, through direct or indirect effects of changes in energy patterns, radiation levels, chemical and physical constitution and abundances of organisms" (1965). The key aspect of this definition is whether there is an "unfavorable alteration" in the environment. Most human actions alter the environment, but whether or not that action is "unfavorable" is often open to debate.

Characteristics of pollutants

Pollutants can be divided into two major classes, natural and artificial. On a global scale, natural pollutants are more significant; but at a local scale, pollutants produced by human activity can be more significant, as apparent in cities such as Los Angeles or Tokyo.

Whether pollution is the result of natural or human activity, mounting evidence suggests that many types of pollutants diffuse quickly over the entire earth. Radioactive fallout from nuclear tests has been found throughout the world within days or weeks of the event; this was a principal reason for stopping nuclear testing in the atmosphere. Other dramatic evidence of the worldwide diffusion of pollution is the high levels of DDT found in the liver and fat of animals in the Antarctic.

Another significant characteristic of pollutants is that they remain in some areas for an indefinite period of time. Some pollutants break down into harmless compounds quite quickly, whereas others last for a long time. Radioactive materials are among the most dangerous; one of the primary reasons why many environmental scientists oppose the development of nuclear power is that they fear radioactive wastes generated by nuclear power plants will persist in the environment for thousands of years.

The trophic structure of ecosystems can serve as a means of concentrating pollutants so that pollution levels in one part of an ecosystem are much larger than those in other parts. For example, DDT may be found in small quantities in ocean water, then acquatic plants concentrate the DDT. In turn, herbivore fish eat these plants and the DDT becomes even more concentrated. In more complex trophic structures, primary or secondary carnivores may further concentrate the pollutant. As the pollutant becomes more concentrated it becomes more dangerous to the organism.

Effects of pollutants

Pollutants can affect both plant and animal life, as well as inorganic materials. High pollution levels can produce noticeable effects on some plants, leading to retardation of growth or even death of certain species. In some cases the effect of a pollutant may be an increase in plant life, as when an abundance of plant nutrients like phosphorous are introduced into an area.

A smoggy morning in downtown Chicago. (United Nations/Argonne National Laboratory, 1970)

The effect of pollutants on animals has been well documented. Air pollution is known to produce eye and respiratory irritations among animals, and water pollution has been responsible for endangering acquatic life in many areas. The effect of pollution on human health, however, is sometimes difficult to determine. Scientists agree that large doses of some substances are highly toxic; the effect of small doses, however, is variable. In some cases small doses of certain substances are necessary and beneficial, whereas larger doses of the same substance can be harmful. For example, small doses of copper are needed for hemoglobin synthesis, but large doses can produce acute poisoning.

Some substances are not beneficial to humans, and it is essential to know whether small amounts of these materials are harmful. For example, we know lead does not serve any useful function and it can be toxic at blood concentrations above 0.8 parts per million; yet an average American has a concentration of about 0.25 parts per million. According to Laurent Hodges, the fact that low doses appear to have no detrimental effect might be explained by either of two possibilities.

1. There exists a threshold, a dose or level below which there are no effects or at least no permanent effects. The important threshold, if exposures are limited in time, is that between irreversible effects, which cannot be undone, and reversible effects, which result in no permanent injury.

2. Low doses or levels also produce harmful effects, but our techniques are not sophisticated enough to detect them. It is well known that the effects of low levels of exposure are sometimes not apparent until many years have elapsed. . . . A common, conservative assumption for low doses or levels is the linear nonthreshold hypothesis which holds that the effects are directly proportional to dose. (1977, p. 11)

Increasing evidence is being found to show how long-term exposure to low levels of certain substances in the environment can lead to chronic diseases. For example, asbestos is known to be a cause of lung cancer among asbestos workers, but it can take 20 to 30 years of exposure before the disease is detected. Other forms of cancer have also been related to the environment, and the World Health Organization has estimated that 80 to 90 percent of all human cancers are environmentally related or induced. Cancer mortality

TABLE 11–1 Emissions of U.S. air pollutants by source (million tons/year)

Source	Sulfur oxides	Nitrogen oxides	Hydrocarbons	Carbon monoxide	Particulates
Transportation	0.8	10.7	12.8	73.5	1.3
Stationary fuel combustion	24.3	11.0	1.7	0.9	5.9
Industrial processes	6.2	0.6	3.1	12.7	11.0
Solid waste disposal	0.0	0.1	0.6	2.4	0.5
Miscellaneous[a]	0.1	0.1	12.2	5.1	0.8
Total	31.4	22.5	30.4	94.6	19.5

[a]Includes oil and gasoline production

Source: Environmental Protection Agency, in Council on Environmental Quality, *Environmental Quality, 1975*, p. 440.

rates in the United States show a strong correlation with areas that are highly industrialized and urbanized.

Aside from their effect on plants, animals, and people, pollutants may also adversely affect inorganic materials. Metals and building materials are corroded from air pollutants, such as sulfur dioxide gas or sulfuric acid; aerosols and water pollutants can adversely affect industrial equipment, pumps, and bridges. Even the noise associated with sonic booms can break windows and damage buildings.

Air pollution

Air pollution is probably the most obvious form of pollution. It can be seen in almost every major metropolitan area, as well as felt in the eyes or lungs of their inhabitants. Although it is more obvious in urban areas, large portions of relatively uninhabited regions are now afflicted to some degree. Perhaps the best view of air pollution was that of the Apollo astronauts who were unable to see southern California (Fagan, 1974, p. 10).

Air pollution can be categorized in many different ways: by chemical composition, by source of pollutants, by impact on plant and animal life, or by the different types of reactions that take place. The principal types of pollutants and sulfur oxides, nitrogen oxides, hydrocarbons, and carbon monoxide. In addition, there are particulates such as dust, metals and metallic compounds, and insecticide particles.

An analysis of the amounts of pollutants in the United States (table 11–1) points out some interesting relationships. Most air pollution, represented by the first two sources, is the direct result of combustion. As nations become industrialized, an increase in the burn-

ing of fossil fuels occurs, and the combustion of both coal and oil result in sulfur oxides. The bulk of the emissions of carbon monoxide result from engines used in transportation.

There is ample evidence to indicate detrimental effects to human health because of air pollution. The most dramatic example was the London smog disaster of 1952 where almost 4,000 deaths were directly attributed to the smog. Various other pollutants (table 11–2) are the source of a variety of human health problems, ranging from minor eye or throat irritations to cancer.

Water pollution

In a chemical sense, water is almost never pure H_2O. It easily absorbs varying amounts of gases and other substances and is usually considered polluted only when unsuitable for its intended use or when undesirable substances are present. The intended use may be recreation, irrigation, industrial use, or human consumption, and many undesirable substances such as sediment, disease-causing organisms, or chemical substances, may be present.

Types of **water pollution,** like air pollution, may be classified in several ways. One classification system involves the medium in which pollutants occur, such as ground water, surface water, or soil; another involves the habitat in which pollution occurs, such as rivers, estuaries, or the ocean. A classification of eight categories based upon the source or type of contamination was developed by Laurent Hodges (1977, pp. 169–175).

1. *Sewage and other oxygen-demanding wastes.* These primarily include organic compounds found in

TABLE 11–2   Common air pollutants and their effects

Pollutants	Where they come from	What they do
Aldehydes	Thermal decomposition of fats, oil, or glycerol.	Irritate nasal and respiratory tracts.
Ammonias	Chemical processes—dye-making; explosives; lacquer; fertilizer.	Inflame upper respiratory passages.
Arsines	Processes involving metals or acids containing arsenic; soldering.	Break down red cells in blood; damage kidneys; cause jaundice.
Carbon monoxides	Gasoline motor exhausts.	Reduce oxygen-carrying capacity of blood.
Chlorines	Bleaching cotton and flour; many other chemical processes.	Attack entire respiratory tract and mucous membranes of eyes; cause pulmonary edema.
Hydrogen cyanides	Fumigation; blast furnaces; chemical manufacturing; metal plating.	Interfere with nerve cells; produce dry throat, indistinct vision, headache.
Hydrogen fluorides	Petroleum refining; glass etching; aluminum and fertilizer production.	Irritate and corrode all body passages.
Hydrogen sulfides	Refineries and chemical industries; bituminous fuels.	Smell like rotten eggs; cause nausea; irritate eyes and throat.
Nitrogen oxides	Motor vehicle exhausts; soft coal.	Inhibit cilia action so that soot and dust penetrate far into the lungs.
Phosgenes (carbonyl chloride)	Chemical and dye manufacturing.	Induce coughing, irritation and sometimes fatal pulmonary edema.
Sulfur dioxides	Coal and oil combustion.	Cause chest constriction, headache, vomiting, and death from respiratory ailments.
Suspended particles (ash, soot, smoke)	Incinerators; almost any manufacturing.	Cause emphysema, eye irritations, and possible cancer.

Source: From *Ecology and the Quality of Our Environment,* 2nd ed. by Charles H. Southwick, p. 19.© 1976 by Litton Educational Publishing, Inc. Reprinted by permission of D. Van Nostrand Co.

sewage or other industrial wastes, and their chemical or biological degradation leads to a depletion in dissolved oxygen. Fish and other acquatic life require specific levels of oxygen, and a depletion will eventually lead to death of these organisms.

2. *Plant nutrients.*   Phosphorous and nitrogen stimulate plant growth, and quite often it is in the form of algae or plankton. Undesirable effects of these algal or plankton blooms include unpleasant odor or taste, and in some cases toxic products result in fish kills.

3. *Infectious agents and disease-causing organisms.* These organisms include parasites, viruses, and bacteria commonly found in raw human sewage, and are important agents in the spread of water-borne diseases, such as amoebic dysentery, hepatitis, typhoid, or cholera. In recent years many lake and ocean beaches have been closed to public swimming because of high bacterial counts resulting from domestic pollution.

4. *Synthetic organic compounds.*   Included in this category are pesticides and other agricultural chemi-

cals, detergents, a variety of industrial waste products, and products resulting from the decomposition of other organic compounds. Many new chemical products are introduced each year, and little is known about their impact on natural ecosystems. The possibility always exists that at least one of these products might cause irreparable damage before scientists realize it.

5. *Inorganic minerals and chemical compounds.* Many types of inorganic materials find their way into the world's water supply. Among the more dangerous are mineral fibers such as asbestos, heavy metals like mercury, and acids. They can have catastrophic impacts on fish and other acquatic life and can render water useless for either industrial use or human consumption.

6. *Radioactive substances.*   Radioactive materials can be especially dangerous because they persist for such long time periods. The sources of radioactive materials include wastes associated with nuclear power plants, uranium and thorium mining and refining, and

Discharge pipes of a wood pulp plant pollute the waters of a fishing port in Washington. (United Nations/Cahail, 1971)

from medical, industrial, or scientific use of radioactive materials.

7. *Sediments.* These are soil and mineral particles washed into streams or water bodies. They cause a variety of problems, including reducing the amount of sunlight available for plants, plugging turbines or water filters, and filling in stream channels and reservoirs.

8. *Heat.* Large amounts of water are used for cooling purposes, primarily in steam-electric power plants. The water is then discharged into streams at a raised temperature. These temperature changes can drastically change an acquatic ecosystem and in some cases have caused the death of acquatic life.

One interesting aspect of water pollution is that, because the oceans are so vast, people have thought their capacity to absorb waste products is unlimited. However, substantial evidence now indicates that large coastal areas, as well as open oceans, are becoming polluted. Two famous explorers, Thor Heyerdahl and Jacques Ives-Cousteau, have reported that oceanic areas far from human population centers are becoming seriously polluted. Heyerdahl reported finding floating debris and waste oil thousands of miles from land in the middle of the Atlantic Ocean. Cousteau feels that, in the 50 years he has explored the world's oceans, there has been a 40 percent decline in marine life.

Noise pollution

In recent years increased attention has been given to noise as a form of environmental pollution. A by-product of industrialization has been excessive noise. However, recent discoveries associated with hearing loss by some teenagers as a result of exposure to amplified rock music, as well as sonic booms and noise associated with supersonic transports (SST), have brought about increasing public concern. Medical studies suggest that noise can have detrimental effects on human health, including increases in nervous stress, irritability, heart rate, blood pressure, and metabolism. Studies in India and Africa, nonindustrialized societies, have shown that the progressive loss of hearing with age found in industrial societies is not a natural part of aging, but rather a consequence of the noisy, modern industrialized environment (ReVelle & ReVelle, 1974, p. 162).

Noise pollution is becoming more of a threat to health and happiness. According to Paul Ehrlich, "Even if the biosphere is not subjected to the booms of large-scale commercial use of the SST, the need for noise abatement will continue to be serious. . . . this problem will prove to be more readily solvable with technology, imagination, and determination than most pollution problems" (Ehrlich, et. al., 1977, p. 597).

Mining landscape, San Juan County, California.
(Library of Congress, 1940)

Aesthetic pollution

One type of pollution that has received little attention in the past has been *aesthetic pollution.* The "sea of ugliness" engulfing many areas is a form of pollution which threatens the quality of life in a similar manner as air, water, and noise pollution. Aside from the economic value of a beautiful environment, there is an even more basic aspect of aesthetic beauty. According to the geographer Pierce Lewis, "Man's ability to recognize, appreciate, and create beauty is one of the most important qualities which makes man more than just another animal (1970, p. 3).

The measurement of aesthetic beauty is a difficult task, and what holds beauty in the eye of one person may not in the eyes of another. But what remains through all the arguments and hairsplitting, according to Lewis, ". . . is the clearly recognized fact that some things are judged more beautiful than others, and that most people have no trouble identifying them" (1970,

p. 3). The task now for government and private concerns interested in the unattractiveness of an area is to evaluate the causes of this visual blight and initiate public and private actions to help change the quality of the environment.

ENVIRONMENTAL HAZARDS

One important aspect of how people relate to their environment is how they perceive and adjust to *natural hazards.* With increasing affluence and the advent of social security systems, societal members want to insure themselves against the unexpected loss of life or property due to extreme natural events. People must adjust to environmental extremes as they constantly interact with biological and physical systems. In recent years public interest, awareness, and concern over natural hazards has increased as major disasters are brought into our living rooms over television.

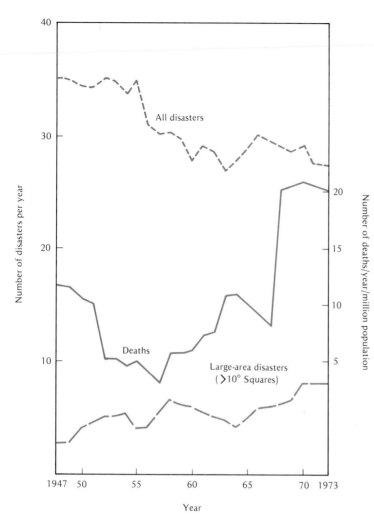

FIGURE 11–6 Major natural disasters, 1947–1973 (5-year moving average, excluding drought). (J. Dworkin, 1974, *Global Trends in Natural Disasters, 1947–1973*. Boulder, CO, Univ. of Colorado, Institute of Behavioral Science, NHRWP No. 26, p. 6.)

Importance and magnitude

An environmental hazard can only exist within the context of human initiative and choice. In order to be a hazard, some type of ***human adjustment*** must be involved. For example, an earthquake is not an environmental hazard unless people either live in or are travelling through the seismic area at the time.

In a time when we are technically more capable of controlling natural events, the global toll in both life and property associated with environmental hazards is increasing. Although the average number of disasters per year has declined slightly, the death rate has increased; so has the areal extent of disasters, as measured by the number of large-area disasters (figure 11–6). The average annual death toll from all hazards is estimated at approximately 250,000 people, and the

extent of property damage is approximately 40 billion dollars.

> Approximately 90 percent of the world's natural disasters originate in four hazard types: floods (40 percent), tropical cyclones (20 percent), earthquakes (15 percent), and drought (15 percent). Earthquakes are probably overestimated because they are so easy to detect. Drought is underestimated because of difficulties in its definition, timing, and siting, and in distinguishing drought impact from perennial seasonal hunger or malnutrition. Floods are the most frequent and do the greatest damage; tropical cyclones cause most fatalities. (Burton, et. al. 1978, p. 2)

Over 95 percent of the deaths associated with natural hazards occur in the developing nations of Asia, Africa, and Latin America. The extent and value of property loss, however, is greater in the wealthy, developed countries, with over 75 percent of property loss occurring in these regions. This increase in the loss of life and property occurs in conjunction with unprecedented programs in hazard control and disaster relief.

The primary reason for the increase in loss of life and property is that populations are growing rapidly, particularly in the developing countries, and people are moving to places that are more prone to environmental hazards. Rapidly expanding populations force people to live in hazardous areas, thus increasing the probability of disaster. Because most people cannot move from a dangerous area, it becomes increasingly more important that systems be developed to enable people to cope with natural hazards.

Natural events and processes occur at several different scales of magnitude. A continuum of events exists, from those of small magnitude, which usually occur daily and are not considered environmental hazards, to those of large magnitude that take place infrequently. Included in this latter category are volcanic eruptions, large earthquakes, and floods. Although the large-magnitude events receive the most attention, they are not necessarily the most important in terms of loss of life or property. For example, the large California earthquake that occurred in 1906 in the San Francisco area received nationwide attention and has been categorized as a major catastrophe. In that earthquake some 700 lives were lost, and over one-half billion dollars of property damage occurred. In the years since 1906, however, there have been more than 15 smaller earthquakes, which have been responsible for the loss of 217 lives and approximately the same amount of property damage. The large-scale catastrophic events certainly are important, but of equal importance in many instances are the hazards of moderate magnitude.

Bangladesh and Tropical Storm Agnes. An interesting comparison can be made between two relatively recent catastrophes: the **Bangladesh** cyclonic storm of 1970 in Asia and **Tropical Storm Agnes** in the eastern United States in 1972. One of the greatest natural disasters in recent years was the Bangladesh cyclonic storm. Although it was identified on November 9 and tracked by satellite, it struck the coastal regions of Bangladesh at 11 P.M. on November 12. Unfortunately the peak of the storm coincided with high tide, and water rose more than 20 feet above the normal high tide.

By the next morning approximately 225,000 people had died, crops worth 63 million dollars had been destroyed, and 280,000 head of cattle had been killed (Frank and Hussain, 1971, p. 439). Although the warning system was inadequate, and some of these disastrous results might have been avoided with better warning systems, the primary reason for the large toll in lives and property was the indirect result of technological change and population growth. Land was reclaimed by the government of Bangladesh, with financial and technical assistance from the United States, and people were encouraged to inhabit these lowlands. The earthen embankments constructed to protect them from the sea were too small and too weak to withstand the onslaught of water. The end result was a tremendous loss of both lives and property.

The Caribbean region, like the Indian Ocean, is known for its generation of tropical cyclones. Tropical Storm Agnes was tracked with sophisticated equipment, and its path was forecast with reasonable accuracy (figure 11–7). It moved inland over Florida, then northward across the coastal and Appalachian regions. The storm generated heavy rains and at least 15 tornadoes.

In New York and Pennsylvania, the storm joined a large system of cold air and generated heavy rainfall. In some places as much as 19 inches of rain fell during a two-day period. Massive flooding occurred, much greater than any previous flooding, and engineering works like dams and floodways were not capable of containing the water. The flooding was responsible for 3.5 million dollars in property damage and the deaths of 118 people.

According to a study by Burton, both Bangladesh and Tropical Storm Agnes had six common features (1978, pp. 11–12):

1. In both cases there was a trade-off between economic return and the social risk involved: the people were aware of the dangers, at least to some degree, but were willing to make some trade-offs. They probably were not, however, fully aware of the magnitude of the danger involved.

2. The hazards involved were the result of the interaction between natural systems and human-use systems. In both cases the people involved relied heavily upon engineering works. In Bangladesh the engineering works were constructed for agricultural use, whereas in

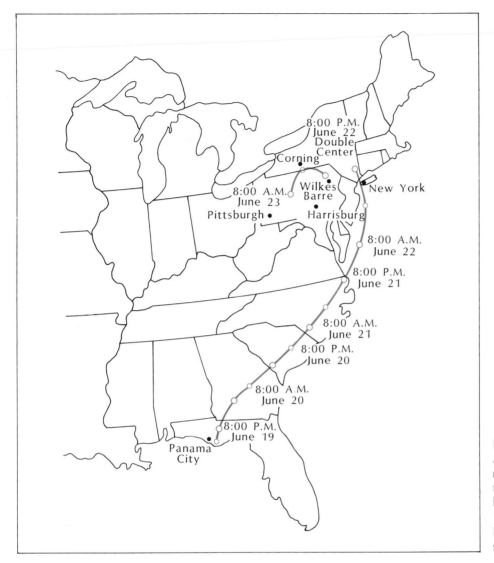

FIGURE 11–7 Tropical Storm Agnes, 1972. (From *The Environment as Hazard* by Ian Burton, Robert W. Kates, and Gilbert F. White. Copyright © 1978 by Oxford Univ. Press, Inc., p. 8. Reprinted by permission.)

Pennsylvania they were constructed for industrial protection. These engineering works did lead to increased productivity, particularly in the short run, but they also led to unprecedented disaster.

3. Both individual and collective governmental decisions were responsible for the choices made and the courses of action taken. In both cases the outcomes were the result of neither individual nor governmental decisions alone, but of both. The residents of Pennsylvania who lived in the flooded area, as well as the peasants in Bangladesh, had some choice.

4. Disasters are inequitable, and it is usually the poorer people who suffer the most.

5. The loss of property and life could have been decreased if certain measures had been taken in advance. These include better advance warning systems and better land-use planning and building design.

6. The final common feature of both disasters is that, in each case, the disaster was followed by preventive measures against future disasters. In Bangladesh a better warning system was developed; in the eastern United States, federal

legislation was enacted relative to insurance and land-use planning in floodplains.

The above six common features, although specifically related to the Bangladesh and eastern United States examples, can also be associated with other natural hazards. These are not unique cases. The principal difference is this: in the United States 250,000 people were evacuated—225,000 died in Bangladesh. As in most disasters, the poor are always more vulnerable.

Types of hazards and human response

Almost every aspect of the biosphere is subject to some type of change, whether annual, seasonal, or daily. If we could perfectly predict what hazards would take place and where, it would be possible to diminish the toll in lives and property. In the following section we will outline some of the major types of hazards and discuss the ways people respond to them.

Flooding.   Millions of dollars in damage and numerous lives are lost annually because of *flooding.* Throughout human history, floods have been thought inevitable. Because flooding occurs on an intermittent basis, people are often misled about the dangers of living in a floodplain. According to an analysis of the hazards of floodplain occupance by Beyer,

> Floods are the most universally experienced natural hazard, tend to be larger in spatial impact, and involve greater loss of life than do other hazards . . . . The problem is compounded for human adjustment by the fact that few other hazards present the ambivalent Januslike aspect of good and evil. (1974, p. 265)

There are several obvious reasons why floodplains are attractive places for human settlement. They generally have rich and thick soils. Their flat topography makes them desirable places to build, the rivers provide cheap and efficient transportation, and water is available for irrigation or municipal supplies.

The water level in most stream channels varies during a year and over the years. Most rivers have higher than normal discharges at several times during the year, but the water level is usually contained within the stream channel; when it does overtake the banks, the stream or river is said to be in *flood stage.* With the help of data from previous floods, it is possible to construct a flood-recurrence interval graph to indicate the probability of a flood of any given height. Although higher water levels cause more damage than lower levels, their recurrence interval is much greater.

The damage associated with flooding can take many forms and can be classified as either direct or indirect. The loss of human life is the most dramatic of the direct forms of damage, and in some areas the loss of livestock can be especially costly. In agricultural regions the inundation of cropland and destruction of crops can be significant. Water can disrupt irrigation systems, damage farm equipment, destroy stored materials like seeds and fertilizer, and disrupt communication. Urban areas also feel the direct impact of flooding. Many types of buildings can be destroyed, transportation facilities damaged, and socioeconomic activities disrupted.

The indirect damages associated with flooding generally relate to the health and general welfare of the community. Public health services are under greater pressure during floods because vital elements like transportation, communication, and water supply are disrupted. Pollution and contamination of water, particularly stagnant water, increases associated health hazards. Flooding also has an indirect impact on recreational services and adversely affects scenic values.

The human response to flooding can take several forms (table 11–3). One course of action is to modify the flood itself, generally involving engineering works like dams, dikes, or terraces. These attempts will contain floods of low magnitude, but perhaps at the expense of increasing the possibility of floods of high magnitude. Another aspect of human response to flooding has been to control flood plain regions by imposing land-use regulations and building codes. Also, flood insurance programs, tax write-offs, and more efficient disaster relief measures are being implemented. Unfortunately, the most widespread human adjustment to flood hazards, particularly in the developing countries, is to do nothing and bear the loss. Hopefully, as floodplain management strategies become more widespread, the do-nothing solution will disappear.

Drought.   Agricultural *drought* generally signifies a water deficiency. However, drought is a function of the specific agricultural system used in a given place. With regard to natural hazards, the occurrence of a drought is a function of the relationship between the natural, physical environment and human adjustments to that environment. According to Hewitt and Burton, a

TABLE 11–3 Adjustments to the flood hazard

Modify the flood	Modify the damage susceptibility	Modify the loss burden	Do nothing
Flood protection (channel phase)	Land-use regulation and changes	Flood insurance	Bear the loss
Dikes	Statutes	Tax write-offs	
Floodwalls	Zoning ordinances	Disaster relief	
Channel	Building codes	volunteer	
improvement	Urban renewal	private activities	
Reservoirs	Subdivision regulations	government aid	
River diversions	Government purchase of lands and	Emergency measures	
Watershed treatment	property	Removal of persons and property	
(land phase)	Subsidized relocation	Flood fighting	
Modification of	Floodproofing	Rescheduling of operations	
cropping practices	Permanent closure of low-level		
Terracing	windows and other openings		
Gully control	Waterproofing interiors		
Bank stabilization	Mounting store counters on wheels		
Forest-fire control	Installation of removable covers		
Revegetation	Closing of sewer valves		
Weather modification	Covering machinery with plastic		
	Structural change		
	Use of impervious material for		
	basements and walls		
	Seepage control		
	Sewer adjustment		
	Anchoring machinery		
	Underpinning buildings		
	Land elevation and fill		

Source: From *The Environment as Hazard* by Ian Burton, Robert W. Kates, and Gilbert F. White. Copyright © 1978 by Oxford University Press, Inc., p. 270. Reprinted by permission.

drought may be defined as ''a period in which moisture availability falls below the current requirements of some or all the living communities in an area and below their ability to sustain the deficit without damage, disruption, or excessive costs'' (1971, p. 97).

Deciding when a drought has occurred is a difficult process, and it can only be defined *ex post facto,* that is, after the drought is well underway or perhaps even finished. Although it can end relatively rapidly, it is difficult to define its beginning.

Damage from drought can be in several forms. The most obvious result in the withering and eventual death of vegetation and crops. This, of course, leads to malnutrition, dehydration, or death of animals and eventually people. Lack of water also has a severe impact on water for public utilities, waste utilities, waste transport, and general public health.

Humans can adjust to drought in several ways. Crops that are more drought resistant and need less wa-

ter can be selected over those consuming more water. Food storage facilities can be improved in order to have more of a food cushion in the event of drought. Irrigation systems can be developed, along with other engineering works for water storage. In general, the more wealthy, technologically advanced nations can usually offset the worst effects of drought through the movement of water and food supplies from one region of the country to another. However, poor countries with low levels of technology continue to experience the worst aspects of water shortage.

Tropical cyclones and tornadoes. Tropical cyclones and tornadoes are intense low-pressure storms, and the hazards associated with them derive from wind, hail, rain, and the resulting waves or floods. A **tropical cyclone** generally forms over a tropical oceanic area and may then move over midlatitude regions (figure 11–8). A **tornado** has a smaller radius

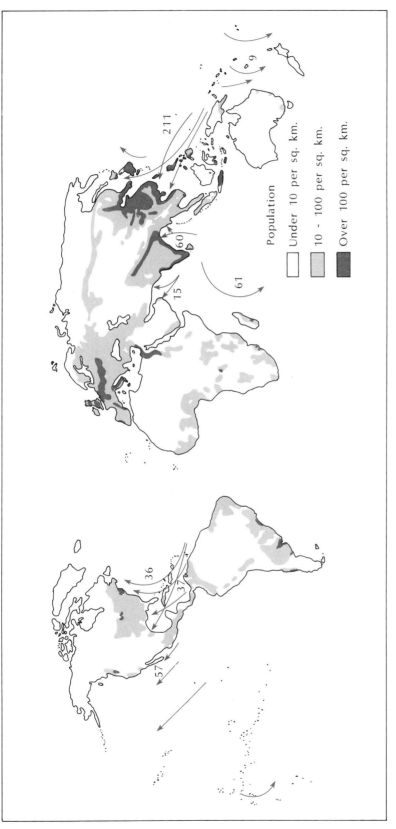

FIGURE 11–8 Tropical cyclone regions. Arrows indicate principal cyclone areas and approximate directions of movement; numbers indicate the frequency of major cyclones per 10 years. (From "Global Summary of Human Response to Natural Hazards: Tropical Cyclones," by Anne U. White, in *Natural Hazards: Local, National, Global*, ed. by Gilbert F. White. Copyright © 1974 by Oxford Univ. Press, Inc., p. 258. Reprinted by permission.)

Population

☐ Under 10 per sq. km.

▨ 10 - 100 per sq. km.

▧ Over 100 per sq. km.

and is generally found over continental areas in the midlatitudes, mainly in the United States.

Damage from tropical cyclones is the result of a combination of several factors: strong winds, marine flooding, riverine flooding, coastal erosion, intense rainfall, and lightning. Tropical cyclones, referred to as *hurricanes* or *typhoons,* last longer and cover a greater area than tornadoes. Their damage is a function of the intensity and size of the storm, as well as the population and economic character of the area affected. In terms of aggregate damage, they are the most severe of all storms. There has been a general upward trend in the amount of damage worldwide because population pressures have forced people to move into low-lying areas where they are more prone to suffer greater damage, as we saw with Bangladesh.

Humans have adjusted to tropical cyclones in several ways (table 11–4). These adjustments may either attempt to alter the nature of the hazard or protect people and property from the intensity of the storm. Storm modification through cloud seeding has had some success in decreasing maximum wind speeds, although more research is needed in order to determine exact cause and effect relationships. Most modification methods, however, attempt to reduce the damage potential by building levees and other protective shore works, developing efficient warning systems and evacuation procedures, developing building and zoning codes that restrict building in hazardous areas, and providing emergency relief services.

Tornadoes, like hurricanes, are cyclonic storms, but they are more well-defined and cover much smaller areas (table 11–5). Most of the damage associated with tornadoes is the result of sudden changes in pressure and high wind velocities. The damage can range from slight structural damage of buildings to complete devastation of everything in a tornado's path.

The sudden onset of tornadoes in conjunction with their tremendous force make effective human response difficult. The primary response mechanism has been the construction of shelters and the development

TABLE 11–4 Adjustments to the hazard of tropical cyclones

	Before the storm	During the storm	Immediately after the storm
Modifications of the extreme event	Seeding of cyclone clouds to lessen the intensity of the storm		
Modifications of the damage potential	Protective shore works; levees		
	Afforestation and dune control		
	Warning system: of the approaching event; of hazardous areas	Evacuation	
	Evacuation	Seeking shelter	
	Construction of raised areas as refuges; designation of shelters	Praying	
	Local regulations governing debris and loose materials		
	Zoning codes		
	Building codes		
	Construction modification		
	Flood- and wind-proofing		
Distribution of losses	Buying insurance		Claims on insurance
	Stockpiling of emergency supplies of water, food, and building materials		Emergency relief and reconstruction Bearing the loss

Source: From *The Environment as Hazard* by Ian Burton, Robert W. Kates, and Gilbert F. White. Copyright © 1978 by Oxford University Press, Inc., p. 260. Reprinted by permission.

San Martin Jilotepeque, Guatemala. People search the rubble for survivors of the earthquake of February, 1976. (United Nations/SYGMA/J. P. Laffont, 1976)

of effective warning systems. According to the Environmental Science Services Administration, the recommended procedures to follow upon receipt of a tornado warning are:

> *SHELTER.*   Seek inside shelter if possible. If in the open, move away from a tornado's path at a right angle. If there is no time to escape, lie flat in the nearest depression, such as a ditch or ravine.
>
> *In office buildings,* the basement or an interior hallway on a lower floor is safest. Upper stories are unsafe. If there is no time to descend, a closet or small room with stout walls, or an inside hallway will give some protection against flying debris. Otherwise, under heavy furniture must do.
>
> *In homes with basements,* seek refuge near the basement wall in the most sheltered and deepest below ground part of the basement. Additional protection is afforded by taking cover under heavy furniture or a workbench. Other basement possibilities are the smallest room with stout walls, or under a stairway. (U. S. Department of Commerce, 1968, p. 15)

Earthquakes.   Energy release associated with sudden movements along a fault cause **earthquakes.** The amount of surface disturbance is a function of how much energy is released at the focus of the earthquake, the distance from the focus, and the nature of the rocks

TABLE 11–5   Average path length of tornadoes in the U.S.

Path length	Percent of record
Less than 0.5 miles	10
0.5 to 5 miles	42
5 to 10 miles	16
10 to 20 miles	15
Greater than 20 miles	17

Note: As of 1959, 95% of all U.S. path lengths (except those which "hopped") were less than 8 miles.

Source: L. V. Wolford, *Tornado Occurrence in the United States,* Weather Bureau Technical Paper No. 21 (Washington, D.C.: U.S. Government Printing Office, 1960).

through which the seismic waves travel. The majority of earthquakes occur in an area called the circum-Pacific belt, although major earthquakes have also occurred in the Trans-Himalayan Zone and the Mediterranean Zone (figure 11–9). In the United States the major seismic areas are in California, the northern and central Rockies, the middle Mississippi River Valley, and parts of the northeast (figure 11–10).

The hazards associated with earthquakes are complex and consist of both direct and indirect effects. The principal direct effect of an earthquake is the movement of the earth's surface. Secondary effects include landslides, subsidence, fire, snow avalanches, soil failure, and seismic sea waves *(tsunamis).* This mul-

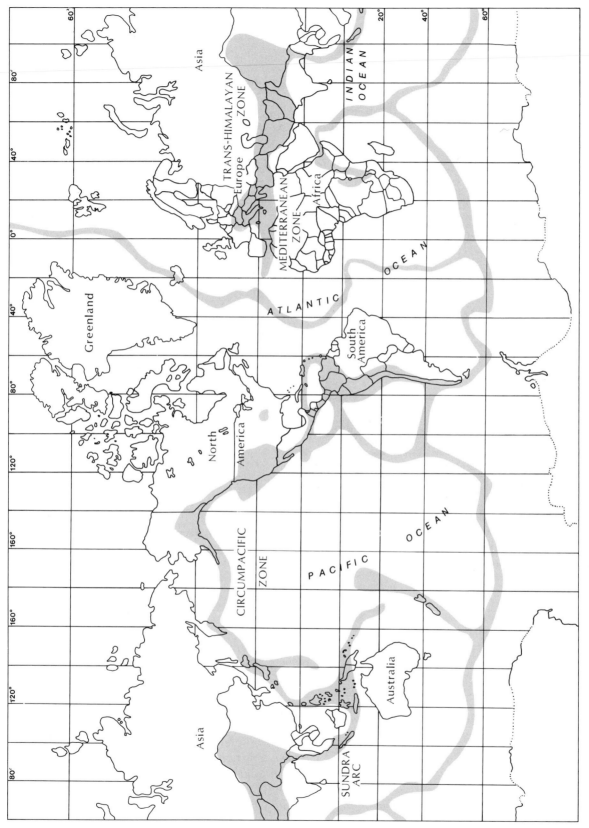

FIGURE 11–9 Major seismic belts. (U.S. Geological Survey.)

233

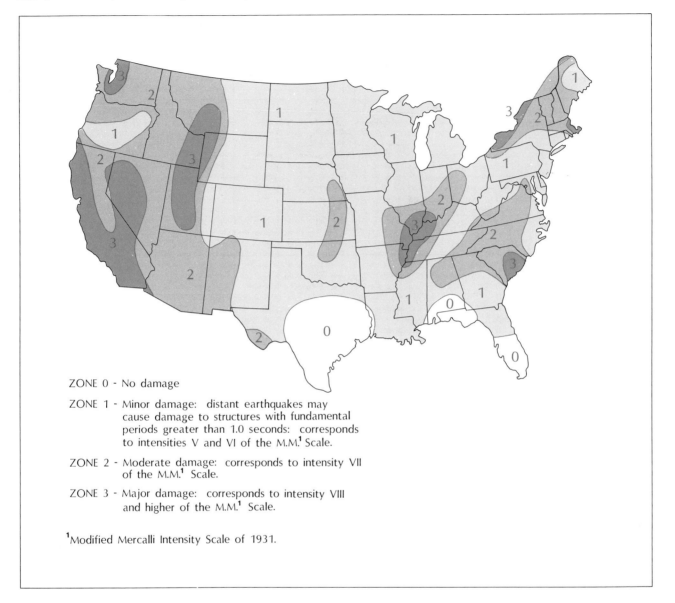

ZONE 0 - No damage

ZONE 1 - Minor damage: distant earthquakes may
cause damage to structures with fundamental
periods greater than 1.0 seconds: corresponds
to intensities V and VI of the M.M.[1] Scale.

ZONE 2 - Moderate damage: corresponds to intensity VII
of the M.M.[1] Scale.

ZONE 3 - Major damage: corresponds to intensity VIII
and higher of the M.M.[1] Scale.

[1]Modified Mercalli Intensity Scale of 1931.

FIGURE 11–10 Seismic risk in the United States, based on the known distribution of damaging earthquakes, their M. M. intensities, evidence of strain release, and consideration of major geologic structures believed to be associated with earthquake activity. The probable frequency of occurrence of damaging earthquakes in each zone was not considered. (U.S. Office of Emergency Preparedness, 1972, *Disaster Preparedness*, Volume 3. Washington, D.C., Office of the President.)

tiple hazard extorts a high toll in anxiety, physical harm, and personal loss suffered by the populace.

Human adjustments to earthquake hazards include warning systems, earthquake prevention, structural protection (including resistance to fire as well as shock), insurance, land use change, fire-prevention measures, relief, rehabilitation, and loss bearing on inaction (Nichols, 1974, p. 281). Although promising research in earthquake prediction and prevention is currently being undertaken throughout the world, the best human adjustments to earthquakes involve living in places that are not hazardous and how to live with the hazard when it cannot be avoided.

CASE STUDY:
The Tangshan earthquake of 1976

Early in the morning of July 28, 1976, an earthquake struck in Hebei (Hopei) province, one of China's most populous regions. The first tremor, which measured 8.2 on the Richter scale, was the most powerful since the Alaska quake of 1964. A second tremor, measuring 7.9, occurred sixteen hours later. Hebei province includes the cities of Beijing (Peking) with 7.6 million, Tianjin (Tientsin) with 4.3 million, and Tangshan with 1 million.

In Beijing the earth shuddered, and some older buildings cracked and crumbled. Fortunately only 50 people died. In the days that followed the quake, many people, fearing further shocks, moved into city parks and streets. The port city of Tianjin also suffered extensive damage. According to the former Australian Prime Minister Gough Whitlam, who was in the city, "It was absolutely terrifying . . . . The building was grinding and bucking and we were crawling around in the darkness. Outside, people were digging under the rubble. Whole facades of buildings had come down" (*Carroll,* 1976, p. 31).

The most serious toll, however, in terms of both life and property, took place in the city of Tangshan, the epicenter of the quake. In some places the earth was actually rent apart; at other places many craters were formed where the ground caved in. Tangshan was an important industrial center where rail locomotives, diesel engines, and other types of heavy machinery were produced. It was also China's largest single coal producer, accounting for over 6 percent of the nation's production. Foreign observers at Tangshan during the quake said the devastation of the city was comparable to that of Hiroshima after the atomic bomb. According to a visiting French friendship delegation, the city was 100 percent ruined.

The final death toll from the quake has not been revealed by the Chinese government, but reliable sources estimate that approximately 750,000 people lost their lives. This makes it the second most disastrous quake in recorded world history. (The worst quake occurred in China's Shaanxi (Shensi) province in 1556, and 800,000 people were killed.) Besides descriptions of the tremendous damage and death toll, there were some interesting revelations about the phenomenon itself.

> Just before the earth began to shudder, residents were awakened by a brilliant incandescence that lit up the dark, early morning sky for hundreds of miles around. The glow was predominantly red and white.
>
> When the quake struck many people were catapulted 6 feet high by what they said felt like a violent, hammerlike subterranean blow. In the quake's aftermath many bushes were scorched on only one side, much like snow accumulates preferentially on the windward side of a tree trunk during a blizzard. Trees and crops were bowled over as if by a colossal steamroller and other plant leaves were burned to a crisp. (*Science News,* 1977)

Chinese scientists had warned that an earthquake in this region of China was imminent, although there was no explicit prediction. Survivors of the quake said it struck suddenly and without warning. The Chinese have an elaborate warning system which includes thousands of "peasant observers," along with many highly trained scientists. They have at least 17 fully equipped seismographic centers and 250 auxiliary stations. Folk wisdom, which has been passed down through over 3,000 years of earthquake watching, primarily focuses on natural signs, such as water levels in wells and observations of birds and animals. An illustrated pamphlet published in 1973 by the Earthquake Office in Tianjin advises peasants that an earthquake may be imminent:

When cattle, sheep or horses refuse to get into the corral.

When rats run out from their hiding place.

When chickens fly up to the trees and pigs break out from their pens.

When ducks refuse to go to the water and dogs bark for no obvious reason.

When snakes come out from their winter hibernation.

When pigeons are frightened and will not return to their nests.

When rabbits with their ears standing jump up or crash into things.

When fish jump out of the water as if frightened.

Although the Chinese had not been able to precisely predict the Tangshan quake they were fast and efficient in carrying out relief efforts. Foreign observers reported long columns of trucks carrying prefabricated houses, temporary bridges, and other relief materials headed for Tangshan.

KEY TERMS

Ecology
Biosphere
Biological community
Ecosystem
Abiotic
Biotic
Trophic structure
Trophic level
Food chain
Pollution
Diffusion
Air pollution
Water pollution

Noise pollution
Aesthetic pollution
Natural hazards
Human adjustment
Bangladesh
Tropical Storm Agnes
Flooding
Drought
Tropical cyclones
Tornadoes
Hurricanes
Earthquakes
Tangshan earthquake

REFERENCES

Beyer, J. L. (1974), "Global Summary of Human Response to Natural Hazards: Floods," in White, G. (ed.), *Natural Hazards: Local, National, Global*. New York: Oxford University Press.

Burton, I., Kates R. W., and White, G. (1978), *The Environment as Hazard*. New York: Oxford University Press.

Clapham, W. B., Jr. (1973), *Natural Ecosystems*. New York: Macmillan, Inc.

Cousteau, J. Y. (1963), *The Living Sea*. New York: Harper & Row, Publishers, Inc.

Ehrlich, P. R., Ehrlich, A. H., and Holdren, J. P. (1977), *Ecoscience: Population, Resources, Environment*. San Francisco: W. H. Freeman & Co., Publishers.

Fagan, J. J. (1974), *The Earth Environment*. Englewood Cliffs, NJ: Prentice–Hall, Inc.

Frank, N. L. and Husain, S. A. (1971), "The Deadliest Cyclone in History," *Bulletin of the American Meteorology Society* 52.6, 438–444.

Hewitt, K. and Burton, I. (1971), *The Hazardousness of a Place: A Regional Ecology of Damaging Events.* Toronto: University of Toronto Press.

Heyerdahl, T. (1971), *The Ra Expeditions.* Garden City, NY: Anchor Press/Doubleday & Co., Inc.

Carroll, R. (1976), "China's Killer Quake," *Newsweek,* August 9, 30–32.

Hodges, L. (1977), *Environmental Pollution,* 2nd ed. New York: Holt, Rinehart & Winston.

Lewis, P. (1970), "Aesthetic Pollution: When Cleanliness Is Not Enough," *Public Management,* July.

Nichols, T. C., Jr. (1974), "Global Summary of Human Response to Natural Hazards: Earthquakes," in White, G. F. (ed.), *Natural Hazards.* New York: Oxford University Press, 280–285.

President's Science Advisory Committee, Environmental Pollution Panel (1965), *Restoring the Quality of our Environment.* Washington, D.C.: U.S. Government Printing Office.

ReVelle, C. and ReVelle, P. (1974), *Sourcebook on the Environment.* Boston: Houghton Mifflin Co.

Science News (1977), "Tangshan Quake: Portrait of a Catastrophe," Vol. 111, 388.

U.S. Dept. of Commerce, Environmental Science Services Administration (1968), Environmental Hazards: Occurrences, Deaths, Injuries, and Property Damage; Annual Basis. Washington, D.C.: U.S. Government Printing Office.

People make their livelihood through a variety of economic activities. In this section we discuss the nature of economic activities and the associated spatial patterns. Chapters 12 and 13 focus on agriculture and industry as major types of economic activities. In the final two chapters we discuss the nature of urbanization, its historical evolution, and spatial patterns.

Economic activities and urbanization 4

Toronto, Canada
(United Nations/Toronto Transit System, 1973)

12

Land and livelihood: Sustenance from the earth

Our major purpose in this chapter is to survey the primary ways in which people produce their food supplies. We look at various food production systems, the locations of these systems, and finally the associated landscapes.

Food production systems are evolving and are related to modernization. A key change in inputs in agriculture is energy, and generally modernization increases the demand for energy in agriculture. Thus, we try to relate the various agricultural systems to energy requirements and then, locationally, to underdeveloped and advanced countries.

Major food production systems in the underdeveloped countries are hunting and gathering, nomadic herding, shifting cultivation, and intensive subsistence agriculture. In the developed countries we look first at a theoretical model of agricultural land use patterns, then at dairy farming, mixed farming, Mediterranean agriculture, and commercial grain farming.

Next we consider food production and the growth syndrome, focusing on ways to expand food production to feed a growing population. We also look at the pattern of world food consumption. Finally, the chapter ends with a brief survey of house types and settlement patterns in agricultural landscapes.

From hunting and gathering to modern agriculture

As we have seen, population growth has been limited by the supply of food throughout most of human his-tory. People took what sustenance they could find from their landscapes, mainly what animals they could kill and what plants they could safely eat. Of course, no record remains of those who ate what their bodies could not tolerate.

Beginning some 10,000 years ago, the domestication of plants and animals increased people's food supplies. People could exercise more control over their environment and use it to greater advantage. Improvements in crop production resulted in population growth, forcing people to further expand the biosphere's productivity; intricately related in a mutually reinforcing way are the twin phenomena of population growth and advances in food production (Brown, 1970, p. 160). The current demand for food is greater than ever, and it continues to advance as a result of both population growth and increasing affluence. Yet pressure on the biosphere already raises questions about our ability to sustain growth in the food supply.

Current world patterns of food production systems reflect the various levels societies have reached in their attempts to provide sustenance, as well as the various cultural, economic, and ecological constraints on food production. In order to view this complex pattern of food supply systems, we must simplify and generalize to a considerable extent. Simplification requires classifying the various food production systems. However, various classification schema have been used by geographers. Agricultural activities, for example, are sometime classified on the basis of the types of tools used—hoe, plow, or primitive hunting and gathering.

Agricultural activities can also be classified on the basis of the frequency of cultivation and length of fallow, which we shall discuss in more detail later.

For our purposes such classifications, though useful, are insufficient. We have viewed the world as divided into cores and peripheries, or into developed and developing countries. Furthermore, we have suggested a major concern with the ecological implications of development. Thus, we would like to view agricultural systems as they fit in with the core–periphery worldview and with ecological systems.

A consistent thread running throughout the range of various food production systems, from hunting and gathering to the most advanced modern agriculture, is the need for energy as an input. The amount of energy required, as well as the form of energy used, varies considerably from one system to the next and among different levels of income and technology within any one system. Thus, food-producing activities in the peripheral or developing countries generally use less energy per unit of food produced than do those in the developed countries. Of course, as we shall see, the pattern of food-producing systems is far more complicated by other constraints.

Steinhart and Steinhart (1974) provided a view of energy and food production which related energy input to food output on a calorie-by-calorie basis. They measured the food supply by the caloric content actually consumed and the amount of all energy required in its production. Thus, a ratio of caloric input to output provided a useful index for contrasting food supply systems (figure 12–1).

FOOD PRODUCTION SYSTEMS IN THE DEVELOPING COUNTRIES

Figure 12–1 provides an idea of the energy input–output ratios of several different food-producing activities, though many other activities are not shown. If we arbitrarily divided activities at the one-to-one ratio, that is at the point where one calorie of input is producing one calorie of output, then the activities below that line would be low-energy input activities. Many of these food production systems are located in portions of the developing countries; a few can be found in very isolated peripheral portions of developed countries. Although our generalization holds neither for every type of production system nor for every crop, we feel

it is a useful way of organizing an overview of world agricultural patterns.

Hunting and gathering

Too often today people in the urban-industrial nations are so isolated from food production that they are unable even to imagine life in the preindustrial era, let alone the preagricultural era. However, until about 10,000 years ago people either lived by hunting, fishing, and gathering edible plants, tubers, and roots, or they perished. Early people learned the secrets of their environment and developed increasingly sophisticated tools and techniques for providing their next meal. The only energy input was human energy.

By the beginning of the Upper Paleolithic, about 40,000 years ago, group cooperation had helped solve the basic problem of survival. During the Upper Paleolithic "hunters began to stabilize their food supplies through more specialized hunting of one or two species of the larger mammals, through intensive gathering of selected vegetable foods, and through fishing activities" (Fagan, 1974, p. 117). A thorough knowledge of the environment was a prerequisite to maximizing food resources. As humans established themselves as ecological dominants, they began to affect the ecological balance, altering both plant and animal communities.

Some scholars have argued that **Pleistocene overkill** occurred in certain areas. Evidence in North America suggests that the extinction of camels, horses, elephants, mammoths, dire wolves, and other large mammals closely coincided with the appearance of Early Mongoloid hunters and gatherers (Boughey, 1975, p. 137). Evidence of overkill has also been found in Africa. Thus, we can scarcely suggest that humankind has only recently begun to alter its environment.

Today only a few societies survive by hunting and gathering. As you might expect, their numbers are small, and they are located in harsh and relatively isolated environments. The Eskimos of Canada, Alaska, and Greenland and the Bushman of Africa's Kalahari Desert are examples. Others live in parts of Brazil, Southeast Asia, and Australia. The actual numbers of hunters and gatherers today is small and their population densities are quite low.

Besides hunting and gathering, a few people still live by **nomadic herding,** again usually in isolated

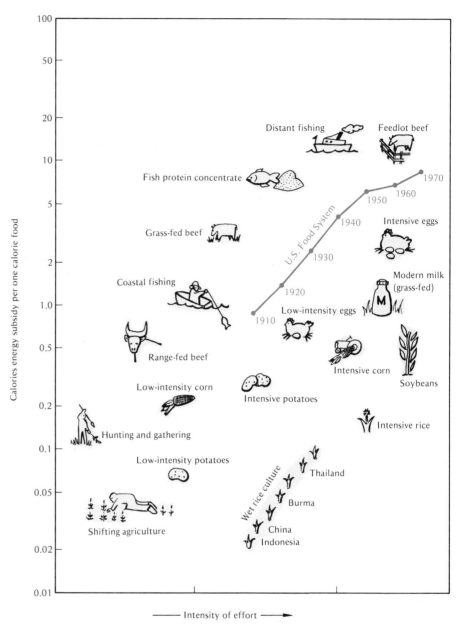

FIGURE 12–1 Energy subsidies for various food crops. The energy history of the U.S. food system is shown for comparison. (From *Energy: Sources, Use, and Role in Human Affairs* by Carol Steinhart and John Steinhart.: © 1974 by Wadsworth Publishing Co., Inc., Belmont, CA 94002, p. 84. Reprinted by permission of the publisher, Duxbury Press.)

areas. Examples include the Masai in East Africa and the Tuareg of Africa's Sahel region.

Shifting cultivation

With respect to agriculture, ***shifting cultivation*** (or slash-and-burn) systems have received considerable attention from cultural geographers. Unlike the settled farmers and their neat arrangements of barns, homes, and silos, shifting cultivators raise crops in one place only so long as the inherent fertility of the soil provides a sufficient yield; then they move on and let the tropical forests rejuvenate. Note that shifting cultivation is quite energy efficient, in that there is a low ratio of calorie input to output. As with hunting and gathering, the energy input is human energy.

The system is rather simple. Farmers chop away the low-growing vegetation in an area, then kill the trees by girdling them. The dried debris is burned, and its ashes add to the soil. A variety of crops are then sown in the cleared area. Essentially the system can be seen as one in which farmers rotate fields rather than crops, or as one where crops are rotated, with a long fallow period.

The number of people practicing shifting cultivation is not precisely known but may be around 200 million. They are found in the tropical forests of South and Central America, Africa, and Southeast Asia. Crops grown include maize, rice, manioc, yams, and millet. Thus, diets are high in carbohydrates; hunger and malnutrition are constant threats.

The Danish economist Ester Boserup (1965) has studied the relationship between agricultural systems and population growth in underdeveloped areas and suggests that the intensification of land use is a response to population growth. She views the increased frequency of cropping in isolated areas not as a *cause* of population growth (as we saw with Malthus's ideas) but as an *effect*.

Boserup suggested a classification of land use according to increased intensity. Our use of energy inputs fits well with her view because, at least in general, an increase in the intensity of land use requires more inputs to the production process, including more energy. Boserup used the following five types of land use, listed in order of increasing land-use intensity (1965, pp. 15–16):

1. ***Forest-fallow cultivation.*** A shifting agricultural system in which an area is cleared, cropped for one or two years, then left fallow for twenty to twenty-five years, during which the area returns to forest. Human energy requirements are low.

2. ***Bush-fallow cultivation.*** As with the above system, this is a shifting agricultural system. However, the fallow period is shortened to between six and ten years. Rather than forest, the land returns to a growth of bush and shrubs, but not true forest. The period of cultivation varies from one or two years to as many as ten years.

3. ***Short-fallow cultivation.*** Land lies fallow for only one or two years. Only wild grasses return.

4. ***Annual cropping.*** The land is fallow for only part of one year, between harvests and sowing. Boserup includes annual rotation systems within this category as well.

5. ***Multicropping.*** Land is used for two or more successive crops every year. The period of fallow is reduced to almost nothing.

Boserup states her main thesis as follows:

> Under the pressure of increasing population, there has been a shift in recent decades from more extensive to more intensive systems of land use in virtually every part of the underdeveloped regions. In some parts of the world, cultivators under the forest-fallow system have been unable to find sufficient secondary forest. They have then had to re-cultivate areas not yet bearing fully grown forest. In this way, the forest has receded and been replaced by bush. Again, in regions of bush fallow the cultivators have changed to short-fallow systems or annual cropping and many short-fallow cultivators have changed to systems of annual cropping with or without irrigation. In the densely populated regions of the Far East, the growth of population during this century has caused a rapid spread of multi-cropping. (1965, p. 16)

As population pressure forces an intensification of land use and a decrease in the length of fallow, it is essential that people do more to restore fertility and maintain or increase yields. Fertilization becomes a necessity, and in most cases, people will have to work harder in fertilizing, cultivating, and tending crops. Ultimately irrigation and other capital investments are required, especially for multicropping.

Though Boserup has been criticized considerably, her ideas have yet to be replaced with more widely accepted alternatives. Of course, exceptions and variations on the basic theme are likely to be found, especially as modernization spreads to the more isolated regions in which hunting, gathering, herding, and shifting cultivation are still practiced.

Intensive subsistence farming

Intensive subsistence farming is practiced throughout the densely populated areas of the Far East and in a few other areas (figure 12–2). Though the output per unit of land is quite high, intensive subsistence farming requires a considerable amount of human energy and produces a relatively low output per worker. Farm machinery is virtually nonexistent, though draft animals are used in some places. However, new crops and new technology have recently had an impact throughout most of the area, resulting in the "green revolution" which we will discuss in detail subsequently.

Crops are extremely important and include rice, wheat, barley, and millet. Though grains are heavily emphasized, farmers supplement their diets with

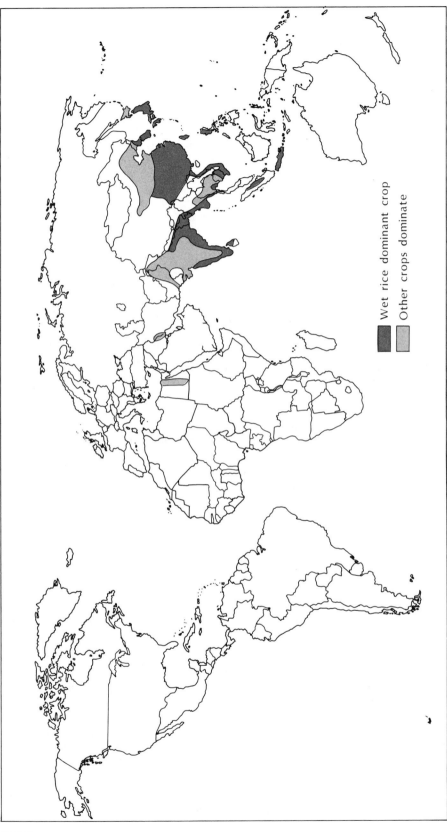

Wet rice dominant crop

Other crops dominate

FIGURE 12–2 Intensive subsistence farming. (John W. Alexander, Lay James Gibson, *Economic Geography*, 2nd ed., © 1979, p. 36. Reprinted by permission of Prentice-Hall, Inc., Englewood Cliffs, NJ.)

Simultaneously uprooting and transplanting rice, Jamalpur, India. (J. Breitenbach for IDA, 1969)

beans, peanuts, and other fruits and vegetables. Cotton for clothing is also grown by many farmers. Fishing and fish farming also provide dietary supplements, especially protein.

Rice is the most widespread grain grown by intensive subsistence farmers for at least two reasons: it produces more food per acre than any grain except corn, and it keeps well in humid climates. Though both wet and dry rice cultivation are practiced, **wet rice cultivation** is by far the more important. Yields of wet rice may, under good conditions, reach 3000 pounds per acre annually. Despite its importance as a major food crop in the Far East, wet rice cultivation occupies a relatively small area. According to Loomis (1976, p. 101), the dominance of a particular crop in a region is the result of a combination of ecological and economic factors, including environmental adaptation, yield, reliability, and farm management practices.

Rice adapts to a wide range of soils and environmental conditions. It requires relatively high temperatures during the growing season and sufficient, but not excessive, moisture, though neither of these requirements particularly restrict the cultivation of wet rice. The major restriction, rather, is its need to be submerged below gradually moving water for the first three-fourths of its growing period, which restricts it to flatlands near rivers (Griggs, 1974, p. 75). As a result most wet rice cultivation occurs on deltas and along the lower portions of rivers. Examples include the Mekong and Irrawaddy.

Wet rice farming generally occurs on small farms in scattered small plots. The family is the entire labor supply. High population densities are sustained in most wet rice producing regions, with maximum densities in parts of the Ganges delta and much lower densities in the more recently settled Mekong and Irrawaddy deltas.

The importance of rice in the developing countries is paramount. Among the developed countries, only the United States produces a significant amount of rice, and our production methods differ considerably from those used in the Far East. For example, airplanes are used to sow the rice and apply herbicides, and large mechanical harvesters quickly move through the fields at harvest time.

Banana harvester in the Naranjal–El Guabo region of Ecuador. (Larry Daughters for World Bank Group, 1971)

Wheat is another important crop in the developing countries (especially China, India, and Pakistan) and, unlike rice, in the developed countries, as well. As with rice, of course, production methods differ considerably between the developed and the developing countries. In the former wheat production is generally capital intensive and occurs on large farms, whereas in the latter wheat production is more labor intensive and occurs on small farms.

Plantation agriculture

We have mentioned **plantation agriculture** previously in our discussion of core–periphery relationships.

Plantations are located primarily in the peripheral tropical areas but serve the needs of the industrial areas of the core. Among the exceptions to the peripheral country locations are cotton plantations in the southeastern United States and sugar plantations in Hawaii.

Plantations in the developing countries differ from local subsistence agricultural systems in several ways: They are commercial rather than private systems, established to produce excess rather than subsistence amounts. Plantation products are exported rather than consumed locally, so they are involved in international trade patterns. They are generally highly mechanized and require more energy inputs, both in production and distribution. They involve large, consolidated landholdings rather than small, fragmented plots. They usually specialize in the production of one crop.

Workers reside on the plantation and are distinctly separated socially and economically from the managing class. Plantations use as many unskilled laborers as possible and try, within the bounds of economic profitability, to maximize the ratio of unskilled laborers to the higher cost of managerial employees.

Plantations may be categorized on the basis of ownership: private individuals, families, limited liability companies, partnerships, cooperative societies, and state ownership (Beckford, 1972, p. 7). According to Beckford there has been a major shift as private individual and family plantations have changed to limited liability companies, which are the dominant plantation type today. Foreign ownership prevails in the developing countries, thus center dominance on the periphery.

Products of plantations in developing countries include sugar cane, bananas, pineapples, coconuts, coffee, tea, and rubber. Because these products are bound for distant markets, plantations locate on or near coasts when possible to minimize distribution costs. The greatest concentration of plantations is in the Caribbean, though larger populations are involved in plantation agriculture in Southeast Asia and Ceylon.

AGRICULTURE IN THE DEVELOPED COUNTRIES

Compared to the subsistence agriculture practiced throughout the developing countries, we find commercial agriculture predominant in the developed countries. Whereas labor was a major input in subsistence agriculture, capital, technology, and energy are major inputs in the agricultural systems of developed countries. As figure 12–1 illustrated, more energy is required than is produced in many products, thus we actually find an energy subsidy in agriculture in places such as the United States, where in 1970 approximately eight calories of input were required for each calorie of consumable output. For feedlot beef, a favorite on the American table, the caloric input–output ratio rises above ten to one, without considering the ecological problems associated with the system.

Another major difference between food supply systems is the need for transportation. In subsistence agricultural systems, most of what is produced on farms is consumed on the farms as well, though the small remainder may go to local markets. However, in the developed countries, most of the food produced on farms is consumed by people living elsewhere, mainly in the cities. High productivity per worker in developed countries frees most of the labor force for other jobs, mainly in manufacturing and service activities, which are concentrated in the cities. Thus, not only does modern commercial agriculture require high energy inputs to the production process, but also it requires considerable energy in transportation to the market.

Location of commercial agricultural activities

As we previously suggested, the location of a particular crop is the result of a combination of economic, ecological, and cultural variables. Agricultural regions evolve as a response to various combinations of factors and, though sometimes portrayed as homogeneous regions, usually vary from place to place with respect to crops. For example, in the United States we can and do speak of the Corn Belt. However, within the Corn Belt we find livestock, especially hogs, and other important crops, such as soybeans.

In order to try to explain the pattern of commercial agriculture in a market economy such as the United States, we can proceed along a path which will at least provide some assistance. At the outset, we need to recognize that the individual farmer is motivated by profit, though it need not be a maximum profit. Thus, we might ask what a particular piece of land might be used for in a particular location.

Let's assume for a moment that we have a farmer who wishes to make as much profit as possible each year. What considerations are important to the decision? Some obvious considerations are the cost of producing the crop (or crops) and the price it brings, the natural fertility of the soil (including climatic situation), and the relative location of the land. Without getting unnecessarily bogged down in mathematical and economic details we'll attempt to look at each of the three considerations.

Relative location. Because most food in the United States is consumed in cities, we should suspect that land near cities is going to be profitable for farmers because, all else being equal, transportation costs will be

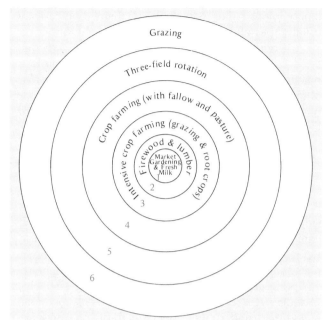

FIGURE 12–3 Sequence of land use in *Der Isolierte Staat*. (Reproduced by permission from the *Annals* of the Association of American Geographers, Volume 57, 1967, Robert Sinclair.)

lower. However, as a result, the land is likely to be more expensive.

A 19th century German, Johann Heinrich Von Thünen, explored the spatial organization of agriculture in a book entitled *The Isolated State* (Hall, 1966). After studying agriculture, Von Thünen acquired an 1146-acre estate, which he called Tellow, in 1810. There he spent most of his life and carried out the detailed studies necessary for his model of agricultural production. Like most models, Von Thünen's has a set of assumptions to simplify reality and allow us to focus our attention on a specific variable, in this case distance.

Von Thünen assumed an isolated state with a single large town at its center and soil of good and uniform fertility throughout. The central town must supply the rural areas with manufactured goods, whereas the town gets all its food from the surrounding area. Furthermore, he assumed that the surface was flat and uninterrupted by rivers or mountains. He also assumed that farmers would transport their products to the market themselves by oxcart via a straightline route; so transport costs were assumed to be directly proportional to distance. Assuming that farmers behaved rationally, Von Thünen wished to know what pattern of cultivation would evolve in the isolated state, and what would be the role of distance in determining the pattern.

He concluded that land use would fall into a series of concentric zones of varying size around the town. He recognized six different zones (figure 12–3) market gardening, forestry (for firewood), intensive crop farming, crop farming with a fallow period, three-field crop rotation, and grazing. Beyond the sixth ring would be only wasteland, because the cost of transportation was too great to allow any agricultural pursuit to be carried on profitably. This pattern of agricultural land use may surprise you, especially the location of forestry, but keep in mind that he was writing early in the 19th century in Germany, where the Industrial Revolution was just beginning. Thus, what is important is not whether we find identical concentric land-use zones around cities today, but whether we find any concentric land-use patterns in some similar fashion.

For a century or more, scholars have reported such patterns around various cities, and they continue to do so. Examples include a four-zone pattern from Durban, South Africa, to the interior, a five-zone gradation around Buenos Aires, and a five-zone pattern of decreasing farm intensity in a southwesterly direction from Chicago (Gregor, 1970, pp. 59-60). Of course the patterns found are not at all perfect concentric zones, nor are they solely restricted to one type of use. Climatic, topographic and soil differences alter local land-use patterns, as do farmers who make nonprofit-maximizing decisions about what to produce. How-

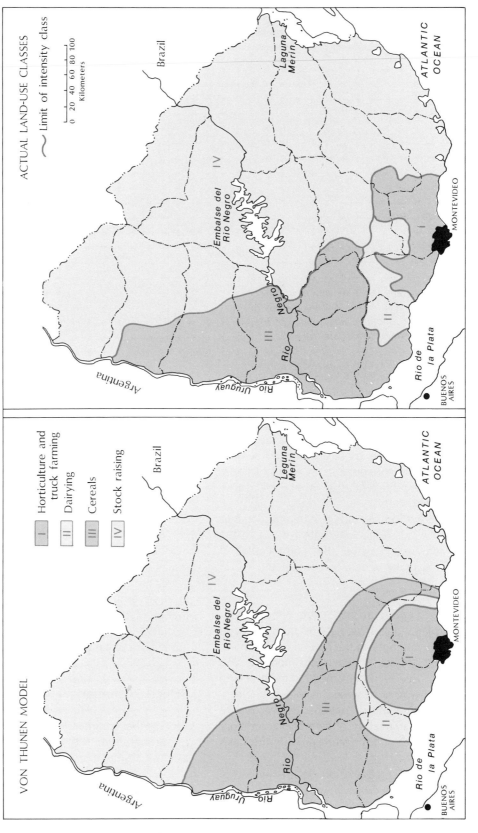

VON THUNEN MODEL

Horticulture and
truck farming
Dairying
Cereals
Stock raising

I
II
III
IV

Brazil

Embalse del
Rio Negro

Laguna
Merin

Argentina

Rio
Negro

Rio
Uruguay

Rio de
la Plata

BUENOS
AIRES

MONTEVIDEO

ATLANTIC
OCEAN

ACTUAL LAND-USE CLASSES

Limit of intensity class

0 20 40 60 80 100
Kilometers

Brazil

Embalse del
Rio Negro

Laguna
Merin

IV

Argentina

Rio
Negro

III

II

I

Rio
Uruguay

Rio de
la Plata

BUENOS
AIRES

MONTEVIDEO

ATLANTIC
OCEAN

FIGURE 12–4 Comparison of actual land-use classes with patterns based on the Von Thünen model. (Ernst Griffin, October, 1973, "Testing the Von Thünen Theory in Uruguay," in the *Geographical Review* 63, p. 510, with the permission of the American Geographical Society.)

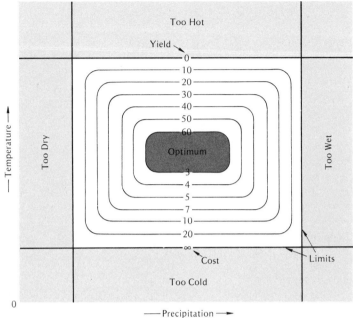

FIGURE 12–5 Optima and limits schema of temperature and precipitation. (Harold H. McCarty, James B. Lindberg, *A Preface to Economic Geography,* © 1966, p. 61. Reprinted by permission of Prentice-Hall, Inc., Englewood Cliffs, NJ.)

ever, strong evidence favors the operation of distance as *one* major factor in agricultural land-use patterns.

A recent study of agricultural land use patterns in Uruguay by Griffin (1973) found considerable agreement between the Von Thünen model and actual land-use patterns (figure 12–4). There are deviations from the theoretical pattern, of course, as a result of variations in soil fertility, differences in inputs, and variations in settlement patterns.

Even at the world scale, it is possible to see signs of Von Thünen zones, especially with respect to the intensity of land use. However, the complexities of land-use patterns make generalizations at the world scale difficult.

Environmental considerations. We already suggested one explanation for deviations from the Von Thünen model—variations in the natural environment which affect soil fertility. A schematic model developed by Harold McCarty and James Lindberg (1966) provides a useful way of viewing the role of environmental factors in agricultural patterns (figure 12–5). Their schema is an adaptation of central place theory in which temperature and moisture provide the basis via **optima and limits.**

Temperature and precipitation requirements vary considerably for different crops; however, for any crop some optimum set of conditions exists. Away from that optimum we can believe that yields either decline or can be maintained only at higher costs. For example,

corn yields decrease as we move from optimum precipitation toward drier conditions, but yields can be maintained by irrigation. Beyond some point, however, a crop may be impossible to grow, though given sufficient capital most obstacles could probably be overcome. Thus variations in environmental conditions may be considered along with Von Thünen's model in explaining agricultural land-use patterns.

Costs and prices. For the individual farmer concerned with making a profit, costs and prices are primary determinants in decision making. Production requires land, labor, and capital in varying proportions. Prices are determined by supply and demand, as well as by government policies. Thus, we need to remember that agricultural patterns develop in response to a set of different variables, which themselves vary in importance from place to place.

Selected commerical agricultural patterns

Among the commercial agricultural activities carried on primarily in the developed countries, we shall briefly consider dairy farming, mixed farming, Mediterranean agriculture, and commercial grain farming.

Dairy farming. Three major belts of commercial **dairy farming** can be identified. The North American belt runs from New England, through Pennsylvania and

Dairy farm, Lancaster, Pennsylvania. (United Nations/John Isaac, 1975)

Ohio, on through Wisconsin, Minnesota, and on into the Canadian provinces of Manitoba, Saskatchewan, and eastern Alberta. Smaller areas of commercial dairying occur in Utah and the Pacific states. Local supply areas are also found around major cities throughout the country, in keeping with Von Thünen's model.

American dairy farms average 37 cows on 250 acres, though variations in farm and herd size are considerable (Alexander, *et al.*, 1979). Close to 80 percent of the income of most dairy farmers comes from milk sales, either to local markets as fresh milk or to manufacturers of dairy products. Large capital investments are required, especially for buildings.

Dairy farms located near growing metropolitan areas are often forced to move outward as urban use competes for the available land. Dairies don't make good neighbors for new residential developments; hence citizen pressure, if not economic pressure, usually forces them to relocate.

A second major belt of commercial dairying extends from Ireland and England, across Northern France and Germany, Denmark, southern Norway, and Sweden, and on into the U.S.S.R. European dairy farms are generally only about one-fifth the size of their American counterparts, and feed is usually purchased by the dairy farmer rather than grown, as it is on most American dairy farms. In both Europe and America, dairy farms are closely related to urban areas because of the high demand for fresh milk and its perishability.

The area of milk production around a city is sometimes referred to as a *milk shed*.

A smaller dairy farm belt occurs in southeastern Australia and New Zealand, again in association with a Western culture realm. Among other cultures, fresh milk is far less important in people's diets.

Mixed farming. **Mixed farming** refers to farming which involves both crops and livestock. Though confined mainly to the developed countries, mixed farming does occur elsewhere, especially in parts of Latin America.

In the developed countries, two main areas of mixed farming may be identified. One is in the American Midwest, mainly in what has long been identified as the *Corn Belt*. Corn is grown primarily as feed for hogs and cattle. The Corn Belt is an example of agricultural land use where the idea of optima and limits applies rather well, especially to the north and west, where corn production is limited by the cold and dryness, respectively. Within the Corn Belt other crops are grown, of course, including oats and hay for feed, as well as soybeans and wheat.

Major markets also play a role in the location of mixed farming, because the United States population is heavily concentrated in the Midwest and the Northeast. Also (in Von Thünen fashion) on an automobile trip from Chicago to Denver, you would observe a decreasing pattern of agricultural intensity. Around Chi-

Wheat field in Daykin, Nebraska. (United Nations/Krishna Singh, 1974)

cago dairy farms are a major use of land, but westward mixed farming, with corn the predominant crop, would be found. Depending on your route, you would begin to see less corn as you travel through Iowa or northern Missouri into eastern Nebraska or Kansas, as mixed farming gives way mainly to grazing or to wheat farming as a cash-grain crop.

The other major mixed farming region extends from Northern Spain and Portugal, across most of Europe, and into and across the U.S.S.R. Smaller areas of mixed farming occur in South Africa, Mexico, Argentina, Chile, and southeastern Brazil.

We should note that mixed farming is a response to diets centered on meat, a luxury offered mainly to those in the developed countries. In terms of caloric input–output, meat production is above one except for range-fed beef. Animals are inefficient converters of food energy from grains, so they are expensive to produce.

Mediterranean agriculture. Ecologic factors are important determinants of **Mediterranean agriculture,** which produces an abundance and variety of both plants and animals. This type of land use is found in five regions of Mediterranean climate, characterized by mild winters, long dry summers, and relatively low annual rainfalls. The classic area of Mediterranean agriculture is found, as you might well have guessed, around the Mediterranean Sea. Others occur in California, Chile, South Africa, and Australia.

A variety of crops are grown in both winter and summer. Winter crops are sown in the fall and harvested early the following summer to take advantage of the winter rains. Summer crops are sown in early spring and harvested in late summer or fall. Winter crops include wheat and barley. Locally, winter vegetables are also important and include broccoli and cauliflower. Summer crops include peaches, citrus, tomatoes, grapes, olives, and figs. The cuisine of the Mediterranean reflects the abundance of tomatoes, peppers, onions, summer squash, and olives. Think about spaghetti sauce or ratatouille! Livestock are also important, especially cattle, goats and sheep.

The degree of commercialism, the size and type of farm, and the techniques used vary considerably, of course, from one area to the next. Though California is not entirely Mediterranean, we can see the variety of land uses is complex (figure 12–6a). Topography and local microclimates, as well as population distribution, are important determinants of agricultural land use. Furthermore, areas often specialize in nationally sold crops, such as artichokes, lettuce, and broccoli. Thus, the pattern of vegetable production alone is of interest (figure 12–6b).

Commercial grain farming. Grains are essential to people's diets, though the type of grains consumed and the forms in which they are consumed vary considerably from place to place. Wheat may be preferred in two different places, though as noodles and other

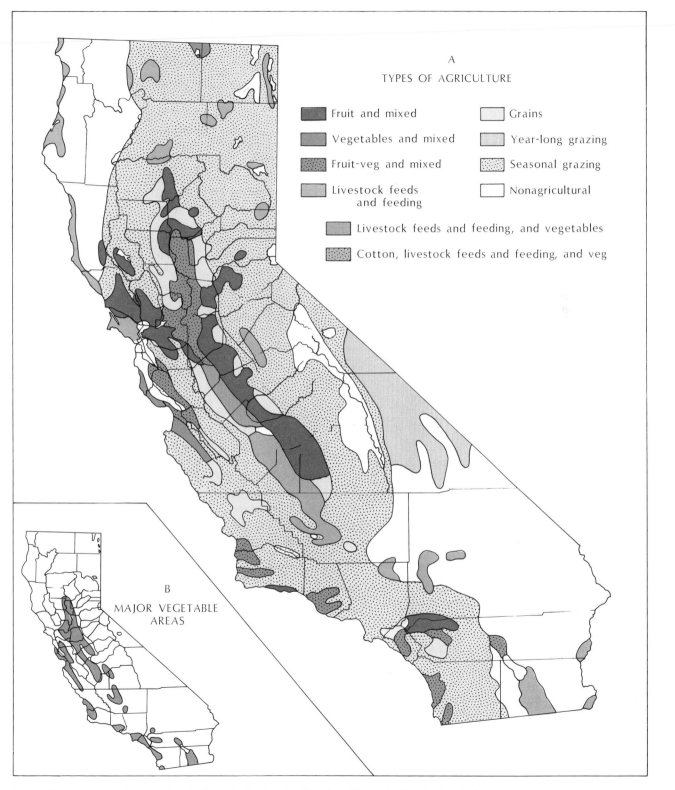

FIGURE 12–6 General types of agriculture in California. (Reprinted from *California: Land of Contrast*, 3rd ed., by David Lantis, Rodney Steiner, and Arthur Karinen. © 1977, with permission of Kendall/Hunt Publishing Co., pp. 441 and 445.)

253

forms of pasta in one, such as Italy, and bread in the other, such as the United States.

Four major areas of **commercial grain farming** can be identified: the United States, Argentina, Australia, and the U.S.S.R. Production is limited to the middle latitudes, and farms usually concentrate entirely on the production of one grain. Though grains can be grown over a rather wide range of environmental conditions, only a few regions appear to specialize in commercial (as opposed to subsistence) production.

Of the various grains grown by commercial grain farmers, wheat is the most important. Wheat is produced in developing countries—especially China, India, Pakistan, and Mexico—as well as in the developed countries; however, farming methods differ considerably. Small subsistence farms with little or no mechanization are the rule in the developing countries, whereas large, highly mechanized farms are the rule in the developed countries, especially in the United States.

Populations densities associated with wheat producing regions differ also, with high population densities characteristic in the developing countries and low population densities in the developed countries. Whereas the need for labor in the developing countries encourages high fertility among farm families, the high capital costs and low labor needs in the developed countries encourages not only lower fertility but also out-migration. In parts of North America, only nine hours are required to sow, grow, and harvest a hectare (about 2.5 acres) of wheat, whereas in 1830, 148 hours were required (Grigg, 1974, p. 257).

In terms of both tons harvested and acreage planted, wheat is the world's leading crop. By volume it is also the major food commodity in international trade, with the United States and Canada accounting for about two-thirds of trade volume. The U.S.S.R. has become a net importer—a fact of which Americans became rather suddenly aware in 1972, when large sales of American wheat to the Soviet Union were followed by a rapid rise in the cost of wheat products, especially bread.

Population growth in many areas has forced wheat producers farther afield, as rising land values required that more intensive land uses replace wheat production. Wheat has been far removed from its optimum growing conditions, pushed mainly onto drier lands with attendant lower yields. In some cases, as in the Virgin Lands project in the U.S.S.R., expansion of wheat production into marginal areas has been unsuccessful.

FOOD PRODUCTION AND THE GROWTH SYNDROME

Associated with the gradual evolution of food production systems over the past 10,000 years, we can see a long process of diminishing variations in human diets. As people have specialized in growing certain crops, major ecosystems have been greatly simplified, thus diminishing their stability.

Between 1965 and 1970 the world's population increased by about one billion people, the majority of whom were added to the hungry developing countries. Population growth, coupled with increasing affluence, annually creates an enormous increase in world food needs. Increasing affluence increases the demand for meat in the diet, hence the need for more cereals to fatten livestock

On the one hand, people are faced with a constantly growing demand for food; on the other hand, concern is focused on the various ways that the productivity of the land itself is undermined by accelerated soil erosion, creeping deserts, increased flooding, and a general decline in soil fertility (Eckholm, 1976, p. 5). In recent years crops have been grown on roughly 3 billion acres, nearly 10 percent of the earth's land surface. Nearly 70 percent of this cultivated acreage has been planted to cereals, which in turn provide about half of the caloric intake of the world's population. However, food is not necessarily produced and distributed where it is needed, mainly for cultural, political, and economic reasons.

To an economist the demand for food (or any other item, for that matter) is not synonymous with need. No one doubts that a hungry person represents a demand for food, but for that demand to become effective in the marketplace, the person must also have the ability to pay. Thus, the effective demand for food in a given place is different from the number of hungry people. For example, many conscientious and well-meaning people have suggested that Americans should eat less meat, thus freeing more grain for shipment to where it is sorely needed, such as India, Bangladesh, and Pakistan. However, one of the obvious paradoxes in the world of food supply and demand is that the hungry people are those who have little or no money to spend on food. American farmers would be more than willing to ship grain to India, providing, of course, that they receive their asking price.

If Americans suddenly cut their meat consumption drastically, a chain of events would likely take place. Meat producers would see falling prices and cut

Socorro County, New Mexico. It would be difficult to make this land productive because of lack of moisture. (Library of Congress, 1940)

their production accordingly. Then farmers who produced grains and other crops for livestock would see prices for their products falling and would also cut back production. They would have to shift to other crops, find new markets, or sell their land and move to the city.

Food consumption patterns

Food consumption varies considerably from place to place. At the world scale significant variations in the amounts of food eaten and in the protein content of diets are particularly important. Of course, the specific content of diets is related to cultural differences in tastes, food taboos, religious dietary restrictions, and historical traditions.

In recent decades food production has outpaced population growth, though not by a very wide margin. For example, between 1954 and 1973 population grew at about 2.0 percent annually, while food output increased at an annual rate of 2.8 percent. However, most of the increase in food production occurred in the developed countries, whereas most of the population growth occurred in the developing ones.

Expanding food output

Considering the built-in momentum of population growth and the probability of continually increasing

affluence, it is essential that world food supplies be expanded over the decades ahead. Three major ways of increasing food supplies are: increase the amount of land under cultivation, increase the yields on currently cultivated acreage, and increase the output from oceanic fisheries.

Increase the amount of land under cultivation. This at first appears to be an easy and practical choice for increasing food supplies. If farmers are currently cultivating only 10 percent of the earth's land surface, then we have just begun, so to speak. However, before we become overly optimistic, consider our discussion of agricultural location, especially the optima and limits schema.

Though, theoretically, we could produce bananas or strawberries at the South Pole, the cost would be prohibitive. So when we talk about environmental limits, we are really talking about economic limits resulting from environmental constraints. Only about 25 percent of the earth's surface is considered arable; another 25 percent is suitable for grazing.

The potential for expanding the acreage under cultivation doesn't look quite as great now, but if 25 percent of the land surface is considered arable, and we are currently cultivating only 10 percent, then we should be able to increase the cultivated acreage by 150 percent (figure 12–7). However, good reasons still exist to prohibit cultivation on currently uncultivated

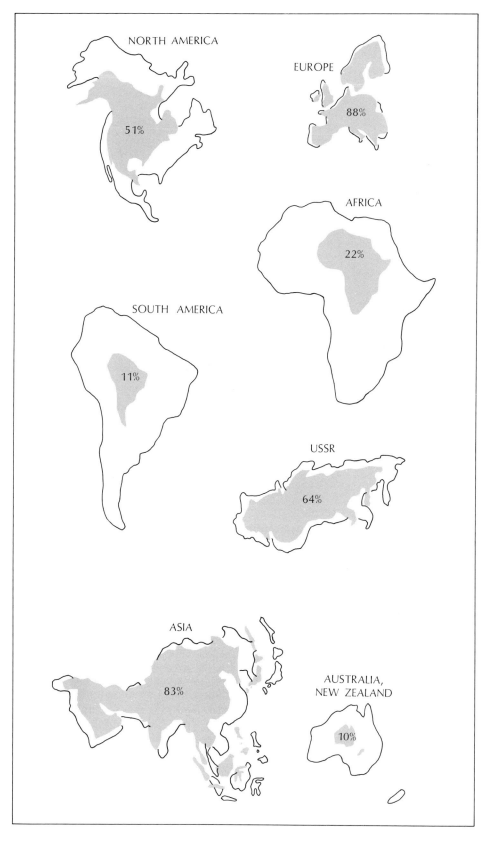

FIGURE 12–7 Expansion of farming to arable but uncultivated land is one way to increase the world's food supply. The outline maps show major land masses in proportion to their potentially arable land, and the silhouette maps within show how much of it was being cultivated as of the mid-1960s. (From W. David Hopper, "The Development of Agriculture in Developing Countries." Copyright © September, 1976 by Scientific American, Inc., p. 199. All rights reserved.)

256

but arable land, including insufficient water supplies, the effect of diseases and pests, and economics. Water, of course, can always be provided, but cost quickly becomes a problem. A Von Thünen principle operates also, because currently unused arable land is often far from major food markets, in which case transportation costs make farming unprofitable, even if production costs could be controlled. Diseases often make areas virtually uninhabitable; for example, arable land in some areas of Africa is unused because of the presence of the tsetse fly, a carrier of sleeping sickness which threatens both people and livestock. A more serious limitation may be the danger of expanding food acreage and yields sufficiently to allow the world's population to grow beyond the numbers that could be sustained on natural sources of nitrogen (Loomis, 1976, p. 103). Thus, expanding food supplies will further increase ecological stresses in a variety of ways.

Increase the yields on currently cultivated acreage. From the beginning of the agricultural revolution until about 1950, most gains in agricultural production have resulted from expanding the amount of land under cultivation. Since 1950, however, this pattern has changed. Prospects for bringing new land under cultivation are not good, yet the population continues to grow; this leaves us with the major alternative of increasing food output from the currently cropped acreage (Brown, et al., 1974, p. 75). At the same time, of course, we need to consider ways of curbing the rate of population growth, thereby slowing the increase in demand for food.

Among the major ways of increasing crop yields are fertilizers, herbicides and pesticides, irrigation, and genetic improvement of plants. Of course none of these are new, though only recently have some of them been employed in the developing countries. The history of fertilizer usage is long, though modern chemical fertilizers are a product of the 20th century. Historically the mainstay in most areas was manure; today manure is still important, though it may be supplemented by chemicals (figure 12–8). In some areas manure is also used as an energy source. Even human wastes have sometimes been used by farmers as fertilizers, especially in the Far East, where it is called *night soil.*

Dramatic yield improvements are possible with the addition of chemical fertilizers, especially under favorable conditions. However, decreasing returns occur at some point as the amount of fertilizer is increased.

Average fertilizer usage varies considerably from country to country, though it is generally high in the developed countries and low in the developing ones. For example, in 1972 West Germany used 363 pounds of fertilizer for each acre of arable land, whereas the United States used 72, China 35, India 14, and Nigeria one (Brown, et al., 1974, p. 116).

Nitrogen, mainly in the form of anhydrous ammonia, is the major ingredient in chemical fertilizers. Ammonia may be applied directly or used as an ingredient in other fertilizer products, such as urea. Unfortunately the manufacture of ammonia requires hydrogen, which must be derived from hydrocarbon compounds such as natural gas, naptha, or even coal. Because of the steep rises in coal and petroleum prices during the 1970s, chemical fertilizers have also shown rapid price increases, which in turn make it impossible for most farmers in the developing countries to use much, if any. Its use in developing countries is also limited to some extent by the cost of associated equipment.

Another major fertilizer ingredient is phosphate, which is generally strip-mined. Thus, in the developed countries especially, concern over environmental degradation makes it difficult to expand phosphate output rapidly.

Farmers in the developing countries could benefit from the increased use of chemical fertilizers, but again, they can least afford it. High prices and uncertain, irregular supplies mean that the major users of chemical fertilizers will remain the farmers in the developed countries. If supplies were more equitably distributed, world agricultural output would probably increase. However, no such redistribution appears likely, mainly because of a combination of economic and political reasons. In the richest countries lawns and golf courses will continue to grow lush and green; in the poorest countries subsistence farmers will continue to harvest their meager yields of rice and wheat.

Many scholars suggest that perhaps half of the world's entire food production is consumed not by people, but by hungry hordes of insects and animals. Pesticides can help prevent some of the losses, but again we run headlong into an environmental dilemma. Many chemical pesticides are highly toxic and remain in the environment for a long time. Furthermore, they are concentrated as they move up through the food chain.

One example is DDT. Traces of DDT have been found throughout the marine food chains. Because of

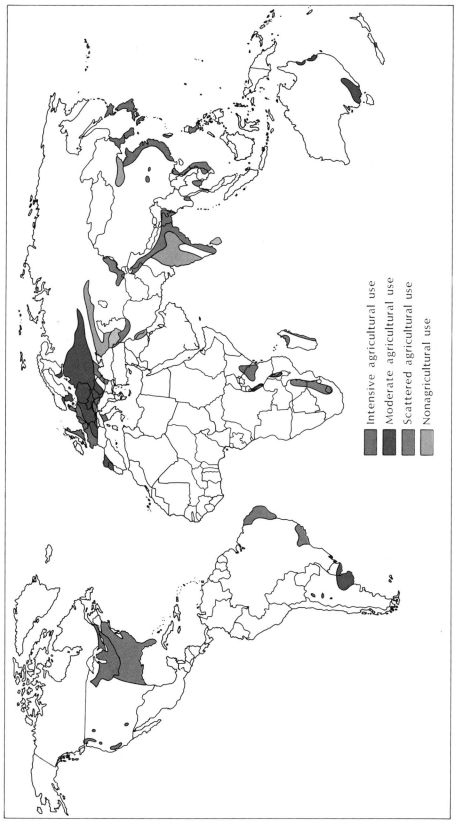

FIGURE 12–8 Manure map of the world. (Eugene Mather, John Fraser Hart, 1956, "The Geography of Manure," in *Land Economics* 32, no. 1, p. 25.)

Intensive agricultural use

Moderate agricultural use

Scattered agricultural use

Nonagricultural use

Khuzestan, southwest Iran. Irrigation canals provide many functions of natural waterways. (Ray Witlin for World Bank, 1972)

its persistence in the ecosystem, DDT may be carried far from where it was originally applied; so we find traces of DDT in the fatty tissue of Eskimos and in penguins at the South Pole. Yet a dilemma persists as well with DDT. Despite its harmful potential in the ecosystem, it has probably extended the lives of countless millions of people, both increasing the food supply and by cutting down the incidence of insect-transmitted diseases, including malaria, sleeping sickness, and bubonic plague.

Weeds are another menace to improving agricultural output. They compete with crops for water, sunlight and nutrients, so controlling them should improve yields. Control of many weeds is possible with herbicides such as 2, 4-D (2,4-dichlorophenoxyacetic acid) and 2, 4, 5-T (2, 4, 5-trichlorophenoxyacetic acid). Use of these chemicals is increasing, and they are not usually lethal to people. They do not persist in the environment for long periods of time; however, they threaten ecosystem stability by diminishing the number of plant species. Agriculture in general simplifies ecosystems, so in a sense herbicides are just another step in the same direction. Many wonder, though, which step might lead us over the precipice into wholesale eco-

system breakdowns and resultant losses in food supplies. Unless we are willing to accept widespread starvation in the developing countries, we must accept some risks and trade-offs. We need to use pesticides and herbicides, at least until safer alternatives are available.

Irrigation is another way to increase yields, but large-scale irrigation projects are costly and take much time to develop. Anyone who has driven through California's Great Central Valley during the summer knows what irrigation can do, even if they are unaware of the complexity and cost of the California Water Project. About 12 percent of the world's cultivated land is irrigated, but about half of the world's food is produced on that irrigated acreage. Half of the irrigated cropland is in China and India, where rice is widely grown. Rice may well be the world's thirstiest crop.

Besides large-scale river irrigation projects, small-scale projects are also important in some areas. For example, tubewells have been rapidly increasing in India and Pakistan.

As with other methods of improving yields, though, irrigation schemes often run into ecological troubles. Water tables may be raised to the point where

Examining experimental, high-yield corn at the Uttar Pradesh Agricultural University in Pantnagar, India. (Philip Boucas for World Bank, 1968)

root systems become waterlogged, and salinization may occur as salts are concentrated by evaporation at or near the surface. In turn cropland is abandoned. Not only are present countries threatened; past civilizations in Mesopotamia and elsewhere, according to archaeologists and historians, have declined as a result of undermined irrigation systems.

Since the beginning of the agricultural revolution, genetic improvements in plants and livestock have made significant contributions to expanding food supplies. In the process, the number of different plant species used by humans has greatly declined. Farmers have accepted improved species and let others disappear. Improved plants may be developed to better tolerate adverse environmental conditions or various dis-

eases, or to be more responsive to fertilization. Hybrid corn has been grown for decades in the United States with good results. Furthermore, the breeding of a corn which would ripen during a shorter growing period has allowed the northern margin of the United States Corn Belt to be extended 500 miles farther than it was with the earlier varieties.

Since the mid-1960s worldwide attention has been focused on the **Green revolution,** a revoltuion based on the "miracle strains" of rice and wheat developed in the Philippines and Mexico, respectively. They are shorter and stiffer than earlier varieties and are more responsive to fertilization. Also, because of their reduced sensitivity to variations in the length of day, they can be used in multiple cropping.

Pakistani farmers gather to hear agricultural broadcasts every morning from the agricultural college in Lyallpur. (Kay Muldoon for World Bank and IDA, 1970)

Following 1965 high-yielding varieties of wheat and rice spread quickly among developing countries, especially the Philippines, Indonesia, India, and Pakistan. By 1970 agricultural economists became optimistic as it appeared that food production would easily outdistance population growth. Such optimism, though, was short-lived: by the mid-1970s it was apparent that the green revolution was not a panacea for the problems of the developing countries. Furthermore, some countries became more complacent about the threat of population growth.

Increase the output of oceanic fisheries. Finally, many people feel we can turn increasingly to the oceans for food, especially for the proteins lacking in so many diets. But the prospects are hardly encouraging. On a caloric input–output basis, modern long-distance oceanic fishing ranks up with feed-lot beef production at just over ten to one, requiring a substantial energy subsidy.

Between 1950 and 1970 the world annual fish catch increased from 21 to 70 million tons. However, since 1970 the world catch has fluctuated between 65 and 70 million tons, and prospects for significantly increasing catches are dismal (Brown, 1978, p. 7). Because population growth has continued since 1970, the per capita fish catch has obviously declined. Also,

anyone who has been to a fishmarket recently knows that prices have soared.

Energy and agriculture

The 1980s should prove interesting. Energy is bound to be a central issue, and energy prices will probably continue to escalate. Environmental concerns may take a back seat as political pressure is applied to maintain, if not substantially increase, energy supplies. Political problems in energy-producing nations remain a threat to world energy supplies, as became apparent in Iran in 1978.

Modernization, as we have mentioned before, is closely associated with increases in per capita energy consumption. In agricultural modernization, two factors tend to increase the caloric input–output ratio. First, agricultural development requires more inputs per unit of labor—thus, more irrigation, more machinery, more chemical fertilizers, and, as a result, more energy. Energy is required to run pumps on wells, to fuel the new machinery, and to produce and distribute the fertilizers.

Second, as per capita productivity rises in the agricultural sector, surplus laborers will leave for jobs in industry and commercial activities, thus redistributing the population from rural to urban areas. With respect to food, this means that more energy will be needed to transport food to consumers, who will increasingly live in cities. Furthermore, as per capita incomes rise, consumers demand more processed foods, and energy is required in the processing. Nowhere do we find better examples of the latter than in the United States, where cooking has become almost a lost art, as people more and more frequently sit down to TV dinners or eat out at their favorite fast-food restaurant. Recently TV dinners have even appeared in China.

IMPRINTS ON THE AGRICULTURAL LANDSCAPE

Before leaving the topic of agricultural systems, we would like briefly to look at some imprints on the agricultural landscape. These imprints—including settlement patterns, house types, crop patterns, field patterns, and barns—vary considerably from place to place and have long attracted the interest of cultural geographers.

All farmers have at least one thing in common: a fond appreciation of, and deep attachment to, the land. The intensity of feelings toward the land varies, of course, and is probably lowest in large-scale corporate agriculture in places like the United States.

Farmers have known for centuries that the land they use is a fragile part of the natural ecosystem. Soil that has formed over hundreds or thousand of years can be quickly destroyed by accelerated erosion, often human-induced. One example is the American Dustbowl, which set in motion a stream of migration toward California—a saga made famous by John Steinbeck in *The Grapes of Wrath*. In one description of dustbowl conditions, historian William Manchester commented, "Wives packed every windowsill, door frame, and keyhole with oiled cloth and gummed paper, yet the fine silt found its way in and lay in beach-like ripples on their floors" (1974, p. 99). Through the centuries farmers have tried to understand the land, to nourish it, and to give to it as well as take from it. They have not always been successful.

Rural buildings

In a short space we cannot hope to capture the essence of agricultural landscapes. The sights and smells, the narrow country roads, the houses, the barns, the fences, the fields of ripening crops, the long furrows in plowed fields—all are elements of a landscape which, for many, is something of an ideal. For others, of course, it is a landscape demanding sweat and toil, one to be escaped at the first opportunity.

House types.   Rural house types are infinitely varied, yet we can find some general features in certain areas. Our concern with house types focuses on folk architecture, not on great architectural masterpieces. Housing is a major aspect of material culture and deserving of our careful attention.

Folk housing tends, first of all, to be functional in design; it tends, also, to fit harmoniously into the physical environment. For example, seldom if ever would you find a Pennsylvania barn that looked as if it did not fit into its natural setting. Furthermore, many elements of house types can be associated with culture regions and the diffusion of culture traits. According to architect Amos Rapoport, "Buildings and settlements are the visible expression of the relative importance attached to different aspects of life and the varying ways of perceiving reality" (1969, p. 47).

We can hardly imagine the variety of house types which exists; differences in size, shape, color, and building material creates an endless list. However, some designs are sufficiently widespread that they may be viewed as types, though we must allow for numerous variations on general themes. Consider the problem, for example, created by people who continue to add on to houses as families grow and expand the need for space. An original house type may end up so modified that it is unrecognizable.

House types vary from one region to another for a variety of reasons—from environmental to economic and from personal preference to functional necessity. Climate, for example, dictates certain needs. Cold climates require houses which maintain heat, whereas warm climates require houses with good ventilation. Yet in any climate different people may come up with different styles of housing to meet basic climatic needs. Before the advent of central heating and air conditioning, housing often represented a definite response to climatic determinants. For example, the Eskimo igloo and the European and early American log cabins were built to help people survive harsh winters.

In the United States log cabins were associated with the cultural hearth centered in the Delaware valley and southeastern Pennsylvania. Log construction, however, was a European invention, and early American log building techniques derived mainly from Ger-

Shotgun houses are common in the American South. (Chester E. Zimolzak, Charles A. Stansfield, Jr., 1969, *The Human Landscape: Geography and Culture.* Columbus, OH, Charles E. Merrill Publishing Co., p. 211)

many, a case of diffusion of a cultural trait. From the Delaware valley log construction techniques moved west through Appalachia; however, the log cabin's spread westward was limited as settlement moved onto the grasslands.

In warm climates the simplest shelters were probably poles supporting a grass roof, though they would hardly suffice for most agricultural purposes. After all,

farmers have tools and usually have a variety of storage needs. In the southeastern United States one common house type, found in both rural and urban areas, is the **shotgun house,** so named because you could supposedly fire a shotgun in the front door and out the back door without hitting anything (Vlach, 1977). In the United States, the shotgun house seemed to have originated in a cultural hearth around New Orleans. How-

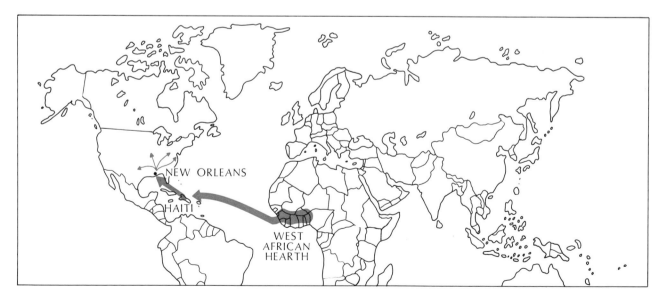

FIGURE 12–9 Diffusion of shotgun houses. (Chester E. Zimolzak, Charles A. Stansfield, Jr., 1979, *The Human Landscape: Geography and Culture.* Columbus, OH, Charles E. Merrill Publishing Co., p. 212.)

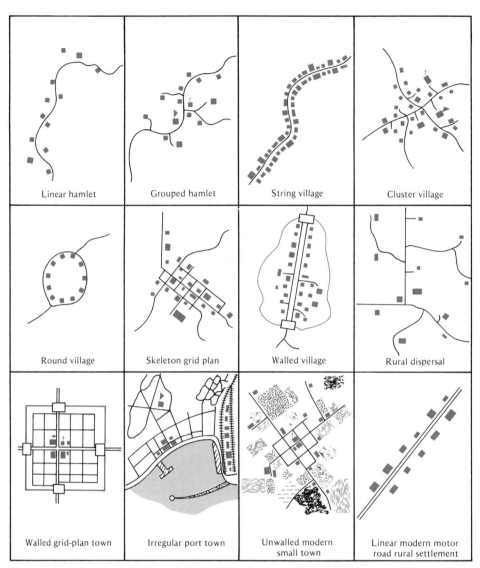

Linear hamlet	Grouped hamlet	String village	Cluster village
Round village	Skeleton grid plan	Walled village	Rural dispersal
Walled grid-plan town	Irregular port town	Unwalled modern small town	Linear modern motor road rural settlement

FIGURE 12–10 Basic settlement forms. (J. E. Spencer, William Thomas, *Introducing Cultural Geography*, 2nd ed. Copyright © 1978 by John Wiley & Sons, Inc., p. 65. Reprinted by permission of John Wiley & Sons, Inc.)

ever, its origin has been traced to Blacks who came to New Orleans early in the 19th century from Haiti, and to there from West Africa (Vlach, 1977). Thus, the shotgun house presents an excellent example of cultural diffusion. Furthermore, tracing the diffusion of a material culture trait in this manner allows geographers also to see evidence of past migration patterns.

Other factors which affect house types include construction methods and knowledge, types of materials available (especially in developing countries, where it may be difficult to transport materials from place to place), economics, and even religious beliefs and attitudes. The latter, within the broader realm of culture, seems particularly important in determining house type; whereas materials, technology, and construction methods, only facilitate creating the desired housing type.

Religion affects the form, plan, spatial arrangements, and orientation of the house, and may be the influence which leads to the existence of round and rectangular houses. The reasons for a culture never having had round houses may well be due to the needs of cosmic orientation—a round house cannot easily be oriented. (Rapoport, 1969, p. 41)

Of course we must be careful to remember that religion is not the sole determinant of house type.

Barns. Though house types are important elements of the rural landscape, barns probably represent to many the major elements of material culture in the agricultural landscapes where they are found. The origin of the word *barn* may be traced back to the Old English word *bereaern,* literally a barley place (Hart, 1975, p.

Because of traffic on the Triunfo–Guayaquil highway, numerous markets have sprung up at junctions of secondary routes. This market is in one such town, "Kilometro 26." (Larry Daughters for World Bank Group, 1971)

124); *bere* meant "barley," and *aern* meant "place" in Old English.

Like houses, barns appear in great variety. In western Europe the term *barn* applies only to buildings which are used for grain storage; however, in the United States barns are used for both livestock and grain storage. Among the major types of barns in the United States are the basement barns of upstate New York, the Pennsylvania barn, and the Appalachian crib barns. Dairy barns, tobacco barns, and even round barns can also be found.

Barns are a vanishing feature of the American landscape. As geographer John Fraser Hart has commented,

> On a modern farm the barn is a relict feature; the hayloft is obsolescent, the threshing floor is obsolete, and who needs stalls for horses? Of course some use can be found for the old building, if it is still structurally sound, but as soon as it starts to

deteriorate the best thing to do is to pour kerosene on it and light a match. (1975, p. 136)

Settlement forms

Houses may be arranged in a variety of patterns, from the widely spaced individual farm houses common in many parts of the United States to closely clustered farm villages typical of Japan or China (figure 12–10). Many of these arrangements have evolved over a long period of time and are clearly related to the perceived needs of local people.

Settlement patterns can generally be divided into two broad categories, **agglomerated** and **dispersed.** In agglomerated patterns, houses are collected into villages or hamlets, whereas dispersed settlements are widely scattered across the rural landscape. Dispersed settlement patterns tend to be associated with frontier development, as in the United States, and with areas previously colonized by Europeans.

In agricultural areas, agglomerated settlements often develop as service centers for surrounding farms, though at one time agglomeration may have been motivated by the need for a common defense. They serve as central locations for schools, churches, post offices, and markets, and often provide places where farmers and others can get together informally.

As figure 12–10 suggests, agglomerated settlements may be found in a variety of patterns, many of which reflect cultural preferences as well as economic and environmental needs. The case study by geographer Frederick Scantling illustrates the significance of cultural differences in the settlement patterns of selected villages in one area of New Mexico.

CASE STUDY:
The influence of values and value systems on the cultural landscape
Frederick H. Scantling

The values held by a cultural group comprise a basic element in the ordering of the cultural landscape. In a closely settled area, discrete evidence of these values is often obscured by the proximity of the cultural groups and consequent accelerated acculturation. For this study an areal separation of cultural groups was desirable, and an area of the Colorado Plateau in western New Mexico centered on the village of Ramah met this requirement.

The Ramah area of New Mexico, comprising about 1700 square miles, lies directly south of the cities of Gallup and Grants. It is characterized by a short growing season, thin, sandy soils, a general lack of surface water, a lack of any marketable resource (except for several hundred acres of timber), sparse grass, and inadequate and unreliable precipitation. In this relatively harsh and uniform physical environment live six different cultural groups, each of which has occupied and developed its own ecological niche. Referring to the map these are, from the right the Hispanics in San Rafael, Anglo miners, the Navajo on their checkerboard reservation, the Mormon village of Ramah, the Zuni in Zuni Pueblo, and Fence Lake, a settlement of Texan homesteaders at the southern limit of the area (Figure 12 – 11).

San Rafael was founded in 1869 by Hispanic farmers and sheepherders, and in its first fifty years was a dynamic settlement. After World War I it began to decline, mainly because of competition from Grants on the railroad three miles distant, and now is rather somnolent with a population of about 500.

Approaching from the north the village profile offers no clues to the cultural affinity of the residents. On the right side of the main road, set out 100 yards from the other houses, is a large, two-story, cast-stone mansion. Proceeding down the left fork of the road (old Main Street) the houses are one- and two-story, in the Anglo styles of the period; the flat-roofed, adobe dwellings are located across the main road on the west side of the village. This pattern relates to the patrón system in the Hispanic social organization. The patrón of San Rafael was a child when the village was founded, but in a relatively short time he became the wealthiest and most influential man in the village and gradually assumed the patrónship. By 1912 he was sufficiently established to

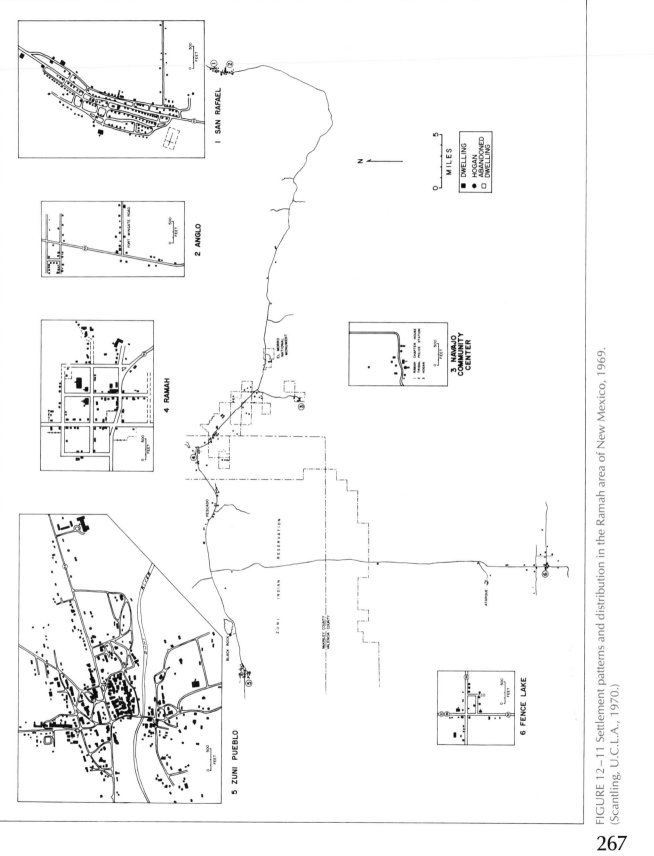

FIGURE 12–11 Settlement patterns and distribution in the Ramah area of New Mexico, 1969. (Scantling, U.C.L.A., 1970.)

267

build the cast-stone mansion at the main (north) entrance to the village. The other houses in the style of the period were occupied by members of his extended family and other prominent residents of the village; the flat-roofed adobes were occupied by families lower on the socioeconomic scale.

More common evidence of the Hispanic tradition is the location of the Catholic Church and adjacent, small plaza near the center of the village, and the presence of two cantinas. The church is a religious institution and the cantina a social institution; no Hispanic village of any import would be without at least one of each.

The skeleton grid pattern of the *the Anglo settlement* one mile south of San Rafael implies more organization and regularity than exists in reality. The settlement appears to have grown quite casually, and according to each individual family's means and choice of building materials, but without benefit of a building code. Migrants from West Virginia, who came to work in the uranium mines near Grants, comprise the majority of the residents, and all are Anglo. Cultural factors observable in this small settlement are neither distinctive nor diagnostic. The skeleton grid pattern is noticeable more for its contrast with the pattern of San Rafael than for its uniqueness. This grid pattern, as well as similar types, styles, and arrangements of dwellings can be duplicated on the fringes of many of the larger towns in New Mexico, occupied by either Anglos or Hispanics.

The Navajos moved into the area in the vicinity of what is now Ramah between 1870 and 1880, and subsequently spread south and east under pressure from the Mormon settlers. The Navajos are not village dwellers. In a broad sense, their settlement pattern is dispersed; but more precisely, it is an irregular distribution of small clusters of hogans, cabins, ramadas, and corrals, usually associated with small, irregularly shaped, cultivated fields. These clusters, called *establishments,* may be as close together as one-half mile or separated by several miles, and each is occupied by the members of an extended family group. Clustering in establishments relates to the dynamics of Navajo social organization; geographic and consanguinal proximity are the two principal conditions necessary for social interaction. The Navajo Community Center is a nontraditional settlement necessitated by coordination with government agencies.

The nuclear village of *Ramah* was founded as a Mormon agricultural colony in 1882, and continued as such through two-thirds of its history. Now, irrigated farming has all but disappeared, and the basic economy of the village of 250 has shifted to cattle ranching and wage work. Upon entering the village, several features stamp it as belonging to the Mormon tradition—wide, tree-lined streets crossing each other at right angles and narrow irrigation ditches between the borders of the streets and the lot lines. The regular plan of the village and its associated fields establish this settlement as Mormon. Genetically, this plan derives from the Plat of the City of Zion.

The Zunis, one of the several Western Pueblo cultures, have lived in their present territory at least since the first Spanish contact in 1540, and by 1705 the several villages had been reduced to one main village (the present Zuni Pueblo) on a low knoll beside the Zuni River. The Zuni population, most of which is concentrated in Zuni Pueblo, is about 6,000. It is not the plan of the village, with its irregular and meandering streets, which is distinctive, but the older houses near the center. These traditional houses are single story, apartment style, and house an extended family, usually of matrilocal units. Newly married couples would add a room or rooms to the existing house for their own use, and in the course of time some of these houses have grown to over 200 feet in length. In the last decade there has been an increasing trend toward single family housing, indicative of the change that is taking place from the extended family of a predominantly matrilocal pattern, to the nuclear family of the Anglo, with its independent locale pattern.

Fence Lake was established in 1932 by homesteaders from Texas who came from the Dust Bowl to start farming anew. They brought their dispersed settlement tradition with them and laid out their farms and farmsteads within the framework of the public land survey. The population peaked at about 250 in 1940, but now farming is no more and the population has dwindled to about 40.

The uniformly marginal nature of the physical environment for crop growing has fostered the development of grazing as the predominant land use pattern in the study area, and viewed from afar the areas of closest settlement are inconspicuous in the vast expanse of grasslands and woodlands. On the other hand, the individual settlements contrast sharply with the surrounding open spaces, and each ecological niche is clearly recognizable. Elements of the value systems of each group, expressed in cultural features on the land, have made each of the ecological niches distinctive—social organization and religion in San Rafael, social organization for the Navajo, religion in Ramah, social organization in Zuni Pueblo, and tradition in Fence Lake.

From "Factors and Processes in the Establishment of Cultural Boundaries: A Study of Discreet Boundaries on the Landscape." Ph.D. dissertation, U.C.L.A., 1970.

Modernization may have an impact on settlement patterns in many agricultural areas—especially as increased productivity lowers the requirements for labor, and people move to the cities in search of work. Improved transportation systems, for example, often mean that the smallest villages are no longer viable. In the United States small towns in some major agricultural areas are either declining or growing very slowly as fewer people are needed in agricultural activities.

Exceptions are small towns with colleges or universities, those located on or near major highways, and those located within perhaps 50 miles of large cities.

House types, barns, and settlement patterns give agricultural landscapes a distinctive appearance, though in many developed countries the distinction between rural and urban populations is sometimes not well-defined.

KEY TERMS

Caloric input–output ratio
Hunting and gathering
Pleistocene overkill
Nomadic herding
Shifting cultivation
Forest-fallow cultivation

Bush-fallow cultivation
Short-fallow cultivation
Annual cropping
Multicropping
Intensive subsistence farming
Wet rice cultivation

Plantation agriculture
Von Thünen's model
Optima and limits schema
Dairy farming
Mixed farming
Mediterranean agriculture

Commercial grain farming
Green revolution
Shotgun house
Agglomerated settlement
Dispersed settlement

REFERENCES

Alexander, J. W. and Gibson, L. J. (1979), *Economic Geography*, 2nd ed. Englewood Cliffs, NJ: Prentice–Hall, Inc.

Beckford, G. L. (1972), *Persistent Poverty: Underdevelopment in Plantation Economies of the Third World*. New York: Oxford University Press.

Boserup, E. (1965), *The Conditions of Agricultural Growth: The Economics of Agrarian Change under Population Pressure*. Chicago: Aldine Publishing Co.

Boughey, A. S. (1975), *Man and the Environment: An Introduction to Human Ecology and Evolution*, 2nd ed. New York: Macmillan, Inc.

Brown, L. R. (1970), "Human Food Production as a Process in the Biosphere," *Scientific American* 233, 160–170.

Brown, L. R. (1978), *The Global Economic Prospect: New Sources of Economic Stress*, Worldwatch Paper No. 20. Washington, D.C.: Worldwatch Institute.

Brown, L. R. with Eckholm, E. P. (1974) *By Bread Alone*. New York: Praeger Publishers, Inc.

Eckholm, E. P. (1976), *Losing Ground: Environmental Stress and World Food Prospects*. New York: W. W. Norton & Co., Inc.

Fagan, B. M. (1974), *Men of the Earth: An Introduction to World Prehistory*. Boston: Little, Brown & Co.

Gregor, H. F. (1970), *Geography of Agriculture: Themes in Research*. Englewood Cliffs, NJ: Prentice–Hall, Inc.

Griffin, E. (1973), "Testing the Von Thünen Theory in Uruguay," *Geographical Review* 63, 500–516.

Grigg, D. B. (1974), *The Agricultural Systems of the World: An Evolutionary Approach*. London: Cambridge University Press.

Hall, P. (ed.) (1966), *Von Thünen's Isolated State*, English edition of Von Thünen, J. H., *Der Isolierte Staat*, Wartenberg, C. M., trans. Oxford: Pergaman Press, Inc.

Hart, J. F. (1975), *The Look of the Land*. Englewood Cliffs, NJ: Prentice-Hall, Inc.

Loomis, R. S. (1976), "Agricultural Systems," *Scientific American* 235, 99–105.

Manchester, W. (1974), *The Glory and the Dream: A Narrative History of America, 1932–1972*. Boston: Little, Brown & Co.

McCarty, H. H. and Lindberg, J. B. (1966), *A Preface to Economic Geography*. Englewood Cliffs, NJ: Prentice–Hall, Inc.

Rapoport, A. (1969), *House Form and Culture*. Englewood Cliffs, NJ: Prentice–Hall, Inc.

Sloane, E. (1974), *Our Vanishing Landscape*. New York: Balantine Books, Inc.

Steinhart, C. and Steinhart, J. (1974), *Energy: Sources, Use, and Role in Human Affairs*. North Scituate, MA: Duxbury Press/Wadsworth Publishing Co., Inc.

U.S. Department of Agriculture (1976), *The Face of Rural America*, 1976 Yearbook of Agriculture. Washington, D.C.: U.S. Government Printing Office.

Vlach, J. (1977), "Shotgun Houses," *Natural History* 86, 50–57.

Zimolzak, C. E. and Stansfield, C. A. Jr. (1979), *The Human Landscape: Geography and Culture*. Columbus, OH: Charles E. Merrill Publishing Co.

13

An industrializing world: Patterns and prospects

Our central concern in this chapter is the location of industrial activities. However, first we look at the Industrial Revolution—its origin, diffusion, and impact on people and on the landscape.

Our consideration of industrial location begins with an overview of locational factors, including basic inputs and costs, and of locational decision making in different economic systems. We then look at Smith's model of industrial location and the concepts of space cost curves and spatial margins to profitability.

A discussion of general orientations for industrial locations, including raw material, market, and other orientations, is followed by the introduction of a still tentative theory of manufacturing places. Then we look briefly at the world pattern of manufacturing, the world iron and steel industry, world industrial regions, and the manufacturing regions of North America.

We look again at the growth syndrome as it relates to manufacturing activities. Economic and environmental trade-offs, environmental controls in the United States, and the Environmental Protection Agency are considered.

The chapter ends with a view of industrial impressions on the landscape. We offer not only our own impressions but also those of artists and poets who have looked in their own ways at industrial landscapes.

THE INDUSTRIAL REVOLUTION: A MAJOR EVENT

It is virtually impossible for most people in the developed countries today to even imagine lives and landscapes without industrialization. Yet this multifaceted revolution, which affects both developed and developing countries, began in earnest less than 300 years ago. In other words, despite its dramatic influences on people, on society, and on the landscape, it is so new that we are just beginning to understand its many ramifications.

Origin of the Industrial Revolution

The essential ingredients in the **Industrial Revolution** were machines and the use of inanimate energy to drive them; with these the productivity of labor could be greatly increased, and a new era was born. At the same time, however, machines became a threat to laborers because they could replace people. Thus the Industrial Revolution, like the Roman god Janus, has two faces. One face looks upon the increasing abundance of material goods, and the other on such evils as child labor and the squalor portrayed by Dickens. However, as the eminent art historian Sir Kenneth Clark pointed out, the beginning of the Industrial Revolution "coincided exactly with the first organised attempt to improve the human lot" (1969, p. 321).

Disagreements among scholars are common with respect to the causes of the Industrial Revolution, as well as to its precise beginning date. Here we accept the view that the Industrial Revolution began in England with the sharp upward turn in industrial output during the 1780s (Redford, 1960). For example, English pig iron production rose from 25,000 tons in 1720 to 125,000 tons in 1796.

Leland Stanford's special train en route to Promontory, Utah, where the last spike of the first U.S. transcontinental railroad was driven on May 10, 1869. (Richard S. Thoman, 1978, *The United States and Canada: Present and Future.* Columbus, OH, Charles E. Merrill Publishing Co., p. 9)

Of course the stage upon which the first act of the Industrial Revolution was played had been prepared well in advance. Major stimula were the market growth following the geographical discoveries of the 15th and 16th centuries and England's natural and human resources (Redford, 1960, pp. 3–4). By the end of the 17th century, Liverpool was growing rapidly and Bristol's trade was on the rise. Expanding imports of sugar, tobacco, and cotton from Colonial America stimulated the expanding English economy. Between the beginning of the 18th century and 1760, England's overall trade doubled.

Other events also contributed. Toward the end of the 17th century, science became institutionalized with the founding of the Royal Society of London. Early in the 18th century, Darby developed a successful process for smelting iron ore with coke, and Newcomen designed the first engine to be delivered for use at coal mines.

With new innovations and various technical improvements, the size and scale of production in English industries increased. In turn new markets were needed. Though the English population grew only slowly during the first half of the 18th century, its rate of growth began to accelerate around 1750, thus expanding the domestic market for industrial goods. Also, by 1750 many English industries had cultivated sizable and expanding foreign markets.

Major roles in the earliest phase of the Industrial Revolution were played by mining, textiles, and manufactured metals. According to Rostow, the role of the textile industry was particularly important. It was large relative to the total size of the English economy and, from the 1780s on, a large proportion of textile output was being sold in foreign markets. In turn the growth of this early industrial giant was affecting the development of urban areas, the demand for coal and working capital, and the demand for cheaper and better transportation (Rostow, 1971).

Cheaper transportation was a further stimulant to industrial development, and railroads became the major initiator of the Industrial Revolution in the United States, Canada, France, Germany, and the Soviet Union (Rostow, 1971). Lower transportation costs allowed industries to exploit new markets and new sources of raw materials and were essential in the large-scale development of the coal and steel industries.

We tend to see the Industrial Revolution mainly in economic terms, yet we need to remember that the whole fabric of society was altered—from essentially agrarian to what would ultimately be described as urban-industrial, with accompanying intellectual, political, and social changes (table 13–1). Even the atti-

TABLE 13–1   Polar distinctions between preindustrial and urban–industrial society

	Preindustrial society	*Urban–industrial society*
Demographic	High mortality, fertility	Low mortality, fertility.
Behavioral	Particularistic, prescribed. Individual has multiplex roles.	Universalistic, instrumental. Individual has specialized roles.
Societal	Kin-group solidarity, extended family, ethnic cohesion. Cleavages between ethnic groups.	Atomization. Affiliations secondary. Professional influence groups.
Economic	Nonmonetary or simple monetary base. Local exchange. Little infrastructure. Craft industries. Low specialization.	Pecuniary base. National exchange. Extensive interdependence. Factory production. Capital intensive.
Political	Nonsecular authority. Prescriptive legitimacy. Interpersonal communications; traditional bases.	Secular polity. Elected government. Mass media participation. Rational bureaucracy.
Geographical	Parochial relationships. Close ties to immediate environment. Duplication of sociospatial groups in a cellular net	Regional and national interdependence. Specialized roles based upon major resources and relative location within urbanspatial system.

Source: Brian J. L. Berry, 1973, *The Human Consequences of Urbanization.* New York: St. Martin's Press, Inc., Macmillan & Co., Ltd., p. 13.

tude toward change was changed. The redistribution of people and jobs altered the entire structure of England's space economy. Furthermore, people's capacity for altering the natural landscape increased severalfold. As Earl Cook commented, "Coke, coal, and the steam engine powered the Industrial Revolution, which gave man power to change the face of the earth and to devour in a few centuries resources that had taken hundreds of millions of years to accumulate" (1976, pp. 9–10).

Machinery and the energy to power it were the essential ingredients of the Industrial Revolution. As our continuous need for feeding the energy appetites of industrial nations suggests, they remain essential. Before the use of inanimate sources of energy began, machines were driven by draft animals and human

Traditional farming by human muscle in Ecuador. (Larry Daughters for World Bank Group, 1971)

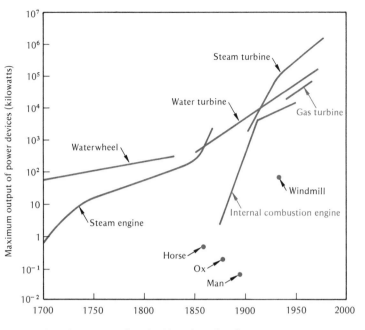

FIGURE 13–1 The power output of basic machines has increased since the start of the Industrial Revolution, about 1750. (From Chauncey Starr, "Energy and Power." Copyright © September, 1971 by Scientific American, Inc., p. 38. All rights reserved.)

muscle. Since 1750, however, with numerous technological innovations, the power output of basic machines has increased considerably (figure 13–1). Early in the Industrial Revolution, energy resources were major determinants in the location of industrial centers.

Diffusion of the Industrial Revolution

England was the first country to experience the Industrial Revolution and, as you might easily imagine, it was not keen on sharing this new-found wealth with everyone else. However, technological innovations could not be kept secret for long and during the 19th century, industrialization and modernization began to spread. According to Rostow (1971, p. 38), tentative take-off dates for other countries are: France 1830–1860, Belgium 1833–1860, United States 1843–1860, Germany 1850–1873, Sweden 1868–1890, and Japan 1878–1900. The Industrial Revolution continues to spread to new places even today.

Two factors have been especially important in the diffusion of the Industrial Revolution. First, coal production played an essential role because of its growing industrial uses. Steam engines were improved rapidly in the 19th century and were especially important in the textile and metallurgical industries; and steam power was also increasingly important for transportation. Second, the spread of railroads was an important stimulus to industrialization.

Dual economies in the developing countries

Earlier we distinguished between urban-industrial core regions and exploited, developing peripheral regions. Furthermore, we examined the concept at various scales, from the international to the local. At the international scale, the core areas were modern urban-industrial countries, whereas the peripheral countries were considered to be developing and dependent on the core. However, within selected regions of the peripheral countries, we see the Industrial Revolution speading from core to peripheral ones. The regions selected are usually metropolitan, often coastal, and destined to become core areas within the peripheral countries.

Thus a *dual economy* in a developing country exists when one part of the economy is engaged in modern industrial production, usually for export, whereas the remainder of the population is engaged in traditional preindustrial pursuits, primarily subsistence agriculture. We find economic dualism reflected in landscapes when, for example, we compare Rio de Janeiro with Brazil's interior.

LOCATIONAL FACTORS FOR MANUFACTURING ACTIVITIES

The location of manufacturing enterprises depends on several major factors which enter into locational decision making to various degrees. The importance of different factors of location differs among various industries and over time within an industry.

Basic inputs and costs

Three different sets of costs are associated with manufacturing: ***procurement costs,*** the costs of bringing together the raw materials to be used; ***production costs,*** the costs required to change the raw materials into finished products; and ***distribution costs,*** the costs involved in getting products from factories to consumers. Obviously costs must be considered if we are to explain the geographic distribution of industries, though we must not be led to believe that other locational factors are unimportant. However, for some industries cost may be an overriding factor in their decision to locate.

Procurement costs. Procurement costs include the cost of raw materials and the cost of transporting them to the manufacturing site. Classical location theory emphasized the importance of minimizing transportation costs for bringing raw materials together and for distributing finished products—in other words, choosing the ***least transport cost location,*** at which the total transportation costs for a firm are minimized.

Production costs. Production costs include the many costs involved in transforming raw materials into finished products. Production requires land, labor, capital, and management; because the costs of each of these ***factors of production*** vary from place to place, they may influence locational decisions.

Industries require various amounts of land for factories, storage, parking, and future expansion. A steel mill would require a considerable amount of land, whereas an electronics plant may require far less. Large parcels of land may be more difficult to locate than small ones, especially in or near metropolitan areas. Land costs vary considerably from place to place, though generally they tend to decrease as we move away from urban centers.

Both the amount of labor needed by firms and the kind of labor required differ from industry to industry. Labor, unlike land, can move to where it is needed. Wages for a particular type of labor vary from place to place and tend to be highest in urban areas.

Capital may be subdivided into ***financial capital*** and ***physical capital.*** Financial capital is a prerequisite for purchasing physical capital, which includes plants, machinery, and other equipment. The interest rate represents the cost of financial capital, and it normally does not vary widely from place to place in industrial nations. Notice that financial capital is easily moved from one region to another, but physical capital tends to be immobile. Because of this immobility, industrial areas tend to exist even after their original locational advantages have disappeared, a phenomenon referred to by geographers as ***industrial inertia.***

Management provides the skills necessary to organize the firm and to combine the various inputs in the manufacturing process. Early in the Industrial Revolution, management usually consisted of one individual who made all important decisions. Today, however, major corporations are too complex to be managed by a single individual, and they are ususaly run by a Board of Directors. The locational impact of management varies. In some cases it may be a major determinant: Boeing Aircraft Corporation located in Seattle because that was where Mr. Boeing wished to live.

Before going on we should point out two things. First, some costs, as we will soon see, vary more than others from place to place; costs which don't differ from one place to another obviously have no affect on locational preferences. Second, the locational importance of any one cost depends on its proportion of the total cost; for example, if half of an industry's operating cost is the transportation of one raw material, then the industry would tend to locate near the source of that raw material. However, most industries today have complex cost structures which make such extreme cases virtually nonexistent.

Distribution costs. The locational impact of distribution costs depends on two things—their size relative to total costs and who is paying them, the consumer or the producer. Furthermore, transportation costs do not increase directly with distance; rather, they tend to increase proportionately more slowly for long distances.

Miscellaneous. Other factors may sometimes affect industrial location decisions: taxes, climate, amenities, political factors (such as defense spending), water availability, air and water pollution regulations, community attitudes, and even the personal preferences of locational decision makers.

Beyond all the locational factors mentioned already, the location of an industry may depend on two related considerations. First the size of a plant is im-

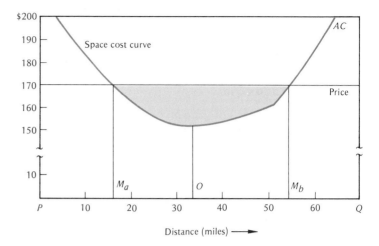

FIGURE 13–2 Smith's space-cost curve. (D. M. Smith, *Industrial Location: An Economic Geographical Analysis.* Copyright © 1971 by John Wiley & Sons, Inc., p. 195. Reprinted by permission of John Wiley & Sons, Inc.)

portant, because costs of production vary with the scale of production. In most industries larger scales of production are associated with lower per unit production costs, a phenomenon referred to as **economies of scale.** Second, for an individual firm, choosing a profitable location depends not only on costs but also on revenues, which means that the firm must consider the location of its competitors. In some industries firms may benefit by locating together, whereas in other industries firms do best when they are spread out.

Thus the study of industrial location is rather complex, and we can barely touch upon its main features here. Readers interested in a more solid theoretical treatment are referred to Foust and deSouza (1978).

Decision making in different economic systems

Before we explain the location of manufacturing activities, we need to consider who makes locational decisions and what motivates them. We can recognize three different possibilities, private capitalists, corporate capitalists, and the State (Hamilton, 1967). For either the private capitalist or the corporate capitalist, decision making is motivated by profit, whereas national interests and perceived social costs may affect the State's decisions. Though we tend to associate State decision making with planned economies, such as the Soviet Union, we must remember that government decisions at various levels, from national to local, affect business decision making in most countries, including the United States. Examples with locational impacts include zoning laws in metropolitan areas and subsidies

to industries locating in depressed regions, such as Appalachia.

For the most part, we are concerned with the location pattern of industries in Western industrial nations. Thus, the models we discuss assume profit is the major motivation for choosing one location over another. However, profitable locations need not necessarily be those which maximize profits, despite an emphasis on profit-maximization in many models. Though it may be desirable for a firm to maximize profits, locational decision makers may not have all the knowledge necessary to choose that location.

Smith's model of industrial location

Most of the groundwork for industrial location studies was done by economists. However, because of space constraints, we will focus on one developed by geographer David Smith (1971), which synthesizes much of the earlier work of location theorists.

Derivation of Smith's model is beyond the scope of this text; however, we feel that the essence of his approach may be comprehended without it. We can view any firm in an industry as having both costs and revenues which will vary according to location. Furthermore, we can assume that the firm will continue to produce so long as it is making a profit—that is, so long as its total revenues equal or exceed its total costs.

Smith's model (figure 13–2) basically shows a **space-cost curve** and a **space-price curve.** The space-cost curve represents variations in average cost from *P* to *Q*, whereas the space-price curve shows a constant average revenue from *P* to *Q.* Costs are lowest at point

O. Conceptually, producers may locate profitably anywhere along the line PQ where price (or average revenue) exceeds average cost. M_a and M_b mark the points along PQ where average cost equals price, and they are referred to as the **spatial margins to profitability.** Thus, firms choosing locations along PQ could operate profitably between M_a and M_b, but elsewhere they would operate at a loss. The maximum profit location in the model would be at point O.

Smith's model provides guidelines for explaining patterns of industrial location by considering spatial variations in average costs. We need not consider a single optimum location for an industry, but rather an area within which it could operate profitably. The area boundaries would be the spatial margins to profitability. Even if firms originally chose locations elsewhere, a pattern would emerge over time because those with unprofitable locations would go out of business. Of course, over a long period of time, costs and revenues would change, and new firms entering the industry at later dates may seek different locations.

General orientations for industrial locations

Despite what appear to be complex problems, many industrial location patterns can be rather easily understood. As we previously suggested, the reason is that for some industries, a single cost may stand out and the industry will tend toward locations which minimize that cost. Several different orientations occur, but we will use two as examples, **raw material orientation** and **market orientation.**

Raw material-oriented industries. **Primary industries** are industries which use raw materials as inputs and whose function is to change the form of that material; for example, the steel industry produces pig iron from iron ore. Changing the form of a raw material increases its value, referred to as **value added** by manufacturing. **Secondary industries** use as inputs materials which have already undergone some manufacturing. For example, the automobile industry uses steel as a major input. Again value is added in the process. Thus, value added is a basic measure of the contribution made by manufacturing.

Industries tend to be raw material-oriented under either of the following conditions: the industry uses one primary raw material, and in the manufacturing process, a significant weight loss occurs; or the industry uses a perishable raw material.

In the case of high weight loss, raw materials industries are attracted to a site because of savings in transportation costs; after all, the firm pays for hauling such raw materials of which some part will ultimately become waste. Fuels are an extreme example because their weight is entirely used up in the manufacturing process, though of course fuels are not in this sense "raw materials."

With respect to a space-cost curve, we are looking at industries for which average costs rise steeply away from raw material sites. How steeply they rise, however, depends on the amount of weight loss the raw material will undergo and the importance of transportation costs relative to total costs.

The copper concentrating industry is an excellent example of raw material orientation. Concentrating is the first step in deriving metallic copper from copper ore. For every 100 tons of copper ore mined in the United States, about 97 tons will be waste after the concentration process; thus copper concentrating occurs on, or very close to, the mine site. Similarly, copper smelting, which removes most of the impurities not removed by the concentrating process, carries nearly a 60-percent weight loss; copper smelters tend to locate near copper concentrators (figure 13–3). Exceptions occur, however; Tacoma, for example, uses imported copper concentrate.

Perishable products also draw processors, mainly because of high transporation costs induced partly by such special needs as refrigeration. An example of such a raw material-oriented industry is fish-canning. Can you imagine canning tuna in Des Moines rather than in the tuna ports of San Diego and Los Angeles? Again, in terms of the space-cost curve, costs would rise steeply away from the place of raw material production.

Market-oriented industries. Market-oriented industries are those for whom location at or close to consumers is essential. In terms of the space-cost curve, costs would tend to rise away from consumer locations, such as cities. Keep in mind, however, that consumers are different for different types of manufactured goods. Four general situations lead to market orientation: bulk is added to products which are available at similar costs almost everywhere; items produced are

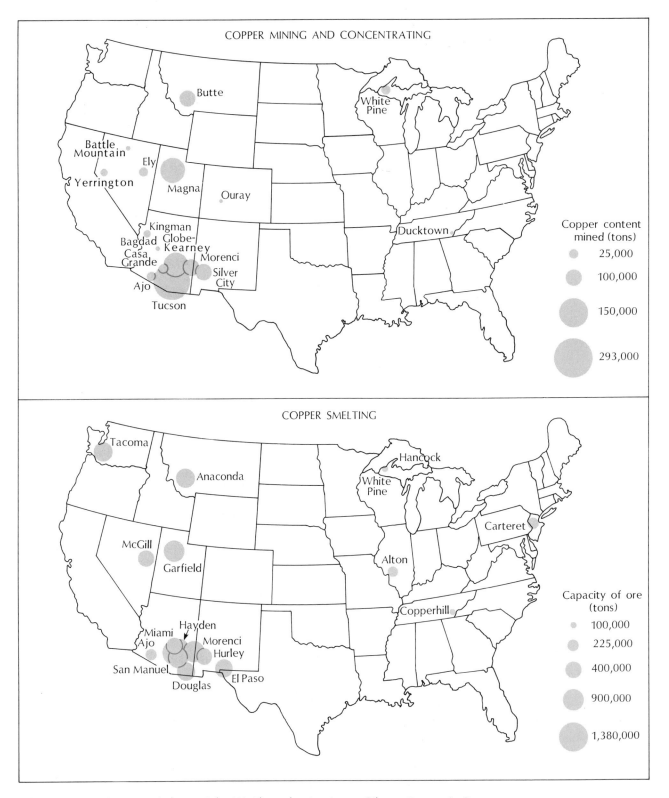

FIGURE 13–3 U.S. copper industry. (John W. Alexander, Lay James Gibson, *Economic Geography*, 2nd ed., © 1979, pp. 248–249. Reprinted with permission of Prentice-Hall, Inc., Englewood Cliffs, NJ.)

An industrializing world: Patterns and prospects **279**

either fragile or perishable; items produced are subject to rapidly changing fashions and tastes; and fabricated items are substantially bulkier than the raw materials from which they are produced.

An excellent example of the first situation is the soft drink industry. Soft drinks are composed primarily of water and syrup. If bottling were to take place far from consumers, bottlers would incur large transportation costs for carrying a product which is mainly water.

Producers of perishable goods also tend to be oriented toward consumers. Imagine a cream puff which arrived at your favorite lunch counter after a 500- or 1000-mile journey. Bread is not baked where wheat is grown, then distributed throughout the country; rather, the wheat is milled into flour and then transported to bakeries which serve a nearby clientele.

The clothing industry is one example of market orientation because of changing tastes and styles, though it tends to concentrate in major markets such as New York and Paris.

Finally, many fabrication industries tend to choose locations near markets, because transportation costs are lower when their raw materials are in unassembled form. Containers, such as cardboard boxes and barrels, are good examples.

Other orientations.   Not all industries are oriented toward any one locational factor, though many are. So far we have viewed raw materials and markets as locational determinants for selected industries; however, other orientations are also possible.

Energy sometimes operates as a localizing factor. Early in the Industrial Revolution, water power was important in determining industrial locations. Then coal increased in importance, and industries were drawn to coalfield locations, though coal was certainly more mobile than rivers. With the rising cost of energy worldwide, more industries may have to consider energy as a major locational factor.

Labor has sometimes had a localizing influence on some industries, especially those where labor costs comprise a large proportion of total costs. For example, the location of the textile industry in the United States—primarily in the nonunionized South—has often been influenced by the presence of relatively low wages.

However, the locational patterns of many industries result from two or more interacting locational factors. Careful study of cost structures may be required before we can understand the shapes of their space-cost curves. Furthermore, in an era of conglomerates

and factories producing a variety of products, the locational questions become even more difficult to answer.

Toward a theory of manufacturing places

For several reasons, the importance of transportation costs relative to total costs has declined in recent decades for many industries. Improved transportation technology, for example, has lowered transportation costs and increased speed and reliability. According to Norcliffe, "For the majority of lighter industries transportation costs do not vary greatly from location to location within the industrial heartland, although in peripheral regions remote from important markets, costs do begin to rise more steeply" (1975, p. 23). Norcliffe suggested that the following three factors exert a major influence on locational decisions today: infrastructure availability, internal and external economies of scale, and linkage and contact fields. Norcliffe stressed that these influences are characteristics of places, specifically manufacturing places, and that their locational impact is greatest on **footloose industries,** those for whom transportation costs are relatively unimportant locational factors. Manufacturers of electronics components, such as transistors, are often considered footloose.

At the outset Norcliffe assumed the following: the existence of a differentiated and bounded space economy, industrial development sufficient to have defined a heartland manufacturing belt, and a mature system of cities with many larger ones located in the heartland. His basic question, then, is "given the economic, social and technical conditions prevailing in the latter part of the twentieth century, what relationships may one anticipate at the regional and urban level between the existing structure and the location of manufacturing industry?" (1975, p. 37).

Norcliffe approaches the answer by dividing industries into four categories: processing activities, whose major inputs are raw materials; fabricating activities, whose major inputs are processed goods; integrative activities, whose inputs are processed goods undergoing little change other than assembly; and administrative activities, which generally involve neither inputs nor outputs (1975, p. 38). He then suggested that three types of relationships between manufacturers and cities could be expected. First, Norcliffe focused on plant size as an important locational consideration. He argued that, whereas small plants might be located in towns of any size, larger plants would tend to locate

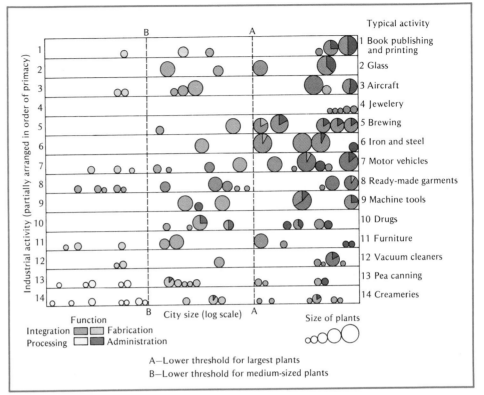

FIGURE 13–4 A summary of the proposed relationship between city size and the function, size, and activity of a plant. (Lyndhurst Collins, David F. Walker, *Locational Dynamics of Manufacturing Activity.* Copyright © 1975 by John Wiley & Sons Ltd., p. 43. Reprinted by permission of John Wiley & Sons Ltd.)

in larger towns (figure 13–4). Thus, urban orientations are more likely for the larger industries. Second, he specifically argued that administrative activities would be oriented toward major metropolitan locations in the heartland. Similarly, plants engaged in integrative activities are attracted to large cities, whereas fabricating industries are attracted to intermediate-sized towns, and processing activities to small towns. Finally, he suggested a relationship between industrial composition and city size. Industries which have substantial economies of scale with increased plant size will be attracted to large urban centers, as will those with specialized service needs, such as the need for air transportation.

Given our previous discussions of various industrial orientations, coupled with the shift toward higher value-added and more footloose industries, Norcliffe's approach extends our ability to explain various patterns of industrial location. Furthermore, Norcliffe's theory ties together industrial location decisions and the existing framework of national and regional urban systems. However helpful these ideas are, though, we are likely to find some patterns that they don't explain, especially as we begin to look more carefully at partic-

ular manufacturing regions. For example, the American manufacturing belt has been losing ground recently to peripheral areas (Rees, 1979).

THE WORLD PATTERN OF MANUFACTURING

The world pattern of manufacturing is, as one would expect, markedly similar to the world pattern of economic development (figure 10–1). Obviously manufacturing is unevenly distributed throughout the world, as we suggested in our examination of the diffusion of the Industrial Revolution. One reason for the similarities in the two patterns was suggested by Colin Clark (1940): because of differences in the elasticity of demand for the output of the primary, secondary (manufacturing), and tertiary (services) sectors of an economy, economic development would be accompanied by changes in the proportions of the population employed in each sector. With economic development, the percent of the labor force employed in agriculture should drop, the percent employed in manufacturing should increase (to a maximum of 40 to 50 percent), and the percent employed in services should also increase.

However, the general pattern of worldwide manufacturing is too broad and diverse to be considered as a whole, though obviously it helps to view the overall pattern within our core–periphery framework. Our discussion of locational factors, though so far viewed in general terms, can be applied to only one industry at a time.

Of course we cannot examine each industry's distribution in our survey because of the limitation of space; rather, we can analyze the distribution of selected industries as examples of the way geographers approach such studies. We must also consider another geographic approach to the study of manufacturing activity, namely the regional approach. In other words, we can look at manufacturing regions or *belts*. Again, in this chapter we cannot consider all the world's manufacturing regions, so we must be content with a sample.

Thus, two approaches to the locational study of manufacturing are commonly used. One focuses on the locational factors which determine the geographic distribution of specific industries, whereas the other focuses on regional concentrations of manufacturing industries. However, the two approaches often overlap.

The world pattern of iron and steel production

We cannot begin to examine the locational patterns of all of the world's manufacturing activities, so we have chosen to examine the spatial distribution of only one industry, iron and steel. Our justification for this selection is simple: the iron and steel industry is one of the most important in modern industrial societies. Furthermore, for purposes of illustrating the geographic approach to industrial location, the iron and steel industry is a good example; raw materials, especially coal and iron ore, markets, and industrial inertia all play a role in explaining the spatial distribution of this essential industry.

As we have already mentioned in other contexts, geographic studies may be done at various scales. The models of industrial location we have discussed are designed mainly to explain locational patterns at the national scale in the developed countries, though we can extend their basic principles to the international scale. In this section we will begin at the world scale but,

when it appears of value to our understanding of industrial patterns and their determinants, we will move to the national or regional scales.

People began to produce iron from iron ore as early as 1500 B.C. in several different places using charcoal, so we are hardly considering a new industry. However, the industry only began to really grow in the 15th century with the development of the charcoal furnace in western Europe. With the Industrial Revolution, the iron and steel industry was swept into the prominent position it continues to occupy. Coal replaced charcoal as the major fuel for the industry when the puddling furnace was developed in England in 1784. Locational decisions during the late 18th and early 19th centuries still influence the geographic distribution of this important industry.

Locational considerations. The two major raw materials for the production of pig iron are coke, which is produced from bituminous coal, and iron ore. Limestone is also required, but its locational impact is insignificant. During the 18th and 19th centuries, several tons of coal were required to smelt one ton of iron ore, so coalfields exercised considerable influence in the location of iron furnaces. For example, early centers of iron production in Britain were found in the Midlands, Yorkshire, Derbyshire, and South Wales (Miller, 1977, p. 181).

Around 1800, nearly ten tons of coal were required to produce one ton of iron, whereas slightly under one ton is required now. Technological advances rapidly reduced coal requirements and, as a result, coalfields have lost their dominant influence on the location of the iron and steel industry. The role of iron ore became relatively more important. For example, the iron and steel industry in the Soviet Union has developed on iron ore deposits in the Urals using coal brought in from the Kuznetsk Basin (Miller, 1977, p. 182). Scrap iron has become increasingly important in the 20th century steel industry with the development of the electric furnace and the open-hearth furnace. Steel recipes often call for a ton or more of scrap per ton of pig iron, thus scrap sources are also exerting some pull on the steel industry. Most of the scrap comes from junkyards and from the motor vehicle and machinery industries.

Recently the market has increased its locational pull on the steel industry. Steel is sold to fabricating industries, which further process it into such items as

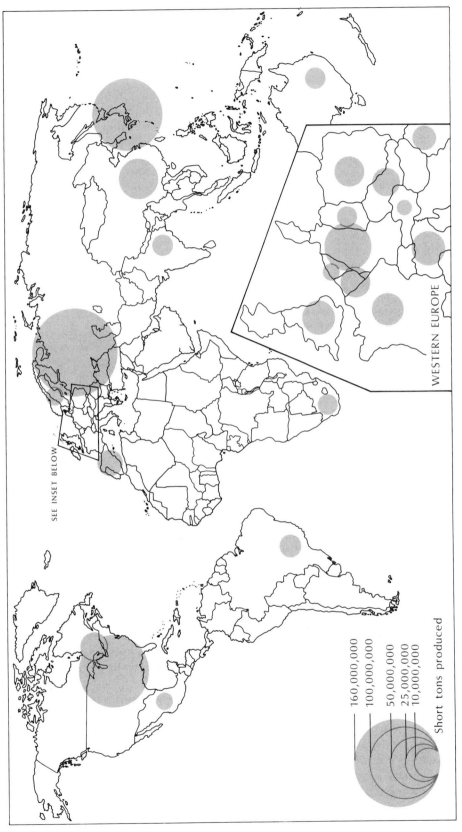

FIGURE 13–5 World distribution of raw steel production. (John W. Alexander, Lay James Gibson, *Economic Geography*, 2nd ed., © 1979, p. 271. Reprinted by permission of Prentice-Hall, Inc., Englewood Cliffs, NJ.)

WESTERN EUROPE

SEE INSET BELOW

160,000,000
100,000,000
50,000,000
25,000,000
10,000,000

Short tons produced

steel sheets and wire, and to final consumers such as the construction industry. Market locations allow for the benefits derived from economies of scale, and market areas are also often major sources of scrap.

Iron and steel locations. As one would expect, the iron and steel industry, with its need for capital, skilled labor, and markets, is concentrated mainly in the developed countries (figure 13–5). Three major steel producing regions can be identified: the United States and Canada, Europe, including the Soviet Union, and Japan. Other steel-producing regions include Mexico, Brazil, the Republic of South Africa, India, China, and Australia.

Iron and steel production in the Big Three. The Soviet Union is the world's largest producer of raw steel. Iron and steel production is concentrated in three major regions; the oldest is the southern Ukraine, which is similar to the Chicago area in the United States with respect to relative locations of coal, iron ore, and transportation. Nearly 40 percent of Soviet steel production now occurs in the Urals, though the region largely depends on outside coal; steel is produced at several locations within the Urals, including Magnitogorsk and Sverdlovsk. The third region is the Moscone Basin, where scrap has been an important element in location of the industry. It also reflects, obviously, the increasing influence of the market on location. In Lipetsk, some 200 miles southeast of Moscow, the Soviets began operation of their largest blast furnance in 1973.

The United States ranks second in steel production, and together, these two industrial giants produce nearly 40 percent of the world's raw steel. According to E. Willard Miller, "The iron industry was one of the first types of manufacturing to develop in the United States, with the first iron furnaces being built in Massachusetts in 1629" (1977, 189). The importance of markets, coupled with the industrial inertia so characteristic of the steel industry, helps us to understand the current pattern of steel production in the United States. About 90 percent of raw steel production occurs in the American Manufacturing Belt, which includes major markets, low-cost water transportation, Appalachian coal, and iron ore from the Mesabi Range in Minnesota and from Labrador. The three major steel-producing regions in the United States are the Chicago area, including East Chicago, Gary, and Hammond; the Lake Erie district, which reaches to Detroit; and the Pittsburgh region, which has undergone a relative decline in recent decades.

Japan ranks third as a world steel producer. However, unlike the Soviet Union or the United States, Japan's steel industry depends almost entirely on imported raw materials. Japan's steel industry benefitted from technological developments elsewhere, because its rapid growth following World War II allowed it to install modern large blast furnaces and other innovations, such as oxygen converters. The Japanese steel industry often is cited as a thorn in the side of the United States. Japanese steel, produced at lower cost, can often be sold in the United States for less than domestic steel despite the greater transportation costs. Within Japan steel mills are drawn to coastal locations to minimize transportation costs for imported raw materials and steel exports.

WORLD INDUSTRIAL REGIONS

Within the context of people and place, an overview of the world's manufacturing regions offers us more than an industry-by-industry approach. Industrial regions are concentrated in the developed countries and, to a lesser extent, in the urban core regions of developing countries. The world's major manufacturing regions have highly urbanized populations, high incomes, high energy consumption levels, and such urban–industrial problems as traffic congestion and air and water pollution. However, many differences also exist among major manufacturing regions.

As always, the problem of scale returns to haunt us. At the world scale manufacturing regions appear as small islands in a nonmanufacturing sea of people employed in primary and tertiary activities (figure 13–6).

Economically the world's manufacturing regions have an importance far beyond their relatively small spatial extent. These are centers of the modern urban–industrial world, centers of trade and commerce, and centers of new inventions and innovations. It is no accident, no unlikely locational coincidence, that we find four major industrial regions in the world coinciding geographically with the four major iron and steel producing regions we just examined. Steel is a fundamental industry, not only because of its size, but because steel is an essential input for so many other major industries, including the automobile and machine-tool industries.

FIGURE 13–6 Major industrial regions. (Anthony R. de-Souza, J. Brady Foust, 1979, *World Space-Economy.* Columbus, OH, Charles E. Merrill Publishing Co., p. 369.)

Raw materials, including fuels, move toward industrial regions from wherever they are found and produced. Manufactured goods, however, are mainly consumed within the world's industrial regions, though not necessarily within the region where they were produced. World trade in manufactured products takes place mainly among the developed countries. Cars are a good example. Despite the giant American automobile industry, many Americans drive Datsuns and Toyotas from Japan and Volkswagens from Germany, and American cars can be found on the streets of Tokyo and Bonn. Cars are considered a necessity in these countries, yet in the People's Republic of China, owning a car is beyond the wildest dreams of almost everyone. The demand for manufactured goods depends not only on the desires and tastes of individuals, but also on their ability to pay. Thus, the developing countries, despite their populations, are not large markets for such major manufactured items as automobiles, refrigerators, and freezers.

Just as manufacturing regions differ among countries, we can also recognize differences between manufacturing regions within a country. For example, the manufacturing region surrounding Pittsburgh, with its dominance of steel and related heavy industries, is quite different from that of Los Angeles, which is dominated by aerospace industries.

MANUFACTURING REGIONS IN NORTH AMERICA

Even on the world map of manufacturing regions (figure 13–6), it is apparent that several manufacturing regions exist in the United States and Canada. It is also apparent that the manufacturing region of the Northeastern United States and adjacent portions of Canada is far larger in extent than all of the other manufacturing regions combined. A somewhat closer focus on manufacturing regions within North America (figure 13–7) will help us relate people to industrial regions.

The manufacturing heartland of North America

Within the United States and Canada, a definite core region of manufacturing can be identified (figure 13–8); it extends from Megalopolis in the east to Chicago and Milwaukee in the west, and includes numerous major cities in both countries. Though the region

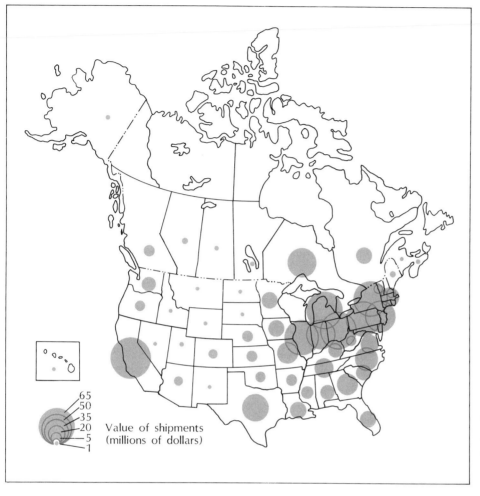

FIGURE 13–7 Distribution of manufacturing in the United States and Canada. (Richard S. Thoman, 1978, *The United States and Canada: Present and Future.* Columbus, OH, Charles E. Merrill Publishing Co., p. 195.)

occupies only 3 percent of the combined land area of the United States and Canada, it produces 80 percent of their steel, nearly 80 percent of their motor vehicles and parts, and contains the headquarters of 17 of North America's 20 largest corporations (Birdsall and Florin, 1978).

Life in the manufacturing heartland is primarily urban-oriented, though the region includes some significant agricultural areas as well. Industrial cities have been both praised for their many amenities and damned for their many faults, and evidence can be accumulated to support either view. We shall have more to say about industrial cities later in this chapter and in subsequent chapters.

Locational considerations for the heartland.

The North American industrial heartland, often referred to in the United States as *the Manufacturing Belt*, owes its existence to many of the locational consider-

ations we have already considered, especially raw materials, transportation, labor, and markets. Of course, historical development and industrial inertia have also been important.

Mineral fuels occur throughout the Manufacturing Belt. Appalachian coal has played a major role in industrial development, primarily by localizing the iron and steel industry. Oil and natural gas were also historically important in the region's industrial development; the first commercial oil well in the United States, for example, was drilled at Titusville, Pennsylvania.

Transportation has played a crucial role in bringing together raw materials and distributing manufactured products. Internal modes of transportation have varied in importance through the years and have included rivers, canals, railroads, highways, and airlines. Furthermore, foreign material sources and markets have been accessible both from east coast and Great Lakes ports.

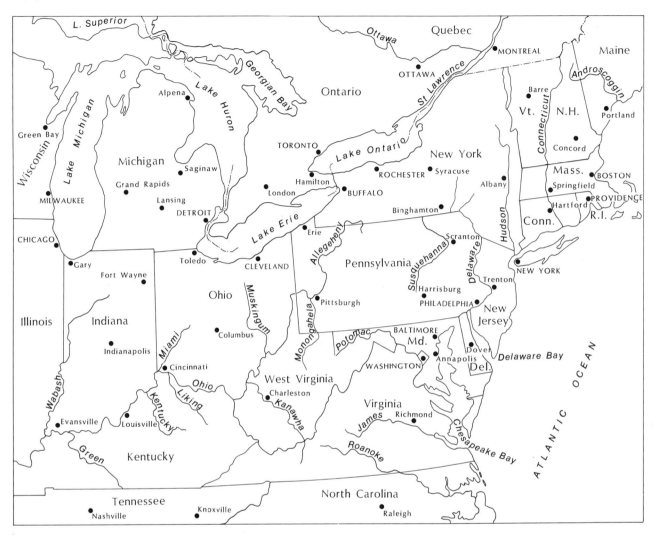

FIGURE 13–8 North American manufacturing core region. (Stephen S. Birdsall, John W. Florin, *Regional Landscapes of the United States and Canada.* Copyright © 1978 by John Wiley & Sons, Inc., p. 77. Reprinted with adaptation by permission of John Wiley & Sons, Inc.)

Because Europeans first settled America, both labor and markets were first concentrated in Eastern North America. Future immigrants supplied cheap unskilled labor for growing factories as well as ethnic enrichment of urban cultural landscapes. To a considerable extent, industrial inertia, especially in major industries like iron and steel, has helped maintain the Manufacturing Belt's dominant position, though its locational attraction for new industries is not as great as it once was (figure 13–9).

Other manufacturing regions in North America

In recent years the Manufacturing Belt has been beset by a variety of problems. Manufacturing industries are increasingly footloose and seem to be responding to such locational considerations as pleasant climates, clean air, availability of various types of recreation facilities, and other amenities. In one recent study, Greenberg and Valente concluded that,

Whether through explicit or implicit federal, state, and local decisions about transportation and governmentally funded projects, or private enterprise forces pressing upon raw material and market costs, or adverse public reaction to urban problems, the Northeast has experienced an accelerated relative

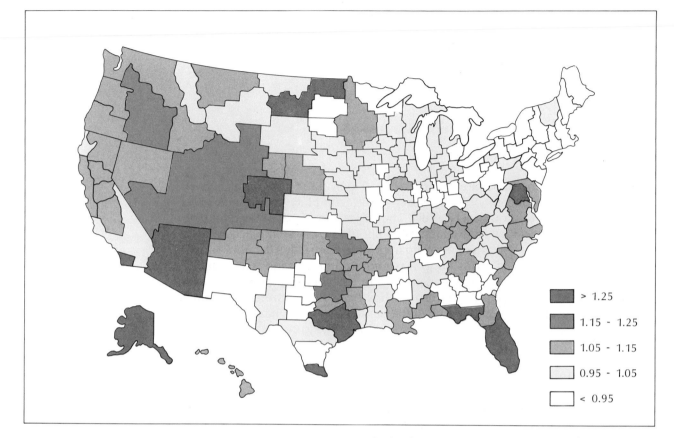

FIGURE 13–9 Employment change, 1965–1970 (U.S. = 1.0). (Reproduced by permission from *The Professional Geographer* of the Association of American Geographers, Volume 31, 1979, p. 37, figure 1, W. B. Beyers.)

> decline and in some cases an absolute decrease, in employment during the 1970s. (1975, p. 97)

Not only are manufacturing activities finding the Manufacturing Belt less attractive, but people are also less satisfied there than they have been in the past. Between 1970 and 1976, for example, New York City lost 473,000 people, leaving the city with its lowest population since the 1930s (Population Reference Bureau, 1979). During the same period Chicago, Philadelphia, Detroit, Baltimore, Cleveland, and many other northeastern cities lost population. On the other hand, San Antonio, Houston, San Jose, San Diego, and Phoenix were the fastest growing major metropolitan areas during the 1970s.

The South.   Nearly 30 percent of total manufacturing employment in the United States is found in the South,

with the largest concentrations currently in Houston and Dallas. Plentiful natural resources and cheap labor supplies have attracted some industries to the South, whereas tax incentives and other governmental amenities have attracted others. Local markets, though growing rapidly, have been too small to provide the necessary economies of scale for some industries.

Textiles, apparel and food processing have been especially important in Southern manufacturing; aircraft production and petrochemicals have also found the South attractive.

The Pacific.   Along the West Coast several areas have emerged as important manufacturing regions. Los Angeles is by far the largest, though San Francisco and Seattle are also important. Aerospace, electronics, lumber, and food processing are major activities in the West.

Population growth in the West is likely to continue, producing a growing market for goods and services. However, in some areas, such as Los Angeles, environmental restrictions are likely to be important obstacles to the location of many manufacturing activities.

We have outlined some of the basic trends operating to change the distribution of economic activities in the United States during the 1980s. The following special study indicates one practical application of understanding what is happening to the geography of economic activity.

CASE STUDY:
Taking stock — Geography and the market
James Fraser

Growth-oriented investors need to take a broad look at the geographical background within which companies operate, so they can place their funds where business is likely to grow most rapidly. The migration of people and industry to the South and Southwest is a factor that should be taken into account.

The 1950s and 1960s saw a strong migration from cities to suburbs, with "strip cities" developing — Boston to Washington and Chicago to Milwaukee, for example. Since 1970, however, people in growing numbers have been going rural. National population growth has been concentrated in smaller cities, villages and the countryside. At the same time, there has been a trend toward states that have warmer weather and lower living costs.

Strong incentives

The Northern winters of recent years, including the fierce cold and blizzards in the Midwest this year and the extraordinary snows in the Northeast last year, have made more people aware of an easier climate not far away where life is not a continual struggle against nature.

The energy crisis also makes the sun belt more attractive. Retired people find living there more comfortable. Homes require less heat, and fresh produce is readily available for longer periods.

Companies that create jobs in the warmer region are likely to benefit from this movement.

Sun City, the retirement community built by Del E. Webb outside Phoenix, illustrates what is happening. Housing in Sun City, with a population close to 50,000, has been sold out. Sun City West, a new self-sustained community, is under construction, with 15 to 20 homes being completed every day. The backlog of orders is in the thousands.

Among businesses that thrive on such growth are real-estate firms, financial-service corporations, construction companies, newspapers serving smaller cities and some regional airlines. The stocks of many of these companies are not well known nationally, though the issues are strong in their own region. The companies tend to operate more efficiently than similar ones in the North because they are less apt to be affected by "featherbedding" and union organizing.

Among the first manufacturers to move south in the 1950s were the textile producers, who had to reckon with outmoded plants in New England and lower wage rates in the South.

New England then staked its future on development along Route 128 around Boston, where many of the first wave of high-technology companies located large plants—among them Polaroid, Raytheon and Honeywell. At one time, this area was the technology center of the United States, built on the basis of superior educational facilities in the Boston area.

Now that has changed. The new technology center is in "Silicon Valley" between Palo Alto and San Jose in California, where Stanford University provides academic leadership. The area around Los Angeles also has many high-technology firms. Others are located eastward around Phoenix and Tuscon in Arizona, around Dallas, Austin, San Antonia and Houston in Texas, and in some parts of Florida. Southern educational institutions have improved, so that business managers no longer think that academic wisdom is confined to the Northern climes.

Growth climate

For the investor, the upshot of all this is that a department-store chain in the South is likely to be increasing sales faster than inflation—and faster than a similar firm in the North—because it is receiving a steady flow of additional customers. A well-run Southern bank has greater opportunity for expansion compared with a well-run bank in the North, where the population is stagnant or declining.

Forest products also flourish in this area because of the long growing season and abundant rainfall. Fast-food restaurants that specialize in Mexican fare are rapidly gaining in popularity.

Such growth adds up to opportunities for investors who realize these migration trends are not likely to be reversed for many years to come.

MANUFACTURING AND THE GROWTH SYNDROME

Economic growth, beyond some optimal level, was one of the three parts of Zelinsky's view of the *growth syndrome* (1971). Because manufacturing forms one of the major cogs in the wheel of economic growth, we need to further consider it in the context of the growth syndrome.

Economic and environmental trade-offs

We have already elaborated upon the contrasting views of ecologists and economists. So far the modern industrial world has opted for the path prescribed by economists where trade-offs must be made between environmental preservation and economic growth, though the nature and extent of such trade-offs vary from place to place.

In the United States many people consider economic growth a necessity. Whereas some still support an attitude of "growth at any cost," increasing numbers are becoming aware of the environmental costs of sustained economic growth. During the 1970s public dissatisfaction with *growthmania* appeared in a variety of ways. Oregonians, for example, were saying that visitors were welcome but new residents were not. In Colorado bumper stickers decried the *Californication* of Colorado. In California voters passed Proposition 20, which placed tight controls on all coastal zone developments. Communities in many places became more selective about the types of industries which they were willing to accept; *clean* industries were considered desirable, but *dirty* industries were not.

Among other trade-offs, locational ones are likely to be more apparent in industrialized countries in the decades ahead. Some areas may be unable to absorb more dirty industries because of environmental controls on air and water pollution. We cannot expect manufacturing to grind to a halt in order to preserve the environment in its present condition, though some suggest we should. However, we are not likely to see Los Angeles continue to attract industries which would significantly lower air quality in the Los Angeles Basin.

Environmental controls in the United States

One way to insure that trade-offs are made with the environment in mind is through government interference. Too often air and water are treated as free goods by decision makers, thus allowing air and water pollution to continue. In the United States during the 1970s, environmental legislation was actively pursued, though critics liken it to the death of the free-enterprise system. Others argue, however, that expanded production in recent years has increasingly come at the expense of the environment. We have our automobiles and airplanes, our refrigerators and freezers, our all-electric push-button homes, but we also have our Appalachias, our pock-marked landscapes where mining came and went, and rivers that are considered fire hazards.

The Environmental Protection Agency. The **Environmental Protection Agency (EPA)** was established in December of 1970 and charged with the mission of attacking environmental pollution, including air pollution, water pollution, solid waste disposal problems, pesticides, noise, and radiation. The EPA's first task was to establish and enforce environmental standards for pollution control; they would limit the amounts and types of pollutants that can be tolerated without endangering human health and welfare. Among the first major steps in the development of national environmental pollution control programs were the Clean Air Act of 1970 and the Water Pollution Control Act of 1972. Since then these acts have been amended and supplemented by other environmental legislation.

From the view point of industrial location, environmental protection is often an additional cost. For example, a company may have to install scrubbers or other devices to decrease the emission of designated pollutants. If the cost of pollution control does not vary from place to place, of course, its locational impact will be relatively insignificant. However, emission allowances are usually least in areas which are already having air or water quality problems. The result, then, would be peaks in an industry's space-cost curve over polluted areas. Thus, industries with pollution problems may seek different locations than before the enactment of environmental legislation. Phrased a different way, many industries face a new type of trade-off between pollution abatement costs and location.

INDUSTRIAL IMPRESSIONS ON THE LANDSCAPE

No matter how we consider it, the Industrial Revolution has had a considerable, and sometimes brutal, impact on the landscape. As Sir Kenneth Clark said,

> Imagine an immensely speeded up movie of Manhattan Island during the last hundred years. It would look less like a work of man than like some tremendous natural upheaval. It's godless, it's brutal, it's violent—but one can't laugh it off, because in the energy, strength of will and mental grasp that have gone to make New York, materialism has transcended itself. (1969, p. 321)

Industrial landscapes are neither always ugly, though many may be, nor always depressing to those who work in or live near them. Nevertheless, ugliness is a common feature of many industrial landscapes, especially older ones and those in which dirty industries are major elements. Dingy buildings with broken windows and belching smokestacks are still common, though in many new industrial parks landscaping is required of new tenants, and aesthetics are given due consideration.

We have all seen the gamut of industrial landscapes, from flowers and ponds to unbelievable ugliness, but seldom do we give these landscapes a second thought. Yet in ugliness, as well as in other characteristics associated with factories and the people who work in them, we find the other face of Janus.

Artists, poets, and industrial landscapes

During the 1970s ecology became a household word, though the suddenness with which people discovered ecological problems was rather surprising. After all, the Industrial Revolution was already at least two centuries old. Various facets of the relationship between industrialization and ugliness had been pointed out before, however usually by sensitive individuals such as artists and poets, people who were not so immersed in the industrialization process.

The task of art, according to Yi-Fu Tuan, may be viewed as follows:

> Art does not aim to duplicate reality. It does not aspire to reproduce in its beholder the pleasant or lacerating emotions of people in the real world. Art provides an image of feeling; it gives objectified form and visibility to feeling so that what is powerful but inchoate can lead a semipublic life. (1975, p. 161)

Certainly the artist bears a responsibility to others, and geographers can learn from what artists have to say, if we would listen.

Industrial landscapes have changed through time, and so have the ways in which people, including artists, have perceived them. Unfortunately artists have not always been attracted to industrial landscapes; many have turned their backs and painted idyllic landscapes as if nothing had happened. However, some artists and poets did focus rather early on industrial scenes, and some, had people been listening, were raising questions about the benefits of industrialization.

Though early in the Industrial Revolution, artists sometimes found a new hope for humankind because people might be freed from many dreary tasks, this hope gave way to pictures of broken landscapes and such social ills as child labor. In some early English factories, for example, only one laborer in four was an adult male.

Industrialization needed not only labor but also raw materials, and mining to produce those materials increased in scale and in impact on the landscape. According to Lewis Mumford,

> Mining originally set the pattern for later modes of mechanization by its callous disregard for human factors, by its indifference to the pollution and destruction of the neighboring environment, by its concentration upon the physico-chemical processes for obtaining the desired metal or fuel, and above all by its topographic and mental isolation from the organic world of the farmer and the craftsman, and the spiritual world of the church, the University, and the City. (1970, p. 147)

Artists and poets have not been alone in warning against the new machine age ushered in by the Indus-

trial Revolution. However, some did voice reservations quite early. For example, Robert Burns scratched these words on a window pane at the Carron Iron Works in 1787 (Clark, 1969, p. 321):

> We cam na here to view your works,
>   In hopes to be mair wise,
> But only, lest we gang to Hell,
>   It may be nae surprise.

Perception of industrial landscapes

Industrial landscapes have been, and today continue to be, perceived differently from place to place and from person to person. To a miner on his way to work in a West Virginia coal mine, the environmental impact of mining does not appear the same as it might to an outsider on vacation from Los Angeles or Chicago. The miner's paycheck is drawn from the landscape, whereas the visitor collects mainly aesthetic impressions. What seems ugly to the outsider may symbolize security to residents of an area, thus we must be careful to consider various perceptions of the industrial landscapes.

Again we need to emphasize the idea of trade-offs, including locational trade-offs. Modern industrial societies, with their tremendous and ever-increasing appetites for raw materials and energy, will not be stopped by environmentalists who want nature left unadulterated. But, if we are going to give credence to the quality of life in industrial societies, the voices of the environmentalists must be heard. We do not have to accept the conflict between having jobs and having a decent environment as an either/or situation, though all too often both growth advocates and environmentalists make it sound that way.

However, trade-offs are not always easy to make, nor can we always include all essential variables in our decision making, though we must try. Too often we fail to draw on the subjective, yet we feel it is essential to understanding our current predicament and prescribing ways to grow in the future. Resolving conflicts is often difficult, but ignoring them may be far worse. Our feelings are best summarized in this comment:

> The rivers along which lovers might formerly have wandered may be deserted as hydrogen sulfide replaces the old smells of springtime. But it is a bold economic calculus that balances the increase in sewage costs against the decline in lyric poetry. (Ward and Dubos, 1972, p. 73)

KEY TERMS

Industrial Revolution
Dual economy
Production costs
Distribution costs
Least transport cost location
Factors of production
Financial capital
Physical capital
Industrial inertia
Economies of scale

Space-cost curve
Space-price curve
Spatial margins to profitability
Raw material orientation
Market orientation
Primary industry
Secondary industry
Value added
Footloose industry
Environmental Protection Agency (EPA)

REFERENCES

Alexander, J. W. and Gibson, L. J. (1979), *Economic Geography,* 2nd ed. Englewood Cliffs, NJ: Prentice–Hall, Inc.

Beyers, W. B. (1979), "Contemporary Trends in the Regional Economic Development of the United States," *The Professional Geographer* 31, 34–44.

Birdsall, S. S. and Florin, J. W. (1978), *Regional Landscapes of the United States and Canada.* New York: John Wiley & Sons, Inc.

Clark, C. (1940), *The Conditions of Economic Progress.* London: Macmillan & Co., Ltd.

Clark, K. (1969), *Civilisation: A Personal View.* New York: Harper & Row, Publishers, Inc.

Cook, E. (1976), *Man, Energy, Society.* San Francisco: W. H. Freeman & Co., Publishers.

deSouza, A. R. and Foust, J. B. (1979), *World Space–Economy.* Columbus, OH: Charles E. Merrill Publishing Co.

Estall, R. C. and Buchanan, R. O. (1973), *Industrial Activity and Economic Geography,* 3rd ed. London: Hutchinson University Library.

Foust, J. B. and deSouza, A. R. (1978), *The Economic Landscape: A Theoretical Introduction.* Columbus, OH: Charles E. Merrill Publishing Co.

Greenberg, M. R. and Valente, N. J. (1975), "Recent Economic Trends in the Major Northeastern Metropolises," in Sternlieb, G. and Hughes, J. W. (eds.), *Post-Industrial America: Metropolitan Decline and Inter-Regional Job Shifts.* New Brunswick, NJ: Center for Urban Policy Research, Rutgers University, 77–99.

Griffin, P. F., et al. (1976), *Culture, Resource and Economic Activity: An Introduction to Economic Geography,* 2nd ed. Boston: Allyn & Bacon, Inc.

Hamilton, F. E. I. (1967), "Models of Industrial Location," in Chorley, R. J. and Haggett, P. (eds.), *Models in Geography.* London: Methuen & Co., Ltd., 361–424.

Miller, E. W. (1977), *Manufacturing: A Study of Industrial Location.* University Park, PA: Pennsylvania State University Press.

Morrill, R. L. (1979), "Stages in Patterns of Population Concentration and Dispersion," *The Professional Geographer* 31, 55–65.

Mumford, L. (1970), *The Pentagon of Power.* New York: Harcourt Brace Jovanovich, Inc.

Norcliffe, G. B. (1975), "A Theory of Manufacturing Places," in Collins, L. and Walker, D. F. (eds.), *Locational Dynamics of Manufacturing Activity.* New York: John Wiley & Sons, Inc., 19–57.

Peters, G. L. and Anderson, B. L. (1976), "Industrial Landscapes: Past Views and Stages of Recognition," *The Professional Geographer* 28, 341–348.

Population Reference Bureau (1979), "Urban Dwellers Moving Out," *Intercom* 7, 14–15.

Redford, A. (1960), *The Economic History of England, 1760–1860,* 2nd ed. London: Longmans, Ltd.

Rees, J. (1979), "Technological Change and Regional Shifts in American Manufacturing," *The Professional Geographer* 31, 45–54.

Rostow, W. W. (1971), *The Stages of Economic Growth: A Non-Communist Manifesto,* 2nd ed. Cambridge: Cambridge University Press.

Smith, D. M. (1971), *Industrial Location: An Economic Geographical Analysis.* New York: John Wiley & Sons, Inc.

Thoman, R. S. (1978), *The United States and Canada: Present and Future.* Columbus, OH: Charles E. Merrill Publishing Co.

Tuan, Y. (1975), "Place: An Experiential Perspective," *Geographical Review* 65, 151–165.

Ward, B. and Dubos, R. (1972), *Only One Earth: The Care and Maintenance of a Small Planet.* New York: W. W. Norton & Co., Inc.

Zelinsky, W. (1971), "Beyond the Exponentials: The Role of Geography in the Great Transition," *Economic Geography* 46, 498–535.

14

Cities and an urbanizing world

Gideon Sjoberg has observed that people began to live in cities some 5,500 years ago; however, the proportion of the human population concentrated in cities did not increase significantly until about 100 years ago (Sjoberg, 1960). In order to understand urbanization, we need to investigate two principal issues: we must identify the factors which brought about the origin of cities, and we need to understand the evolutionary stages through which cities passed prior to the modern epoch of urbanization.

This chapter and the following one are devoted to the study of cities and the process of urbanization. It is appropriate that a discussion of cities is taken up in the final two major chapters of this volume. The perspective on human geography offered throughout this book relates population, economic growth, and modernization to the ever-changing manner in which people perceive and use the resources of the earth. We have observed that, as technology develops, and the intellectual, political, economic, social, and psychological elements of cultural systems are transformed through time, changes occur in the way human groups use the surface of the earth. If we could freeze time and explore a given point in history, the artifacts which typify that historical landscape would be the sum of the technological achievements of past civilizations, as well as the level of modernization of groups at that moment.

If we could take such a historical snapshot, we would probably want to focus on an urban area. The city represents the place in which the process of modernization and the level of technology are given form.

Reflection on the spatial, social, and economic organization of cities should reinforce the notion of the city as a general summation of modernization and cultural systems: think for a moment of the ways in which the major cities in your area are the result of the interaction between the subsystems of cultural systems.

The city is both the product and mirror of all the facets of peoples, environments, and places which we have discussed to this point. Here we will deal with the difficult questions of the definition of a city and the origin of the first cities. A progression of topics follows, including the history of cities, present day urbanization, and the city in the developing world.

The definition of a city

There is an immense body of academic study which focuses on the question, What is a city? We may define a *formal* city of buildings and roads, political or legal boundaries, and statistical entities. If we define a regional or *functional* city, then perhaps political boundaries are not used as the determinants of the edge of the city; activity patterns, such as the distance from which suburban commuters come to work in the city, might be used as a criterion for urban definition. In addition to assigning either formal or functional definitions is the problem of whether an urban definition is for intellectual purposes or for specific and applied use.

Several terms should be identified and defined at this point. We often use the words *urbanization, urbanism, urban,* and *city* interchangeably, but each term describes a different facet of the phenomena of cities. **Urbanism** refers to the conditions or characteristics of the way of life of those who live in cities. A person interested in the study of urbanism might consider the elements of cultural systems as found in cities. **Urbanization** is the process which brings people into cities; it may also describe the number of cities or the size of the population living in cities in a region, usually expressed as a percentage.

Despite some conceptual differences, we will use the terms *city* and *urban place* synonymously. Sjoberg proposed the following definition of a city: a community of substantial size and population density containing a variety of nonagricultural specialists, including a literate elite (1960). Cities as defined by Sjoberg have existed for a considerable period of time.

Most urbanized societies have done so through a three-stage process:

1. First being a pre-urban and pre-literate folk society of small groups absorbed in the quest for food, with no specialization of labor;

2. followed by a civilized pre-industrial "feudal" society having a surplus of food, specialization work, social classes, and some wind and water power;

3. finally places having mass literacy, a fluid class system and use of inanimate energy (Sjoberg, 1960).

It must be understood that each urban nation did not undergo this exact process; United States cities, for example, did not evolve in exactly this way. According to Sjoberg's tricomponent levels of human organization, clusterings of people in both the feudal era and the society of mass literacy would qualify as urban.

The fundamental elements of virtually any definition of *urban* are incorporated into the criteria proposed by Sjoberg. Population size is a factor in nearly all urban definitions, and population density figures in many. The final two parts of Sjoberg's definition are difficult to assess. A certain percentage of nonagricultural workers is used in urban definitions in some developing nations; India demands that a specific percentage of the population be involved in nonagricultural work if a place is to be considered urban. The final criterion, a place housing a literate elite, would be difficult to use in the determination of what is urban.

Population size is the principle factor defining cities in most nations: in the United States, a place of more than 2500 people is considered to be a city, in

Canada a city must have a population greater than 1000, in Switzerland more than 10,000, and in Denmark 250. The number of people in a place is also used to define urban organization within nations. The **Standard Metropolitan Statistical Areas (SMSA)** of the United States are based on population size within a metropolitan region. An SMSA consists of a central city (or twin cities) of at least 50,000 population, plus the county containing the city and those adjacent counties that are metropolitan in character.

The definition of a city is often developed to fit specific needs. A straight numerical definition is the easiest criterion from which to develop data to either support or refute the claim that a place is a city. If a population of 2500 is the prime consideration for defining a city, it is a much less complicated matter to determine whether or not a place is urban than if the criteria includes something as abstract as the existence of a literate elite. Thus, academic definitions of a city are often far different from the definitions used by urban scientists involved in applied practice.

A simple numerical definition, however, is not without problems. Suppose a place has a population of 20,000 inhabitants but is simply a "bedroom" community of commuters who work in a major city. If the bedroom community is only a collection of residences, and has no real economic base, cultural opportunities, or social diversity, is that place a city?

The questions and problems inherent in defining a city have been subject to great debate. In exploring what constitutes a city we see more than just problems of definition. We have our first taste of the complexity involved in any question dealing with urban places. Throughout the remainder of this chapter, and in the following chapter, our definition of a city will roughly follow Sjoberg.

THE ORIGIN OF CITIES

The original impetus for the development of cities was the shift to settled agriculture from other forms of economy. Many other factors—commerce, religious and political centers, defense, early processing, and manufacturing—were also instrumental in the establishment of cities. Compared to modern 20th century cities, most of the early urban agglomerations would be considered small. Many early cities or villages served as agricultural bedroom communities from which people commuted on foot to their farms two or three miles from the village center (Thomlinson, 1976, p. 405).

Many conclusions about ancient cities are based on speculation, and the archaeological evidence is fragmentary. Certainly an important early step in the urbanization process was the development of agricultural technology, including the wheeled cart, the ox-drawn plow, the art of metallurgy, the development of new crops, and improved irrigation techniques (Johnson, 1967, p. 3). When we consider the factors which facilitated the development of early cities, the importance of what we have learned of peoples, environments, and places to this point becomes clear. Cities are forged from the product of technological innovation, which in turn is the heart of modernization. In essence we are discussing the evolution of cultural systems, population growth, and agricultural and other economic development when we study the origins of cities.

Many scholars have speculated why people first clustered together in what were undoubtedly small agricultural settlements. Lewis Mumford believes the process involved ceremony.

> In the development of permanent human settlements, we find an expression of animal needs similar to those in other social species; but even the most primitive urban beings reveal more than this. Soon after one picks up man's trail in the earliest campfire or chipped stone tool one finds evidence of interests and anxieties that have no animal counterpart; in particular, a ceremonious concern for the dead, manifested in their deliberate burial. . . . In one sense the city of the dead is the forerunner, almost the core, of every living city. (1961, pp. 14–15).

Mumford's argument is that people involved in hunting and gathering, and indeed even in primitive agriculture, had little disposition to settle in one place permanently. The ceremony involving the burial of the dead, however, occurred at a specific location and therefore was a tie of people to a place.

Mumford raises two important points. First, that ceremony may have been an essential reason why people first gathered in cities (although some argue this was a minor factor). Second, perhaps more important, is his allusion to the delicate nature of the catalyst required to bringing people together; groups of people were working in primitive agriculture in many parts of the world between 6000 and 9000 years ago, though they apparently lacked only a critical set of circumstances to force them into what would become cities. We could liken this situation to pieces of metal slowly but inexorably drawn together once a magnet is intro-

duced into their area. What we are searching for is the magnet which influenced the grouping of people into urban places. We must be mindful that this undoubtedly was a very slow evolutionary process. Mumford's point is that ceremony, or even the gracious nature of human beings, may have been the key factor which influenced early urban settlement.

Mumford is not alone; Professor Paul Wheatly found evidence that the ceremonial complex was probably the starting point of urbanism. He proposed the process of compacting many very small centers into one urban place (1971).

V. Gordon Childe is often credited with coining the term *Urban Revolution* (1954). He postulated that improvements in agriculture lead to a surplus of wealth and to power, because some form of political hierarchy would be necessary to regulate the surplus, and a fixed place would be necessary to store it. Clustering in one location would be a logical outcome of both the needs of leaders and the necessity to store food stuffs; in other words, economy and technology were triggering elements in the origins of the first cities.

Technology plays an important part in the theories which assume that urban origins and the development of cities were clearly related to the development of irrigation systems. Professor Karl Wittfogel has termed a society which develops partially because of irrigation practices a **hydraulic civilization** (1956). He contended that early agriculturalists would have had to dig and redig ditches and other parts of the water system, terrace the land if it were uneven, and regulate the flow of water. In all of these activities, direction and supervision would have been necessary. Thus, a hydraulic civilization would have developed through an organizational rather than technological revolution.

Two requirements of a society emphasizing water resources would have been a clear and well-defined division of labor and governmental organization to regulate the water resources, organize the labor force, and control the agricultural surplus. Wittfogel does not specifically claim that urban centers sprang from the need for complex irrigation systems in all parts of the world. Many, however, have used his theory of hydraulic civilizations to support a case that cities developed as a result of the need for organization and the need for places from which to regulate people and resources.

Many scientists continue to speculate on the origins of the earliest cities. We have examined a small sample of ideas about urban beginnings; however, in all probability some combination of needs for social or

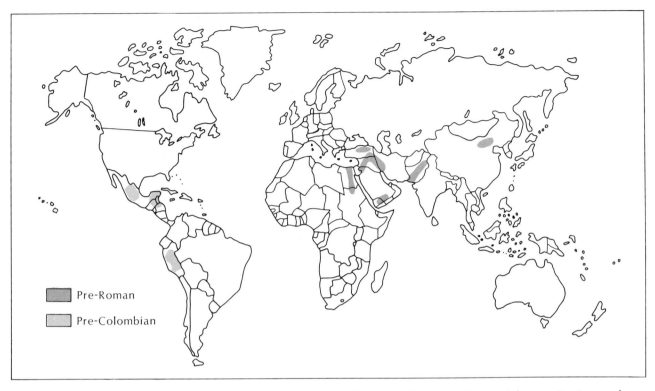

FIGURE 14–1 Early centers of urbanism. (Chester E. Zimolzak, Charles A. Stansfield, Jr., 1979, *The Human Landscape: Geography and Culture.* Columbus, OH, Charles E. Merrill Publishing Co., p. 241.)

economic regulation, religious practices, technological innovations, and defense brought people together in the first cities. Regardless of other factors involved, an agricultural surplus was the cornerstone upon which cities were built. Without a surplus of food, clustering in cities larger than small agricultural hamlets would have been virtually impossible. It was the interaction between cultural systems, technological development, and the first of a series of agricultural revolutions that gave rise to the first cities.

The sites of earliest urbanization

Substantial evidence suggests that cities developed in a number of areas during approximately the same era. The distribution of the centers of urbanization parallel the location of cultural hearths (figure 14–1). Sjoberg cites three conditions for a favorable environment from which cities could develop: "a favorable ecological base, an advanced technology (relative to pre-urban forms) in both the agricultural and non-agricultural

spheres, and a complex social organization—above all, a well-developed power structure" (1960, p. 27).

These preconditions for urban life, coupled with the various forces which drew people together, apparently first acted toward city formation in Mesopotamia (figure 14–2). The cities in this region were undoubtedly small, with buildings made from mud bricks; streets were apparently narrow and winding, with little drainage and no pavement. Early Mesopotamian cities were politically independent but with common cultural elements (Mumford, 1961). Artifacts recovered from temples and tombs indicate the existence of a class of artisans who served the wealthy. Slavery must also have existed, given the size of some construction projects undertaken.

The hinterlands around early Mesopotamian cities were necessarily devoted to agricultural use. Lack of transportation, few methods of preserving foods, and a need for a market for agricultural products meant that the agricultural practices took place in plots within, or immediately beyond, the city boundaries. Early cities were undoubtedly limited in both land area and population. A city of 10,000 people in early Mesopotamia would have been considered extremely large, and the majority were much smaller (Childe, 1957).

FIGURE 14–2 Ancient cities of the Tigris-Euphrates Valley. Key: 1–Ergani, 2–Cayönü Tepesi, 3–Edessa, 4–Tell Halaf, 5–Dura-Europas, 6–Mari, 7–Mosul, 8–Guagamela, 9–Tepe Gawra, 10–Nineveh, 11–Nimrud, 12–Tell Hassuna, 13–Ashur, 14–Kirkuk, 15–Jarmo, 16–Behistun, 17–Samarra, 18–Choga Mami, 19–Mandali, 20–Eshnunna, 21–Baghdad, 22–Akkad, 23–Sippar, 24–Agade, 25–Seleucia, 26–Clesiphan, 27–Kish, 28–Babylon, 29–Jamdet Nasr, 30–Nippur, 31–Isin, 32–Shuruppak, 33–Umma, 34–Uruk, 35–Larsa, 36–Tell al'Ubaid, 37–Eridu, 38–Ur, 39–Lagash (Telloh), 40–Susa, 41–Tepe Sialk. (L. King, R. Golledge, *Cities, Space and Behavior: The Elements of Urban Geography,* © 1978, p. 22. Reprinted by permission of Prentice-Hall, Inc., Englewood Cliffs, NJ.)

Other regions in which early cities emerged include the valleys of the Nile, Indus, and Hwang Ho Rivers and the Yucatan Peninsula. However, it is difficult to determine the timing and extent of urbanization in areas other than Mesopotamia. The independence of urban development in Egypt is questionable; we don't know the degree to which cities along the Nile were an extension of Mesopotamian cities. In the remaining areas, especially in Meso-America, the archaeological evidence is incomplete and data difficult to obtain, thus a complete picture of the cities in these areas is nonexistent.

The city in history

The evolution of cities has been built upon developments in agriculture and transportation, increases in the ability to acquire and utilize natural resources, and changes in social and economic systems. We will take up the study of the city when the Greeks were dominating much of the Mediterranean and the Middle East.

Greek cities were tied initially to the agricultural production in surrounding lands. However, as the resources adjacent to Greek cities were consumed, long distance trade became an important cultural aspect. The site and situation of the nation of Greece is excellent with respect to developing a strong tradition of commerce. Greece is a long peninsula with many fine harbors along the coastline. The Aegean Sea is a well-protected body of water with many small islands which served as stepping stones for the early Greeks in their efforts to trade with the Middle East. The Mediterranean Sea also offered a similar trade route on a larger scale.

Trade and interaction along such water routes served Greek cities well. Innovation in transportation at this time, five centuries before Christ, allowed for the growth of Greek cities as localized resources were depleted.

The cities of Greece are noteworthy for several reasons. One was the city's function as the center of political authority over the surrounding territory. Political control over the hinterland was not unique to Greek cities, but in no preceding civilization were city and specific region wedded as they were in the Greek **city-state.**

A second important contribution of the Greek city was its social role. According to Mumford, "The transformation of the village into the **polis,** the place where people come together not just by birth and habit, but consciously, in pursuit of a better life, takes place before our eyes in Greece" (emphasis added) (1961, p. 240).

The early Greek cities of **Olympia, Delphi,** and **Cos** exemplify a transition in urban function. Olympia was a city devoted to athletic development, the site of the first Olympic games. Delphi was the location of the Shrine and sacred oracle of Apollo and centered around literary pursuits. Cos was a great health resort and the training center for physicians. Although each city served more than the one function, a great many scholars point to Olympia, Delphi, and Cos as the first truly specialized cities (Mumford, 1961).

We tend to think of superb monuments when we visualize Greek cities, but the course of daily life took place in far different surroundings. Greek houses were small and simple, with little furniture. The road systems were generally winding paths, with little drainage or pavement to allow the flow of waste water or materials.

The debt developing Western cities owe the Greeks is an intellectual one. Greek cities reflected achievements in literature, philosophy, science, and art. The simple and reasoned life enjoyed by urban Greeks allowed for speculation and discussion, which in turn produced a series of philosophies emphasizing the development of the mind, body, and spirit. As the Roman civilization began to develop into the dominant group in the Mediterranean, much of Greek language, religion, literature, and art was diffused westward to the Italian Peninsula.

Several hundred years before the birth of Christ an empire was established in the Mediterranean and ruled from the city of Rome. Through massive public works projects, such as road and aqueduct systems, some of the traditional constraints to urban size were diminished. As cities grew larger, they became increasingly dependent on more than the surrounding hinter-

land for resources. Satisfying the demands of some Roman cities for food and materials caused the natural environment of places far away to be converted to agricultural production. In reciprocal fashion the Roman system of roads and political control in conquered territories allowed the flow of ideas and materials to extend outward from Roman cities to the countryside. One of the most valuable achievements of the Roman Empire was the founding of towns and the establishment of a network for cultural diffusion.

As with Greek cities, one imagines Rome to be composed of massive public works and great monuments. However, the homes of the masses were obviously far less imposing: the rich lived in single family dwellings built around an open courtyard or *atrium,* whereas the majority of people lived in multiple family dwellings. Neither dwelling held much furniture.

The towns and cities founded by the Romans exist to this day, as do many of their roadways and aqueducts. In the 5th century A.D., Roman influence in the world faltered and the Empire was destroyed. The network of commerce and interaction developed by Rome was similarly stalled, and a period of urban decline, which was to last several hundred years, began.

Medieval cities. A resurgence of urbanization occurred in the 11th century, though scholars are not in agreement about the causes. Rorig summarized the factor most believe led to the rejuvenation of urbanization:

> The medieval town should not be thought of as a small, self-contained unit, but only within the framework of the organic interrelationship of towns. Long distance trade provided the basis on which urban life on a grand scale was founded and prospered. Each town was dependent on another for its functioning. . . .(1971, p. 181)

Long distance trade is generally credited as the factor which inspired medieval urban development and growth. Many medieval cities were reconstructed Roman cities. In other cases, a good situation with respect to trade routes (where a stream was easily forded, at a harbor entrance, or where major roads intersected) was responsible for urban development.

The early medieval city was often a part of the feudal system. Urban residents and rural serfs owed their allegiance to the lord of the region. Through a variety of means a great many people became free of the lord, and over the course of 500 years a well-defined class system developed throughout Europe.

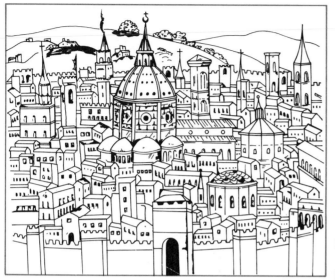

FIGURE 14–3 Florence in the 15th century. (Fritz Rorig, 1967, *The Medieval Town*. London, B. T. Batsford Ltd., p. 29.)

The medieval city was the home of a middle class of merchants, artisans and professional people, the clergy, nobles, and peasants.

Significant differences within classes began to appear during the 13th and 14th centuries. The ***burghers,*** long distance traders, owned property and began to wield great political power. The artisans lived mainly on property they did not own and were dependent upon the upper classes for survival. As Rorig observed, "Nothing could be more mistaken than to assume that in German, French, and English towns of the eleventh or twelfth centuries there was any kind of economic or social equity" (1971, p. 21). Among the key contributions of medieval cities were the development of a complex set of social and economic strata and the emergence of the middle class.

The visitor approaching a medieval city passed through miles of open fields and saw in the distance a city which most often resembled a fortress. Walls, towers, gates, and drawbridges were generally incorporated into urban design (figure 14–3), and are apparent in some European cities today (figure 14–4). Above narrow, winding, poorly paved streets within the city, the upper stories of houses jutted out, because of the need to maximize the use of even the smallest space within the city walls.

Water was often obtained from polluted streams and wells, and all manner of refuse was simply dumped into the street. In this environment it was little wonder that plagues were such a problem. The streets were crowded with people by day, and scavenged by dogs and pigs by night.

A prominent feature of most medieval cities was a market square in the center of the town, where much of the city's economic activity took place.

Medieval urbanization gave rise to the city of the Renaissance in Europe. Gradually key cities became the centers of political control for entire nations. In the 18th century one of the most important events in the urban history of the western world occurred, the ***Industrial Revolution.***

Industrial cities. We have already discussed the underlying causes of the Industrial Revolution. The importance of that period to the evolution of cities is that industrialization lead to a wholly different urban pattern. Preindustrial cities were generally small in land area and population size. Wind and water were used as energy sources, as was human and animal power. Social classes existed, as did a somewhat specialized labor force, and people generally lived in or near their place of work.

Industrial cities featured a new source of energy, the extensive burning of coal. The place of work and residence became separated as factories were developed. A social class of unskilled or semiskilled workers developed. Well-defined districts of both social groups and economic activities evolved within cities. Coal fields, canals, and eventually rail lines became prime factors in the location of cities such as Birmingham, which is at the confluence of two canals in the center of England.

In the century between 1750 and 1850 a major shift in population distribution began to occur: citizens

FIGURE 14–4 The growth of Paris. (From *The Urban Pattern* by A. Gallion and S. Eisner, p. 78. © 1963 by D. Van Nostrand Co., New York.)

Wall A built by Phillip Augustus, Twelfth century
Wall B built by Charles V, Fourteenth century
Wall C built by Louis XIII, Seventeenth century
Wall D built by Louis XV, Eighteenth century
Wall E built by Napoleon III, Nineteenth century

Shaded streets show the Haussmann Programme

Seine River

of industrializing nations started to settle in cities in unprecedented numbers.

The harnessing of an inanimate power source had many ramifications on industrial activity and the ability to transport people and materials. Large industrial complexes were developed to take advantage of the power of steam-driven machines. The Industrial Revolution gave rise to the contemporary western city.

So far we have concentrated on the western city. Urbanization played an important, but somewhat different, part in the development of other cultural systems. A contrast between urban functions in Western Europe and China exemplifies the distinction between the role of the city in each culture.

The role of the city in western Europe and China

Rhodes Murphy delineated fundamental differences between Chinese and Western cities: whereas the Western city functioned primarily as a trade and market center, the Chinese city was primarily an administrative center (1954). Chinese cities were apparently larger and more complex than their European counterparts until the 19th century. It was the commercial expansion of European economic activity, with the city as the heart of trade networks, that thrust European cities into the forefront of world urbanism.

In addition, at least one fundamental geographic element proved advantageous to European development. China was basically isolated from the main stream of world political, social, and economic activity. The process of the diffusion of innovation and information was therefore a much greater factor in the development of European cities than in Chinese cities.

In each cultural system, cities play an integral and varied part in development and modernization. We have examined, in a broad overview, urbanization from the origins of cities to the city of the Industrial Revolution. The Industrial Revolution sets the stage for

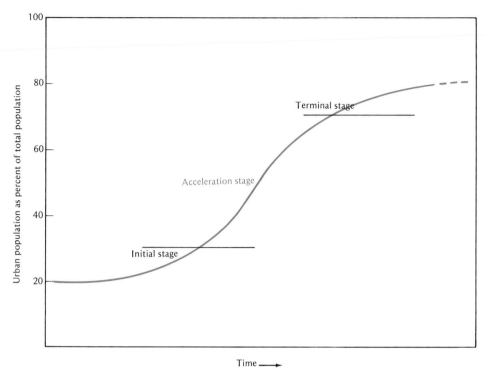

FIGURE 14–5 The urbanization curve and the stages of urbanization. (Ray M. Northam, *Urban Geography*, 2nd ed. Copyright © 1978 by John Wiley & Sons, Inc., p. 53. Reprinted by permission of John Wiley & Sons, Inc.)

the patterns of urbanization in our world today. Before we discuss the nature of the post–Industrial Revolution North American city, it is important to realize the true extent to which we live in an urban world. We shall see the dynamics of city development in a review of the process of urbanization and regional examination of urban demography.

RECENT URBANIZATION: REGIONAL COMPARISONS AND CONTRASTS

The population of the world as a whole has been increasing rapidly, but the increase of the urban population has taken place even more rapidly. An analysis of recent urbanization shows a three-stage process (figure 14–5). In the *initial stage,* the population is primarily rural, engaged in agricultural pursuits, and dispersed. In the second stage, or the *acceleration stage,* an increasingly larger share of the population lives in urban centers, and there is a marked redistribution of the population, with the urban component rising from under 25 percent to over 70 percent of the total population (Northam, 1978, p. 35). This stage also involves a basic restructuring of the economy which concentrates economic activity in the city. Large numbers of people are employed in manufacturing industries and service and trade activities.

The final stage in the urbanization process is referred to as the *terminal stage.* The urban population is approximately 60 to 70 percent of the total population. Above 70 percent, the urbanization curve tends to flatten out; for example, the urbanization curve for England and Wales since 1900 has flattened above the 80-percent level.

A worldwide regional analysis of urbanization shows the world's nations in various urbanization stages. Generally, the developed nations are in the terminal stage, and the developing nations are in the acceleration stage, although some largely agarian nations could be considered in the initial stage.

The primate city

The regularity between the sizes of cities and their rank was noted as early as 1913 by Auerbach. A common factor in the regularity of cities is that one city, the **primate city,** is usually much larger and more powerful than the rest. Not only does the primate city have the largest population, but it usually dominates the nation with respect to most commercial, industrial, educational, and political concerns (Jefferson, 1939). The primate city is commonly at least twice as large as the next largest city and usually more than twice as significant.

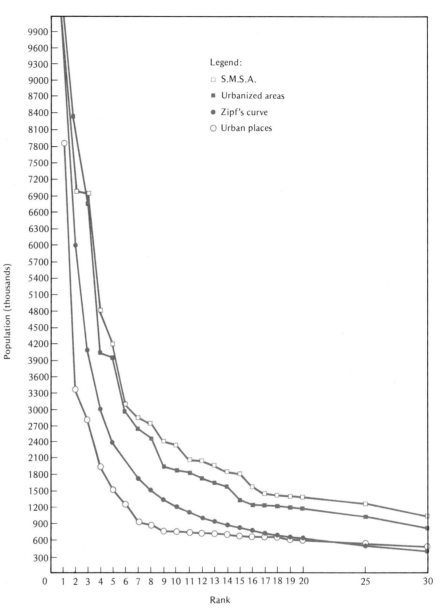

FIGURE 14–6 City size and rank in the United States, 1970, compared with Zipf's theoretical curve. (U.S. Bureau of the Census, 1971, *1970 Census of Population,* "Number of Inhabitants: United States Summary," PG(1)–Al. Washington, D.C., U.S. Government Printing Office, pp. 87, 120, and 189.)

The concept of the relationship between the rank and size of cities was formalized by G. K. Zipf in the *rank-size rule* (1949). It can be stated in the following equation:

$$P_r = P_l / r$$

where P_r is the population of a city of rank r, P_l is the population of the largest city, and r is the rank of a given city. Comparisons can be made between Zipf's ideal curve and United States cities, urbanized areas, and Standard Metropolitan Statistical Areas (figure 14–6). According to Zipf, deviations from the curve

are indicative of improper balance in the patterns of urbanization.

The rank-size ideas of Zipf and the primate city concept of Jefferson are used in international comparisons of the primary rate—the population of the largest city compared with that of the second largest city. As Thomlinson noted,

Countries with high primacy rates tend to be characterized by a low percent urban, low income, and recent political or economic dependency on another country; almost always the primate city is the national capital. . . . Most industrial countries have

A

B

Urban housing is rapidly growing in Third World cities. Many people are forced to live in this type of environment. (A) El Salvador. (World Bank Photo by Jaime Martin, 1975) (B) Rio de Janeiro, Brazil. (United Nations/John Littlewood, 1974)

303

San Salvador, El Salvador. Urban housing: where many children live and play. (World Bank Photos by Jaime Martin, 1975)

moderate or low primacy rates, generally traceable to strong pressures toward regionalism. (1976)

URBANIZATION IN DEVELOPING COUNTRIES

The growth of large cities is a well-recognized characteristic of the developed nations, but most people do not realize that urbanization in the developing countries is equally strong. The shift of people from the farm to the city has enormous consequences. Because of overcrowding and lack of jobs in the rural areas, families leave the poverty-stricken countryside with the hope of making a livelihood in the city. Unfortunately, in many cases jobs are equally difficult to find in the cities, and the result has been unemployment and growing slums in urban areas. Robert S. McNamara,

Unidad Kennedy in Mexico City. Urban housing is one method of attacking urban problems. (Hilda Bijur for World Bank, 1970.

then President of the World Bank, has commented on the problems of the developing countries with regard to urbanization.

> To understand urban poverty in the developing world, one must first understand what is happening to the cities themselves. They are growing at a rate unprecedented in history. Twenty-five years ago there were 16 cities in the developing countries with populations of one million or more. Today there are over 60. Twenty-five years from now there will be more than 200. (Population Reference Bureau, 1976, p. 17)

How has this happened? It is, of course, a function of rapid population growth in the less developed countries, but it is more than simply that. An analysis of population growth shows that, although the total population in these countries is growing at about 2.5 percent, the population of urban areas is growing at nearly twice that rate. Approximately one-half of urban growth is due to migration from the rural areas.

These figures imply that cities in the less developed countries will find it increasingly difficult to provide decent living conditions and employment for the hundreds of millions of new urbanites. According to Robert McNamara,

> An even more ominous implication is what the penalties of failure may be. Historically, violence and civil upheaval are more common in cities than in the countryside. Frustrations that fester among the urban poor are readily exploited by political extremists. If cities do not begin to deal more constructively with poverty, poverty may well begin to deal more destructively with cities. (Population Reference Bureau, 1976)

Current patterns

Prior to 1975 the majority of the world's urban population was located in what the United Nations calls the *more developed* nations. However, since 1975, according to U.N. estimates, there has been a shift; presently the majority of urban residents live in the developing countries (United Nations, 1975). This pattern is expected to accentuate; between 1950 and 2000 estimates are that the urban population in the developing countries will have increased eight-fold, compared with the urban population of the developed countries of 2.4 times. By the end of this century approximately two-thirds of the world's 3.1 billion urban residents will be located in the developing countries; by comparison, in 1950 only one-third of the urban population resided in developing countries. At the end of the century the urban population of developing countries will be close to 41 percent of the total population, compared to less than 16 percent in 1950 (figure 14–7) (Beier, 1976).

In the countries that are now highly urbanized— the leading industrial countries of the developed regions—urbanization proceeded slowly at the begin-

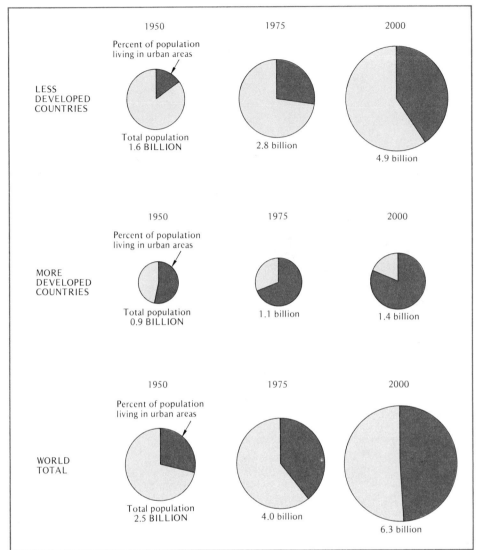

FIGURE 14–7 World Urbanization: 1950, 1975, 2000. Includes Temperate South America, Northern America, Japan, Europe, Australia, New Zealand, and the Soviet Union. (U.N. Population Div., April, 1975, "Trends and Prospects in Urban and Rural Population, 1950–2000, as Assessed in 1973–1974," ESA/P/WP–54. New York, United Nations, Table C, medium variant. As found in G. Beier, September, 1976, "Can Third World Countries Cope?" in *Population Bulletin* 31. Courtesy of the Population Reference Bureau, Inc., Washington, D.C.)

ning of the development process, then rose sharply in the beginning stages of industrialization, and finally tapered off when a saturation point was reached. Because of the relatively low rate of urbanization in Europe, the emergence of new political, social, and economic institutions kept pace with the urban influx. Urban growth in the developing countries is taking place under much more difficult conditions. Several important differences have resulted in rapid and dramatic urban growth, as outlined in a Population Reference Bureau study (Beier, 1976):

1. The increase in population growth in the 20th century is the single most important factor distinguishing present from past urbanization. Population growth rates in Europe during its period of urbanization were 0.5 percent a year,

whereas in the developing countries today, population growth rates are from 2 to 3 percent. These significantly higher growth rates mean that the developing countries have both a larger natural population increase within their cities and a larger absolute population movement to their cities.

2. Because of widespread communication facilities, people in the developing countries are provided more information about urban amenities and opportunities. Also, the cost of migration is cheaper because of better means of transportation.

3. Unlike the urbanization experience of most of the developed countries, urbanization taking place in the developing countries is confined within

relatively fixed territorial boundaries; there is little chance for people to move to other countries.

In total, these factors mean that developing countries will find it much more difficult to urbanize than did the developed countries and will have to accomplish the task in a shorter time. Although there certainly will be country-by-country differences, approximately one-half of the residents of these cities will have been born there. These urbanites will most likely be relatively poor, unskilled laborers.

India is a case in point. In 1951 India was 11-percent urbanized, a level reached by many European countries between 1850 and 1900. At this point slightly over one-half of the population of European countries derived their livelihood from agriculture, whereas two-thirds of India's population were agriculturalists. Approximately 10 percent of India's population was engaged in manufacturing, whereas about one-fourth of Europe's labor force was already engaged in manufacturing (Westebbe, 1970).

Although there is a common thread of rapid urban growth in the developing countries, there are considerable differences between countries in the extent of future urban growth and in the resources to deal with such growth. The Population Reference Bureau looked ahead over the next 25 years and identified four patterns of urbanization (table 14−1) (Beier, 1976).

Type 1. Those countries in which urbanization is well under way are included in this category. There is little pressure on natural resources and arable land and relatively high per capita incomes. They are more than one-half urban now, and most of their populations will live in urban areas by the end of this century, when the urbanization process will decline. This description fits most of Latin America (Daland, 1969; Rabinowitz and Trueblood, 1971).

Type 2. The urbanization process is more recent in these countries. Incomes in these areas are relatively low, and there is often a shortage of arable land. Over one-half of the population reside in rural areas. If re-

TABLE 14−1 Urbanization patterns in selected developing countries

| Country | Per capita GNP level (in 1972 U.S.$) | Size of population (in millions) | | | | Percentage of population that is urban | | Compound growth rate of urban population | | Compound growth rate of rural population | |
| | | 1975 | | 2000 | | | | | | | |
		Urban	Rural	Urban	Rural	1975	2000	1970–75	1990–2000	1970–75	1990–2000
Type 1											
Argentina	1290	20.3	5.1	29.3	3.6	60.0	89.2	2.0	1.2	-1.1	-1.6
Mexico	750	37.4	21.8	103.6	28.7	63.2	78.3	4.6	3.8	1.3	0.9
Colombia	400	16.0	9.9	40.4	11.1	61.8	78.4	4.8	3.2	0.9	0.2
Brazil	530	65.2	44.5	162.2	50.3	59.5	76.3	4.5	3.3	0.8	0.3
Type 2											
Algeria	430	8.4	8.4	26.0	10.7	49.9	70.8	5.7	3.9	1.0	0.7
Egypt	240	17.9	19.6	41.5	23.1	47.7	64.3	3.9	3.1	1.2	0.4
Korea	310	16.1	17.9	36.0	16.0	45.9	67.0	4.8	2.5	-0.1	-0.6
Philippines	220	16.0	28.5	45.6	47.1	36.0	50.9	4.8	3.9	2.7	1.2
Malaysia	430	3.6	8.4	9.9	12.1	30.2	45.1	4.7	3.5	2.2	0.8
Type 3											
Senegal	260	1.3	3.2	3.5	4.7	28.4	42.7	4.1	4.1	1.8	1.4
Ivory Coast	340	1.0	3.9	3.7	5.9	20.4	38.7	6.5	4.8	1.7	1.8
Nigeria	130	11.4	51.5	40.9	94.0	18.2	30.3	5.0	5.2	2.2	2.4
Sudan	120	2.4	15.9	8.9	30.0	13.2	22.9	5.5	5.1	3.0	2.9
Kenya	170	1.5	11.8	6.4	24.6	11.3	20.7	6.1	5.8	3.0	2.9
Upper Volta	70	0.5	5.6	1.7	9.2	8.3	15.7	5.2	4.9	2.1	2.0
Type 4											
Pakistan	130	19.0	51.6	62.3	84.6	26.9	42.4	5.3	4.4	2.4	1.5
India	110	131.7	481.4	342.1	717.2	21.5	32.3	3.7	3.7	2.1	1.2
Indonesia	90	26.2	109.8	74.7	162.8	19.3	31.4	4.7	3.9	2.2	1.2
China, People's Republic of	170	196.9	641.9	414.1	733.8	23.5	36.1	3.3	2.9	1.2	-0.4

Sources: U.N. Population Division, "Trends and Prospects in Urban and Rural Population, 1950–2000, as Assessed in 1973–1974," ESA/P/WP−54 (New York: United Nations, April 25, 1975); World Bank *Atlas*, 1974.

Rio de Janeiro, Brazil. (United Nations, 1953)

source restraints can be overcome and population pressures eased, it is possible for these countries to be as urbanized by the year 2000 as Type 1 countries are today.

This category includes the semi-industrialized nations of North Africa and East Asia (Renaud, 1974). A continued successful development of these nations, because of their limited natural resources in most areas, will depend largely upon slowing the population growth.

Type 3. The third type of urbanization pattern is typical of the nations of sub-Saharan Africa (Kuper, 1965). Recent urban growth in these countries—incipient manufacturing and other productive activities—has been the result of large differences in the income levels of the rural and urban areas. Agriculture will probably continue to absorb the growing number of people in the rural areas because of the relative abundance of land. By the year 2000 these countries will still be predominantly rural. The urbanization process will be more manageable than in other less developed countries because of the relatively small size of the urban population.

Type 4. The final type of urbanization pattern is found in the large countries of Asia: Indonesia, India, Bangladesh, Pakistan, and the People's Republic of

China (Bose, 1974). By the year 2000, if present trends continue, these countries will still be dominated by large and growing rural populations living in absolute poverty. However, urban population will continue to grow; for example, India's urban population is estimated to increase by 210 million people between 1975 and 2000, compared with a rural increase of 236 million, without allowing for any substantial push out of rural areas.

Unlike other countries in this category, the People's Republic of China appears to be managing a decline in population growth rates with migration to urban areas and at the same time bringing about an increase in income and a more equitable distribution.

Cities in developing countries

An analysis of individual cities in the developing countries shows that many are already as large as the major cities of the developed regions, and in a few years they will be considerably larger. The projected size of several cities in developing countries at the end of this century, as well as four major cities in developed countries, is estimated in table 14–2. Some interesting contrasts are shown; for example, if the current growth rate of 4.4 percent continues, Mexico City will be the

TABLE 14−2   Populations of selected urban areas (in millions)

Urban area	1950	Average annual rate of growth (percent)	1975	Average annual rate of growth (percent)	2000
Developing countries					
Type 1					
Mexico City	2.9	5.4	10.9	4.4	31.6
Buenos Aires	4.5	2.9	9.3	1.6	14.0
Sao Paulo	2.5	5.7	10.0	3.9	26.0
Rio de Janeiro	2.9	4.4	8.3	3.5	19.4
Bogota	0.7	6.5	3.4	4.2	9.5
Type 2					
Cairo	2.4	4.3	6.9	3.5	16.4
Seoul	1.0	8.3	7.3	3.8	18.7
Manila	1.5	4.4	4.4	4.3	12.7
Type 3					
Kinshasa	0.2	9.7	2.0	6.2	9.1
Lagos	0.3	8.1	2.1	6.2	9.4
Type 4					
Shanghai	5.8	2.6	10.9	2.3	19.2
Peking	2.2	5.6	8.5	3.3	19.1
Jakarta	1.6	5.1	5.6	4.5	16.9
Calcutta	4.4	2.4	8.1	3.6	19.7
Bombay	2.9	3.7	7.1	4.0	19.1
Karachi	1.0	6.2	4.5	5.2	15.9
Developed countries					
New York	12.3	1.3	17.0	1.3	22.2
London	10.2	0.2	10.7	0.7	12.7
Paris	5.4	2.1	9.2	1.2	12.3
Tokyo	6.7	3.9	17.3	1.7	26.4

Source: U.N. Population Division, "Trends and Prospects in the Populations of Urban Agglomerations, 1950−2000, as Assessed in 1973−1975," ESA/P/WP−58 (New York: United Nations, November 21, 1975, Table C).

world's largest urban area by the year 2000, with 31.6 million inhabitants. It is interesting to note that in 1950 Mexico City, with 2.9 million, was less than one-fourth the size of New York City. The next largest city in the year 2000 will be Sao Paulo with 26.0 million people. Sao Paulo will be more than twice the size of London, although in 1975 these two cities had almost the same number of inhabitants, 10.0 and 10.7 million, respectively.

There will be a continued concentration of people in the larger cities of both the developed and the developing countries (figure 14−8). Cities with more than 5 million inhabitants will undergo the most rapid increases, particularly in the developing countries.

Most of the increase in urban population will occur through the expansion of existing cities. There will be few new cities, except where new resources are discovered. Because most choice urban locations are already taken, and because it is less costly to expand these areas than develop new cities, there is little likelihood that many new urban centers will develop.

Migration impact

A significant aspect of urban growth is the migration of people from the rural areas. The significance of this rural to urban migration varies over time and from country to country. In Latin America and other areas that

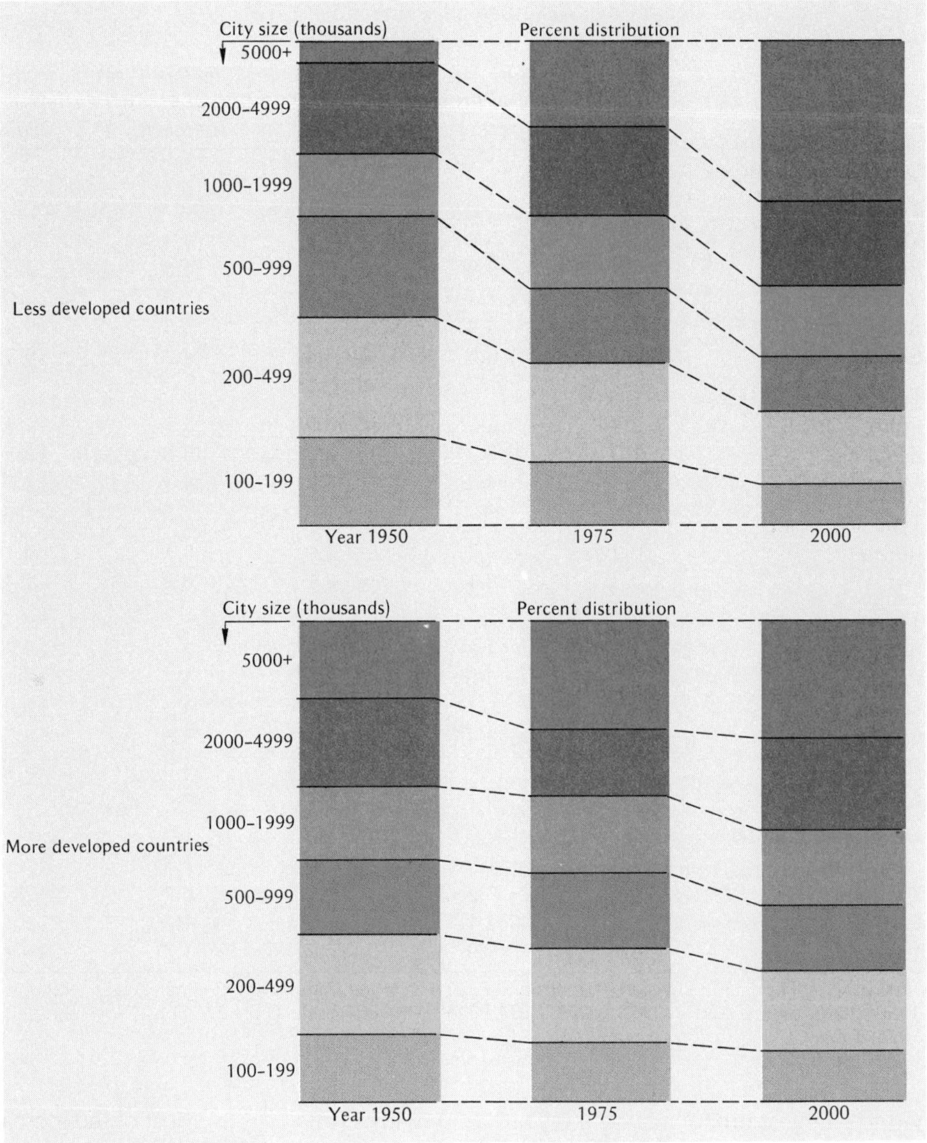

FIGURE 14–8 Population distribution in cities over 100,000 in 1970: 1950, 1975, 2000. (U.N. Population Div., November, 1975, "Trends and Prospects in the Populations of Urban Agglomerations, 1950–2000, as Assessed in 1973–1975," ESA/P/WP–58. New York, United Nations, Table C. As found in G. Beier, September, 1976, "Can Third World Cities Cope?" in *Population Bulletin* 31. Courtesy of the Population Reference Burea, Inc., Washington, D.C.)

already have a significant proportion of their populations living in urban areas, there will most likely be a decline in rural to urban migration in another decade. However, in those nations that are largely rural, like many of sub-Saharan Africa, migration will continue to play a key role in urban growth and distribution patterns for some time.

The reasons people migrate are many and varied, but the economic motive seems to predominate. In most cases, the expectations of economic improvement held by migrants are met: migrants who stay in cities do seem to be better off. Immediate employment is not found by everyone, but a large fraction of mi-

grants find jobs in a reasonably short period. Even for the unskilled, incomes are higher, and many who start out in relatively undesirable jobs manage to find better ones in time (Yap, 1975).

Although migrants come from varying cultural and socioeconomic environments, they are remarkably similar in many respects. On the whole they have little education, although they do have a higher average education than nonmigrants, and they are typically young, under 30.

Migration flows are an important variable in explaining why large cities in developing countries are growing relatively faster than the medium-sized and

Singapore—a target for migration from rural areas. (World Bank Photo by Edwin G. Huffman, 1975)

smaller cities. An interesting pattern of movement has occurred. Migration is often a two- or three-step move, from the rural areas to small local cities and then to urban areas. This step-migration occurs primarily during the early stages of the urbanization process. However, evidence suggests that migrants are increasingly bypassing the smaller cities and moving directly to urban areas. There are several reasons for this pattern. First, better economic opportunities are available in the larger cities. Second, with improved communication and transportation facilities, it is easier for prospective migrants to obtain more accurate information about a place and thus lower the risks of resettlement. Third, friends and relatives of prospective migrants are sources of support and information; when an urban area contains a large proportion of a nation's total population (15 to 20 percent), it is likely that a potential migrant will have a friend or relative living there.

Urban population trends in Latin America

The per-capita economic growth rate and the rate of population growth during the past decade have been higher in Latin America than in any other developing region of the world. The growth rate of the population has been 3 percent per year, yielding a doubling time of 23 years. This demographic expansion has had serious implications for urbanization in Latin America.

Over the past several decades, Latin American urban populations have increased rapidly (figure 14–9). According to a recent study by the Inter-American Development Bank, "Every year Latin America accumulates the equivalent of a city of seven million people in its aggregate urban centers, while the rural population expands by 1.5 million people" (Fox, 1975). The rapid rate of population increase and the exodus of people from rural to urban areas are the principle demographic trends today. They are important factors in reshaping the social, economic, and demographic fabric of Latin American countries, and their impact is felt most heavily in the medium-sized and large cities.

Much of the population increase in urban areas has taken place since 1950 and is the result of two mutually reinforcing factors: the rate of population increase has been largely due to rapidly declining mortality and a consistently high birth rate, and there has been a steady movement of people from rural to urban areas.

In 6000 years—literally the blink of an eye over the age of the earth—world society has moved from hunting and gathering and primitive agriculture to modern urban society. Urbanization goes hand-in-hand with the process of modernization. The elements of human cultural systems described throughout the preceding chapters of this book are all reflected in the urban world of today.

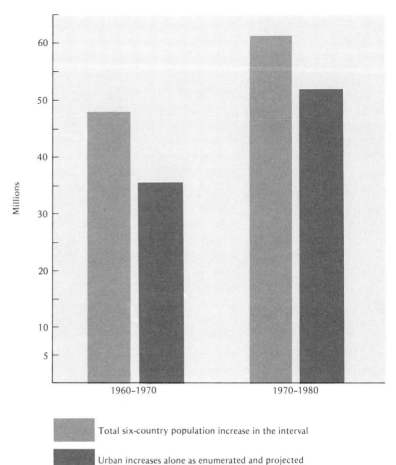

FIGURE 14–9 Regional population growth trends: Argentina, Brazil, Chile, Mexico, Peru, Venezuela. (Robert W. Fox, 1975, *Urban Population Growth Trends in Latin America*. Washington, D.C., Inter-American Development Bank, p. ii.)

Total six-country population increase in the interval

Urban increases alone as enumerated and projected

KEY TERMS

Formal city
Functional city
Urbanism
Urbanization
Standard Metropolitan Statistical Area (SMSA)
Hydraulic civilization
City-states
Polis

Olympia
Delphi
Cos
Burghers
Industrial Revolution
Industrial city
Primate city

REFERENCES

Auerback, F. (1913), "Das Gesetz der Bevolkerungskozentration," Petermann's Mitteilugen 59.

Beier, G. (1976), "Can Third World Cities Cope?" *Population Bulletin*. 31. Washington, D.C.: Population Reference Bureau, 4.

Bose, A. (1974), *Studies in India's Urbanization 1901–1971*. New Delhi: Tata McGraw–Hill Publishing Co.

Childe, V. G. (1954), "Early Forms of Society," in Singer, C., et al. (eds.), *A History of Technology, Vol. I*. Oxford: Clarenden Press/Oxford University Press.

Childe, V. G. (1957), "Civilization, Cities and Towns," *Antiquity* 31, 36–38.

Daland, R. (1969), *Comparative Urban Research.* Beverly Hills, CA: Sage Publications, Inc.

Davis, K. (1965), "The Urbanization of the Human Population," *Scientific American* 213, 43.

Fox, R. (1975), *Urban Population Growth Trends in Latin America.* Washington, D.C.: Inter-American Development Bank.

Jefferson, M. (1939), "The Law of the Primate City," *Geographical Review* 29, 226–232.

Johnson, J. (1967), *Urban Geography.* New York: Pergamon Press, Inc.

Kuper, H. (1965), *Urbanization and Migration in West Africa.* Los Angeles: University of California Press.

McNamara, Robert S. (See Population Reference Bureau, below.)

Murphy, R. (1954), "The City as a Center of Change: Western Europe and China," *Annals of the Association of American Geographers* 24, 349–362.

Northam, R. (1978), *Urban Geography,* 2nd ed. New York: John Wiley & Sons, Inc.

Population Reference Bureau (1976), *World Population Growth and Response 1965–1975.* Washington, D.C.: Population Reference Bureau.

Rabinowitz, F. and Trueblood, F. (1971), *Latin American Urban Research,* Vol. 1. Beverly Hills, CA: Sage Publications, Inc.

Renaud, B. (1974), "The Evolution of the Urban System in Korea, 1910–1970," *Bulletin of the Population and Development Center* 3. Seoul: Seoul National University.

Rorig, F. (1971), *The Medieval Town.* Berkeley, CA: University of California Press.

Sjoberg, G. (1960), *The Pre-Industrial City.* New York: Free Press.

Thomlinson, R. (1976), *Population Dynamics,* 2nd ed. New York: Random House, Inc.

U.N. Population Division (1975), *Trends and Prospects in Urban Rural Population, 1950–2000.* New York: United Nations, ESA/P/WP.54.

Westebbe, R. (1970), "Urbanization Problems and Prospects," *Finance and Development* 7.

Wheatly, P. (1971), *The Pivot of the Four Quarters.* Chicago: Aldine Publishing Co.

Wittfogel, K. (1956), "The Hydraulic Civilizations," in Thomas, W. L., Jr., et al. (eds.), *Man's Role in Changing the Face of the Earth.* Chicago: University of Chicago Press, 152–164.

Yap, L. (1975), "Internal Migration in Less Developed Countries: A Survey of the Literature," *World Bank Staff Working Paper* No. 215.

Zipf, G. K. (1949), *Human Behavior and the Principle of Least Effort.* Reading, MA: Addison-Wesley Publishing Co., Inc.

15

The urban environment

In this chapter we present a general overview of the form and functioning of cities. We explore two methods of urban analysis: the city as a system unto itself and the city as a component in a system of cities. The distinction between the city as a system and the system of cities will become clear as we proceed.

Once again the reader must be mindful of the city-forming processes discussed throughout this volume. We are simply focusing the phenomena involved in modernization on the city in this chapter.

Introduction

Diversity is the keystone of the study of cities; urban analysts question whether or not there is an order to such diversity. People observing the city note the physical form, the buildings, roads, parks, unique neighborhoods, and so on, but are often unaware of the processes which are taking place before their eyes. The same intellectual, political, economic, social, and psychological elements which we have described as the basis of cultural systems are, in microcosm, interacting to give form to the city. The question is, how does one make sense of this complexity of interrelationships? We need a special approach if the city is to be understood: an ecologist could never begin to describe or explain a tropical rainforest without a highly systematic method of illustrating the manner in which diverse variables interact to form the forest, and those studying urban areas cannot effectively deal with the city without a similar systematic approach.

Consider for a moment a forest. A person wishing to understand this biosystem looks not only at the physical features, such as the forms of vegetation, but explores the processes which created those features as well. The locations of the elements of the forest ecosystem are not the result of chance occurrences but the products of a systematic sequence of events. The local landforms, soils, and plant and animal communities must be examined, and the local patterns of weather and climate must be considered. Human influences should also be reviewed to complete the ecosystem. Noted physical geographers Alan and Arthur Strahler have described the importance of the systems concept to ecological study:

> A systems approach is concerned with interrelationships, unification and the flow of matter and energy. . . . with this approach the significance of an item can be grouped more readily if its place in a system can be discovered. A knowledge of the workings of a system often explains the inevitability of certain results. (1973)

The use of the systems methodology allows us to study the interrelations between the variables which create the forest. The same technique can be applied to our study of the city.

A casual glance at the physical form of the city produces the same impression of structures as did the first look at the forest. The components of the urban system, often referred to as the *urban ecosystem,* interact like the elements of the biological system. Instead of the interrelationships between the atmosphere, hy-

Downtown Manhattan, New York City. (United Nations/Jan Ralph, 1975)

drosphere, biosphere, and lithosphere needed to create the forest, the urban scholar studies the manner in which economic, social, political, and decision making processes work together to produce a city. The systems approach to urban analysis allows the discovery of how each part of the process affects the others. The city is viewed as a living organism, a dynamic place with a vitality causing growth and allowing decay, just as the forest.

A second approach to urban study undertaken in this chapter considers the city in its place within a system of cities. The urban ecosystem allows us to study the internal structure of the city, whereas the systems of cities method places each city in a country, or even the world, in the perspective of its relationships to other larger and smaller cities.

ELEMENTS OF THE URBAN ECOSYSTEM

In discussing the dynamics of urban growth, James E. Vance, Jr., identified several stages of **urban evolution** (1966). Together they provide a sound framework for our study of cities. Among them are inception, exclusion, segregation, extension, replication and readjustment, and redevelopment. Vance was focusing on the

downtown or central business district (CBD); however, these stages serve to tell the story of the city in general.

The process of *inception* refers to the factor which gives rise to a city in a particular place. It may be that transportation, such as we find with a port city like New York or New Orleans, or resources, or climate formed the impetus for urban location, such as Palm Springs, California. An examination of the basic processes of economic activity may provide a clue to the reasons for urban settlement in a given place. We often use the terms *mining town, mill town, agricultural service center,* or *fishing village* to describe cities. They indicate the types of activities which help support cities and perhaps were responsible for their initial location.

Exclusion is the pattern of forcing activities out of an area. The costs of rent in the central business district may be so high that many activities can not locate there; a large supermarket may be excluded from a location in the central business district because of a combination of its need for a large area and the relatively lower return per square foot of floor space.

Segregation is much like association: similar industries may tend to locate in a particular area. For example, Vance observed that, "In New York we find the stock exchange on Wall Street, the ship company area on Park Row, advertising several miles away on Madison Avenue, and corporate headquarters, other than those noted, on Park Avenue'' (1966, p. 116). Segregation is the process through which separate functional districts, those identified with a particular set of goods or services, come about.

Innovations in transportation produced the process of extension. As the term implies, *extension* is the outward, often radial, movement of activities from the center. This phenomenon became an important part of urban development following the beginning of the 20th century.

The large suburban shopping centers and malls are examples of the occurrence of *replication and readjustment*. The downtown area of most cities was generally the center of retail sales activity. As the urban-to-suburban population shift has taken place during the past 40 years, many activities have shifted from central city to suburban locations, as evidenced by suburban shopping centers. As a consequence of this movement, the downtown areas of many cities have had to readjust from their traditional functions in an attempt to maintain economic and social viability. In turn, attempts at revitalizing downtowns have become commonplace.

The final element in Vance's progression is *redevelopment*. It implies physical transformation—an altering of the morphology of the city which reflects changing functions. This may result from the conversion of one type of commercial activity to another, or from the renewal of residential areas within the city.

CASE STUDY:
Urban evolution

The site of the city of San Francisco is rather inhospitable. San Francisco is located on a peninsula which was, at the time of first settlement, basically sand dunes and mud flats with little fresh water or timber. The major advantage of the physical site of San Francisco was its safe harbor. The situation of the city was also not particularly impressive, although a fine river and bay system allowed relatively easy access to the interior of California. There was, however, little to recommend settlement in the Great Central Valley or the Sierra Nevada foothills.

The situation of San Francisco underwent a dramatic change with the discovery of gold in California in 1848. The physical location of the city obviously did not change; however, San Francisco became one of the most important cities in North America almost instantly. Ocean-going ships were often too large to sail into the very shallow San Francisco Bay, so cargo was unloaded at San Francisco and transferred to smaller ships. San Francisco became the "warehouse" for the gold fields (Vance, 1964, pp. 9 – 13).

Following inception, land use exclusion and segregation rapidly occurred, creating specialized districts of economic activity and social groups. As a result, an urban region based on water transportation began to develop around San Francisco Bay. These settlement patterns extended inland with the coming of railroads and railroad towns which began in the 1860's (figure 15 – 1). Inland settlement was expanded as electric interurban and traction rail lines were extended outward from the skeleton of sea and rail transportation (figure 15 – 2).

The transportation network that facilitated settlement became even more extensive in the 20th century with the introduction of the automobile. The flexibility of the automobile allowed the urban realm of the San Francisco Bay Area to greatly expand (figure 15 – 3). This expansion has caused major readjustments in the function of the San Francisco central business district, which

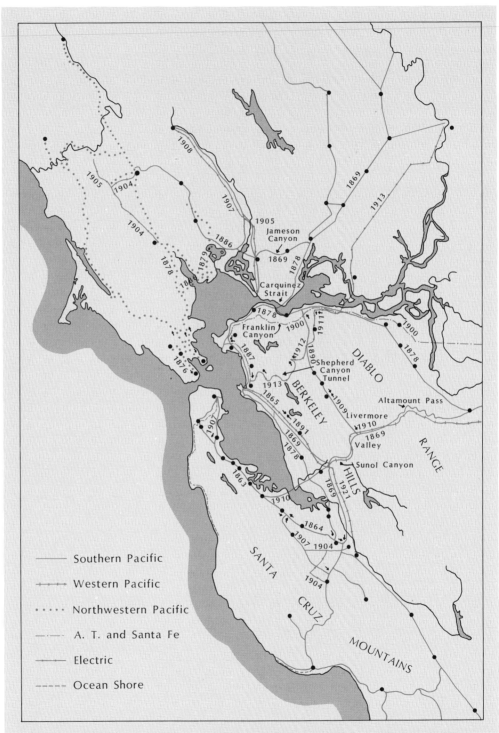

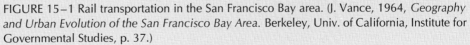

FIGURE 15–1 Rail transportation in the San Francisco Bay area. (J. Vance, 1964, *Geography and Urban Evolution of the San Francisco Bay Area*. Berkeley, Univ. of California, Institute for Governmental Studies, p. 37.)

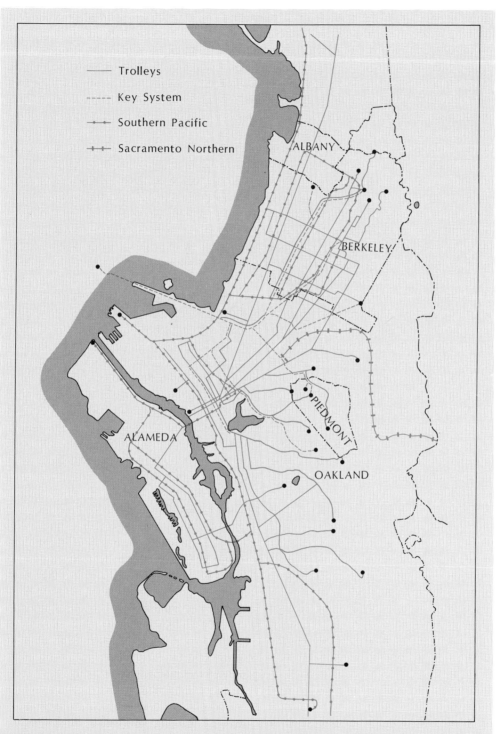

FIGURE 15–2 Small rail systems in the eastern Bay area. (J. Vance, 1964, *Geography and Urban Evolution of the San Francisco Bay Area*. Berkeley, Univ. of California, Institute for Governmental Studies, p. 49.)

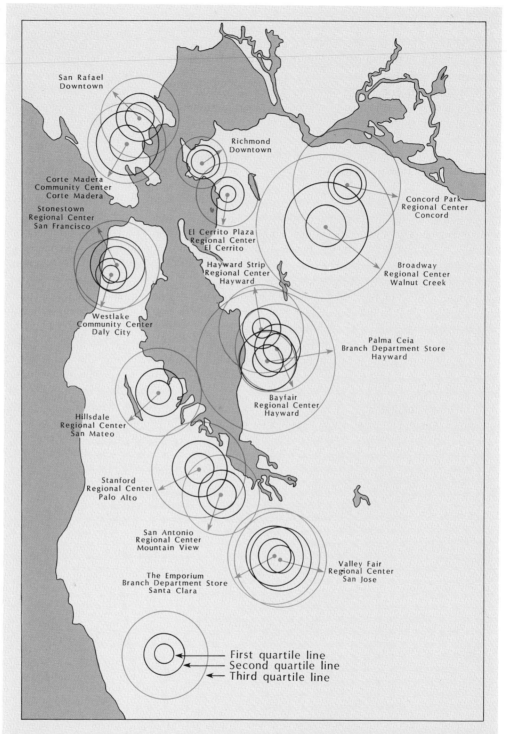

FIGURE 15–3 Urban realms of the San Francisco area, as indicated by major shopping facilities. The three concentric circles centered on each facility enclose the residence of the nearest quarter of its customers, the nearer half, and the nearer three-quarters, respectively. Thus, the space between successive circles indicates the density of customer residence. (J. Vance, 1964, *Geography and Urban Evolution of the San Francisco Bay Area.* Berkeley, Univ. of California, Institute for Governmental Studies, p. 73.)

is currently evolving primarily into a financial center as retail establishments are moving outward.

Vance demonstrated the manner in which transportation encouraged urban expansion. The method of study he used to examine San Francisco could be applied to many cities.

The economic basis of cities

Two terms used to describe the economic activities found within cities are **basic** and **nonbasic**. A basic activity is one which generates a flow of income into the city, so is "basic" to the economic health of the city. Automobile manufacturing in Detroit or steel in Pittsburgh are examples of cities dominated by basic industries. The so-called *nonbasic activities* provide goods and services to residents of the city, rather than people in other regions. The term *nonbasic* should not be confused with nonessential: the nonbasic sector must be present if a city is to function. Grocery stores, barber shops, and local bakeries are examples of nonbasic activities.

Determining the basic-to-nonbasic ratio for cities is a difficult task. Defining what constitutes a basic industry is not as simple as it may seem. It is a fairly straightforward exercise to determine the number of workers at a given automobile manufacturing plant, but

how does one classify the workers who provide the power, water, or services related directly to production from that particular plant? Furthermore, some of the autos are consumed locally, as a walk through downtown Detroit will quickly confirm.

Estimates have been derived to determine the minimum number of workers in different occupational categories for cities of various sizes (figure 15–4). The percentage of the total working population is given on the X axis; the Y axis indicates population size of cities. It is evident that as city size increases, the requirements for service (nonbasic) employment increase relatively slowly (with the exception of professional services). Nonservice (basic) employment categories show a much greater increase in minimum requirements as population increases. Numerical ratios have been computed in an attempt to determine the employment basis of cities. It is difficult, however, to generalize about basic–nonbasic ratios and population size (table 15–1).

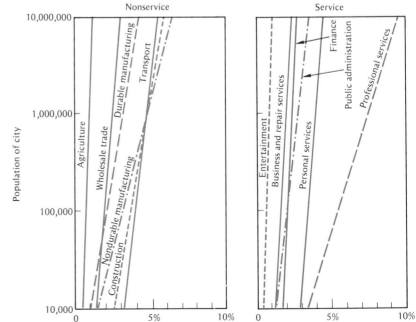

FIGURE 15–4 Minimum requirements for the functioning of cities of different sizes. (E. L. Ullman, M. F. Dacey, 1962, *Symposium in Urban Geography*, International Geographical Union, p. 129.)

TABLE 15–1 The basic/nonbasic ratio of selected U.S. cities

City	Total population	Basic/nonbasic ratio
New York	12,500,000	100 : 215
Detroit	2,900,000	100 : 117
Cincinnati	907,000	100 : 170
Brockton	119,000	100 : 82
Albuquerque	116,000	100 : 103
Madison	110,000	100 : 82
Oshkosh	42,000	100 : 60

Source: J. Alexander, "The Basic/Non-Basic Concept of Urban Economic Function," *Economic Geography* 30, 1954, p. 259.

If such problems exist with determining the basic–nonbasic ratio, why is it computed? In planning for a city's economic growth, basic industries are often those most encouraged to locate in a city; the nonbasic industries will follow. Without a solid base of fundamental nonservice (basic) industries, the economic soundness of a community may be questioned. A knowledge of the basic–nonbasic components of a community is essential by those who promote community growth.

City classification. Employment categories have been used to determine the economic classification of cities. Early studies of city classification used a strict numerical limit to define a manufacturing city or a transport city. Harris used 60 percent of the work force involved in manufacturing as a threshold for the definition of a manufacturing city (1943). If a city were determined to be a retail city, 50 percent of the labor force had been found to work in retailing operations (figure 15–5).

Classification of cities is more than an academic exercise. A knowledge of the relative importance of the basic industries in a given city provides a tool for planning and impact assessment. If a particular manufacturing industry is in a state of decline, an estimate can be made of the effects of that decline on specific cities and urban regions.

The location of economic activities within cities has traditionally been a function of land costs and linkages, the routes of interaction between commercial establishments. The lines along which linkages occur are comprised of communication and transportation systems. Distance is the main determinant of the cost of moving goods or services along a linkage path.

Some industries find it advantageous to cluster within groups of similar industries to share the costs of specialized goods and services. One example is the electronics industry in such cities as Colorado Springs, Houston, and San Jose. In these cities large groupings of electronics firms are found in relatively small areas with all manner of companies producing equipment or developing related technology. This clustering minimizes the distance that materials to be assembled and finished products must travel, which in turn reduces the costs of manufacturing and distributing the particular commodity. One aspect of the process of economic land use segregation is the attraction of industries to competitive industries. Other factors also operate, one of the most important being land value.

One model which summarizes the economic competition for land is the *bid-rent curve* (figure 15–6). The vertical axis represents the cost of land, and the horizontal axis represents the distance from the central business district. Note that land is most valuable at the central business district. Those involved in land use A are willing to bid (pay) more for the land than those practicing land use B. This is true up until point 1, at which land use B bids more at that location than land use A. We therefore have a zone of land use A-type activities near the city center, extending to the point at which land use B becomes predominant. If all else were equal, then we would end up with concentric bands of different land uses.

In a real sense, an activity in the A category might be a financial institution or a specialized retail store. As we move outward from the central business district, we find enterprises which do not find a central location important enough to pay the high costs of prime land. These firms might be nonspecialized retail establishments, wholesalers, or small corporations.

In our model land use C is the next major type of activity. Land use C becomes dominant at the point where the curve for C intercepts the curve for B. In other words at point 2, activity C will pay more for the land than any activity. This category could include a land-intensive business, such as a lumber yard, commercial nursery, or a large supermarket. The bid-rent curve demonstrates a straightforward competition for the use of land. There are several interesting ways in which the principle demonstrated by the bid-rent curve can be applied.

Robert Sinclair suggested that the impacts of land speculation at the edge of the city could be assessed by a device similar to the bid-rent curve. He postulated

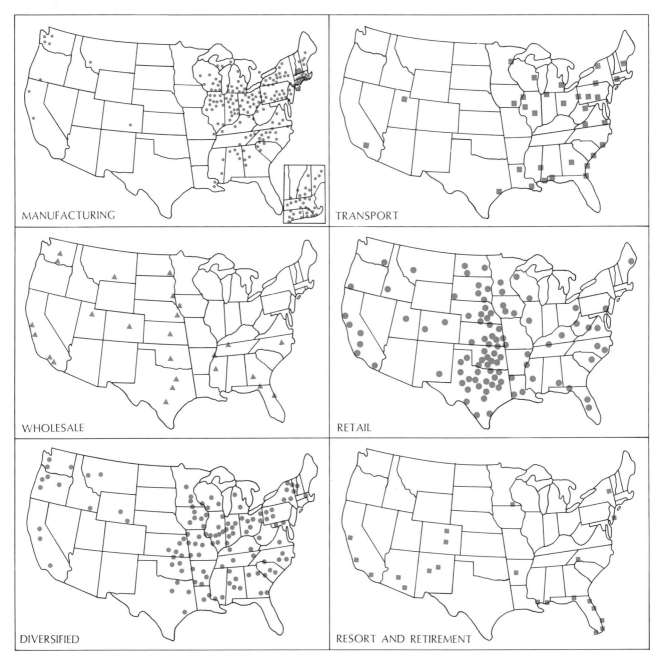

FIGURE 15–5 Functional types of U.S. cities (C. Harris, 1943, "A Functional Classification of Cities in the United States," in the *Geographical Review* 33, p. 92, with the permission of the American Geographical Society.)

that, as land became more valuable at the point where agricultural land was likely to be converted to urban uses, land speculation would occur. This would tend to drive land prices upward and could also create a change in agricultural land use. The person owning land which may undergo a change from agricultural to urban uses would probably not be inclined to invest in crops which were expensive to plant and maintain.

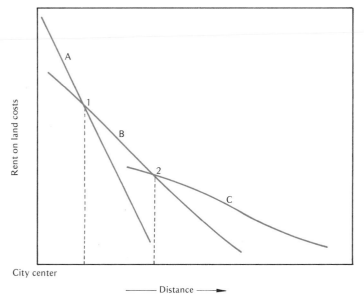

Rent on land costs

City center

———— Distance ————▶

FIGURE 15–6 The bid–rent function.

Thus orchards might be allowed to decline and cereal grains planted. Sinclair modeled his theory on a reverse of the bid-rent curve (figure 15–7). The vertical axis is the value of the land for agriculture, and the horizontal axis distance from the city. Land use A would be agricultural and require low capital or labor input. There is a distance between the city and the curve of land use 1 in which no activity is indicated. This zone would be of speculation so intensive that no real value for agriculture existed. Land use 1 follows this area, and finally land use 2 becomes dominant at point Z. Agricultural practices in the 2 zone could include orchards, vineyards, or specialized crops which might once have been grown in other areas but, due to land speculation, are pushed farther away from the city and suburbs.

The pattern of agricultural land use proposed by Sinclair is the opposite of the spatial organization of agricultural land use predicted by Von Thünen. Recall, however, that Von Thünen was dealing with a rural agricultural area in the 19th century, and Sinclair was studying an area on the fringe of a city in the 20th century. Although Von Thünen and Sinclair based their models on the same underlying theory, economic competition for land, the fact that they obtained such different results should alert us to the importance of the temporal and spatial contexts in which models are applied.

The models which we have introduced can be used to describe the organization of economic activity within cities as well as in the suburbs. These are static models of a very dynamic process, thus we find limitations in their use. Urban models have also been developed to explain the social structure of cities.

The human mosaic

Any discussion of the social organization of cities would be incomplete without the inclusion of three models used to describe the groupings of people within cities.

One of the first attempts to model urban social structure, the **concentric zone model,** was by Robert Park and Ernest Burgess in the second decade of this century. Park was particularly concerned with the concept of human ecology. He reasoned that humans as well as plants and animals competed for space and that the ecological concepts of invasion, succession, and dominance might be used to explain the manner in which people organize themselves in the city.

Following a great deal of study of the city of Chicago, Burgess developed a model of urban social organization consisting of a series of concentric zones (figure 15–8). Burgess termed these areas of the city (I) the central business district, (II) the zone in transition, (III) the zone of independent workers' homes, (IV) the zone of better residences, and (V) the commuters' zone (1928). It is important to note that the zones show continual increase in social and economic status with distance from the central business district.

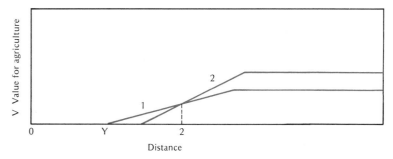

FIGURE 15–7 The Sinclair model. (Reproduced by permission from the *Annals* of the Association of American Geographers, Volume 57, 1967, Robert Sinclair.)

The first zone, the central business district, is the hub of urban economic and cultural life. The zone of transition is an area of deterioration caused by the encroachment of business and industry from Zone I; people moving into Zone II are often immigrants or those with little financial resources. As people began to attain relative wealth, movement from Zone II became possible, and at this point that the concepts of urban ecology become important. As individuals and families moved from Zone II, they "invaded" Zone III. This invasion resulted in displacement of those already in Zone III and left a supply of housing in Zone II for those entering the urban ecosystem—more poor and unskilled, and typically recent immigrants and minorities.

Those moving into a city tended to move into areas which were inhabited by people of similar backgrounds; this was especially true of immigrants. There were two underlying causes for this clustering pattern. First, there was discrimination in housing, whether overt social discrimination or the inability to acquire

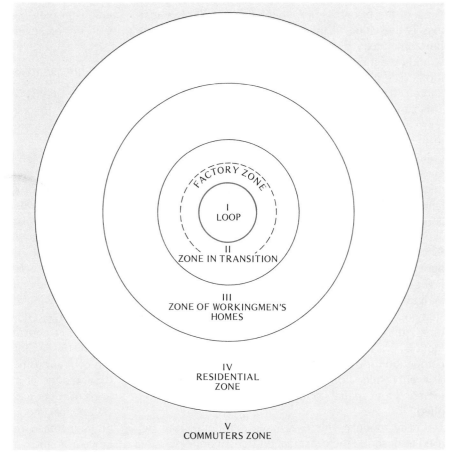

FIGURE 15–8 The Burgess model. (R. Park, E. Burgess, 1925, *The City*. Chicago, Univ. of Chicago Press, p. 19. © 1925, 1967 by The University of Chicago. All rights reserved.)

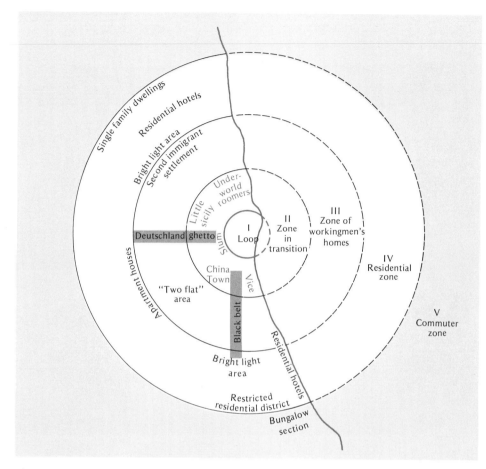

the necessary financial support required in many other areas of the city. A second factor was the understandable inclination to live with people sharing their heritage: imagine moving from a country in which you were the majority to a country in which you suddenly became the minority. In most cases the language, social customs, and way of life are very much different. It is little wonder that an Irish, Italian, or Chinese community in an American city would be appealing to immigrants from those countries. Thus, people concurrently were "pulled" into communities by ethnic ties and were "pushed" into communities by social and economic discrimination.

The results of this community formation process are illustrated in the Burgess model (figure 15–9). As members from these groups began to move from Zone II into Zone III, a process of invasion was initiated. As people were displaced by the invasion and as more members of a particular group entered an area, that group could be said to dominate the community. The Burgess model features a continuous movement of

people within the city striving to relocate outward into the better residential areas. This transition weakened the strength of communities when families reached the outer zones of the city, because social groups became more diffuse.

There have been many criticisms and interpretations of the Burgess model. The fundamental value of this approach to the study of urban social structure is in the ecological analogy used: like an alpine lake which is gradually transformed into a swamp, then a marsh, an area of shrubs and deciduous trees, and finally a forest, the city undergoes such changes. Housing is built and decays, but building continues to take place in other areas and people move constantly; thus invasion and succession, slow evolutionary processes, are constantly occurring.

The mechanism which allows for such a continual transition in housing is referred to as ***filtering:***

> An indirect process for meeting the housing demand of a lower income group. When new quality housing is produced for higher income households, houses

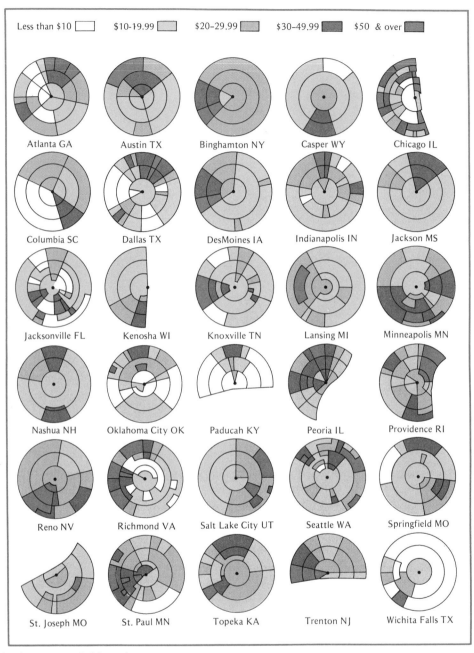

Less than $10 □ $10-19.99 □ $20-29.99 □ $30-49.99 ■ $50 & over ■

Atlanta GA   Austin TX   Binghamton NY   Casper WY   Chicago IL

Columbia SC   Dallas TX   DesMoines IA   Indianapolis IN   Jackson MS

Jacksonville FL   Kenosha WI   Knoxville TN   Lansing MI   Minneapolis MN

Nashua NH   Oklahoma City OK   Paducah KY   Peoria IL   Providence RI

Reno NV   Richmond VA   Salt Lake City UT   Seattle WA   Springfield MO

St. Joseph MO   St. Paul MN   Topeka KA   Trenton NJ   Wichita Falls TX

FIGURE 15–10 The Hoyt model of urban residential patterns. (H. Hoyt, 1939, *The Structure and Growth of Residential Neighborhoods in American Cities*. Washington, D.C., U.S. Government Printing Office, p. 17.)

given up by these households become available to the lower income group. (Smith, 1964, p. 1)

The process of filtering is a basic component in the sector theory of urban social structure proposed by Homer Hoyt. Hoyt's model is often used as an alternative to the Burgess model, but as we shall see it is really a refinement of the concentric zone model. Hoyt criticized the Burgess model on several counts. He maintained that widespread use of the automobile would

vastly distort the concentric zone patterns. He further charged that rents do not always increase with distance, and that, "It is not true that one progresses from dilapidated dwellings in the center to an encircling belt of mansions at all points on the periphery of the city (1939, p. 23).

Simple geometry will illustrate another problem of the concentric zone model. Consider the amount of space in the commuter zone and areas of higher social

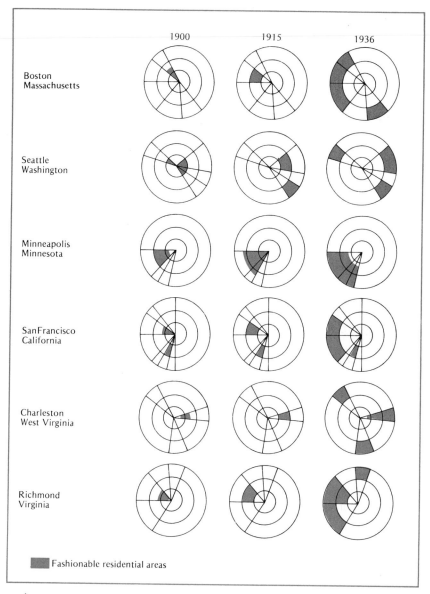

1900 1915 1936

Boston
Massachusetts

Seattle
Washington

Minneapolis
Minnesota

SanFrancisco
California

Charleston
West Virginia

Richmond
Virginia

■ Fashionable residential areas

FIGURE 15–11 Changing locations of fashionable residential areas. (H. Hoyt, 1939, *The Structure and Growth of Residential Neighborhoods in American Cities*. Washington, D.C., U.S. Government Printing Office, p. 17.)

and economic status. Far more urban land is devoted to these activities than to any other land use in the city. This proportion of high status residential areas does not occur in many cities.

Hoyt answers these criticisms with a pattern of urban form which incorporates sectors into concentric zones (figure 15–10). The **sector model** is predicated on the notion that high rent areas are found in wedge shapes and extend out in sectors along radial lines from the city center to the periphery. High rent areas dictate much of the other urban social structure in this model. It is assumed that areas of slightly less social status will be juxtaposed to the high rent areas, and in turn a pro-

gression of areas of slightly lower housing value will be found in sectors as one moves away from the rich. The locations of the areas of the most expensive housing change through time, so Hoyt suggests that urban social structure is in a constant state of adjustment and change (figure 15–11).

The sector model has also received some strong criticism. It has been said that Hoyt placed far too much emphasis on the role of the rich as a determinant of social structure. Questions have also been raised as to the exact definition of a sector. A third major criticism was that Hoyt not only allowed the rich to dominate the spatial organization of the city, but also failed

FIGURE 15–12 The multiple-nuclei and sector models of urban land-use patterns. Key: 1—central business district, 2—wholesale and light manufacturing, 3—lower class residential, 4—middle class residential, 5—higher class residential, 6—heavy manufacturing, 7—outlying business district, 8—dormitory suburb, 9—industrial suburb. (Reprinted from "The Nature of Cities" by C. D. Harris and E. L. Ullman in volume no. 242 of *The Annals* of The American Academy of Political and Social Sciences, © 1979. All rights reserved.)

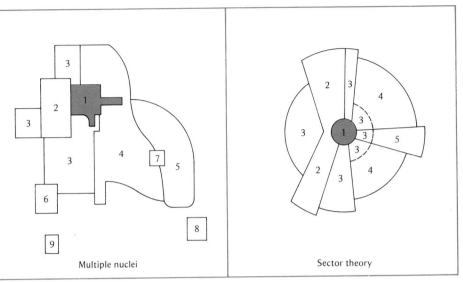

Multiple nuclei   Sector theory

to give adequate coverage to the other social and economic groups. Hoyt's theory, first published in 1939, does add an important ingredient into our understanding of urban spatial structure. The sector theory incorporates the importance of transportation systems into the evolution of the social structure of the city.

One persistent criticism of both Burgess and Hoyt is that both theories assumed rational "economic man," that is, a decision making process designed to maximize the economic and social profit for the individual. People were considered to behave in a manner that would make the most economic sense. Walter Firey's research indicates this is not necessarily the case (1945). In studies of why people moved to a particular place in Boston, Firey discovered that people chose a location often for sentimental, historical, or cultural reasons and not simply out of economic motivation.

A second basic problem with the Burgess and Hoyt models has been created by the evolution of metropolitan America. In the beginning of this chapter, we discussed Vance's concept of urban extension. In the case study of the evolution of the San Francisco Bay Area, we observed the manner in which changes in transportation created urban patterns not necessarily focused upon the central business district. This nonconcentric pattern of urban growth has created places of importance other than the central business district.

Harris and Ullman anticipated this problem and in 1945 published what was to become the third major model of urban structure, the ***multiple nuclei model***. They argued that multiple centers or nuclei were responsible for urban growth, rather than development springing from the single central business district. Four

reasons were given for the multiple nuclei development of a city:

1. Some land uses need special facilities; for retailers these include accessibility, which has traditionally been greatest in the CBD, but parts and industries require water fronts which may be eccentrically located within the city.

2. Like activities often cluster for external scale economics (the benefit of being near similar organizations) as in the office districts and industrial complexes.

3. Certain activities are detrimental to each other, such as noxious industries and high status residential areas.

4. Certain activities cannot afford the high rents of most accessible locations and form their own subsidiary clusters. This happens, for example, within the CBD where the space consuming furniture stores and car sales rooms are usually on the fringe. (Johnston, 1971, p. 95)

The model developed by Harris and Ullman indicates a number of centers from which urban development takes place (figure 15–12). This model is a better representation of the urban structure of the automobile age than are either the Hoyt or Burgess models. Constant movement is a necessity if the viability of the city is to be maintained; however, we have yet to address the question of why people move.

Intraurban mobility

Urban residents with geographic mobility may move for several basic reasons (Lowry, 1960; Grigsby, 1963).

Restored house in San Francisco. (Christopher Exline)

Houses may have become technologically obsolete; the plumbing, wiring, or heating systems may be outdated, making the house an expensive or impractical place to live. Secondly, the architectural style of the home, including the building materials, may have lost status. Or the home may simply have depreciated to the point at which upkeep and repair is economically unwise. Fourth, the physical site of the home may have become undesirable; a change in zoning may allow unwanted land use practices near the residence. The fifth consideration is one basic to the models we have discussed; the composition of the neighborhood may have changed over time through the processes of invasion and succession, thus causing the perceived need for relocation in the form of out-migration. Sixth, job changes may stimulate a move, especially if the new job requires a substantially longer journey to work. Seventh, changes in the life cycle, such as grown children leaving the home, change housing needs.

It is an interesting note that the first three of these elements which influence the decision to move—technological obsolescense, style, and depreciation—are now often attracting forces. There has been a shift in some cases back toward houses which are in some way unique. The desire to renovate a brownstone in New York City or a Victorian home in San Francisco is a factor drawing movers toward housing stock in which traditional models assume deterioration. Several

other changes in the model of downward filtering of housing units are occurring in major cities.

Supported by Federal, State, and local governments, **urban homesteading** is taking place in many cities. This is a process through which a person can secure a low-cost loan to repair a home in poor physical condition. Homesteading rejuvenates housing stock which might otherwise become uninhabitable. In some urban areas the middle and upper middle social and economic groups are returning to the central city. The rising costs of petroleum and transportation, as well as the upward spiral in the price of suburban housing, are creating this movement. In-migration to the central city may be an important factor in the future dynamics of urban social structure.

Attendant to the question of why people move is the related issue of where they move. John Adams has determined that movers have a *directional bias* in their locational decision making process (1969)—that people tend to move within relatively well-defined sectors of the city. These are wedge-shaped areas closely related to transportation lines which radiate outward from the city center.

A *distance bias* is present in the pattern of intraurban relocation; the term refers to the inclination of people to purchase a new home relatively close to the house from which they are moving (Greer-Wotten and Gilmour, 1972). Distance and directional biases result from the amount of information the mover can accumulate about prospective sites for relocation. It is likely that a person planning an intraurban move has the greatest knowledge of the areas adjacent to where he or she already lives. The high proportion of short distance moves within the city should therefore be of little surprise.

While the physical shell of the city remains more or less fixed, the movement of people and the formation of neighborhoods are ongoing processes. When we look at the skyline or an aerial photograph of a city, we often concentrate on the structures of the city to the point of excluding thoughts on the human activities taking place. Returning to our analogy of the forest and the city, we should at this point be viewing the city in terms of social and economic processes. This is the same frame of reference which is used by the ecologist who sees the forest as a series of interactions rather than a collection of trees.

Identifying urban communities. We are concerned with the location of people in particular places in the city. Often the name of an area brings forth an image of both the place and its residents. For example, in Colorado Springs the *Broadmoor district* connotes magnificent houses and an upper income community to anyone who knows the city. Similarly, in Los Angeles the name *Watts* is synonymous with a Black community, San Francisco's *Chinatown* is obviously an Asian area, and in St. Louis *the hill* refers to a predominantly Italian neighborhood. In your city what place names produce images of both people (social identifiers) and the physical environment (geographic identifiers)?

Factorial ecology

One method of determining the spatial distribution of social groups within a city is **factorial ecology.** Based on a series of statistical techniques, its principal use is to determine subareas of a city or suburb by identifying the main dimensions of urban social structure. Factorial ecology operates from a set of input variables chosen to cover a wide range of demographic, social, economic, and ethnic characteristics. In essence we are going to statistically devise a map to illustrate where groups of a certain social class, age, or ethnic characteristic reside.

One of the major sources of data used in such a study is the United States census. Information is gathered every ten years from nearly all American households on a wide range of topics. Urban areas are broken down into census tracts (reporting areas), and data appear in the form of summaries of the responses or residents in the tract area. In a hypothetical city, census tract 5 could be examined and a determination made about many of the characteristics of the residents of that area and the homes in which they live.

In a factorial ecology a series of variables are chosen to be examined. We might include such items in our case study as the percent of persons over a certain age, the percent of Blacks, income, home value, and education. We derive this data from census tract information. We enter data from all the census tracts in the city, and through computer processing, a number of *factors* are generated which summarize the data from the census tracts.

In this example the data entered for our city may be summarized by five factors. Factor *A* may show a strong relationship between high income, high house value, and a high level of education. We would conclude that factor one is summarizing high social and economic status census tracts. Factor *B* is perhaps strongly related to a high percentage of Blacks in the population, thus census tracts summarized by factor two would be high in the ethnic component of the population. The remaining factors would illustrate different age, ethnic, and social status elements of the population.

Our computer operation produces a number of lists of census tracts. These tracts have been clustered or grouped together based on the way they relate to the factors. The computer printout may indicate that census tracts 1, 5, 19, 21, 101, 102, 103, and 119 are best summarized by factor *A*. We now know that these eight tracts are high in social status, and we can then transfer that statistical information to a map. When our computer program has been completed and we have transferred the results, we can readily see the social organization of the city.

This is obviously a very simplistic overview of what is a complex process. We have made this statistical technique, factorial ecology, rather straightforward; however, there are warnings to issue at this point. Census tract boundaries are derived from road and street patterns. When we map our eight high-status tracts, we know that tract 119 is in this group and tract 120 is not. Will there be an abrupt change once we cross the street into tract 120? Probably not. We encounter a problem in that the actual transition from one social area to another is not a part of our statistical analysis.

As with any statistical technique, the results are only as good as the data and logical approach to solving the problem. A statistical approach to determining the social areas of cities has a wide range of both advantages and drawbacks.

Once places of unique character are determined, the question remains of what factors created these social areas. One of the fascinating aspects of the study of cities is that each urban area has its own set of interesting communities. We have mentioned some of the models and processes used to explain the spatial organization of social groups and economic activities within the city. The emphasis has been on general processes rather than the actual patterns of a given city. We have ignored, to this point, one of the most important elements in the urban ecosystem of the modern North American city today—the suburb.

THE OUTER CITY

Peter Muller uses the term *outer city* to describe suburban America in the 1970s. The suburb has become the most dynamic part of the contemporary American urban mosaic. Suburbia was once stereotyped as an enclave in the middle to upper social and economic classes, and it was generally assumed that the suburban resident commuted to the central city to work. The suburbs of the late 1960s and 1970s have moved beyond the traditional stereotypes to truly become the outer cities of the metropolitan region.

The key to understanding the contemporary suburb is to understand its extremely rapid growth following World War II. This is not to say that suburbs were not somewhat diverse in function prior to the Second World War; however, the widespread transition of many suburbs into urban places did not occur after the 1940s. One of the most important elements in the urbanization of the suburbs was the rapid growth of population on a national scale following World War II. The increased birth rate, coupled with previous waves of immigration, acted to cause a sharp jump in the population of the United States.

There was a tendency for people to come to urban areas following the Second World War. It was a continuation of a historical trend toward migration to urban areas in the United States in response to employment availability. Urban in-migration greatly acceler-

ated following World War II as many of those released from military service sought employment in urban areas.

In the decade following the end of the Second World War, a pattern of rapid growth on the fringe areas of cities occurred. This trend toward suburban settlement was largely the result of the desire for increased dwelling space, lifestyle, and /or freedom from perceived urban problems. The rapid growth of postwar suburbia was made possible by the wide use of the automobile and government subsidization of housing and transportation.

Comparisons of actual central city and suburban growth rates indicate that the decade of the 1930s saw a shift toward a greater percentage of growth in the suburb than in the central city. During the 1950s and 1960s, trends first established in the 1930s were intensified to such a degree that, by the mid-1970s, the suburb was dominant in both growth rates and percentage growth.

American suburban growth would not have taken place on a large scale without the widespread use of the automobile and the development of major highway systems. The creation of such highway systems was largely a function of government subsidization. The interaction between the private sector in constructing homes and the public sector in subsidizing transportation and housing purchases, when combined with population growth, form the major elements in the post–World War II evolution of suburbia in the United States.

It was not until the enactment of the Federal Aid Highway Act of 1944 that the government began large scale programs of highway construction. A governmental program was established in 1916 to provide assistance to cities of less than 2500 population; highway improvement programs were designed to generate employment in the 1930s, but these programs had only minor impacts on the development of major highway systems (Owen, 1966). The Federal Aid Highway Act of 1944, however, allocated $125 million per year over three years for the development of highway systems in urban areas.

One of the major developments stemming from this legislation was a recommendation for a federally subsidized program to develop a national system of interstate highways to connect metropolitan areas, cities, and industrial areas; the result of this recommendation was the Federal Aid Highway Act of 1956. A principal objective of the National Interstate System was to de-

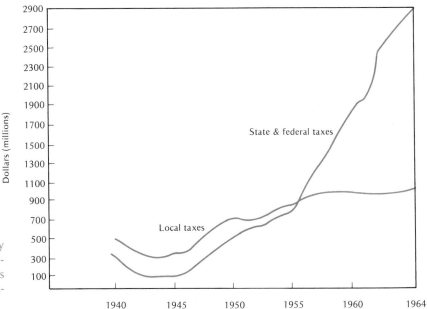

FIGURE 15–13 Trends in urban highway financing. (U.S. Dept. of Commerce, Bureau of Public Roads, Highway Statistics Div., *Highway Finance, 1921–1962*, tables HF–1 and HF–2.)

congest urban areas, and it was estimated that nearly 50 percent of the total expenditure went toward that goal. Approximately 90 percent of the cost of the system was defrayed by the federal government, thus local suburban communities did not directly pay for the transportation systems which provided the accessibility essential to suburban growth (figure 15–13).

In assessing the impact of transportation systems on suburban growth, it is essential to consider both the transportation system itself and the factor of distance from the central city to place of residence. The studies dealing with transportation often illustrate the development of the spatial pattern of suburban growth and urban expansion as a function of the evolution of transportation systems (Vance, 1964). This implies a basic skeleton as established by fixed rail transit, for example, and an interstitial filling of the skeletal structure as transportation becomes more personal and flexible. A consideration of equal importance is the distance the commuter has the ability or desire to travel from home to workplace. It should be noted that the length of the commute is measurable in economic cost, time, and emotional stress, as well as linear distance.

The fundamental influences associated with the move to the suburb—population increase, employment, housing, and transportation—must not be considered independent and unrelated. They function as interworking components of a system which has created the need, desire, and ability to settle on the fringes

of cities. It is interesting that employment and trade, two of the factors which historically have been extremely important in drawing people to the urban region, have not been the factors to "pull" migrants to the suburbs. The move to the suburb has traditionally been related only indirectly to employment; that is, the suburb has been a choice of location made from a set of dwelling place alternatives, but not as a direct result of employment in the suburb. This was largely true until the late 1960s and the 1970s, at which time the central city to suburban shift in economic activity and job opportunities began to gain momentum rapidly.

The suburbanization of economic activity

The rapid rise of economic activity is one of the most important elements in the evolution of the suburb from "bedroom community" to urban place. This trend was a part of the process of the changing economic function of the suburb which began when the first American suburbs served as locations for economic activities. The factor which distinguishes economic functioning in the suburbs since 1940 from that of earlier times is the magnitude of the growth in a wide variety of economic activities which followed the Second World War.

Employment trends. One indicator of this rapid economic growth was the relative proportion of the to-

TABLE 15–2 Annual increase in population and employment (by category)

Population 1960–70	Employment 1958–67			
	Manufacturing	Retail	Wholesale	Services
Central city 0.6	0.7	0.8	1.1	2.6
Suburban ring 2.2	3.1	5.3	7.4	6.1

Source: U.S. Bureau of the Census, *Employment and Population Change—Standard Metropolitan Statistical Areas and Central Cities,* Special Economic Reports, Series ES20(72)–1, 1972.

tal jobs available in the suburb as opposed to the central city, indicating not only the significant increase in the share of suburban jobs which occurred between 1960 and 1970, but also that this shift was a nationwide phenomenon.

The increase of employment in the suburbs was a function of the nearly total range of types of economic activity relocating or being newly established in suburbia. There was, however, considerably more encouragement from most suburban municipalities for the establishment of "clean industries" (nonpolluting), as reflected in the substantial growth in the wholesale and service sectors (table 15–2).

Suburbanization of retail, wholesale, service, and corporate activities. A wide range of factors acted to induce the establishment or relocation of economic activities in the suburbs. A large and rapidly growing population meant major markets to be served by increasing numbers of retailers. A significant locational aspect of the relocation of retail activity, especially since the late 1940s, was the clustering of retail establishments in shopping centers. Suburban population growth, combined with rapidly rising retail sales, induced greater numbers of retail and service establishments to locate in suburban shopping centers.

The culmination of this clustering was in the development of the suburban shopping mall, a massive collection of shops centered around one or two anchor establishments, usually large department stores. The establishment of complex shopping malls produced a signficant change in the pattern of retail activity in the urban region. The advent of the regional shopping mall allowed for the evolution of a noncentric pattern of major retail activity within the urban region, featuring a variety of suburban shopping areas, as opposed to the once traditional downtown shopping district from which the city and suburbs were served.

A second aspect of the process which has acted to create noncentric economic activity patterns was the phenomenon of manufacturing and wholesaling industries locating in the suburbs. The centrifugal factors influencing suburban manufacturing and wholesaling location were mainly the upward spiral of central city land costs, congestion, increasingly difficult transportation access, and decline in the availability of all but vertical space. The suburb offered abundant land (generally at low cost), in some instances tax incentives for nonpolluting industries, and efficient transportation systems, especially as trucks became increasingly important in the movement of materials. In some suburban communities prestige was associated with location and acted as an additional pulling force, inducing some types of wholesaling and manufacturing to locate in the suburbs. The Irvine industrial park in southern California is an excellent example.

The importance of a prestigious location for the corporate image was a major factor in the shift of many corporate operations to the suburbs. They offered a counterpoint to the standard high-rise office, with availability of space providing a variety of possible building types, such as the "campus" structure or single floor sprawling "ranch" pattern, and the additional possibility of such microenvironmental amenities as parklike landscaping.

The corporate move to the suburb was also influenced by residential trends which created a managerial and executive labor force in the suburbs. Location and labor force, when associated with innovation in communication systems and the trend toward a decline in the need for face-to-face communication in many of the subheadquarter-level functions of some organiza-

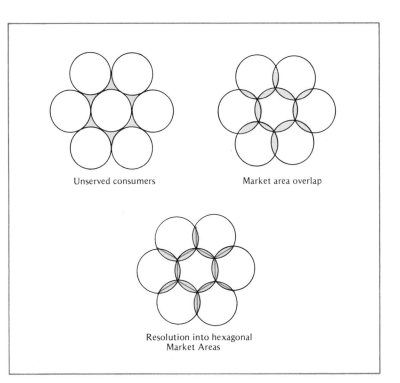

Unserved consumers   Market area overlap

Resolution into hexagonal
Market Areas

FIGURE 15–14 Circular land-use patterns. (J. Brady Foust, Anthony R. deSouza, 1978, *The Economic Landscape: A Theoretical Introduction.* Columbus, OH, Charles E. Merrill Publishing Co., p. 72.)

tions, made the suburbs an attractive place for corporate location.

The suburban landscape of the 1970s reflected a marked contrast to the suburbs from the 1930s through early 1960s. While there is statistical information available detailing the evolution of the function of the suburb from bedroom community to outer city, evidence of this change in form and function is also obtainable from simple observation. The most prominent feature of the suburban landscape of the 1940s through early 1960s was the single family detached home. The tremendous growth of population and economic activity beginning in the 1960s and continuing through the present day has altered the American suburban landscape in such a way that office buildings, industrial parks, large shopping malls, and multiple-unit residential dwellings are now found along most suburban highways.

SYSTEMS OF CITIES

As suburban communities grow in land area and population, the suburbs of one city can expand until they reach the suburbs of another city. If this pattern occurs with regularity, an urbanized region develops, with cities and suburbs blending together to form a vast

megalopolis. Jean Gottmann developed the concept of the megalopolis while studying the urban patterns between Boston and Washington, D.C. He observed,

> The Northeastern seaboard of the United States is today the site of a remarkable development—an almost continuous stretch of urban and suburban areas from the Atlantic shore to the Appalachian foothills. . . . No other section of the United States has such a large concentration of population with such a high average density, spread over such a large area. (1961, p. 3)

The Northeastern seaboard of the United States is not the only place experiencing this pattern of growth. In many major cities of the United States, urban growth and suburban expansion have created megalopolis urbanization. The cities and suburbs in a megalopolis work in concert with each other. A system of urban places exists in what, to the unenlightened observer, might seem to be simply endless sprawl. A knowledge of how cities function with respect to other cities is essential if contemporary urbanization in North America can be understood.

Central place theory

In 1933 Walter Christaller developed the *central place theory* in an attempt to explain the size, function, and

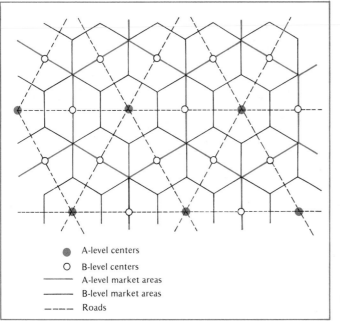

A-level centers
O B-level centers
—— A-level market areas
—— B-level market areas
----- Roads

FIGURE 15–15 Urban hierarchy. (J. Brady Foust, Anthony R. deSouza, 1978, *The Economic Landscape: A Theoretical Introduction.* Columbus, OH, Charles E. Merrill Publishing Co., p. 73.)

distribution of cities. Christaller assumed a featureless land surface (thus mountains, lakes, and deserts would not be a factor), uniform population distribution, and a ubiquitous distribution of resources. He further stated that towns were central places; that is, in every town there were some number of goods and services available.

The size of a city has a great influence on the number of goods and services available. In the smallest of cities only a very basic selection of activities are available. In a somewhat larger city all of the enterprises of the small city will be present plus some additional features. This progression continues until the largest city is reached. The most extensive city in a region has all the attributes of the other cities plus some unique characteristics.

Christaller introduced three factors which would account for this phenomenon. First, cities exist in **hierarchies.** Recall our discussion of the rank-size rule from the preceding chapter: a very few large cities exist at the top with more numerous but smaller cities toward the bottom of the pyramid of urban places. The second basic premise is that people will travel over a certain distance or **range** to obtain goods and services. One might travel a great distance to purchase some special item, but if we need bread or milk, we will probably not be willing to travel far. The attraction of places, therefore, is the result of the variety of goods and services available. A third principle in Christaller's

theory is that a **threshold** or minimum number of people is required if a place is to provide goods and services. A city comprised of a gasoline service station and small food store would not require a large population threshold. These activities simply do not demand great numbers of customers in order to exist. An automobile dealership selling some exotic and expensive type of automobile would require a far greater number of people in a region in order to be viable. This means that, within our hierarchy of urban places, the service station–food store combination will be found in all cities, while the automobile dealer would be located only in the larger cities.

Given the concepts of the interrelated urban hierarchy, range, and threshold, how might one model the spatial distribution of urban places? Christaller, working in southern Germany, determined that a basic geometric shape might provide an answer to the question of spatial patterns (1966). A circular shape presented the problems of overlap and unserved customers (figure 15–14), but a regular hexagonal pattern overcomes these problems (figure 15–15). In this pattern the A-level centers provide all the services found in the B-level centers plus some additional activities. Christaller found this pattern in his empirical study of southern Germany (figure 15–16).

In the United States the concepts of range and threshold can be illustrated by patterns of consumer movements for certain goods. In order to obtain a basic

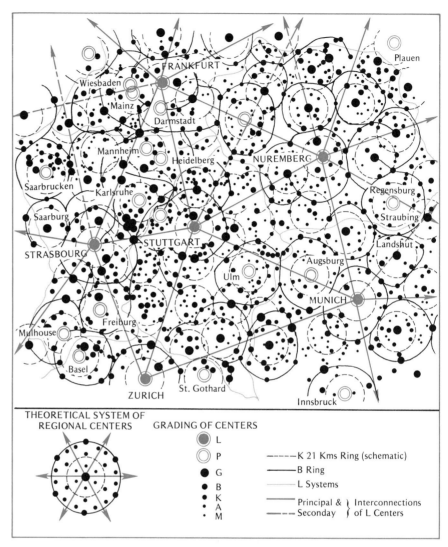

FIGURE 15–16 Distribution of central places in southern Germany. (R. E. Dickinson, 1964, *City and Region*. London, Routledge & Kegan Paul, Ltd.; and Atlantic Highlands, NJ, Humanities Press, Inc., p. 75.)

good such as food, rural residents travel to the closest city or town, while urban residents shop within their city (figure 15–17). In order to obtain dry cleaning services the rural pattern in southwestern Iowa is roughly the same as that for food stuffs; however, the urban pattern shows significant change (figure 15–18). One would assume that the smaller cities, such as Treynor, Hederson, and Lewis, do not provide this particular service, hence residents must travel to a place higher on the urban hierarchy. The purchase of a more specialized product, clothing, demands a trip by both urban and rural consumers to places of larger size (figure 15–19).

The notion of the relationships between cities was clearly stated by Christaller. In the past decade the

concept of a system of cities has taken on new meaning. Social scientists study the linkages and diffusion which occurs between cities, the role of urban systems in national and international development, and planning policies in urban hierarchies.

In our examination of southwestern Iowa, we saw how the ability to provide goods and services attracted consumers. The city which is able to draw customers is going to be economically viable and take on an important role in serving the surrounding region. Christaller demonstrated how even the smallest centers have a place in this scheme. In the study of larger urban systems we are essentially considering the same process. The health and viability of a city is basically the result of its place in a national or international collection of

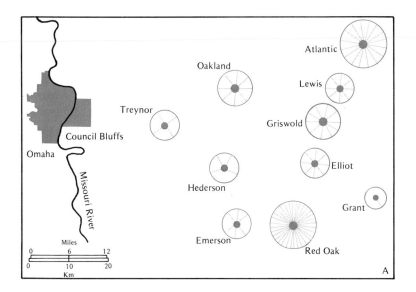

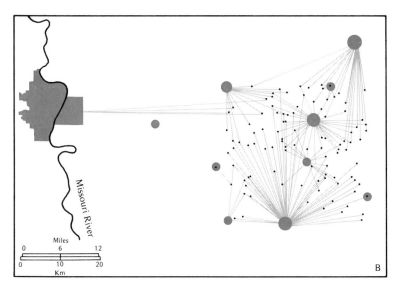

FIGURE 15-17 Purchase movements of urban (A) and rural (B) consumers for food stuffs in south-western Iowa in 1960. (J. Brady Foust, Anthony R. deSouza, 1978, *The Economic Landscape: A Theoretical Introduction.* Columbus, OH, Charles E. Merrill Publishing Co., p. 123.)

cities (Pred, 1974). The economic growth or decline of major cities is of critical importance since, as Bourne and Simmons argued,

> The concepts of the city and region are increasingly interchangeable. The functional or nodal region, centered on a city, is the basic concept. For example, the state of Georgia is increasingly equated with Atlanta; Ontario with Toronto; and Colorado with Denver. (1978, p. 6)

The systems approach can be used for urban analysis on the local, state, national, and even global scale. The process at any level is much like Christaller's hierarchy of central places. Unlike the Christaller model, however, in a system of cities we are concerned not with individual consumers and their travels but with major industries and organizations and decisions made regarding economic inputs to major cities in the hierarchy. The nature of the city as a controlling force over large regions makes understanding the relationships between major urban places essential to understanding how growth and modernization will affect future cultural landscapes.

The city is much like a living organism. Its internal parts may be prospering or decaying, but they are always changing form. The growth of urban and related suburban places has created urban realms so

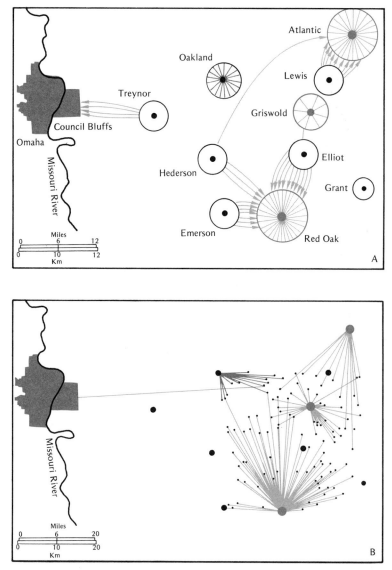

FIGURE 15–18 Purchase movements of urban (A) and rural (B) consumers for dry cleaning in southwestern Iowa in 1960. (J. Brady Foust, Anthony R. deSouza, 1978, *The Economic Landscape: A Theoretical Introduction*. Columbus, OH, Charles E. Merrill Publishing Co., p. 122.)

large that the natural ecosystem has been replaced by an urban ecosystem. Finally, much of what happens to a city and its hinterland is the result of the place of a city in a system of cities.

The investigation of the patterns and processes in the urban ecosystem is both a fascinating and important adventure. As Professor James E. Vance, Jr. noted, "The mortality of man contrasts sharply with the immortality of cities. We must distinguish between the way that human beings transfer their learning to other generations and the way that transfer of experience and

accomplishment is made through cities" (1977, p. 3). This is a fine statement reflecting our contention that the historical study of cities provides insight to the processes of modernization and growth. Once we have dealt with the past, that data becomes an important aspect of our ecological analysis of the present and our speculations of the future. This has been the framework through which we have approached the study of the city as a reflection of cultural systems. The question we now pose is, what does the future hold in store for humankind?

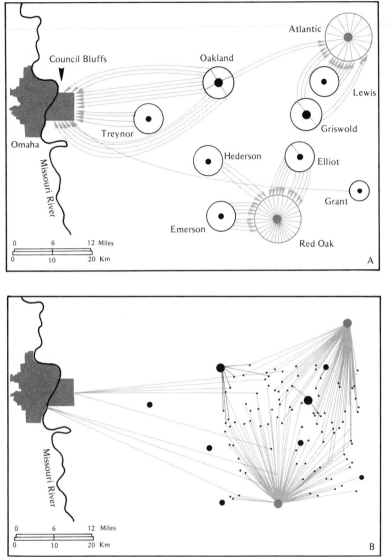

FIGURE 15–19 Purchase movements of urban (A) and rural (B) consumers for clothing in southwestern Iowa in 1960. (J. Brady Foust, Anthony R. deSouza, 1978, *The Economic Landscape: A Theoretical Introduction.* Columbus, OH, Charles E. Merrill Publishing Co., p. 120.)

KEY TERMS

Urban ecosystem
Urban evolution
Basic activity
Nonbasic activity
Concentric zone model
Filtering
Sector model
Multiple nuclei model
Urban homesteading

Directional bias
Distance bias
Factorial ecology
Megolopolis
Central place theory
Urban hierarchies
Range
Threshold

REFERENCES

Adams, J. (1969), "Directional Bias in Intra-Urban Migration," *Economic Geography* 45, 302–323.

Berry, B. J. L. (1969), "City Size Distributions and Economic Development," *Economic Development and Cultural Change* 9, 573–588.

Bourne, L. and Simmons, J. (1978), *Systems of Cities*. New York: Oxford University Press.

Burgess, E. W. (1928), "Residential Segregation in American Cities," *Annals of the American Academy of Political and Social Science* 140, 105–115.

Christaller, W. (1966), *Central Places in Southern Germany*, Baskin, C. W. (trans.). Englewood Cliffs, NJ: Prentice-Hall, Inc.

Firey, W. (1945), "Sentiment and Symbolism as Ecological Variables," *American Sociological Review* 10, 140–148.

Greer-Wotten, B. and Gilmour, G. (1972), "Distance and Directional Bias in Migration Patterns of Depreciating Metropolitan Areas," *Geographical Analysis* 4, 37–49.

Grigsby, W. (1963), *Housing Markets and Public Policy*. Philadelphia: University of Pennsylvania Press.

Gottman, J. (1961), *Megalopolis: The Urbanized Northeastern Seaboard of the United States*. Cambridge, MA: M.I.T. Press.

Hall, P. (ed.) (1966), *Von Thünen's Isolated State*. New York: Pergamon Press, Inc.

Harris, D. C. (1943), "A Functional Classification of Cities in the United States," *Geographical Review* 33, 86–99.

Harris, D. C. and Ullman, E. L. (1945), "The Nature of Cities," *Annals of the American Academy of Political and Social Science* 242, 7–17.

Hoyt, H. (1939), *The Structure and Growth of Residential Neighborhoods in American Cities*. Washington, D.C.: Federal Housing Administration.

Johnston, R. J. (1971), *Urban Residential Patterns*. New York: Praeger Publishers, Inc.

Lowry, I. S. (1960), "Filtering and Housing Standards: A Conceptual Analysis," *Land Economics* 36, 362–370.

Muller, P. O. (1976), *The Outer City*. Washington, D.C.: Association of American Geographers Resource Paper No. 75–2.

O'Keefe, J. J. (1970), *Physical Geography*. Kentfield, CA: College of Marin.

Owen, W. (1966), *The Metropolitan Transportation Problem*. Washington, D.C.: Brookings Institute.

Park, R. and Burgess, E. W. (1925), *The City*. Chicago: University of Chicago Press.

Pred, A. (1974), *Major Job Providing Organizations and Systems of Cities*. Washington, D.C.: Association of American Geographers, Commission on College Geography Resources, Paper No. 27.

Sinclair, R. (1967), "Von Thünen and Urban Sprawl," *Annals of the Association of American Geographers* 57, 72–88.

Smith, W. F. (1964), *Filtering and Neighbor Change*. Berkeley: Center for Real Estate and Urban Economics, Report No. 24, 1–16.

Strahler, A. and Strahler, A. (1973), *Environmental Geoscience: Interaction Between Natural Systems and Man*. New York: Hamilton Publishing Co.

Vance, J. E., Jr. (1964), *Geography and Urban Evolution in the San Francisco Bay Area*. Berkeley: Institute of Governmental Studies.

Vance, J. E., Jr. (1966), "Focus on Downtown: Community Planning Review," in Bourne, L. (ed.) (1971). *Internal Structure of the City*. New York: Oxford University Press, 112–120.

Vance, J. E., Jr. (1977), *This Scene of Man*. New York: Harper & Row, Publishers, Inc.

Appendix: 1980 World Population Data Sheet —Summary

Region or country	Population estimate mid–1980 (millions)	Birth rate	Death rate	Rate of natural increase (annual, %)	Number of years to double population	Population projected for 2000 (millions)	Infant mortality rate	Total fertility rate	Population under age 15 (%)	Population over age 64 (%)	Life expectancy at birth (years)	Urban population (%)	Projected ultimate population size (millions)	Per capita Gross National Product (US$)
WORLD	4,414	28	11	1.7	41	6,156	97	3.8	35	6	61	39	9,832	2,040
AFRICA	472	46	17	2.9	24	832	140	6.4	45	3	49	26	2,051	530
Algeria	19.0	48	13	3.4	20	36.9	142	7.3	47	4	56	55	93.6	1,260
Angola	6.7	48	23	2.4	28	11.2	203	6.4	44	3	41	22	29.2	300
Benin	3.6	49	19	3.0	23	6.6	149	6.7	46	4	46	14	15.0	230
Botswana	0.8	51	17	3.4	21	1.4	97	6.5	50	3	56	12	4.5	620
Burundi	4.5	47	20	2.7	25	7.8	140	6.3	44	2	42	5	19.9	140
Cameroon	8.5	42	19	2.3	30	13.1	157	5.7	41	4	44	29	31.5	460
Cape Verde	0.3	28	9	1.8	38	0.4	105	3.0	36	4	60	20	0.6	160
Central African Rep.	2.2	42	19	2.2	31	3.6	190	5.5	41	4	42	42	8.3	250
Chad	4.5	44	21	2.3	30	7.4	165	5.9	42	4	44	18	17.4	140
Comoros	0.3	40	18	2.2	31	0.4	148	5.2	43	3	46	11	1.4	180
Congo	1.6	45	19	2.6	27	2.5	180	6.0	43	3	46	39	6.9	540
Djibouti	0.4	48	24	2.5	28	0.6	—	—	—	—	—	70	—	450
Egypt	42.1	38	10	2.7	26	64.9	90	5.3	40	4	55	44	90.0	400
Equatorial Guinea	0.4	42	19	2.3	30	0.6	165	5.7	42	4	46	51	1.2	—
Ethiopia	32.6	50	25	2.5	28	55.3	162	6.7	45	3	39	13	136.5	120
Gabon	0.6	33	22	1.1	62	0.8	178	4.3	33	6	44	32	1.3	3.580
Gambia	0.6	48	23	2.4	28	1.0	217	6.4	41	2	41	16	2.4	230
Ghana	11.7	48	17	3.1	22	21.2	115	6.7	47	3	48	36	56.6	390
Guinea	5.0	46	21	2.5	27	8.2	175	6.2	44	3	44	23	22.6	210
Guinea-Bissau	0.6	41	23	1.8	39	0.9	208	5.5	39	4	41	26	1.7	200
Ivory Coast	8.0	48	18	2.9	24	14.0	154	6.7	45	2	46	32	36.1	840

Courtesy of the Population Reference Bureau, Inc., 1337 Connecticut Avenue, N.W., Washington, D.C. 20036.

Region or country	Pop. 1980	Birth rate	Death rate	Nat. inc.	Doub. time	Pop. 2000	Inf. mort.	TFR	Pop. < 15	Pop. > 64	Life expec.	Urb. pop.	Utl. pop.	GNP p.c.
Kenya	15.9	53	14	3.9	18	32.3	83	8.1	50	2	56	10	93.8	320
Lesotho	1.3	40	16	2.4	29	2.1	111	5.4	40	4	50	4	5.1	280
Liberia	1.9	50	17	3.2	21	3.5	148	6.7	48	2	48	29	8.6	460
Libya	3.0	47	13	3.5	20	5.7	130	7.4	49	4	55	60	11.7	6,910
Madagascar	8.7	45	19	2.6	27	15.1	102	6.1	43	3	46	16	39.1	250
Malawi	6.1	51	19	3.2	22	11.5	142	7.0	44	4	46	9	31.3	180
Mali	6.6	49	22	2.7	26	11.6	190	6.7	48	1	39	17	27.9	120
Mauritania	1.6	50	22	2.8	25	2.9	187	6.9	42	6	42	23	7.2	270
Mauritius	0.9	27	7	2.0	34	1.3	35	3.1	37	4	67	44	1.8	830
Morocco	21.0	43	14	3.0	23	37.3	133	6.9	46	2	55	42	70.9	670
Mozambique	10.3	45	19	2.6	27	17.9	148	6.1	45	2	46	8	44.0	140
Namibia	1.0	44	15	2.9	24	1.7	142	5.9	44	3	51	32	4.5	1,080
Niger	5.5	51	22	2.9	24	10.0	200	7.1	47	3	42	11	23.7	220
Nigeria	77.1	50	18	3.2	22	148.9	157	6.9	47	2	48	20	434.7	560
Reunion	0.5	26	6	1.9	36	0.7	41	2.8	38	4	65	56	1.2	3.060
Rwanda	5.1	50	19	3.0	23	9.6	127	6.9	47	3	46	4	24.7	180
Sao Tome and Principe	0.1	45	11	3.4	21	0.1	64	—	—	—	—	24	—	490
Senegal	5.7	48	22	2.6	27	9.7	160	6.5	44	3	42	32	23.5	340
Seychelles	0.1	26	8	1.8	38	0.1	43	4.5	42	6	65	37	—	1,060
Sierra Leone	3.5	46	19	2.6	26	6.0	136	6.4	41	5	46	16	13.6	210
Somalia	3.6	48	20	2.8	25	6.3	177	6.1	44	2	43	31	17.0	130
South Africa	28.4	38	10	2.8	25	46.3	97	5.1	42	4	60	48	107.5	1,480
S. Rhodesia (Zimbabwe)	7.4	47	14	3.4	21	14.0	129	6.6	47	3	54	20	37.2	480
Sudan	18.7	48	18	3.1	22	31.8	141	6.6	44	3	46	20	88.8	320
Swaziland	0.6	47	19	2.8	25	0.9	168	6.4	48	3	46	8	2.7	590
Tanzania	18.6	47	16	3.1	22	35.0	125	6.5	46	3	50	13	93.9	230
Togo	2.5	49	19	3.0	23	4.7	163	6.7	46	3	46	15	11.9	320
Tunisia	6.5	33	8	2.5	28	9.7	125	5.7	44	4	57	50	14.4	950
Uganda	13.7	45	14	3.0	23	25.5	120	6.1	45	3	52	7	57.9	—
Upper Volta	6.9	48	22	2.6	27	11.8	182	6.5	44	3	42	5	24.2	160
Zaire	29.3	46	19	2.8	25	48.1	160	6.1	45	3	46	30	121.9	210
Zambia	5.8	49	17	3.2	22	10.7	144	6.9	46	3	48	39	28.6	480
AMERICA	**247**	**16**	**8**	**0.7**	**98**	**289**	**13**	**1.8**	**23**	**11**	**73**	**74**	**296**	**9,650**
Argentina	27.1	26	9	1.6	43	32.9	45	2.9	28	8	69	80	41.0	1,910
Bahamas	0.2	25	5	2.0	34	0.3	25	3.5	44	4	69	58	0.4	2,620
Barbados	0.3	16	8	0.9	80	0.3	27	2.2	32	10	70	44	0.4	1,940
Bolivia	5.3	44	19	2.5	28	8.9	168	6.8	42	4	47	34	19.4	510
Brazil	122.0	36	8	2.8	25	205.1	109	4.4	41	3	64	61	341.0	1,570
Canada	24.0	15	7	0.8	88	29.0	12	1.9	26	8	73	76	30.3	9,170
Chile	11.3	21	7	1.4	48	15.2	40	3.0	35	5	66	80	18.6	1,410
Colombia	26.7	29	8	2.1	33	42.2	77	3.9	45	3	62	60	55.2	870
Costa Rica	2.2	31	4	2.7	26	3.4	28	3.8	44	4	70	41	4.7	1,540
Cuba	10.0	18	6	1.2	59	12.7	25	2.5	37	6	72	64	16.5	810
Dominica	0.1	21	5	1.6	43	0.1	20	—	—	—	58	27	—	440
Dominican Republic	5.4	37	9	2.8	25	8.5	96	5.4	48	3	60	49	15.1	910
Ecuador	8.0	42	10	3.1	22	14.6	70	6.3	44	4	60	43	25.7	910
El Salvador	4.8	40	7	3.3	21	8.6	51	6.0	46	3	62	39	13.7	600
Grenada	0.1	27	6	2.2	32	0.1	24	—	—	—	63	15	0.2	530
Guadeloupe	0.3	17	6	1.1	65	0.4	35	3.2	32	6	69	48	—	2,850
Guatemala	7.0	43	12	3.1	23	12.3	76	5.7	45	3	58	36	23.2	910
Guyana	0.9	28	7	2.1	33	1.2	50	3.9	40	4	69	40	2.0	550
Haiti	5.8	42	16	2.6	26	9.9	130	5.9	41	4	51	24	16.3	260
Honduras	3.8	47	12	3.5	20	7.1	103	7.1	48	3	57	31	15.3	480
Jamaica	2.2	29	7	2.2	31	2.8	15	3.7	46	6	70	41	5.3	1,110

Region or country	Pop. 1980	Birth rate	Death rate	Nat. inc.	Doub. time	Pop. 2000	Inf. mort.	TFR	Pop. < 15	Pop. > 64	Life expec.	Urb. pop.	Utl. pop.	GNP p.c.
Martinique	0.3	16	7	0.9	80	0.4	32	3.0	32	6	69	50	—	3,950
Mexico	68.2	37	6	3.1	22	128.9	70	5.2	46	3	65	65	203.5	1,290
Netherland Antilles	0.3	28	7	2.2	32	0.4	25	3.1	38	6	62	48	—	3,150
Nicaragua	2.6	47	12	3.4	20	4.8	122	6.6	48	3	55	49	9.3	840
Panama	1.9	28	6	2.2	31	2.9	47	4.1	44	4	70	51	4.5	1,290
Paraguay	3.3	39	8	3.1	22	5.6	64	5.8	45	3	64	40	9.2	850
Peru	17.6	40	12	2.8	25	29.2	92	5.3	44	3	56	62	54.6	740
Puerto Rico	3.5	23	6	1.7	42	4.5	20	2.4	36	6	73	62	—	2,720
St. Lucia	0.1	35	7	2.8	25	0.1	36	—	50	5	67	17	—	630
Suriname	0.4	30	7	2.3	30	0.7	30	—	46	4	67	66	1.8	2,110
Trinidad and Tobago	1.2	25	6	1.9	37	1.4	29	2.6	38	4	67	49	2.2	2,910
United States	222.5	16	9	0.7	99	260.4	13	1.8	22	11	73	74	265.5	9,700
Uruguay	2.9	21	10	1.1	65	3.5	46	2.7	27	10	69	83	4.5	1,610
Venezuela	13.9	36	6	3.0	23	25.7	45	4.9	43	3	66	75	40.1	2,910
ASIA	2,563	28	11	1.8	39	3,578	103	3.9	37	4	58	27	5,573	760
Afghanistan	15.9	48	21	2.7	26	26.4	226	6.9	45	3	37	11	65.8	240
Bahrain	0.4	44	9	3.6	20	0.7	78	7.4	44	3	63	78	1.1	4,100
Bangladesh	90.6	46	20	2.6	27	156.7	153	6.3	44	3	46	9	334.5	90
Bhutan	1.3	43	21	2.2	31	2.0	147	6.2	42	2	43	4	4.0	100
Brunei	0.2	28	4	2.4	29	0.3	20	5.1	43	3	66	64	—	10,640
Burma	34.4	39	14	2.4	29	53.7	140	5.5	40	4	52	24	92.3	150
China	975	18	6	1.2	58	1,212.3	56	2.3	32	6	64	26	1,530.0	460
Cyprus	0.6	19	8	1.1	64	0.7	17	2.1	25	10	73	53	1.0	2,110
Dem. Kampuchea	6.0	33	15	1.8	39	9.1	150	4.7	42	3	44	12	36.5	—
East Timor	0.8	44	21	2.3	30	1.1	175	6.1	42	3	42	12	—	—
Gaza	0.4	53	18	3.5	20	0.7	137	—	48	5	52	87	—	—
Hong Kong	4.8	18	5	1.2	56	6.2	12	2.6	29	6	72	92	7.3	3,040
India	676.2	34	15	1.9	36	976.2	134	5.3	41	3	52	21	1,642.8	180
Indonesia	144.3	35	15	2.0	34	210.6	91	4.1	42	2	50	18	356.0	360
Iran	38.5	44	14	3.0	23	66.1	112	6.3	44	4	58	47	101.0	—
Iraq	13.2	47	13	3.4	20	24.5	104	7.0	48	4	55	66	49.1	1,860
Israel	3.9	25	7	1.8	38	5.5	15	3.5	33	8	73	87	7.5	4,120
Japan	116.8	15	6	0.9	79	129.4	8	1.8	'24	8	75	76	133.4	7,330
Jordan	3.2	46	13	3.3	21	5.9	97	7.0	48	3	56	42	11.8	1,050
Korea, North	17.9	33	8	2.4	28	27.4	70	4.5	40	4	62	33	42.9	730
Korea, South	38.2	23	7	1.6	44	51.1	38	3.2	38	4	62	48	64.1	1,160
Kuwait	1.3	42	5	3.7	19	3.1	39	7.0	44	2	69	56	5.3	14,890
Laos	3.7	44	20	2.4	29	5.7	175	6.2	42	3	39	15	11.1	90
Lebanon	3.2	34	10	2.5	28	4.9	65	4.7	43	5	65	60	7.6	—
Macao	0.3	30	8	2.2	32	0.3	78	—	38	5	—	97	—	1,460
Malaysia	14.0	31	6	2.5	28	20.7	44	4.4	41	3	61	27	29.5	1,090
Maldives	0.1	50	23	2.7	26	0.2	119	—	44	2	—	11	—	150
Mongolia	1.7	37	8	2.9	24	2.7	70	5.3	43	3	62	47	3.9	940
Nepal	14.0	44	20	2.4	29	22.0	133	6.4	40	3	43	4	51.4	120
Oman	0.9	49	19	3.0	23	1.7	142	7.2	45	3	47	5	3.2	2,570
Pakistan	86.5	44	16	2.8	25	152.0	142	6.3	46	3	52	26	334.6	230
Philippines	47.7	34	10	2.4	28	78.1	80	5.0	43	3	61	32	127.9	510
Qatar	0.2	44	14	3.0	23	0.4	138	7.2	45	3	48	69	0.8	12,740
Saudi Arabia	8.2	49	18	3.0	23	15.5	150	7.2	45	3	48	24	30.8	8,040
Singapore	2.4	17	5	1.2	59	3.0	12	1.9	31	4	71	100	3.7	3,260
Sri Lanka	14.8	28	7	2.2	32	20.0	42	3.4	39	4	63	22	30.3	190
Syria	8.6	45	13	3.2	21	16.2	114	7.4	49	4	57	49	32.7	930
Taiwan	17.8	25	5	2.0	35	23.8	25	3.1	35	4	71	77	29.6	1,400
Thailand	47.3	32	9	2.3	30	75.5	68	4.5	43	3	60	13	104.7	490

Region or country	Pop. 1980	Birth rate	Death rate	Nat. inc.	Doub. time	Pop. 2000	Inf. mort.	TFR	Pop. < 15	Pop. > 64	Life expec.	Urb. pop.	Utl. pop.	GNP p.c.
Turkey	45.5	35	10	2.5	28	69.6	119	5.0	40	4	58	45	97.8	1,210
United Arab Emirates	0.8	44	14	3.0	23	1.6	138	7.2	34	3	48	65	2.5	14,230
Vietnam	53.3	41	18	2.3	30	80.9	115	5.8	41	4	48	19	149.4	170
Yemen, North	5.6	48	25	2.3	30	9.5	160	6.8	47	4	45	11	20.4	580
Yemen, South	1.9	48	21	2.7	26	3.4	155	7.0	49	4	45	33	6.9	420
EUROPE	484	14	10	0.4	176	521	19	2.0	24	12	72	69	560	5,650
Albania	2.7	30	8	2.2	32	3.8	87	4.2	37	5	69	34	5.7	740
Austria	7.5	11	12	-0.1	—	7.6	15	1.6	23	15	72	52	7.8	7.030
Belgium	9.9	12	12	0.1	990	10.7	12	1.7	22	14	71	95	10.4	9,070
Bulgaria	8.9	16	10	0.5	139	9.5	22	2.3	22	11	71	60	10.4	3,200
Czechoslovakia	15.4	18	12	0.7	100	17.2	19	2.4	23	12	70	67	19.0	4,720
Denmark	5.1	12	10	0.2	385	5.3	9	1.7	22	14	74	67	5.4	9,920
Finland	4.8	14	9	0.4	161	5.1	9	1.7	22	11	72	59	5.2	6,820
France	53.6	14	10	0.3	198	57.5	11	1.9	24	14	73	73	60.7	8,270
Germany, East	16.7	14	14	0.0	—	16.6	13	1.8	21	16	72	76	17.7	5,660
Germany, West	61.1	9	12	-0.2	—	59.8	15	1.4	21	15	72	92	60.8	9,600
Greece	9.6	16	9	0.7	98	10.6	19	2.3	24	12	73	65	10.9	3,270
Hungary	10.8	16	13	0.3	267	11.2	24	2.2	21	13	70	52	11.8	3,450
Iceland	0.2	19	6	1.2	57	0.3	11	2.3	30	9	76	87	0.3	8,320
Ireland	3.3	22	10	1.1	61	4.0	16	3.4	31	11	71	52	5.5	3,470
Italy	57.2	12	9	0.3	224	61.3	18	1.9	24	12	72	67	62.6	3,840
Luxembourg	0.4	11	12	-0.0	—	0.4	11	1.5	20	13	70	68	0.4	10,410
Malta	0.3	17	10	0.8	92	0.4	16	2.0	25	9	71	94	0.4	2,160
Netherlands	14.1	13	8	0.4	158	15.5	10	1.6	25	11	75	88	15.8	8,390
Norway	4.1	13	10	0.3	248	4.4	9	1.8	24	14	75	44	4.5	9,510
Poland	35.5	19	9	1.0	71	40.9	22	2.3	24	10	71	57	46.8	3,660
Portugal	9.9	17	10	0.7	99	11.6	39	2.5	28	10	69	29	13.6	2,020
Romania	22.3	20	10	1.0	69	25.7	31	2.6	25	10	70	48	29.7	1,750
Spain	37.8	17	8	0.9	75	43.9	16	2.6	28	10	72	70	50.0	3,520
Sweden	8.3	11	11	0.0	1,386	8.6	8	1.7	21	15	75	83	8.2	10,210
Switzerland	6.3	11	9	0.2	301	6.4	10	1.5	22	13	73	55	6.8	12,100
United Kingdom	55.8	12	12	0.1	1,155	56.5	14	1.7	23	14	72	78	60.1	5,030
USSR	266	18	10	0.8	82	311	31	2.4	24	10	70	62	360	3,700
Yugoslavia	22.4	17	9	0.9	80	25.7	34	2.2	26	9	68	39	28.6	2,390
OCEANIA	23	20	9	1.1	61	30	42	2.8	31	8	69	71	37	6,020
Australia	14.6	16	8	0.8	86	17.9	12	2.1	27	9	73	86	18.5	7,920
Fiji	0.6	27	4	2.3	30	0.8	41	4.0	41	2	71	37	1.2	1,440
New Zealand	3.2	16	8	0.8	83	3.9	14	2.2	29	9	72	83	4.6	4,790
Papua-New Guinea	3.2	41	16	2.5	27	5.1	106	6.0	44	4	50	13	9.3	560
Samoa, Western	0.2	37	7	3.0	23	0.2	40	5.8	50	3	63	21	0.5	—
Solomon Islands	0.2	41	10	3.1	22	0.4	78	6.2	44	3	57	9	—	430

Glossary

Abiotic   The nonliving component of an ecosystem.

Acculturation   The modification of a culture by adopting new cultural traits from another group.

Age structure   Refers to the percentage of people in various age groups in a population. Age structure is best described by a population pyramid.

Annual cropping   Land is used for crops each year, thus it lies fallow only for part of each year.

Antecedent boundary   Boundaries that were allocated and delimited before significant settlement in an area.

Apartheid   The policy of the government of South Africa that calls for "separate development" of racial groups.

Allocation   The first stage in the evolution of a boundary line. It involves a general agreement between two or more political entities on the division of a specific territory.

Area-studies tradition   One of the four traditions of geography developed by William Pattison. This tradition is concerned with the character of places and how they evolved to their present organization. Regional geography is an outgrowth of this tradition.

Bangladesh   Formerly East Pakistan and the site of a disastrous cyclonic storm in 1970.

Basic activity   An economic activity that exports beyond the boundary of a city and generates income within the city.

Basic demographic equation   An equation linking population change through the major demographic variables: births, deaths, and migration. The equation views the population of a place at some future date as a function of its present population plus births over the time interval, minus deaths over the time interval, plus in-migrants over the time interval, minus out-migrants over the time interval.

Bilingualism   The ability to speak two distinct languages.

Biological community   A natural population of plants or animals that occupy a common area.

Biosphere   The envelope of life that encompasses the earth, from the deep sea trenches to the upper levels of the atmosphere.

Biotic   The living component of an ecosystem.

Black English Vernacular (BEV)   Characteristic speech patterns spoken by some segments of the Black community in the United States.

Boundary   An agreed-upon demarcation line marking the limits of the jurisdictions of two different political authorities.

Buffer zone   An area between major power blocks that keeps competing powers apart.

Burghers   Long distance traders of the 13th and 14th centuries who owned property and began to wield great political power.

Bush-fallow cultivation   A shifting agricultural system in which the fallow period is six to ten years, thus allowing fallow land to return to bush and shrubs, but not to true forest.

Caloric input–output ratio   A ratio between the amount of energy required to produce a food and the caloric value of the food. It provides a useful index for comparing food supply systems.

Capital city   The primary political and cultural center of a state.

Carrying capacity   The number of people who can be sustained by a particular land area at a given technological level.

Central place theory   A theory developed by Walter Christaller which says that large cities or central places offer a more complete array of goods and services and are spaced farther apart than smaller cities or towns.

Centrifugal force   A force that disrupts or weakens a state.

Centripetal force   A force that unifies or brings together a state.

Charring   The earliest form of energy from fire was the charring or burning of wood.

City-states   Those states whose territory was limited to the city and its surrounding hinterland. They were common in ancient Greece.

Clines   This refers to gradients of change in a measurable genetic characteristic.

Coking   A method developed at the time of the industrial revolution that used fire to produce coke.

Colonialism   The rule of a group of people by a foreign state or power.

Compact state   The most efficient form of a state and, in theory, all boundary areas are the same distance from the center.

Concentric zone model   A model developed by Robert Park and Ernest Burgess which asserts that the urban social organization of a city consists of a series of concentric zones that form around the central business district.

Contiguous zone   An offshore zone that generally extends from 12 to 24 nautical miles. A state does not have complete sovereignty in this zone, but it generally has the right to intercept and search vessels suspected of smuggling and may extend its control of fisheries and mining rights.

Core area   The area in which or about which a state originates.

Core–periphery model   Treats economic development as a set of linkages and interactions between core areas, usually cities, and peripheral areas, usually composed of smaller towns and rural areas.

Cos   An ancient Greek city that was a great health resort and training center for physicians.

Cracking   The process of breaking down fossil fuels to produce combustion.

Creationism   The idea that differences among species were the result of an original creative act.

Crude birth rate   The annual number of births per one thousand people in a given population.

Crude death rate   The annual number of deaths per one thousand people in a given population.

Crude population density   See *population density*.

Cultural hearths   The places of origin from which the major cultural systems of the world have evolved.

Cultural landscape   The uses people make of the earth in providing food, shelter, and defense leaves an imprint on the landscape. This cultural landscape is a distinctive, artificial landscape.

Cultural realm   A large area, such as a continent, that has a relatively homogeneous culture.

Cultural region   An area exhibiting some degree of homogeneity in culture or cultural traits and artifacts.

Cultural relativity   The idea that each culture is specific to a particular group and that there is no way to evaluate the aspects of one culture relative to other cultures.

Cyclical changes   With respect to population growth, changes in growth rates upward and downward in response to changing food supplies, epidemics, and wars.

Delimitation   The second stage in the evolution of a boundary. It involves the actual definition of a boundary in a treaty or agreement.

Delphi   An ancient Greek city that was a center of literary pursuits and the location of the shrine and sacred oracle of Apollo.

Demarcation   The final stage in the evolution of a boundary and involves the precise marking of the boundary on the ground.

Demographic transition   The transition from a demographic regime characterized by high birth and death rates to one characterized by low birth and death rates.

Demography   The scientific study of the human population, focusing on population composition, change, and distribution.

Demonstration effect   An effect in which people in one area are encouraged to imitate the behavior of people elsewhere. In population studies, the small family norm established in European countries after the demographic transition acted as a demonstration effect in other countries, encouraging lower fertility.

Developed countries (nations)   Countries that have industrialized and have relatively high levels of per capita income and per capita productivity.

Developing countries (nations)   Countries that have not industrialized and have relatively low rates of per capita income and per capita productivity.

Diffusion   The outward spread of an idea, innovation, or piece of material culture, usually from a center or hearth of invention or innovation. The process may proceed quite unevenly in space and time, as both physical and cultural barriers affect the rate of adoption of new ideas and innovations.

Directional bias   The process whereby people tend to move within relatively well-defined sectors of the city. These are wedge-shaped areas closely related to transportation lines which radiate outward from the city center.

Distance bias   The inclination of people to purchase a new home relatively close to the house from which they are moving.

Distribution cost   The cost of shipping a finished product from the plant to the market.

Domestication   The process of selective breeding through which wild plants and animals are genetically improved and adapted to use in agriculture.

Dominant   The name give to genetic traits that are predominant.

Dual economy   Characteristic of many developing countries. It is an economy in which both a modern sector and a traditional sector can be found. It gives rise to such scenes as fields being plowed by horses not far from cities filled with modern skyscrapers.

Earthquakes The release of energy associated with a sudden movement along a fault. They can cause enormous loss to both property and life.

Earth-science tradition One of the four traditions of geography developed by William Pattison. This tradition deals with the study of the biosphere, the interface of land, water, and air.

Ecology The science that deals with the interaction between plants, animals, and the physical/biological environment.

Economic development In simplest terms, it is the process of increasing per capita productivity in an economy.

Economies of scale Money saved or earned through purchasing and processing large quantities of raw materials and through modern, large-scale marketing. Generally the average cost of production decreases as plant size increases, at least up to some point.

Ecosystem A complex of living and nonliving material that function as a unit in nature.

Elongated or attenuated state A state that is at least six times as long as its average width.

Energy The ability to do work.

Environmental determinism The belief that human cultures are strongly influenced and conditioned by aspects of the physical environment, primarily climate.

Environmental population theory Attempts to explain demographic behavior through cultural processes.

Epidemiologic transition The transition a society goes through in which death rates decline and the major causes of death shift from communicative diseases to degenerative diseases.

Evolution The process by which an organism attains its character through a series of steps or slow changes.

Exclusive economic zone (EEZ) It extends from shoreline to 200 nautical miles. States have certain rights relative to the exploring and exploiting of natural resources in this area.

Expansion diffusion The spread of ideas or information by one person telling another. This creates a snowballing effect.

Factorial ecology A statistical method used for determining the spatial distribution of groups within a city.

Factors of production The necessary inputs for production, or factors of production, include land, labor, capital, and enterprise.

Family planning Policies and programs designed to help families achieve their desired family size.

Faustian bargain A situation in which an immediate resource shortage leads to short-sighted resource policy decisions that may have long-lasting, regrettable effects.

Fertility trend Any observed or predicted course of fertility over some period of time.

Filtering An indirect process for meeting the housing needs of low income groups. When new housing is produced for higher income groups, houses given up by these groups become available for low income groups.

Financial capital Cash required by businesses and other users and consumers, as opposed to physical capital.

Flexibility A measure of the ability to find adequate substitutions for a resource in order to satisfy demand.

Food chain The arrangement of organisms in an ecosystem such that each level uses the next lower level as a food source.

Footloose industry One in which transport costs are relatively small compared to total costs, thus allowing a fair latitude of locational choice among possible production areas. These industries are often attracted to cultural centers and areas of pleasant climate.

Forced migration A movement of individuals or groups of people in which they participated without choice. The slave trade is a major example.

Forest-fallow cultivation A shifting agricultural system in which an area is cleared, cropped for one or two years, then left fallow for twenty or twenty-five years, allowing it to return to a true forest.

Formal city A means of defining the boundaries of a city according physical properties such as buildings or roads, or through political or legal boundaries.

Fragmented or divided state A state that consists of two or more individual parts separated by land or international water.

Frontier An indefinite area of political control. Usually a zone and not a distinct demarcation line.

Functional city A means of defining a city based upon activity patterns associated with the city.

Generality Characteristics that a place has in common with other places.

Genetic classification A classification of boundaries that involves relating the origin of a boundary to the cultural landscape through which the boundary is drawn.

Genetic drift The process whereby the genetic characteristics of populations change over long time periods.

Genetics The branch of biology that deals with heredity and the variation in the features and constitution of groups of plants and animals.

Geography of religions The study of the origin and diffusion of religious systems.

Gross National Product (GNP) The total monetary value of all goods and services produced by an economy during a one-year period.

Growth syndrome It involves three basic parameters: continuing growth of the human population in both developed and developing countries, rapid increase in the production and consumption of commodities, and misapplication of old and new technologies, leading to an increasing abuse and pillage of the human habitat.

High seas   Most oceans are included in this zone, and this is part of the earth's surface that cannot be claimed by any political entity.

Human adjustment   The ways humans adjust to natural hazards.

Hunting and gathering   A primitive form of economy in which people subsist by gathering fruits, berries, nuts, tubers, and other various edible plants and by hunting and fishing for whatever is available.

Hurricanes   Tropical cyclonic storms that form over oceanic areas and move inland. In terms of aggregate damage, they are the most severe of all storms.

Hydraulic civilization   A civilization based upon large-scale irrigation systems.

Immigration   The movement of people into one country from another one.

Incipient cultivation   The beginning of cultivation, dating back to around 10,000 B.C.

Industrial city   A city that developed around an industrial base.

Industrial inertia   The tendency for a plant, once it has been established, to remain in that location, even though other locational factors may become less favorable, mainly because of the high cost associated with abandoning a plant and moving to another one.

Industrial Revolution   Based on the rapid utilization of inanimate energy sources, more complex machinery, and the factory system, it began in England in the 18th century and continues today. However, the groundwork for the Industrial Revolution was laid over a long period of time and in a variety of places. The scale of industry, transport facilities, mining, and agriculture were altered considerably by it, as was the cultural landscape in general.

Intensive subsistence farming   An agricultural system requiring a considerable amount of human energy and producing a relatively low output per worker.

Internal sovereignty   The supremacy of a person or body of persons in the state over the individual or association of individuals within the area of its jurisdiction.

Intervening obstacles   See *Lee's migration model*.

Least transport cost location   The point at which a plant could be located and have the least total transport costs.

Lee's migration model   A model that views migration as a result of four sets of factors: (1) factors associated with place of origin, (2) factors associated with place of destination, (3) intervening obstacles, and (4) personal factors.

Life cycle   The series of events that a person's life passes through from birth to death. Between those extremes, major life cycle events include marriage, divorce, graduation from school, and job acquisition.

Lingua franca   Any mutually understood language, generally for the purpose of trade, business, or government, that is not the native language of most of its users.

Linguist   A scientist who studies human speech patterns and the structure, nature, and evolution of language.

Location   Refers to the absolute or relative position of a certain object or activity. *Absolute location* means the exact place where something is found, whereas *relative location* refers to the location of an object or activity relative to other objects or activities.

"Man-land" tradition   One of the four traditions of geography developed by William Pattison. This tradition emphasizes the ecological nature of geography, that is, the interaction between people and the physical environment.

Market orientation   Characteristic of industries for whom location near consumers is essential.

Mean information field   A method of weighing the chances of knowing of an innovation if you are close to the source by giving certain numerical values to those places close to the teller. A way to simulate the way in which information spreads.

Migration   The movement of people from place to place, usually across some political boundary, for the purpose of changing their permanent place of residence.

Migration differentials   Migrants are not random samples of the population from which they came. Rather, they are selected by certain characteristics, such as age or educational level; thus, they are differentiated from the general population. One example of this is the age differential: most migrants are young.

Migration selectivity   The idea that migrants do not represent a random sample of either their origin or destination populations. Rather, they tend to be selected for certain characteristics; for example, migrants tend to be young. See also *migration differentials*.

Migration stream   An established movement of people between two places. For example, there is a migration stream between Los Angeles and Chicago.

Minimata disease   Mercury poisoning, so named because it first came to public attention in 1953 at Minimata Bay in Japan, where a number of people died of it. Mercury from a plastics plant was released into the bay and absorbed by marine organisms, which were in turn eaten by local residents.

Modernization   An inclusive term used to indicate both economic development and the sweeping changes in the cultural fabric of a society that accompanies it.

Monte Carlo simulation   A method of estimating how information will diffuse using probabilities.

Morphological classification   A type of boundary classification system based upon conspicuous physical features of the landscape.

Multicropping   Land is used for two or more crops per year, allowing almost no time for a fallow period.

Multiple nuclei model   A model developed by Chauncey Harris and Edward Ullman which asserts that multiple centers or nuclei were responsible for urban growth.

Mutation   The process through which an organism's genetic composition changes through a slight chemical change in the genes.

Nation   A cultural unit, a group of people with a common culture, that may or may not constitute a state.

Nation-state   A distinct cultural unit with a common language and tradition that has the territorial base and internal sovereignty of a state.

Natural hazards   A state of nature that has hazardous consequences for human populations.

Naturalistic population theory   Attempts to explain demographic behavior through mechanistic ideas, stressing the inexorable operation of biological processes and sometimes failing to allow for human adaptive ability.

Natural selection   A theory that suggests that those organisms with attributes allowing adapation to the physical environment would be more likely to prosper, and those that did not adapt were more likely to die off. The result is the survival of individuals or groups who are best adjusted to their living conditions.

Neocolonialism   The development and maintainance of military, cultural, or economic control over a state after it has achieved sovereignty.

Neo-Malthusian   A modern revival of interest in Malthus's ideas. Neo-Malthusians feel that population growth will outrun the food supply and that the world cannot continue to support a growing population.

Neutral stuff   Natural materials in the environment that are, under the prevailing technology, not classified as resources.

Nomadic herding   Primitive livestock herding in which people follow, and sometimes guide, animals from place to place in search of pastures and water. This activity is usually confined to arid or semiarid areas.

Nonbasic activity   An economic activity that provides goods and services to the residents of the city, rather than people in other regions.

Nonrenewable resources   A resource which, once used, cannot be replaced. Oil and coal are examples, as are such minerals as gold, silver and copper.

Olympia   An ancient Greek city that was devoted to athletic development, the site of the first Olympic games.

Perception   The problem of different people selectively observing and interpreting different items in the same environment, usually because of their varying cultural heritages. Perceptual differences may in turn lead to different assumptions and conclusions about landscapes and to different spatial behaviors within those landscapes.

Perforated state   A state that is completely surrounded by the territory of another state.

Physical capital   Capital in the form of plants and equipment, as opposed to financial capital.

Pidgin   A simplified speech pattern used for communication by people of different linguistic groups generally involved in international commerce.

Plasticity   The ability of plants or animals to adapt to change.

Pleistocene overkill   The extinction of various large mammals that coincided with the appearance of Early Mongoloid hunters and gatherers.

Plural society   A society that contains several distinct cultural groups that interface but do not intermix.

Polarized development   A process that leads to a concentration of economic development in a core region, often to the detriment of the peripheral region's economy.

Polis   The place in ancient Greece where people came together in pursuit of a better life. The polis established the social function of the city.

Population density   Generally expressed as the number of people per unit of land.

Population policy   A policy designed to influence one or more of the three major demographic variables: births, deaths, and migration.

Population equilibrium   A point where population is in balance with the natural resource base of an area. Because of the cultural nature of resources and the adaptability of people and technology, the idea of population equilibrium is difficult to translate into actual numbers.

Population projection   Projection of the population of some area for some future date, usually based on a set of assumptions about the future course of births, deaths, and migration.

Population pyramid   A graph showing the age and sex structure of a population. They may be constructed for nations, states, cities, or even smaller regions.

Population redistribution   Process of rearranging spatial patterns of populations. Migration plays a major role in most population redistributions.

Preservationist movement   A movement devoted to preserving rather than utilizing natural resources. Often this movement is associated with John Muir and the Sierra Club, an organization that has long served as a watchdog on new resource developments, especially in the western United States.

Primary industry   One which used raw materials as inputs and whose function is to change the form of that material.

Primary population theory   A theory to explain demographic behavior by focusing on understanding the specific factors related to fertility, migration, or mortality. See also *secondary population theory*.

Primate city   A city that is usually the largest and most important in a state. It is commonly at least twice as large as the next largest city, and it dominates the state with respect to most commercial, industrial, educational, and political concerns.

Procurement cost   The cost to a firm of assembling all raw materials at a plant site.

Production cost   For a firm this is the cost of changing raw materials into finished products. It includes such costs as rent, energy, labor, and management.

Prorupt state   It is similar to a compact state but it has an extension of its territory in the form of a corridor or peninsula leading away from the compact portion of the state.

Raison d'être   A unifying idea or "reason for being" that holds a state together.

Range   The average maximum distance people are willing to travel to obtain a good or service.

Ravenstein's laws   The first set of generalizations published regarding migration.

Recessive   The name given to a genetic trait that is not influential or less influential than a dominant trait.

Raw material orientation   Characteristic of industries for whom location near a source of raw materials is essential.

Recoverability   Refers to the length of time involved in the replenishment and viability of a resource.

Regional dialect   A variety of language spoken in different regions.

Relic boundary   A boundary that has been abandoned for political purposes but is still recognizable on the cultural landscape.

Religious geography   The study of the specific imprints religious practices leave on the local landscape.

Relocation diffusion   The spread of an idea or information by people moving to a new area and carrying the information with them to the new area.

Renewable resource   One that can be replaced after it has been removed. Forests are a good example.

Resource   Materials in the physical environment that serve some function within a given cultural context. Resources expand and contract in response to human needs.

Resource availability   Because of the cultural nature of resources, measuring, estimating, and projecting their availability is a complex and difficult task.

Resource conflicts   Conflicts that arise because a resource has more than one possible use and a decision to use it one way precludes using it another. For example, land cannot be both mined for coal and farmed at the same time.

Resource creation and destruction   Because resources are a creation of human culture, they can also be destroyed by

human culture. Technological innovations create resources by finding ways of using materials that previously were unusable. Similarly, what once was a resource may be made obsolete by technological changes.

Rural Renaissance   A term used to describe the renewed growth of nonmetropolitan areas in the United States during the 1970s.

Scientific method   A method of obtaining knowledge using the principles of science such as observation and classification of facts and the establishment of verifiable general laws.

Secondary industry   One that uses as inputs materials that have already undergone some manufacturing.

Secondary population theory   A theory to explain demographic behavior formulated to analyze a much broader class of phenomena that have demographic implications. See also *primary population theory*.

Sector model   A model developed by Homer Hoyt which asserts that land-use patterns in cities will assume wedge shaped sectors extending outward from the central business district. This was a modification of the *concentric zone model*.

Sense of place   Feelings and ideas people have about places. Places have meanings to people, which vary with scale or size, as well as with the degree to which the places have been experienced.

Shifting cultivation   A land-use system that developed mainly in the wet tropics in which farmers clear a patch of land, plant, harvest, and then, after a year or two, move on to a new patch of land and repeat the process. Thus, the land is used in a long-term rotation. This system of land-use is sometimes called slash-and-burn.

Short-fallow cultivation   Land is allowed to lie fallow for only one or two years at a time. Only wild grasses return.

Site   The characteristics of an absolute or fixed location. It refers to the specifics of immediate surroundings.

Situation   The location of a place relative to other places.

Social institutions   Institutions that operate, regulate, and maintain society. They include the principal sectors of society such as education, religion, politics, economics, science, technology, and communication.

Sociocultural   Factors related to the societal and cultural developments of humans.

Space   A term used by geographers that primarily refers to the surface of the earth. Geographers are concerned with the human activities and physical processes that characterize the earth's surface.

Space-cost curve   A curve showing variations of cost over some distance.

Space-price curve   A curve showing variations in price over some distance.

Spatial margins to profitability   Defined by intersections between space cost curves and space price curves. They represent boundaries on the profitable location of industries.

Spatial tradition One of the four traditions of geography developed by William Pattison. This tradition deals with positioning and layout on the earth's surface and with the spatial arrangements or patterns of both physical and human phenomena.

Spatial variation Differences from place to place in whatever phenomena one is interested in. The study of spatial variations is an essential element in geography.

Species A group of closely related organisms that have the potential to breed with one another.

Stages of economic growth Any of several models that suggest that economic development takes place in a series of sequential steps or stages.

Standard language An institutionalized language with a uniform vocabulary, syntax, pronunciation, and meaning.

Standard Metropolitan Statistical Area (SMSA) A census bureau definition used to define an urbanized area.

State An independent and sovereign political unit that has a territorial base and a permanent population.

Stretchability The ability of a resource to produce greater yields as the result of employing more efficient methods of resource manipulation. For example, the addition of chemical fertilizer increases the output from farmlands, at least up to some point.

Subsequent boundary A boundary that was made during the settlement and cultured evolution of a region.

Sunbelt A area of pleasant and attractive climate. In the United States the term is often applied to the entire southern tier of states from Florida to California.

Superimposed boundary A boundary established after the cultural development of an area but does not conform to ethnic or cultural characteristics.

Syncretic culture A culture that combined different belief systems.

Tangshan earthquake A disastrous earthquake that struck Hebei (Hopei) province of the People's Republic of China in 1976. Approximately 750,000 people were killed.

Territorial sea The oceanic boundary of a state whose outer edge is the legal boundary of the state.

Threshold The minimum population needed in an area to provide goods and services.

Toponymy The study of place names.

Tornado A very intense low-pressure storm with a small radius and generally found over continental areas in the midlatitudes, primarily in the United States.

Trade-off In economics it is an often-used term suggesting that resources can be allocated in various ways but that decision-makers must give up some things to get others.

Transformism The idea that differences among species were the result of gradual changes over time.

Transport network The spatial arrangement and connectivity of a transportation system.

Tripod of culture This refers to the three fundamental components in the development of culture: fire, tools, and systematic communication.

Trophic level Part of the trophic structure that is composed of several separate groups of organisms that obtain food in the same general way.

Trophic structure The organization of an ecosystem in order to maximize the use of energy. It is the mechanism that binds together the different population groups in an ecosystem.

Tropical cyclone An intense low-pressure storm that generally forms over a tropical oceanic area and may move over midlatitude regions.

Tropical Storm Agnes A violent storm that caused much property damage along the East Coast of the United States in 1972.

Underdevelopment See *developing countries*.

Uniqueness Individual characteristics of a particular place.

Urban ecosystem The manner in which economic, social, political, and decision-making processes work together to produce a city.

Urban evolution A six-stage process developed by James E. Vance, Jr. The six stages are: inception, exclusion, segregation, extension, replication and readjustment, and redevelopment.

Urban hierarchies This refers to hierarchical arrangement of cities within an urban system.

Urban homesteading The process through which a person can secure a low-cost loan to repair a home in a poor physical condition. Homesteading rejuvenates housing stock which might otherwise become uninhabitable.

Urbanism The conditions or characteristics of the way of life of those who live in cities.

Urbanization May be defined in two ways. First, it is the percent of a population that lives in urban areas. Second, it is the process by which this number increases over time.

Utilitarian viewpoint The view, widely held, that resources are to be used and should serve the general economy.

Value added A measure of the difference between raw material costs and the price of a finished product. It is the result of applications of labor and capital in the manufacturing process.

Vulnerability A measure of how susceptible a resource is to destruction.

Wet rice cultivation Requires that the rice be submerged below gradually moving water for the first three-fourths of its growing period.

Index

Abiotic, 215
Abortion, 36–37, 57–58, 69
Absolute size, 9
Acceleration stage, 301
Access, 145
Acculturation, 95, 97–98
Adams, J., 329
Aerospace, 287
Aesthetic pollution, 224
Afghanistan, 160
Africa, 13, 52, 110, 136, 156
African National Congress, 112
Afrikaner, 110
Age, 66
Age of degenerative and "man-made" diseases, 56
Age of discovery, 95
Age of high mass-consumption, 198
Age of metals, 87
Age of pestilence and famine, 56
Age of receding pandemics, 56
Age structure, 30, 38
Agency for International Development, 48
Agglomerated, 265
Agricultural landscape, 262
Agricultural regions, 247
Agricultural revolution, 14–15, 17, 92
Agricultural surplus, 91
Agricultural systems, 240, 247
Agriculture, 82, 179, 240–41, 259, 261
Air pollution, 220–21
Alaska, 58
Alaskan Pipeline, 174
Alexander, J., 251
Aliens, 58
Allocation, 149
American Indian, 88
Amish, 84
Ancient cities, 295
Anderson, N., 116, 119
Andes Mountains, 155
Anglo-America, 50

Animal power, 89
Animals, 82
Annual cropping, 243
Antecedent boundaries, 151
Apartheid, 111–12
Appalachian states, 58
Appalachians, 66
Arab League, 164
Arable land, 257
Architectural history, 102
Architectural monuments, 101
Architecture, 100
Arctic ecosystem, 218
Arctic Eskimos, 81
Area-studies tradition, 4
Argentina, 31
Arithmetic graph, 12–13
Arithmetic rate, 24
Art, 100
Artifacts, 80, 296
Artists, 291
Asbestos, 220
Asian Gardens, 119
Assimilation, 126, 128
Atlas Mountains, 121
Atomic power, 91
Attenuated state, 142
Auerbach, 301
Autotroph, 216
Average life expectancy, 54

BEV, 131
Bacillus pestis, 20
Backwash effects, 203
Bangladesh, 143, 226
Banton, M., 106–107
Bantu Authorities Act, 112
Barn, 264–65
Barrett, M., 72, 75
Barriers, 95
Basic, 320
Basic demographic equation, 9

Basin and range regions, 54
Beaujot, R. P., 73–74
Beckford, G. L., 199, 247
Behavior, 160
Beier, G., 305–7
Benedict, Saint, 119
Bengali, 137
Benson, P., 123
Berelson, B., 48
Berghe, P. V. D., 109, 114
Berlin Conference, 156
Beyer, J., 228
Bible Belt, 84
Bid-rent curve, 321
Bilingualism, 138
Billington, R. A., 52
Biological community, 215
Biological organism, 92
Biological systems, 210
Biology, 106
Biomass, 216
Biosphere, 215
Biotic, 215
Birth control, 31, 37, 48
Birth rate, 26, 28, 48, 50, 54
Black, C. E., 82
Black Africans, 112
Black Death, 17, 19, 22
Black English, 132
Black English vernacular, 131
Black inferiority, 110
Black migration, 63
Black speech, 133
Blacks, 63–64, 66
Blast furnaces, 283
Blood type, 107
Bloomfield, L., 127
Bo tree, 119
Boas, F., 109
Bogue, D., 41
Bolivia, 146
Bose, A., 308

Boserup, E., 13, 243
Boughey, A. S., 14, 241
Boundaries, 85, 141, 148–49, 156
Boundary line, 148, 150
Bourne, L. and Simmons, J., 337
Bouvier, L., 10
Brahmanism, 116
Brazil, 146, 171
British Empire, 109
British South Africa Company, 162
Brockway, F., 160
Bronowski, J., 80, 87
Brown, D., 112
Bubonic, 20
Buddha, 117
Buddhism, 116–17
Buffer zones, 159–60
Burgess, E., 323
Burgess model, 325
Burghers, 299
Burton, I., 225–26, 237
Bush-fallow cultivation, 243
Bushman, 241
Bushmen, 81
Butler, J., 115

CBD, 315
California, 121
California condor, 172
California drought, 182
California Water Project, 259
Canada, 50, 70, 72–73
Cancer, 56, 220
Cantonese, 137
Cape Liberalism, 110
Capital cities, 145–47
Capital formation, 194
Capitalism, 166
Capitalist, 25
Capitalist system, 166
Carroll, R., 235
Carrying capacity, 8, 12, 44, 92
Cartogram, 30
Catholic, 71
Catholic Church, 123
Caucasoid, 109
Census, 52
Central place theory, 334
Centrifugal forces, 142
Centripetal forces, 142
Ceremonial activities, 102
Ceteris paribus, 177
Champlain, S. d., 70
Chapin, W., 104
Charring, 87
Chemical fertilizers, 257
Cherry, C., 130
Chicago, 323
Childe, V. G., 295–96
Children, 70, 213
Chile, 145
China, 12, 37–39, 116, 235
Chinese city, 300
Cholera, 56
Christaller, W., 334–37
Christianity, 116–17

Christ of the Andes, 155
Church of Jesus Christ of Latter Day
   Saints, 86
Circular and cumulative causation, 203
City, 92–93, 293–94
City-states, 298
Civilization, 88
Clapham, W. B., 218, 219
Clark, Sir K., 271, 290–91
Class struggle, 25
Clean air, 290
Climate, 262
Clinal analysis, 109
Clines, 106
Closed cycle, 197
Closed systems, 195
Clothing industry, 279
Cloud seeding, 231
Coal, 89, 188–89, 274
Coke, 281
Coking, 87
Colonial language, 137
Colonial woman, 56
Colonialism, 128, 160, 162, 198
Colorado Springs, 321
Colosseum, 101
Coloureds, 110, 112
Combustion, 221
Commercial agriculture, 247
Commercial grain farming, 254
Communication, 91
Communist Manifesto, 25
Communists, 25
Compact state, 143
Concentric zone model, 323
Concentric zones, 248
Conflicts, 65, 176, 187
Confucianism, 116
Confucius, 102
Consumer organisms, 216
Consumption, 66, 255
Contiguous zone, 159
Contraception, 36–37, 57
Contraceptive devices, 69
Conversion, 184
Cook, E., 273
Core area, 145–46, 210
Core-periphery model, 201–202
Core regions, 204–205
Corn belt, 84, 247, 251
Correlation, 56
Corsica, 145
Cos, 298
Cost-benefit analysis, 212
Cotton, 52
Counterstream, 40
Cousteau, J., 223
Cracking, 87
Creationism, 125
Crede, 131
Crime rates, 65
Cro-Magnon Man, 13–14
Crude birth rate, 9, 22, 56
Crude death rate, 9, 56, 72
Crude population density, 8
Cultural adaptability, 39

Cultural change, 84
Cultural diffusion, 264, 298
Cultural evolution, 107
Cultural groups, 107
Cultural hearths, 83–84, 86–87, 93
Cultural landscape, 83–84, 86, 151
Cultural mosaic, 115
Cultural neocolonialism, 164
Cultural realm, 83, 86
Cultural region, 50, 83–84, 86
Cultural relativity, 81
Cultural revolution, 13, 37
Cultural systems, 80–84, 86–87, 93, 107,
   115–16, 171
Culture, 50, 80–82, 84
Cyclical changes, 17

DDT, 257, 259
Dairy farming, 250–51
Daland, R., 307
Darwin, C., 125
Data, 70
Death rates, 22, 26, 28, 43–44, 48, 50, 54
de Blij, H., 142, 147
Decade of development, 194
Decomposer organisms, 216
Deevey, E. S., 12–14, 17, 23
Defense, 84
Deforestation, 179, 211
Delaware, 8
Delimitation, 150
Delphi, 298
Demarcation, 148, 150
Demographic data, 10
Demographic transition, 25, 31–36, 56
Demography, 8
Demonstration effect, 36
Denmark, 142
Density, 142
Department of Commerce, 42
Depressed regions, 69
Desertification, 211
de Souza, A., 194, 198–99, 201, 276
Destination, 66
Destruction, 170
Developed, 28, 30, 195
Developed nations, 28, 165, 305, 307
Developed world, 195
Developing, 28, 30
Developing countries, 28, 33–36, 48,
   165, 197–98, 241, 305, 307
Developing societies, 195
Development, 194–95, 199
Development factor, 201
Diabetes, 56
Dialect, 136
Dickens, C., 181
Diepgen, 19
Diet, 107
Diffusion, 17, 84, 95–96, 97, 109, 115–
   17, 119, 123, 204, 263
Directional bias, 329
Discovery, 184
Dispersed, 265
Distance, 62–63
Distance bias, 329

Distribution, 12, 137
Distribution costs, 275
Divided capital, 147
Divided state, 143
Doe v. Bolton, 57
Dogon, 119
Domesticated plants, 82
Domestication, 15, 240
Dominant, 106
Dordogne Valley, 13
Doubling time, 10, 12, 36
Draft animals, 89
Drive to maturity, 198
Drought, 228–29
Druids, 116
Dual economy, 274
Dubois, R., 291
Dubois, W. E. B., 132
Dust bowl, 62, 262
Dutch East India Company, 109

Earthquake, 226, 232
Earth-science tradition, 3
East India Company, 162
Eastern China, 17
Eckholm, E., 254
Ecological changes, 39
Ecological systems, 115, 119
Ecologists, 211, 216
Ecology, 210, 215
Economic base, 179
Economic colonialism, 86
Economic cost, 176
Economic development, 47, 178, 194–95, 197
Economic Development Administration, 69
Economic growth, 54, 66, 210–11
Economic man, 328
Economies of scale, 276
Ecosystem, 82, 121, 179, 215–16, 218–19, 259
Ecuador, 199
Education, 66
Egypt, 92
Ehrlich, P. R., 223
Electrical energy, 184
Elongated, 142
Emigration, 70, 72
Enclosure Acts, 22
Endemic diseases, 56
Energy, 69, 184, 247, 261
England, 22
Entrepreneurs, 198
Environment, 13, 66, 82, 94, 215
Environmental adaptation, 88
Environmental alteration, 89
Environmental degradation, 164–66
Environmental determinism, 4
Environmental disruption, 69
Environmental perception, 171
Environmental protection, 290
Environmental theories, 23
Environmentalism, 4
Epicanthic, 109
Epidemics, 17

Epidemiologic transition, 56
Equilibrium, 48
Eskimos, 50, 70, 101, 241
Ethics, 115
European experience, 35
Eversley, D. R., 23
Evolution, 107, 125
Evolutionary process, 80
Ewing, S., 119
Exclusion, 315
Exclusive Economic Zone (EEZ), 159
Expansion diffusion, 95, 117
Extension, 316
Extinction, 219

Factorial ecology, 330
Factors of production, 275
Fagan, B. M., 241
Fagan, J. J., 221
Family planning, 31, 47, 48
Famines, 17
Faustian bargain, 190
Federal Aid Highway Act of 1944, 331
Females, 72
Fertile Crescent, 15, 83, 91–93, 95, 102
Fertility, 36, 38, 47, 54, 56, 70, 72
Fertility control, 37, 38
Fertilizers, 257
Feudal system, 149
Filtering, 325
Financial capital, 275
Fire, 87
Fishing village, 315
Flexibility, 172–73
Flooding, 228
Floodplains, 228
Food, 240
Food and Agricultural Organization (FAO), 164
Food chain, 216
Footloose industries, 279
Forced migration, 52
Forest, 179
Forest-fallow cultivation, 243
Formal city, 293
Fossil fuels, 172–73, 176
Foust, J., 201, 276
Fox, R., 311
Fragmentation, 143
Fragmented, 143
France, 145
Frank, A., 198
Frank, N., 237
Frankl, P., 101
Fraser, J., 288
French Canadians, 71
Friedmann, J., 201, 203–204
Frontier, 148
Frontier era, 52
Frontiers, 147
Front Range, 182
Fully fledged spatial organization, 204
Functional city, 293
Fung-Shui, 119
Future, 104

Ganges, 245
Gatherers, 17
Gautama, 117, 119
Genetic classification, 151
Genetic drift, 107
Genetic improvement, 260
Genetics, 106
Genocide, 69
Geographic identifiers, 330
Geography of modernization, 199–200
Geography of religions, 115
Geometric boundary, 155–56
Geometric rate, 24
George, E., 205
Germany, 248
Gilbert, A., 199
Gilmour, G., 329
Ginsburg, N., 177–78
Glacken, C., 115, 119
Glassner, M. I., 157, 159
Goldman, M. I., 166
Goodyear, C., 170
Gottmann, J., 334
Gould, P., 95, 199–200
Grain farming, 252
Grapes, 121
Grapes of Wrath, The, 62
Great Basin, 56
Great Lakes, 151, 155
Great Leap Forward, 37
Great Plains, 54, 56, 58
Great Wall of China, 149
Greek cities, 297
Greeks, 100
Green revolution, 260
Greenberg, M. R., 286
Greer-Wotten, B., 329
Griffin, E., 250
Grigg, D., 245, 254
Grigsby, W., 328
Gross National Product (GNP), 66, 174, 195
Group Areas Act, 112
Growth syndrome, 4, 66, 289
Growthmania, 289
Guild system, 26
Guttenberg, J., 91

Haeckel, E., 215
Hall, P., 248
Hamelin, L., 70
Hamilton, F., 276
Hamlets, 265
Handlin, O., 50
Harris, D. C., 321, 328
Hart, J., 264–65
Hartshorne, R., 142, 151
Harwood, J., 106–7
Harvest, 184
Hawkes, H., 173–74
Hazard, 225–26, 228, 231
Heart disease, 56
Hearth, 83
Heat, 184, 223
Hebrews, 116
Heller, W. H., 211

Henripin, J., 71
Herbicides, 257
Herbivore, 216
Hertzler, J., 127, 130
Hewitt, K., 237
Hexagonal pattern, 335
Heyerdahl, T., 223
Hierarchies, 335
High seas, 159
Hinduism, 116–17
Hodges, L., 220–21
Hofstatter, E., 47
Holdrich, T. H., 155
Holistic, 81–82
Homo sapiens sapiens, 13–14
House types, 262
Hoyt, H., 326–27
Hoyt's model, 326
Huang Ho, 84
Hubbard, M., 175
Highes, L., 132–33
Human adjustment, 225
Human evolution, 13
Human geographer, 80
Human geography, 4, 80, 115
Humanistic geography, 3
Humanities, 3
Hunting, 241
Hunting and gathering, 240–41
Hurricanes, 231
Hussain, S., 237
Hwang Ho, 297
Hwang Ho River, 93
Hydraulic civilization, 295
Hydrologic cycle, 181

Illinois, 189
Immigrants, 58, 70
Immigration, 43, 58, 70, 72, 73
Immigration Act, 73
Immigration policy, 73
Imperialism, 198
Inca Empire, 160
Incas, 98
Inception, 315
Incipient cultivation, 15
Incipient industrialization, 204
India, 116–17, 137
Indian subcontinent, 73
Indians, 50, 70
Indus, 297
Indus River Valley, 84
Industrial cities, 299
Industrial inertia, 275
Industrial landscapes, 291
Industrial location, 276
Industrial Revolution, 19, 22, 26, 50, 52, 92–93, 181, 271–74, 299
Industrialization, 166
Infant mortality, 72
Influenza, 56
Initial stage, 301
In-migration, 31, 331
Innovation, 84, 89
Intensive subsistence farming, 243
Inter-American Development Bank, 311

Internal cohesion, 143
Internal migration, 59
Internal sovereignty, 141
International Geophysical Year (1957–58), 157
International migration, 40
International Monetary Fund (IMF), 164
Intervening obstacles, 41
Intraurban, 330
Introduced capital, 147
Iran, 176
Ireland, 179
Iron, 89, 281, 283
Irrawaddy, 245
Irrigation, 257, 259, 295
Islam, 116
Isolated State, The, 248
Isolation, 126, 128
Israel, 117
Italy, 145

Jainism, 116
Jajj, 123
James, P., 3
Japan, 22, 31, 82, 178–79
Java Man, 13
Jefferson, J., 301
Jihad, 119
Johnson, J., 295
Johnston, R. J., 328
Jones, S. B., 149
Judaism, 116–17

Kalback, W. E., 72
Karamojong, 205
Karma, 117
Kenya, 201, 205
Kifigawa, E. M., 56
Kuper, H., 308
Kuznetsk Basin, 281

Labor, 279
Lake Victoria, 205
Land, 179
Land-locked, 156
Landsberg, H., 174–76
Landscape, 80, 100, 291
Land-use, 119
Langer, W., 20
Language, 125–31, 136–38
Lascaux, 14
Late marriage, 37
Latin America, 123, 199, 311
Laws of migration, 40
Lazarus, E., 60
Leaching, 179
League of Nations, 164
Least transport cost location, 275
Lee, E. S., 41
Legal immigration, 59
Leonardo Scholars, 187, 189, 190
Levner, H., 116
Lewis, P., 224
Life cycle, 41
Life expectancy, 19, 30, 72
Lignite, 189

Limits, 250
Lindberg, J., 250
Lingua franca, 138
Linguists, 125, 131
Liverpool, 272
Location, 2, 81–82, 84–85, 87, 89, 119, 247, 275
Locational factors, 275, 279
Log cabins, 262
Logarithmic, 13
London, 221
London Epidemic, 21
Longwood, W., 188
Loomis, R., 245
Los Angeles, 182
Los Angeles Basin, 92, 290
Lowry, I. S., 328
Luten, D. B., 93, 172, 181, 184

Magic, 115
Major languages, 136
Malnutrition, 213
Malthus, T. R., 23–25, 31
Malthusian model, 23
Manchester, W., 262
Man-land tradition, 3
Manufacturing, 280
Manufacturing belt, 54, 285–87
Manufacturing regions, 283–84
Marin County, 182–84
Marin County Civic Center, 104
Marine fisheries, 188
Maritime boundary, 156
Market economy, 247
Market orientation, 277
Marquard, L., 110
Marx, K., 25, 123
Marxism, 36
Masai, 205–10, 242
McCarty, H., 250
McCasland, S., 116, 117
McFee, W., 159
McHale, M. C., 213
McHarg, I., 104
McNamara, R. I., 31, 304, 305
McVey, W. W., 72
Mean information field, 95
Mecca, 116, 123
Medieval cities, 298–99
Mediterranean agriculture, 252
Meinig, D., 86
Mekong, 245
Mercantilism, 162
Meso-America, 17
Mesopotamia, 92, 260, 296
Metropolitan, 65
Metropolitan areas, 63–64
Mexico, 10, 44, 59
Mexico City, 308–9
Microclimates, 252
Microenvironments, 83
Middle Ages, 149
Middle East, 116, 160
Midwest, 56
Migrants, 62, 128

Migration, 31, 36, 39, 40–41, 50, 61–62, 66, 107, 120, 127, 309, 310, 311
Migration differentials, 40
Migration selectivity, 40
Migration streams, 63
Military neocolonialism, 164
Milk shed, 251
Mill town, 315
Miller, E. W., 283
Miller, G. T., 68, 70, 281
Minerals, 172
Mines and Works Act, 112
Minimata disease, 211
Mining town, 315
Minority groups, 142
Mississippi River, 52, 155
Mixed farming, 251–52
Model, 126, 198, 201, 203, 216, 250, 321, 337
Modernization, 32, 34–35, 80–82, 84, 87–89, 93, 98–100, 178, 194–95, 197–98, 200
Mohammed, 116–17, 123
Mohammedanism, 116
Monasteries, 119
Mongoloid, 109
Montana, 189
Monte Carlo simulation, 95
Mormon cultural region, 85
Mormons, 86
Morphological classification, 151
Morphology, 142
Morrill, R., 199
Morrison, P., 64
Mortality, 30, 35, 54, 56, 72
Mosaic, 80
Mountains, 119
Movable type, 91
Muir, J., 173
Muller, P., 331
Multicropping, 243
Multiple cropping, 260
Multiple nuclei model, 328
Mumford, L., 92, 116, 291, 295–96, 298
Murphy, R., 300
Murstein, 57
Mutation, 107
Myrdal, G., 202, 203

Nation, 81, 141
Nation-state, 141
National fertility statistics, 56
National Interstate System, 331
National Man and Resources Conference, 73
Native Land Act, 112
Natural hazards, 224
Natural resources, 177
Natural selection, 106–7
Naturalistic, 23
Navajos, 268
Near East, 17
Negroid, 109
Neocolonialism, 164
Neolithic, 87
Neo-Malthusians, 25, 31

Nested hierarchy, 204
Network for diffusion, 95
Neutral stuff, 170
New France, 71
New Mexico, 266
New Orleans, 264
New Stone Age, 87–88
New World, 121, 160
Nicholls, B., 117
Nichols, T., 234
Nile, 297
Nitrogen, 257
No-growth, 66
No-man's land, 149
Noise pollution, 223
Nomadic herding, 241
Nomadic people, 84
Nonbasic, 320
Nonmetropolitan, 65
Nonmetropolitan areas, 64
Nonrenewable, 171
Nonrenewable resources, 172
Nonwhites, 56–58
Norcliffe, G. B., 279–80
Nordic, 109
North America, 284
Northam, R., 301
Northeast, 56, 64
Nortman, D., 47
Nuclear energy, 91
Nuclear power, 182, 184, 192

Obstacle, 62
Oceanic fisheries, 210, 261
Offshore zone, 157, 159
Oil, 172
Oil pollution, 182
Oil shale, 171–72
Oil spill, 188
Old Stone Age, 87
Old World, 83
Olympia, 298
Omran, A., 56
Organisms, 82
Organization for European Economic Cooperation, 164
Organization of American States, 164
Organization of Petroleum Exporting Countries (OPEC), 176
Origin, 66, 115
Outer city, 331, 334
Overgrazing, 211
Owen, W., 331

Pacific Coast, 52, 54, 81
Pakistan, 143
Palace of Versailles, 100
Paleolithic, 87–88
Pan-African Congress, 112
Pandemic, 19
Paris basin, 146
Park, R., 323
Paterson, J. H., 52

Pattison, W., 3
Peasant societies, 50, 195, 197
Pei, M., 129
Peking Man, 13
Pennsylvania, 227
People's Republic of China, 25, 36–38, 137
Perception, 41
Perforated states, 145
Pesticides, 257
Petrarch, 22
Petro dollars, 176
Petroleum, 175
Philosophy, 115
Phosphate, 257
Physical capital, 275
Physical environment, 164, 171
Physical geography, 3
Pidgin, 131
Pilgrim circulation, 122
Pinchot, G., 173
Place, 2–3
Place names, 121, 130
Plague, 22
Planned economies, 276
Plantation agriculture, 246
Plantation system, 199
Plasticity, 107
Plato, 102
Pleistocene overkill, 241
Plough, 89
Plural society, 110
Pneumonic, 20
Poets, 291
Polarized development, 201, 203
Polarized growth, 204
Polis, 298
Political frontiers, 148
Political geography, 141
Political territory, 141
Pollution, 165, 181, 215, 219–20
Pomo Indians, 81
Poor, 70
Population, 174
Population age-structure, 73
Population Council, 47
Population density, 73
Population distribution, 38, 73
Population dynamics, 40–41, 54, 72
Population essay, 24
Population geography, 8, 52
Population growth, 36, 66, 69, 211
Population growth rate, 10, 17, 30
Population policy, 73
Population pressure, 243
Population projection, 12, 41–42, 44, 48
Population pyramid, 30–31
Population redistribution, 59
Population Reference Bureau, 38, 287, 305, 307
Population Registration Act, 112
Population size, 73, 142, 294
Population structure, 23, 31
Population theories, 31
Populations, 82
Porter, P., 194, 198–99

Potato blight, 179
Poverty, 69
Pre-Colombian Indians, 171
Preconditions for take-off, 198
Pred, A., 337
Predictions, 42
Pregnancy, 57
Prehistoric populations, 12
Prehistory, 115
Preindustrial Phase, 204
Pre-Malthusian theories, 23
Prescott, J. R. V., 148
Preservationist movement, 174
President's Science Advisory Committee, 219
Primary carnivore, 216
Primary industries, 277
Primary theories, 23
Primate city, 204, 301
Prime mover, 89, 91
Primitive, 115
Printing, 91
Private sector, 198
Procurement costs, 275
Production costs, 275
Projections, 42, 66
Proletariat, 25
Prorupt state, 143
Protein, 210
Psychological costs, 62
Push–pull, 132
Pyramids, 100

Quality of life, 194–95
Quebec, 70, 128, 142
Quipa, 99

Rabinowitz, F., 307
Race, 66, 107, 110
Racial types, 109
Radioactive material, 219, 222
Railroads, 274
Raison d'être, 142
Range, 335
Rank-size rule, 302
Rapoport, A., 101, 262, 264
Rate of growth, 73
Rate of natural increase, 9–10, 70
Rate of population growth, 9, 54
Rationing, 182
Ravenstein, E. G., 40
Raw material orientation, 277
Raw materials, 174, 277, 281
Readjustment, 316
Recessive, 106
Reclaimed, 188
Recoverability, 172
Red Guard Movement, 37
Redford, A., 271–72
Redistribution, 64
Reforestation, 179
Region, 81, 84–85
Regional dialects, 134
Regional inequality, 201
Regionalization, 85

Relative location, 83, 247
Relic boundary, 151
Religion, 115–16
Religious fervor, 22
Religious geography, 115, 119
Religious landscape, 119
Religious systems, 115
Relocation, 117, 330
Relocation diffusion, 95
Renaissance, 100
Renaud, B., 308
Renewable, 171, 172
Renewable resource, 181
Replacement, 127
Replication, 316
Resource, 170–72
Resource availability, 174
Resource base, 177
Resource creation, 170
Resource exploitation, 192
Resources, 80, 174, 176
Retirement, 65
Revelle, C., 223
Revelle, P., 223
Revolution, 13
Richter scale, 235
Ripley, W., 109
Risks, 69
Robinson, E. A. G., 142
Robinson, J. L., 2
Rocky Mountains, 54, 56, 58
Roe v. Wade, 57
Roman Empire, 117, 160
Romans, 100
Rome, 298
Rorig, F., 298–99
Rostow, W. W., 197, 272, 274
Royal Society of London, 272
Rubber, 170
Rural Renaissance, the, 64
Rural–urban migration, 54, 64

SST, 223
Salinization, 260
Salter, C., 181
San Francisco, 316
San Rafael, 266
Sauer, C. O., 15, 17, 83, 87
Scale, 81, 83
Scantling, F., 266
Scarlet fever, 56
Schematic framework, 80
Scientific method, 3
Secondary carnivore, 216
Secondary industries, 277
Secondary theories, 23
Sector model, 327
Sedentary, 17
Sediments, 223
Seers, D., 194
Segregation, 315
Semple, E., 100
Sense of place, 3, 52
Septicemic, 20
Sericulture, 179
Settlement frontiers, 148

Settlement patterns, 269
Sex selectivity, 40
Shape, 142
Sharpeville, 112
Shatter belts, 159
Shelter, 84, 101
Shifting cultivation, 242–43
Shogunate, 178
Short-fallow cultivation, 243
Shotgun house, 263–64
Sierra Club, 173
Silvert, K., 110
Sinclair, R., 321
Site, 83, 107, 316
Situation, 83, 107, 316
Size, 142
Sjoberg, G., 293–94, 296
Slash-and-burn, 242
Slavery, 52, 109, 128
Slaves, 52, 110, 133
Smith, D., 124, 276
Smitherman, G., 132
Smith's model, 276
Smog, 221
Social cohesion, 141
Social costs, 176
Social distance, 63
Social identifiers, 330
Social institutions, 130
Social scientists, 195
Social stratification, 110
Socialists, 25
Sociocultural, 127
Socioeconomic, 61, 69–70
Soft drinks, 279
Soil, 179, 262
Soja, E., 201
Sopher, D., 119–21
Soul, 133
South, 63–64, 287
South Africa, 109–10, 112, 115
South African, 110
Southeast Asia, 15, 17, 82
Soviet Union, 82, 137, 142, 166, 283
Space, 2, 87, 94, 130
Space-cost curve, 276
Space economy, 204
Space-price curve, 276
Spatial, 141
Spatial diffusion, 200
Spatial distribution, 4, 8
Spatial interaction, 127–28
Spatial organization, 107, 199, 248
Spatial pattern, 56
Spatial structure, 199
Spatial tradition, 4
Spatial variations, 8
Species, 106
Spillover, 65
Spread effects, 203
Spykman, N.J., 160
Stabilizing U. S. Population, 69
Stages of economic growth, 197
Standard language, 134, 136
Standard of living, 30
State, 141

Steam engines, 274
Steel, 281, 283
Steinhart, C., 241
Steinhart, J., 241
Step-migration, 311
Sterilization, 38, 69
Storage, 184
Strahler, A., 314
Strangeland, C. E., 25
Steinbeck, J., 63
Stream, 40
Stretchability, 172
Strip-mining, 187–88
Stroke, 56
Strong, C. F., 141
Structures, 102
Subsequent boundary, 151
Subsistence, 24
Subsistence agriculture, 240
Subsistence farms, 254
Subsystems, 80, 82
Suburban, 332
Suburbanization, 63, 332, 333
Suburbs, 104, 331, 334
Sun, 216
Sunbelt, 64
Superimposed boundaries, 151
Supertankers, 188
Supranationalism, 164
Supreme Court, 57
Surface mining, 188
Surnames, 131
Switzerland, 136, 142
Symbolic models, 4
Syncretic culture, 110
System of cities, 334, 336–37
Systems approach, 314–15, 337
Szentes, T., 198

Taaffe, R., 199
Taiwan, 31
Take-off, 198
Tangshan, 235
Tanzania, 205–6
Taoism, 116
Target population, 48
Taylor, C., 72, 75
Taylor, D., 117
Technology, 87, 115, 295
Teenage pregnancies, 57
Teenagers, 57–58
Teitelbaum, M. S., 34
Terminal stage, 301
Territorial, 141
Territorial base, 141
Territorial sea, 157, 159
Textile industry, 179
Thailand, 160
Thalweg, 155
Third United Nations Conference on the
    Law of the Sea (UNCLOS III), 159
Third World, 194–95
Thomlinson, R., 23–25, 294, 302
Thompson, L., 115
Thorium, 222

Three Mile Island, 91
Three-mile limit, 159
Threshold, 220, 335
Tietze, C., 57
Tigris-Euphrates valley, 82, 84
Time, 130
Tool-making revolution, 13
Tools, 87–89
Topography, 252
Toponymy, 130
Torah, 89
Tornado, 229, 231
Torrey Canyon, 157, 159
Tower of Babel, 125
Trade-offs, 191, 212, 289–91
Tradition, 128
Traditional society, 198
Trans-America Pyramid, 104
Transformism, 125–26
Transitional stage, 204
Transport, 184
Transportation, 248
Transportation costs, 247
Transportation network, 199
Tregarthen, T., 188
Tribal societies, 195
Tribalism, 142
Tripod of culture, 87
Trophic level, 216
Trophic structure, 216, 218
Tropical cyclone, 229, 231
Tropical ecosystem, 179
Tropical forests, 243
Tropical Storm Agnes, 226
Truce lines, 151
Trueblood, F., 307
Tsunamis, 232
Tuan, Y. F., 3, 291
Tubal ligation, 38
Tuberculosis, 56
Twain, M., 10
Two-child family, 37

U.S.D.A., 189
Ullman, E. L., 328
Underdeveloped, 28, 198
Underdevelopment, 197, 199
United Nations, 42–44, 48, 164, 305
United States, 10, 22, 50, 166
Unlawful organizations, 112
Upper Paleolithic, 241
Uranium, 222
Urban, 294
Urban ecosystem, 314–15
Urban evolution, 315
Urban growth, 92
Urban homesteading, 329
Urban pollution, 69
Urban sprawl, 175
Urbanism, 294
Urbanization, 54, 64–65, 293–94
Urbanization pattern, 308
Urbanize, 63
Urlanis, B., 25
Uruguay, 31

U.S. Commission on Population Growth
    and the American Future, 66, 69
Uspallata Pass, 155
Utilitarians, 174
Utilitarian viewpoint, 173

Valente, N. J., 286
Value added, 277
Vance, J. E., 315–16, 332, 338
Vasectomies, 38
Vatican City, 142
Villages, 265
Vital rates, 38
Vlach, J., 263–64
Von Thünen, J. H., 248, 250
Vulnerability, 172–73

Wagner, P. L., 126
Ward, B., 291
Warning system, 234
Waste materials, 184
Water, 66, 172, 181, 184
Water conservation, 184
Water deficit, 66
Water mills, 89
Water pollution, 166, 220–21, 223
Water Pollution Control Act of 1972, 290
Water tables, 259
Weinberg, A., 192
Weir, 70
West Coast, 287
Westebbe, R., 307
Westward movement, 52
Wet rice cultivation, 245
Wheat, 246, 254
Wheatly, P., 295
Wheeler, J. P., 64
White man's burden, 113
White superiority, 110
Whites, 57, 66
Whittlesay, D., 84, 145
Wind, 89
Wither, G., 21
Wittfogel, K., 295
Women, 56
Woodlands, 17
World Bank, 305
World Health Organization (WHO),
    164, 220
World Population Conference, 44
World Population Year, 44
World War II, 72
Wright, F. L., 104

Xhosa, 110

Yap, L., 310
Yellow fever, 56

Zelinsky, W., 4, 195, 289
Zimmerman, E. W., 170
Zinser, H., 17
Zipf, G. K., 302
Zulu, 110
Zunis, 268